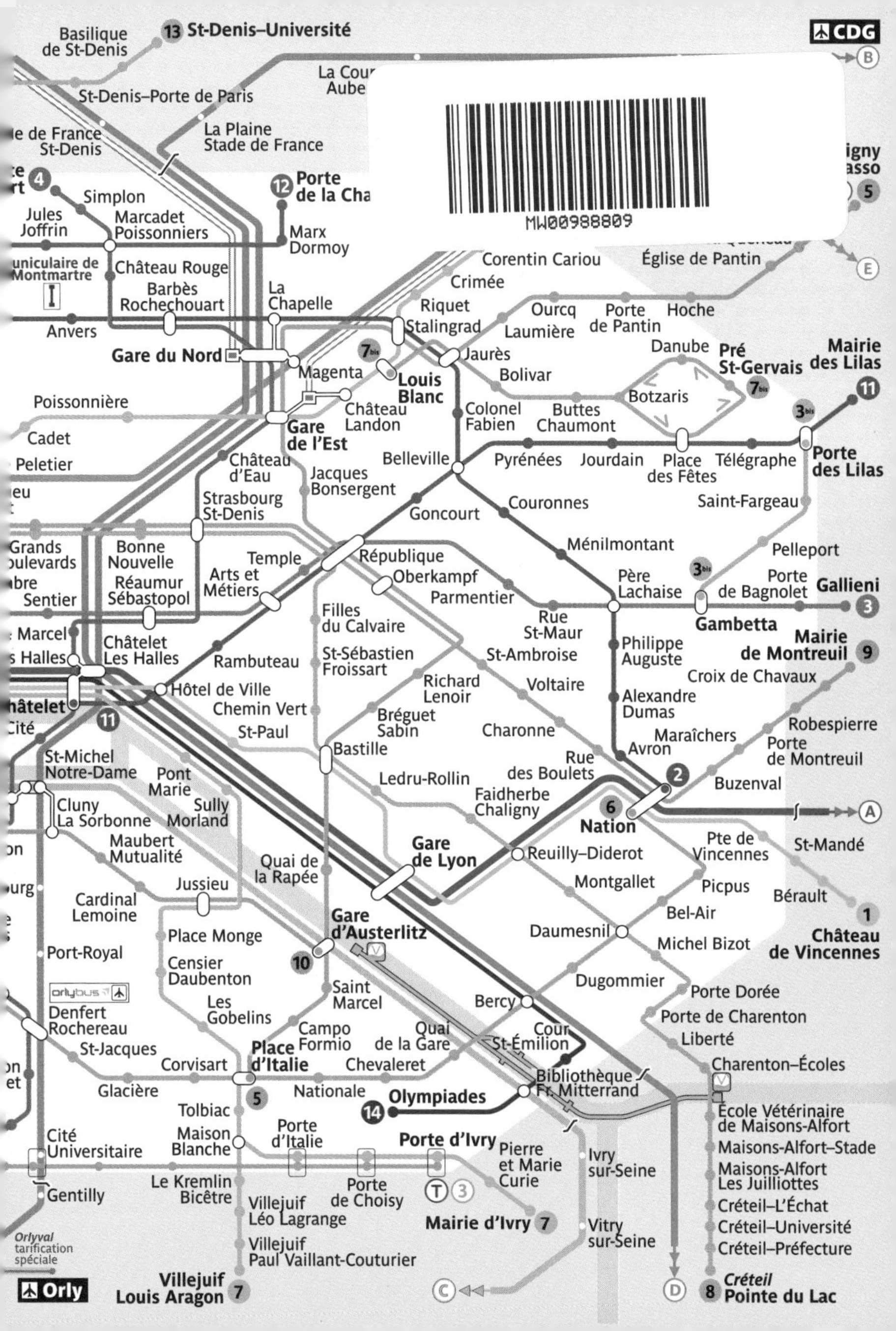

Basilique de St-Denis
13 St-Denis–Université
CDG
B
MW00988809
St-Denis–Porte de Paris
La Plaine Stade de France
4
Simplon
12
Jules Joffrin
Marcadet Poissonniers
Marx Dormoy
5
Funiculaire de Montmartre
Château Rouge
Barbès Rochechouart
La Chapelle
Corentin Cariou
Église de Pantin
E
Crimée
Anvers
Riquet
Stalingrad
Ourcq
Laumière
Porte de Pantin
Hoche
Gare du Nord
7bis
Jaurès
Danube
Pré St-Gervais
Mairie des Lilas
Magenta
Louis Blanc
Bolivar
Botzaris
11
Poissonnière
Château Landon
Colonel Fabien
Buttes Chaumont
3bis
Cadet
Gare de l'Est
Belleville
Pyrénées
Jourdain
Place des Fêtes
Télégraphe
Porte des Lilas
Peletier
Château d'Eau
Jacques Bonsergent
Strasbourg St-Denis
Goncourt
Couronnes
Saint-Fargeau
Grands Boulevards
Bonne Nouvelle
Temple
République
Ménilmontant
Pelleport
Arts et Métiers
Oberkampf
Père Lachaise
Porte de Bagnolet
Gallieni
Sentier
Réaumur Sébastopol
Parmentier
Gambetta
3
Filles du Calvaire
Rue St-Maur
Mairie de Montreuil
9
Châtelet Les Halles
St-Sébastien Froissart
St-Ambroise
Philippe Auguste
Rambuteau
Croix de Chavaux
Hôtel de Ville
Richard Lenoir
Voltaire
Alexandre Dumas
Chemin Vert
Bréguet Sabin
Charonne
Maraîchers
Robespierre
St-Paul
Bastille
Avron
Porte de Montreuil
St-Michel Notre-Dame
Pont Marie
Rue des Boulets
2
Ledru-Rollin
Buzenval
Cluny La Sorbonne
Sully Morland
Faidherbe Chaligny
6
Nation
A
Maubert Mutualité
Gare de Lyon
Pte de Vincennes
St-Mandé
Quai de la Rapée
Reuilly–Diderot
Jussieu
Montgallet
Picpus
Cardinal Lemoine
Bérault
Bel-Air
1
Place Monge
Gare d'Austerlitz
Daumesnil
Château de Vincennes
Port-Royal
Michel Bizot
Censier Daubenton
10
orlybus
Saint Marcel
Dugommier
Porte Dorée
Les Gobelins
Bercy
Denfert Rochereau
Porte de Charenton
Campo Formio
Quai de la Gare
Cour St-Émilion
Liberté
St-Jacques
Place d'Italie
Corvisart
Chevaleret
Charenton–Écoles
Bibliothèque Fr. Mitterrand
Glacière
Nationale
Olympiades
5
14
École Vétérinaire de Maisons-Alfort
Tolbiac
Maisons-Alfort–Stade
Cité Universitaire
Maison Blanche
Porte d'Italie
Porte d'Ivry
Pierre et Marie Curie
Ivry sur-Seine
Maisons-Alfort Les Juilliottes
Gentilly
Le Kremlin Bicêtre
Porte de Choisy
T 3
Créteil–L'Échat
Villejuif Léo Lagrange
Mairie d'Ivry 7
Vitry sur-Seine
Créteil–Université
Orlyval tarification spéciale
Villejuif Paul Vaillant-Couturier
Créteil–Préfecture
Orly
Villejuif Louis Aragon 7
C
D
8 Créteil Pointe du Lac

Discover Paris by metro

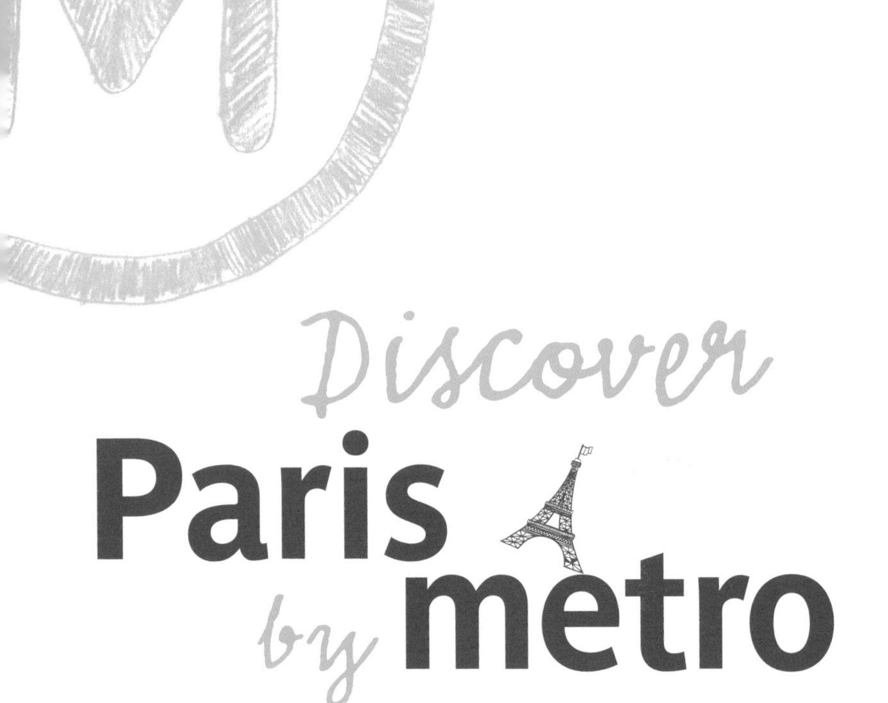
Discover
Paris
by métro

RATP

CHÊNE

MAIRIE DE PARIS

Foreword

Let the Paris Metro be your guide for a different and fun way to discover the beauty of the famous City of Light.

'What makes Paris
Yesterday and today
As beautiful as ever
Is the METRO!' sang actor and singer Yves Montand.

Paris City Hall wanted this Paris, the metro and the city's everyday life, to be available to all, the visitors for a day or the Parisians themselves. And what better way to enter Parisians' Paris than to take a guided tour through the metro? Abbesses, Bastille, Les Halles and Trocadéro, are just some of the stations whose names awaken the imagination and evoke all the magic of Paris.

This is the first guidebook to give everyone, the Paris-lovers who keep coming back and tourists who are just passing through, a fascinating and fun way of discovering the Paris neighbourhoods around the metro, their history, their best addresses, their hidden flower markets, crafts and shops, restaurants and cultural or unusual places, that make up their identity and create the energy of these city villages.

From Raspail to Odéon, Concorde to Châtelet, via Arts et Métiers, Bonne Nouvelle, Ménilmontant or Pigalle, take the metro to a Paris you never imagined being able to visit.
Let me take you on a trip through 300 metro stations.

Jean-Bernard Bros

Deputy Mayor of Paris for Tourism and Local New Media

This is the guidebook we were waiting for. The Paris Metro has over 300 stations and serves more than four million passengers every day, or almost one and a half billion a year. It is itself an integral part of Paris's cultural heritage.
So I am particularly pleased that for the first time there is a guidebook for this fabulous transport network that serves the city and its historical treasures.

This guidebook allows you to discover the metro's history through pictures and various stories brought to you by the RATP, the Paris Metro authority. The origins of the stations' names, their architectural attributes and the works of art they house will hold no mystery for you.

For example, you will learn that a station called 'Chambre des Deputés' was opened in 1910, but was renamed 'Assemblée Nationale' in 1990. Its houses original works by the artist Jean-Charles Blais using a unique technique, and the paintings are renewed according to the parliamentary calendar.

The guidebook also reminds us that the metro is a great way to enjoy the city. It shows us all there is to see and do in Paris along each metro line, station by station—art and culture, monuments, and the essential addresses.

This original guidebook is both practical and fun and makes an ideal companion for anyone just strolling around Paris, for tourists or Paris lovers.

Have a wonderful time.

Isabelle Ockrent

Head of Communications and Branding at the RATP

Introduction

By the end of the 19th century several capital cities already had their own underground railway system. The London Underground had opened in 1863, to be followed by similar transport systems in New York, Berlin, Vienna and Budapest. Paris was considering various proposals at the time and wanted to make its mark, particularly as the World Fair and Summer Olympics of 1900 were about to open. Several projects were put forward. There was already a circular railway called the 'Petite Ceinture', which carried first freight and then people between the railway companies' terminals. The line ran around Paris via the outer boulevards known as the Boulevards des Maréchaux. But it was built without much cooperation between the companies, which made no effort to compromise and stuck to their own positions and lines. And even then, steam trains were not very modern.

The authorities considered a variety of plans, like building viaducts above the buildings of Paris to prevent pollution in the city. This was a radical solution, if not a very aesthetic one. They even envisaged using Paris's underground rivers, but that would have been far too fiddly. Finally, a plan put forward by Edmond Huet, the city's Director of Public Works, and his chief engineer, Fulgence Bienvenüe, was chosen. Paris would have an 'urban railway using electric traction'.

The initial priority was to allow visitors to the World Fair, who came to admire the Eiffel Tower, to travel to the Olympic Games site at Vincennes. The plan finally got underway in 1897 despite some misgivings within the city authorities, the government and the railway companies. The project was declared to be of 'public interest' in 1898. A Paris Metropolitan Railway company was set up, and Compagnie Générale de Traction, owned by the Empain family of Belgium, was chosen as the operator. Fulgence Bienvenüe followed the street layout closely and work progressed very quickly. And so the first line came into service on July 19 1900. Trains with three carriages carried visitors from Porte Maillot to Porte de Vincennes. And construction work could continue. Despite some compromises along the way, and difficulties that were brilliantly resolved, the metro continued its inexorable march and is still being extended to this day. Inner suburbs Montrouge, Montreuil and Bagnolet would, for example, get new stations to serve their areas in the years to come. All this prompted the idea of a rather unusual guidebook dedicated to the metro, using the routes of its 14 lines to look at Paris from a different angle, with one of the best means of transport. Welcome to the age of metropolitan leisure.

You will read the stories of 145 of the 300 metro stations by metro line, from the funniest (the Seine had to be 'frozen' to build Cité), to the most artistic (the original Othoniel sculpture at Palais Royal-Musée du Louvre), not forgetting the most hidden station, Martin Nadaud. For each station walks are suggested to discover parks, history, architecture or unusual or out-of-the-ordinary things, to explore the immediate neighbourhood. There is also a list of addresses, essential for finding interesting local shops or a good restaurant to end the day. All you need to do is arrange to meet at the nearest bistro, café or *brasserie*, which is given for each metro exit. Happy exploring!

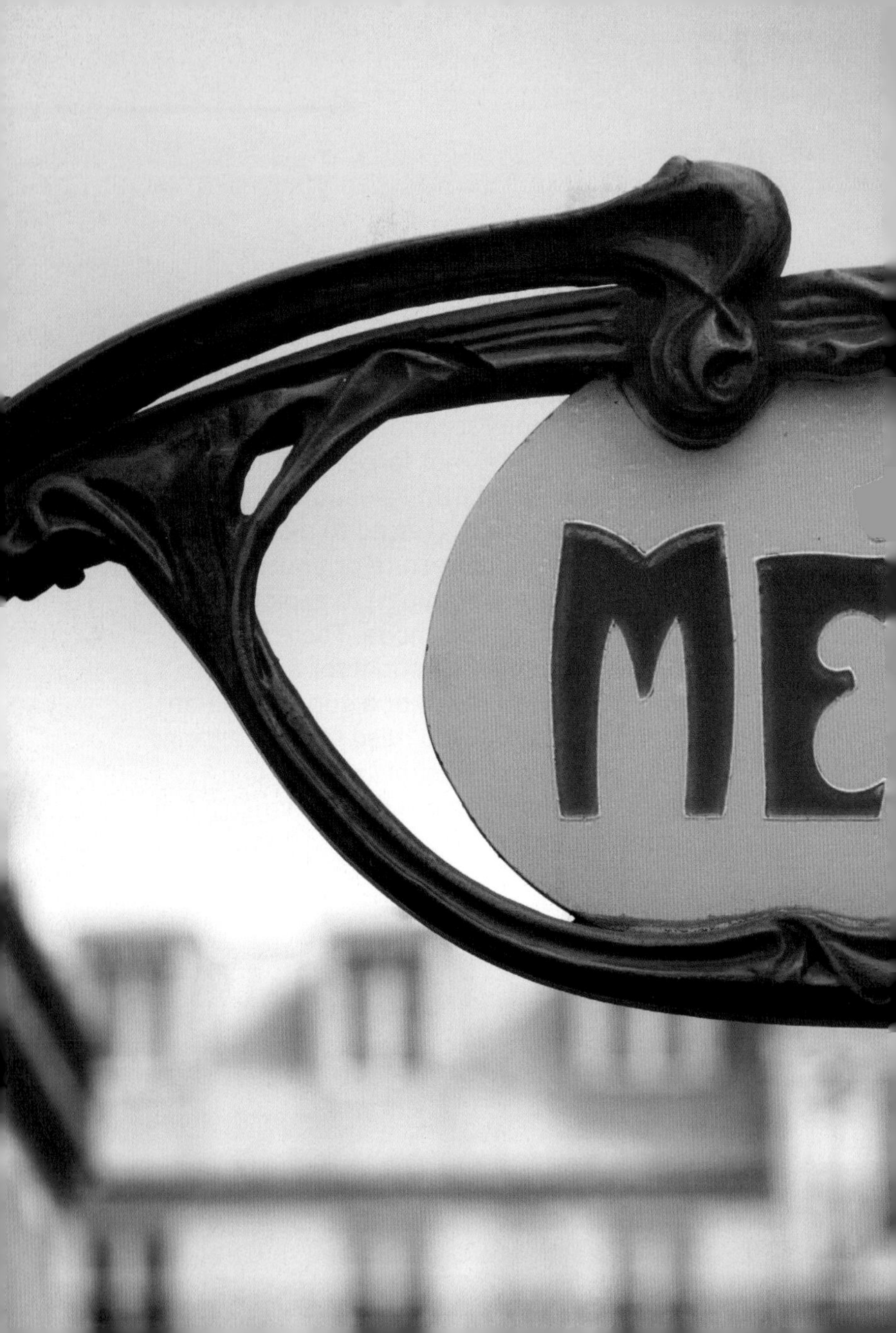
ME

line 1

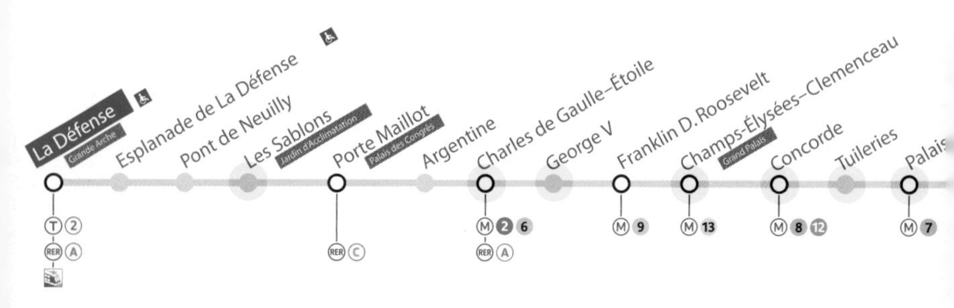

History

The line originally linked Porte Maillot in the west to Porte de Vincennes in the east. It was opened on 19 July 1900, in time for the World Fair. At each terminus there was a platform that allowed trains to turn round, but this is no longer used. That is why Porte de Vincennes is so spacious, but only two rail lines remain out of the original four. Most of the line runs underground, but it surfaces at Bastille, which spans the Saint-Martin canal. The platform at Bastille also bends sharply, with a radius of between 38 and 50 metres (42 and 55 yards). The line was extended east to Château de Vincennes on March 24 1934, and west to Pont de Neuilly on April 29 1937. The original Porte Maillot station was then moved and was later developed into a private conference centre, 'Espace Maillot'. People attending receptions or business meetings could admire the old green Sprague train wagons exhibited there. It has since been renovated and now houses a maintenance workshop. Trains were fitted with rubber tyres from 1963. And soon line 1 will be fully automated, with protective glass and screen doors installed along the route. It will then be equipped with MP05 driverless trains.

La Défense / Château de Vincennes

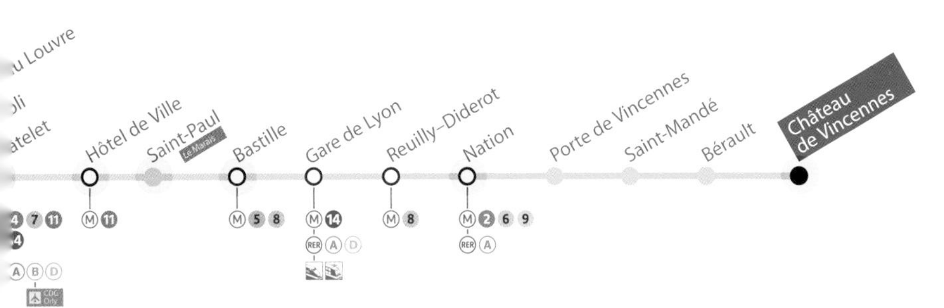

LES SABLONS

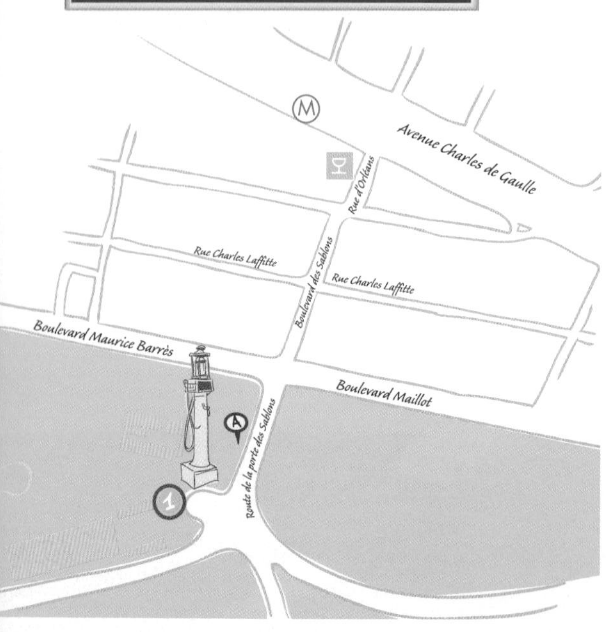

History

The station is named after the surrounding plain from which sand was extracted for construction and building work in Paris. In 1937 this part of the line from Vincennes was extended to Neuilly and this station was built. The famous introduction of Marie-Antoinette to King Louis XVI took place here. The king had returned from Prussia where he had been taken prisoner, and he brought back potato plants grown from a tuber. The potato was thought to be harmful at the time, but he tried to grow it, posting guards at the plantations. Ordinary people got interested and stole a few plants. The king even sported a potato flower in his buttonhole. And the plants flourished. Interest in the potato grew and grew, and continues to do so to this day.

SIGHTSEEING

A walk in the park

1 **Jardin d'Acclimatation:** originally these gardens were to show wild animals which were supposed to 'acclimatise' to the Parisian climate. Napoleon III decided to set aside this part of the Bois

de Boulogne woods for animals. Men and women from far and wide could also be seen walking here. People still come here to walk in the 18-hectare gardens to see the diverse species of flowers and vegetables. Nowadays it's not so much wild animals you will come across but pigs, rabbits, sheep and other farm animals.
Children can also ride on the merry-go-rounds or take a boat on the Enchanted River. There are also puppet shows for kids.
45 avenue de Mahatma-Gandhi, 16th.

Mini-train to the Jardin d'Acclimatation: ideal for the 1.6 km (1 mile) trip from the car-park to the gardens. Since the government's environment forum in 2007 the train no longer runs with an internal combustion engine but is powered by electricity. So the smart red petrol pump that used to refuel the train is no longer needed. Runs between the Palais des Congrès car park (VINCI) and the Jardin d'Acclimatation. Admission fee.

Address book

The place for a rendezvous

Le Jardin
7 rue d'Orléans, 92200 Neuilly-sur-Seine.
Tel.: 01-46-24-45-53.
Open Monday to Friday 6am to 8pm.

Leisure

Ⓐ Christophe Felder cooking classes
At the Maison des Ateliers in the gardens, you can take a class with one of the best pastry chefs in France. Learn the secrets of making macaroons and other tempting sweetmeats.
Further information by email (contact@christophe-felder.com) or on www.christophe-felder.com.
A fee is charged.

Next stations

PORTE MAILLOT

Le Petit Maillot
269 boulevard Pereire, 17th.

ARGENTINE

Café Brunel
2 rue Brunel, 17th.

CHARLES DE GAULLE – ÉTOILE

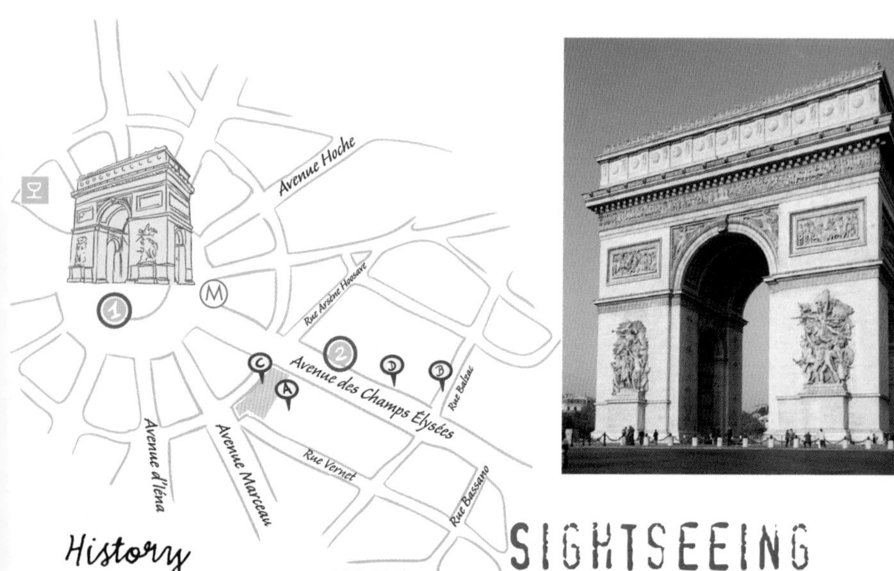

History

Place Charles-de-Gaulle (its official name) honours the memory of General de Gaulle, born in 1890. He organised resistance to the Nazi occupying forces during the Second World War and then took the helm of the provisional government, first in Algiers and then in Paris, between 1944 and 1946. He was elected president in 1959 and again in 1965 but resigned in 1969. He died in 1970, and this is when the station took his name. Until then it had been called 'Étoile', French for star, because of a star-shaped pattern in its red and grey cobblestones which can only be seen from the top of the Arc de Triomphe. There are 12 avenues leading off the square.

SIGHTSEEING

Monument

1 **Arc de Triomphe:** the arch was built in honour of the troops of Napoleon's army. It copies Roman tradition in both its form and symbolism. It is 49.54 metres, or 54.2 yards, high, 44.82 metres, or 49 yards, wide, and has 284 steps. You can climb right up to the top. If you look east to the Louvre and west to La Défense, you are seeing Parisian architecture across the centuries. Inside the monument is the tomb of the Unknown Soldier.

Place Charles de Gaulle, 8th.
Tel.: 01-55-37-73-77.
Open daily 10am to 11pm from April to September and 10am to 10.30pm from October to March.
Entrance fee.

rchitecture

Champs-Élysées street furniture: from traffic lights to benches, this was designed by architect Jean-Michel Wilmotte with simple, clean lines. Also worth seeing are the Morris columns or bus shelters by the English architect Norman Forster.

Address book

The place for a rendezvous

🍸 Le Cristal
6 avenue de la Grande-Armée, 17th.
Tel.: 01-43-80-84-11.
Open daily 6.30am to 2am.

Leisure

Ⓐ Publicis Drugstore
Conceived by Marcel Bleustein-Blanchet, founder of advertising agency Publicis. Perfect to pick up on trends or have a snack or a drink, day or night.

133 avenue des Champs-Élysées, 8th.
Tel.: 01-44-43-77-64.
Open Monday to Friday 8am to 2am and Saturday, Sunday and holidays 10am to 2am.

Ⓑ Le Balzac
Opened in 1935, this kind of cinema is a rarity nowadays. Its director, Jean-Jacques Schpoliansky, comes to present films himself, just as his grandfather did before him. Comfortable red armchairs, rich and varied programming.
1 rue Balzac, 8th.
Tel.: 01-45-61-10-60.
www.cinemalebalzac.com

Restaurants

Ⓒ Atelier Joël Robuchon Étoile
Michelin-starred chef Joël Robuchon, who put French cuisine on the world stage, opened his latest restaurant on the Champs-Élysées. It serves exquisite food modestly, in the restaurant or at the counter. Friendly atmosphere, unusual decor. Main courses around €50.
In the Publicis Drugstore basement.
Tel.: 01-47-23-75-75.
Open daily 11.30am to 3.30pm and 6.30pm to midnight.

Ⓓ Flora Danica
Inside the Maison du Danemark. Contemporary decor with French and Danish food and a *butik* (shop) as well. Full of Nordic exoticism. Prices €40 – 70. Gourmet restaurant on 1st floor, prices €100 – 120.
142 avenue des Champs-Élysées, 8th.
Tel.: 01-44-13-86-26.
www.floradanica-paris.com
Open daily noon to 2pm and 7.15pm to 11pm.

GEORGES V

History

This station, previously called Alma, commemorates the former King of England, George V (1865–1936), who reigned from 1910. It was inaugurated with its new name during his lifetime on May 27 1920. George V is the only king with a metro station named after him, probably in recognition of his commitment during the First World War alongside French forces. The neoclassical entrance to the station is by architect Joseph Cassien-Bernard.

Architecture

1. **Hotel George-V:** one of the oldest luxury hotels in Paris. Built in 1928 by André Terrail in a 1930s style, it has a Michelin-starred restaurant, 245 rooms and 59 suites decorated in Louis XVI style in pastel colours. Luxury, French-style.
31 avenue George-V, 8th.
Tel.: 01-49-52-70-00.

2. **The Lido:** its facade is the work of Jean Desbouis. The building, dating from 1929, was originally to house a radio station. Its architecture is a sharp contrast to neighbouring classical-style buildings.

3. **68 avenue des Champs-Élysées:** Guerlain opened the shop in 1912 in a building designed by Charles-Frédéric Mewes, the architect who designed the Ritz. The ornate steel-framed bay windows and stone wall-lamps were designed by Giacometti. Interior designers

Jean-Michel Frank and Adolphe Chanaux created the beauty parlour on the 1st floor in 1939. The trompe-l'oeil decor is the work of artist and theatre decorator Christian Bérard.

Culture

Espace Culturel Louis Vuitton: this may be a luxury boutique with a brand name of world renown, but feel free to go in and see its exhibitions of top-notch contemporary art on the 7th floor. The journey up in the lift is a real sensorial experience with artwork by Danish artist Olafur Eliasson.

60 rue de Bassano or
101 avenue des Champs-Élysées, 8th.
Tel.: 01-53-57-52-03.

Next station
FRANKLIN D. ROOSEVELT
See line 9, page 254

Address book

The place for a rendezvous

Café George-V
120 avenue des Champs-Élysées, 8th.
Open daily 6.30am to 2am.
Tel.: 01-45-62-33-51.

Shopping

A Ladurée
Renowned for its delicious macaroons and other delicacies. Light meals are also served, a perfect interlude between excursions.
75 avenue des Champs-Élysées, 8th.
Tel.: 01-40-75-08-75.
www.ladurée.fr

Out on the town

B Crazy Horse
One of the best stylised nude dance shows in the world. Detailed choreography and talent. A must for Parisian nightlife.
12 avenue George-V, 8th.
Tel.: 01-47-23-32-32.
www.lecrazyhorseparis.com

C The Lido
Cabaret shows since 1946. Renowned dancers The Bluebell Girls perform there for a spectacular dinner show.
116 bis avenue des Champs-Élysées, 8th.
Tel.: 01-40-76-56-10.
www.lido.fr

Restaurant

D Fouquet's
A luxury *brasserie* founded in 1899. One of the legendary restaurants on the Champs Élysées, it is classed as a historical monument. It was renovated in 1999 by architect and decorator Jacques Garcia. The reception after the César Awards is held here every year. Approximately €80.
99 avenue des Champs-Élysées, 8th.
Tel.: 01-40-69-60-50.

CHAMPS-ÉLYSÉES – CLEMENCEAU

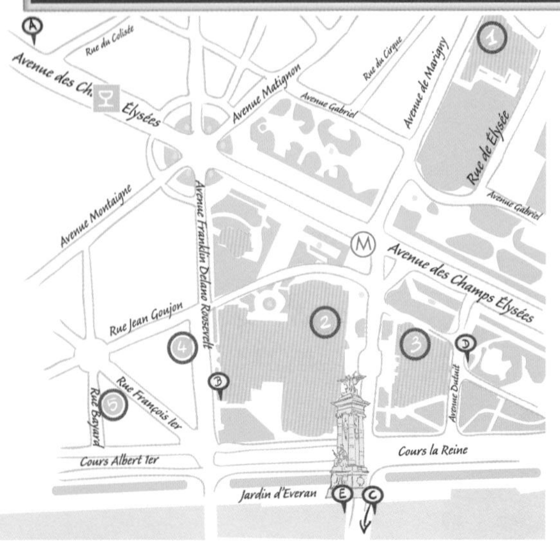

History

Two historical emblems are celebrated here. The first is the Champs-Élysées, a place in Greek mythology where pure and honest souls came to rest. The 'most beautiful avenue in the world' was developed in the 17th century to allow the kings to travel to the forest of Versailles from the Palais-Royal. It measures 1.91 kilometres (1.19 miles) long and 70 metres (77 yards) wide. The other emblem is Georges Clemenceau (1841–1929), former Prime Minister of France, who gave his name to the adjoining square in 1929. The station features balustrades by Cassien-Bernard and is decorated with *azulejos* by Manuel Cargaleiro, donated by the Lisbon Metro in exchange for one Guimard's metro entrances.

SIGHTSEEING

Monument

1 **Palais de l'Élysée:** built in Classical style by architect Armand-Claude Mollet for Louis-Henri de La Tour d'Auvergne from 1718, it then became the residence of Madame de Pompadour. It has been the official seat of the French republic since 1848.
55 rue du Faubourg Saint-Honoré, 8th.
No visits allowed.

Culture

2 **Grand Palais:** inaugurated in 1900 as a monument to the glory of French art. Exhibitions and events are held beneath its spectacular glass roof, the largest in Europe.
Avenue Winston Churchill, 8th.
Tel.: 01-44-13-17-17. www.grandpalais.fr

Petit Palais, Musée des Beaux-Arts de la Ville de Paris: built for the 1900 Universal Exhibition by architect Charles Girault. It is in the shape of a trapezoid with four buildings around a central garden. Features include numerous stained glass windows, ceramics, ironwork, and the Coupole Dutuit, all representing French art.

Avenue Winston Churchill, 8th.
Tel.: 01-53-43-40-00. wwwpetitpalais.paris.fr
Open Tuesday to Sunday 10am to 6pm, and until 8pm on Thursday evenings for temporary exhibitions. Closed on public holidays. Admission free.

Palais de la Découverte : opened in 1931 to popularise science. Suitable for all ages.

Avenue Franklin-Roosevelt, 8th.
Tel.: 01-56-43-20-20.
Open Tuesday to Saturday 9.30am to 6pm, Sundays and public holidays 10am to 7pm. Entrance fee.

Architecture

22 rue Bayard: the legendary headquarters of RTL radio. You can almost feel the sound waves with this building, dating from 1972 and designed by Op artist Victor Vasarely.

Address book

The place for a rendezvous

Le Madrigal
32 avenue des Champs-Élysées, 8th.
Open daily 8am to 2am.
Tel.: 01-43-59-90-25.

Shopping

A Virgin Megastore
Three floors of books and DVDs with a café.
52–60 avenue des Champs-Élysées, 8th.
Tel.: 01-49-53-50-00.
Open Monday to Saturday 10am to midnight, and from noon on Sundays.

Out on the town

B Théâtre du Rond-Point
Contemporary theatre. Also a restaurant.
2 bis avenue Franklin-Roosevelt, 8th.
Tel.: 01-44-95-98-00.
www.theatredurond-point.fr

C Showcase
This concert hall and nightclub is a must.
Under the Alexandre III bridge, port des Champs-Élysées, 8th.
Tel.: 01-45-61-25-43.
www.showcase.fr

Restaurants

D Pavillon Ledoyen
Opened in 1791. A pavilion surrounded by greenery that offers fine dining in a second Empire setting. Five-course dinners priced €200–300.
1 avenue Dutuit, 8th.
Tel.: 01-53-05-10-01.
Open daily except Monday lunch, 12.30pm to 2.30pm and 7.30pm to 10pm.

E Mini-Palais
Located inside the Grand Palais, with views over the terrace, the restaurant is run by Eric Fréchon, three-star chef at the Hôtel Bristol, and Eric d'Aboville. Cuisine inspired by Mediterranean and Asian traditions. Terrace and piano bar in summer. Main courses €25–35.
3 avenue Winston Churchill, 8th.
Tel.: 01-42-56-42-42.
www.minipalais.com
Open daily 10am to 1am.

CONCORDE

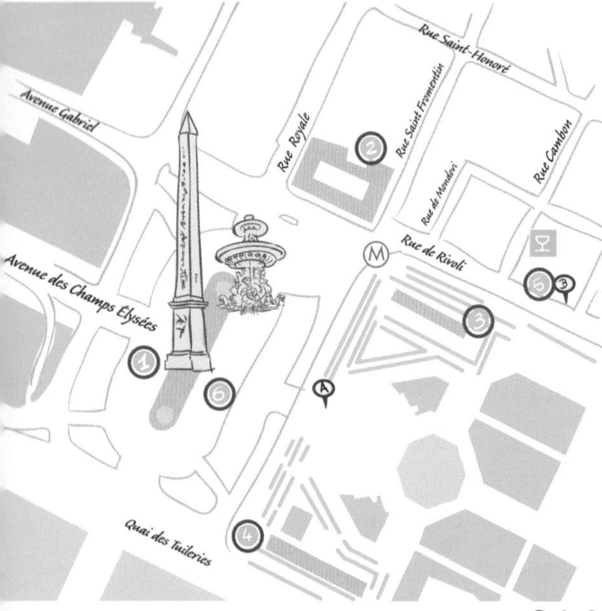

Declaration of the Rights of Man and the Citizen, painted on the walls by the artist Françoise Schein.

History

The original square, Place Louis XV, was completed in 1772 by architect Jacques-Ange Gabriel. It had previously been surrounded by a moat with six bridges. The guillotine was set up here in 1792 for one year, and the square was named Place de la Révolution until 1796 when it finally became Place de la Concorde. Overlooking the square are Hôtel de la Marine and Hôtel de Crillon, both featuring impressive columns, and the United States Embassy. The fountains were built in 1836 and 1846. Inside the station you can read the 17 articles of the Universal

SIGHTSEEING

Monuments

1. **The Luxor Obelisk:** a gift from the Viceroy of Egypt, Mehemet Ali, the obelisk is made of granite and weighs over 230 tonnes. It was placed in the middle of the square in 1836, in the presence of Louis-Philippe.

2. **Hôtel de la Marine:** formerly the Crown's furniture warehouse, it was built from 1757. It is still the Navy headquarters.

Culture

3. **Jeu de Paume:** a reference for photography and visual arts enthusiasts. Quality exhibitions.
1 place de la Concorde, 1st.

Tel.: 01-47-03-12-50.
www.jeudepaume.org. Entrance fee.

Musée de l'Orangerie : a setting with the luminosity for appreciating Claude Monet's *Nymphéas* and other works. Also has temporary exhibitions.

Located in the Jardin des Tuileries.
Tel.: 01-44-77-80-07.
www.musee-orangerie.fr
Open Wednesday to Monday 9am to 6pm.
Entrance fee.

Out of the ordinary

5 **Cercle Suédois:** one of the oldest Swedish clubs abroad, founded in 1891. Alfred Nobel was one of the first members. Promotes good relations between France and Sweden, including in its elegant restaurant.
242 rue de Rivoli, 1st.
Tel.: 01-42-60-75-07.

6 **Sundial:** markings on the ground indicate the presence of the world's largest sundial. It follows variations in the sun, the days and the year. A project devised by the astronomer Camille Flammarion in 1913, it was finally put in place in 1999, making the square the largest 'public clock'.

Address book

The place for a rendezvous

Brasserie Chez Flottes
2 rue Cambon, 1st.
Open daily 7am to midnight..
Tel.: 01-42-60-80-89.
www.brasserie-flottes.fr

Shopping

A Librairie des Jardins
Specialises in gardening books, with over 4,000 to choose from.
Grille des Tuileries, on place de la Concorde.
Tel.: 01-42-60-61-61.
Open daily 10am to 7pm.

Restaurant

B Le Restaurant du Cercle Suédois
Swedish gourmet restaurant with a feast of Nordic flavours.
Menus €28 – 35.
242 rue de Rivoli, 1st.
Tel.: 01-42-60-76-67.
Open Monday to Friday noon to 3pm.

TUILERIES

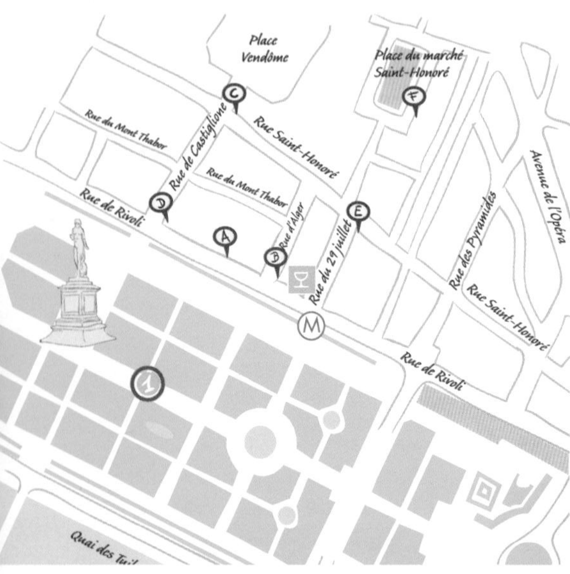

You can spot Marilyn Monroe as well as characters from children's TV.

History

The station is named after the gardens adjoining it. In the 13th century the main activity in the area was the manufacture of tiles, and the station still takes its name from this. But later it became an elegant royal residence thanks to architects Philibert Delorme and Jean Bullard. The Tuileries Palace would be destroyed after the Paris Commune. Louis XIV's gardener André Le Nôtre created the formal French garden there in 1664, and you can still admire his work today. The metro station was redesigned for the year 2000, with large panels portraying key themes from the past century.

SIGHTSEEING

A walk in the park

1 **Jardin des Tuileries:** originally, ordinary people could only access the gardens on Sundays, but nowadays it is open to all. Free guided tours from April to October on Saturdays, Sundays and public holidays take visitors round lesser-known parts of the gardens, which extend over more than 23 hectares. See ducks, sculptures, contemporary art (by Louise Bourgeois or Jacques Maillol for example) and the arch of the Carrousel du Louvre, dating from 1808, which celebrates Napoleon's victories. Opposite rue de Castiglione are 14 steps that have witnessed the vicissitudes of French royal and republican history.
113 rue de Rivoli, 1st.

Address book

The place for a rendezvous

🍸 **Le Welcome**
210 rue de Rivoli, 1st.
Open daily 6.30am to 10pm.
Tel.: 01-42-60-68-53.

Shopping

Ⓐ Galignani
The first English bookstore on the continent, established as

early as 1520. Wide choice of books in English in a wood-panelled setting with cosy old armchairs for comfortable reading. Also a good collection of art books. Karl Lagerfeld often pops in.
224 rue de Rivoli, 1st.
Tel.: 01-42-60-76-07.
www.galignani.com
Open Monday to Saturday 10am to 7pm.

Ⓑ Maison Francis Kurkdjian
A rising star in perfume, he created Jean-Paul Gaultier's *'Mâle'* fragrance.
5 rue d'Alger, 1st.
Tel.: 01-42-60-07-07.
www.franciskurkdjian.com
Open Monday to Friday 11am to 1.30pm and 2.30pm to 7pm, and all day Saturday.

Ⓒ Pierre Barboza
Second-hand jewellery and many other treasures.
356 rue Saint-Honoré, 1st.
Tel.: 01-42-60-67-08.
Open Monday to Friday 10am to 1pm and 2.30pm to 6pm.

Ⓓ Angelina
A confectionery paradise with bakery and tea room in Belle Époque decor. Founded in 1903 by Antoine Rumpelmayer who named his shop after his daughter-in-law. People come especially for the hot chocolate. There is

usually a long queue for the goodies here.
226 rue de Rivoli, 1st.
Tel.: 01-42-60-82-00.
www.angelina-paris.fr
Open daily 9am to 7pm.

Out on the town

Ⓔ Water Bar de Colette
The height of cool! Concept store selling the trendiest wares, with the Water Bar in the basement. Great idea, a water bar!
213 rue Saint-Honoré, 1st.
Tel.: 01-55-35-33-90.
www.colette.fr.
Open Monday to Saturday 11am to 7pm.

Restaurant

Ⓕ L'Absinthe
After shopping at Marc Jacobs, American Apparel or The Kooples, you can take a break in the Rostang family bistro, run by Caroline. Designer interior, a gourmet place to stop. Menus €32–40.
24 place du Marché Saint-Honoré, 1st.
Tel.: 01-49-26-90-04.
www.restaurantabsinthe.com
Lunch served noon to 2pm, dinner 7.30pm to 10.30pm, closed Saturday lunch and Sunday.

PALAIS ROYAL – MUSÉE DU LOUVRE

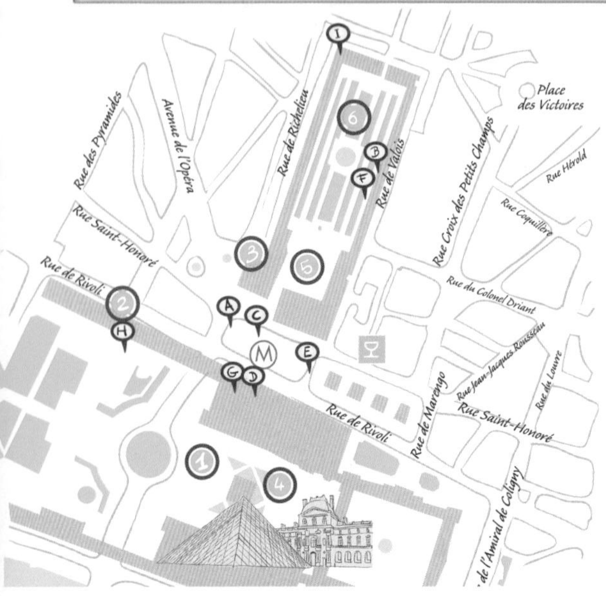

History

From being a bathhouse and spa in Roman times, the Palais Cardinal (under Cardinal Richelieu) took on royal status when the Dukes of Orléans commissioned arcades and shops to be built around the garden in the 18th century. The garden had been used for lovers' trysts and erotic encounters. Wandering around the shops here makes for a pleasant stroll before attending a performance at the Comédie-Française or visiting the Louvre. Contemporary artist Jean-Michel Othoniel created the *Kiosque des Noctambules*, an entrance to the station on Place Colette, to commemorate the Paris Metro's centenary in 2000. The kiosk was a reinterpretation of Hector Guimard's Art Nouveau entrances, with two domes in red and blue Murano glass supported by an aluminium structure. You can also admire the Huichol fresco, a work of native Mexican art by Santos de la Torre, which celebrates Franco-Mexican cooperation, inside the station on the platform and in the corridors of line 1.

SIGHTSEEING

Culture

1. **Musée du Louvre:** a vast collection of art from its origins to the present day in the former French royal palace. You can access the Napoleon, Denon and Sully wings via the Pyramid and admire paintings from

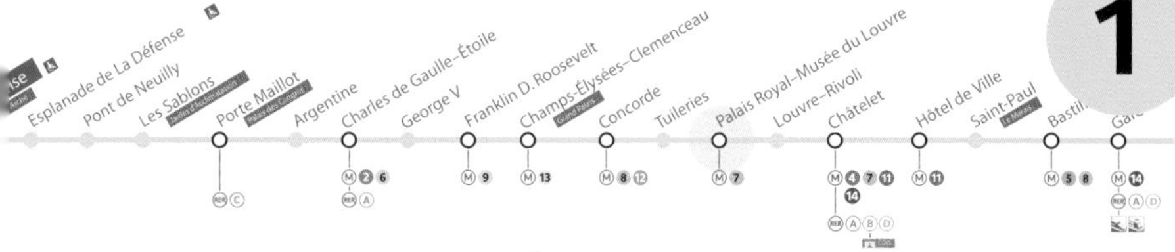

Etruscan, Greek, Roman, and Egyptian antiquity through to the French, Italian, Spanish and northern schools. The Salle des États houses the famous Mona Lisa.

Several entrances, including via the Cour Napoléon or 99, rue de Rivoli, 1st.
Tel.: 01-40-20-50-50.
www.louvre.fr. Open Monday, Thursday, Saturday and Sunday 9am to 6pm and Wednesday and Friday 9am to 10pm. Entrance fee.

Musée des Arts Décoratifs: exhibits showing various techniques using wood, glass and metal as well as plastic, gold or silver, from the Middle Ages to the present day. Thematic exhibitions, textile collections and a depositary of advertising posters.

107 rue de Rivoli, 1st.
Tel.: 01-44-55-57-50.
www.lesartsdecoratifs.fr. Open Tuesday to Sunday 11am to 6pm and Thursdays until 9pm. Entrance fee.

3 **Comédie-Française:** the theatre, built in 1786, contains one of the portraits of Voltaire by Jean-Antoine Houdon. There is also the chair into which Molière supposedly fainted during a performance. There is a padded theatre bar and balconies are open at the intermission with views over the square. For the last available seats go to rue de Montpensier one hour before performances.

Place Colette, 1st.
Tel.: 0825-10-16-80.
www.comedie-française.fr

Monuments

4 **Pyramide de Pei:** commissioned by François Mitterrand in 1989 for the bicentenary of the French Revolution,

the famous Pyramid stands in the middle of the Cour Napoléon. It was conceived by architect Ieoh Ping Pei and is made up of 603 diamond-shapes and 70 triangles of glass which bring natural light into the heart of the museum.

Free access.

5 **Buren columns and Pol Bury spheres:** next to the Palais Royal and

the Conseil d'État you will find strange columns with black asphalt and white stripes. This is a work of contemporary art by painter and sculptor Daniel Buren, which plays on repetition and optical illusion. In the evening, lighting makes it look like a runway. Nearby is the fountain made with metal spheres by Belgian surrealist artist Pol Bury (1922–2005), who was influenced by Magritte, Calder and Mondrian.

Free access.

6 **Jardins du Palais-Royal:** this elegant architectural work was initially carried out for Cardinal Richelieu in the 17th century by Jacques Lemercier, who also designed the Sorbonne. Its three wings were only enclosed in the 18th century. Ladies of the night plied their trade under its arcades and people strolled in its aisles. Then, at the end of the 19th century, the Grands Boulevards became fashionable and the place lost its bustle and liveliness. Today the site is crowded with tourists and Parisians seeking greenery. Colette once lived in the area, and writer Jean d'Ormesson and actress Valérie Lemercier can often be seen here.

2 place Colette, 1th.
Open daily 7.30am to 8.30pm, later in spring and summer.

Address book

The place for a rendezvous

Café Saint-Honoré
194 rue Saint Honoré, 1st.
Open daily 8am to midnight.
Tel.: 01-42-61-49-31.

Shopping

A Hôtel du Louvre

A small hotel (177 rooms) with marble and woodwork and decorated in Napoleon III style. Each side overlooks a major Paris monument: the Louvre, the Comédie-Française and the Opéra Garnier.

Place André Malraux, 1st.
Tel.: 01-44-58-38-38.

B Serge Lutens Perfumery

With the ambiance of a dark baroque boudoir, it is dedicated to delicate fragrances. Original creations redolent of a distant, dream-like past, like *Fumerie Turque, Ambre Sultan* or *Bornéo 1834*. Also try Shiseido's Palais-Royal Salons.

Jardins du Palais-Royal, 142 galerie de Valois, 1st.
Tel.: 01-49-27-09-09.
www.sergelutens.com
Open Monday to Saturday 10am to 7pm.

C Librairie Delamain

Good selection and variety of recent and old books.

155 rue Saint-Honoré, 1st.
Tel.: 01-42-61-48-78.
www.librairie-delamain.com
Open Monday to Saturday 10am to 8pm.

D Apple Store

Avid Apple followers meet in the Carousel du Louvre to see what's new or take advice from other fans.

99 rue de Rivoli, 1st.
Tel.: 01-43-16-78-00.
Open all week 10am to 8pm.

E Le Louvre des Antiquaires

Just by the Louvre, its brochure promises '250 galleries, 30 artistic specialties and works from Europe, Asia, the Middle East, from ancient times until the 1960s, in a historic building from the 19th century'.

Place du Palais-Royal, 1st.
Tel.: 01-42-97-27-27.
www.louvre-antiquaires.com
Free access.

F Jérôme L'Huillier

Fashion and jewellery designer, stocks ultra-Parisian women's clothing, elegant and foxy Showroom.

Jardins du Palais-Royal, 138–139 galerie de Valois, 1st.
Tel.: 01-49-26-07-07.
www.jeromelhuillier.com
Open Monday to Saturday 11am to 7pm.

Out on the town

G Café Marly

Nothing better than sipping a glass of something on the café's terrace, even in winter, facing the Pyramid of the Louvre.

93 rue de Rivoli, 1st.
Tel.: 01-49-26-06-60.
Open all week 8.30am to midnight.

Restaurants

H Le Saut du Loup

Restaurant in the Museum of Decorative Arts, designer interior and terrace, a peaceful place in the heart of Paris. Traditional French cuisine. Main courses €16–22.

107 rue de Rivoli, 1st.
Tel.: 01-42-25-49-55.
www.lesautduloup.com
Open Monday to Friday noon to 11pm, and until 2am Saturday and Sunday.

I Le Grand Véfour

Formerly 'Café de Chartres', this gourmet restaurant opened in 1784 and is closely linked to the Palais-Royal's history. Everyone would love to dine under the gilded ceiling of this temple to French gastronomy, managed by thrice-Michelin-starred chef Guy Martin. In its heyday, Balzac, Lamartine or Cocteau dined here. If you can't eat here, at least go past it. €200–220.

17 rue du Beaujolais, 1st.
Tel.: 01-42-96-56-27.
Service at 12.30pm, 8pm and 9pm from Monday to Friday.

LOUVRE – RIVOLI

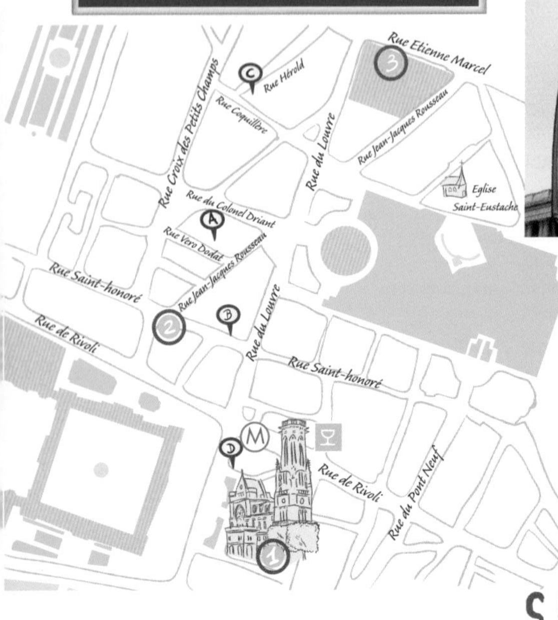

History

The station was renamed in 1989 to avoid confusion with Palais Royal-Musée du Louvre. The famous museum's riches are evoked right on the platform, where the walls are lined with Burgundy stone. Following a decision by André Malraux, then Minister for Cultural Affairs, reproductions of artworks or casts of sculptures were placed in niches in the walls following architect Robert Venter's design. Lighting is dim and there are no garish advertising posters. It is like an underground museum, with Doric columns supporting the ceilings. The second part of the station's name, 'Rivoli', reflects not only the name of the street above but also the battle of Rivoli, where Bonaparte defeated Austria in 1797 during the Italy campaign.

SIGHTSEEING

Monuments

1 **Église de Saint-Germain l'Auxerrois:** next to the Town Hall of the 1st arrondissement. The church dates from the 12th century and is a good example of Gothic building, with an ornate porch. Not to be missed: the bestiary of

stone. The church bells rung out the signal to begin the massacres of Saint-Barthélemy in 1572.

2 place du Louvre, 1st. Tel.: 01-42-60-13-96.

Église Réformée de l'Oratoire du Louvre: a Protestant church with a statue of Admiral Gaspard de Coligny, a leader in the Wars of Religion, who was born in 1519, not in 1517 as engraved on his statue!

145 rue Saint-Honoré, 1st. Tel.: 01-42-60-21-64.

Out of the ordinary

3 **The Central Post Office:** the Central Post Office: It might not seem special on the surface, but this post office is open until midnight. On evenings when an official deadline for submitting tax declarations falls, a huge queue forms here since a postmark is proof of the date of posting.

52 rue du Louvre, 1st.

Address book

The place for a rendezvous

La Coopérative
85 rue de Rivoli, 1st.
Open daily 7am to 10.30pm and Sundays until 9.30pm.
Tel.: 01-42-60-10-89.

Shopping

A Galerie Vero-Dodat
Covered passage with upmarket shops (bookstores, cafés, art galleries). Sumptuous neoclassical decor with mirrors, trompe-l'œil, paving stones in a checkerboard pattern, all to give an impression of depth. The name comes from Mr Vero the butcher and Mr Dodat the financier. On rue Bouloi two statues adorn the facade: Hermes, the god of commerce, on one side and Hercules on the other, with his pelt. This was the terminus for a coach company. People would stop there to shop.

Between 2 rue du Bouloi and 19 rue Jean-Jacques-Rousseau, 1st.
Open Monday to Saturday 11am to 7pm.

B Maison Micro
Ouzo, seeds, herbs, retsina, spices and chickpeas. This store has all the flavours of Greece. It was opened in 1942 by Dimitri Micropoulos (the 'Micro').
140 rue Saint-Honoré, 1st.
Tel.: 01-42-60-15-25.
Open Monday to Saturday 11am to 7pm.

C Ekobo
You cannot miss its bright green facade. Sells tableware made of bamboo, for example.
4 rue Hérold, 1st.
Tel.: 01-45-08-47-43.
Open Tuesday to Saturday 11am to 7pm.

Restaurant

D Le Fumoir
Elegant café, lots of books and comfortable leather chairs. People may no longer smoke here, but there is fine, tasty cuisine at good prices. Its weekend brunch is very popular. Main courses €18–25.
6 rue de l'Amiral-de-Coligny, 1st.
Tel.: 01-42-92-00-24.
Open daily 11am to 2am.

CHÂTELET

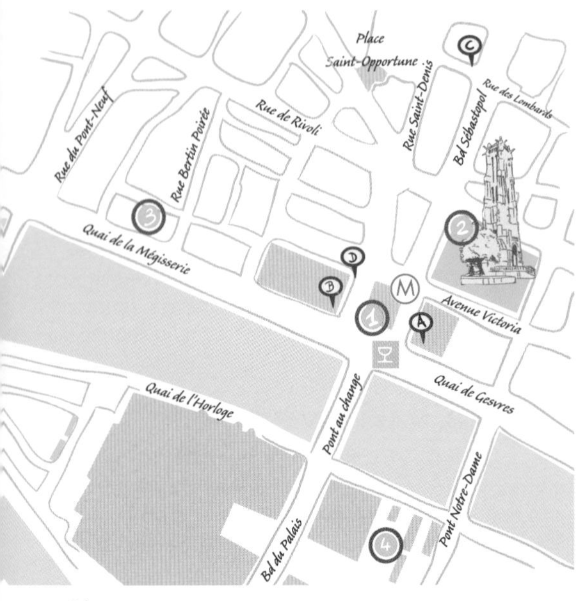

History

The station, which opened on 6 August 1900, takes its name from the square where it is located. First it was called 'Pont au Change', then in 1926 its name was changed to 'Pont Notre-Dame'. In 1934 it finally became 'Châtelet', after the small castle fortified by King Louis VI (1081–1137) to defend that part of the river Seine. The castle would later become a prison, and was demolished in the 18th century. In 1964 Châtelet became the first metro station to be equipped with a moving pavement that transported passengers at 3 km/hr (1.9 miles/hr). At the Place Sainte-Opportune exit there is a Guimard Art Nouveau metro entrance, cast in 2000 for the metro's centenary using plans and moulds left by the inventor. Along the corridors to lines 4 and 11 are ceramics by Hervé Mathieu-Bachelot, artistic consultant for the RATP.

SIGHTSEEING

Monuments

1. **Place du Châtelet:** don't miss the huge Palmier fountain with a central column in the shape of a palm tree, hence its name. The sphinx sculptures were added later by architect Gabrielle Davioud (1824–1881).

2. **Tour Saint-Jacques:** this Gothic tower is 62 metres (68 yards) high. It is all that remains of the Church of Saint-Jacques de la Boucherie, which was destroyed after the Revolution. The church was one of the places from which pilgrim-

ages to Santiago de Compostela in Spain would depart. It is worth lifting your head to appreciate the plethora of detail, like the statue of Blaise Pascal (1623–1662), scientist and philosopher.

Square de la Tour-Saint-Jacques, 4th.

Out of the ordinary

Quai de la Mégisserie: its name derives from the tanning workshops which were once the main trade here. Nowadays there are pet shops and flower sellers, and, on the side next to the river, sellers of old books. There is a good view of the Palais de Justice, the central Paris courthouse.

Place Louis Lépine: known for its wonderful daily flower market. A good way of getting back to nature! The square is named after former police commissioner Louis Lépine, who created a renowned competition for inventors.

Address book

The place for a rendezvous

Brasserie Sarah Bernhard
2 place du Châtelet, 4th.
Open daily 8am to midnight.
Tel.: 01-42-72-00-71.

Culture

A Théâtre de la Ville
For theatre, dance and music.
2 place du Châtelet, 4th.
Tel.: 01-42-74-22-77.
www.theatredelaville-paris.com

B Théâtre du Châtelet
For musicals, opera, dance, recitals and even opera lessons.
1 place du Châtelet, 1st.
Tel.: 01-40-28-28-40.
www.chatelet-theatre.com

C Le Duc des Lombards
One of the best-known Paris jazz venues.
42 rue des Lombards, 1st.
Tel.: 01-42-33-22-88.
www.ducdeslombards.com

Restaurant

D Le Zimmer
Offers a wide variety of dishes from risotto to veal liver, filet of sea bass or cheeseburgers. Founded in the late 19th century by a certain Mr Zimmer, it was renovated by decorator Jacques Garcia, retaining its 19th century *brasserie* charm and elegance. Very popular with theatre-goers and actors from the neighbouring theatres. Main courses €15–18.
1 place du Châtelet, 1st.
Tel.: 01-42-36-74-03.
www.lezimmer.com
Open daily 7.30am to midnight.

HÔTEL DE VILLE

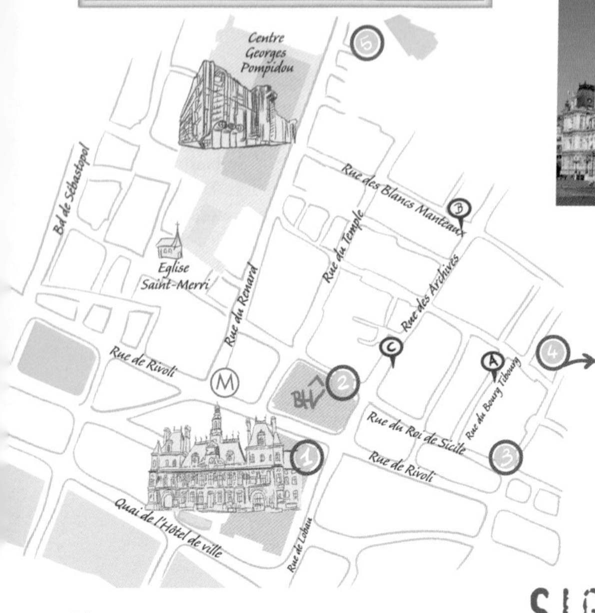

History

This is where French history has often played out its dénouement. Previously called Place de la Grève, labourers and others looking for work would come here to get hired. This went on until workers gathered here and challenged their wages and conditions. This gave rise to the French term *'faire la grève'*, to go on strike. Nothing remains of the original Hôtel de Ville building, as it was burnt to the ground in 1871. It was rebuilt after the Paris Commune in 1883 in a pure Renaissance style. This is where Alphonse de Lamartine, politician, poet and founder of the Second Republic, made his appeal to the people, saying: 'Together we will create the most sublime poetry.' It was also here that De Gaulle gave his famous speech on the liberation of Paris, saying: 'Paris! Paris the oppressed, Paris the downtrodden, Paris the martyr! But now Paris is liberated.'

SIGHTSEEING

Monument

1 **Hôtel de Ville:** guided tours of reception rooms, subject to availability. Totally *'style pompier'* complete with gilding everywhere.
One tour per week, two per week in summer.
Registration: Salon d'Accueil, 29 rue de Rivoli, 4th, on 01-42-76-43-43, 01-42-76-50-49 or 01-42-76-54-04.
Admission free.

Shoppers' paradise

2 **Bazar de l'Hôtel de Ville (BHV):** this department store is legendary for many Parisians. It opened in 1856 and sells just about everything. Interesting ar-

chitecture using metal beams, glass and reinforced concrete. History tells us that its founder, Xavier Ruel, a hosier by trade, courageously saved Empress Eugénie when her horse bolted in front of his stall. She gave him the site as a gift to thank him. At first he called it Bazar Napoléon, and the initials 'B' and 'N' are still visible in its famous rotunda. Don't miss the basement, which is full of every imaginable kind of DIY accessory.

55 rue de la Verrerie, 4th.
Tel.: 01-42-74-90-00. www.bhv.fr

Architecture

3 56 rue du Roi-de-Sicile: the facade of this former horse butcher's shop remains intact, including a mosaic that reads *'achat de chevaux',* or 'horses bought'.

4 High relief at 87, rue Vieille-du-Temple: the sculpture by Robert le Lorrain, *The Horses of the Sun* (1730), can be seen above the entry to the former stables of the Hôtel de Rohan.

Out of the ordinary

5 Musée de la Poupée: a museum where you can learn all about the art of making dolls. There is even a small clinic for dolls to have a check-up!

Impasse Berthaud, 3rd.
Tel.: 01-42-72-73-11.
www.museedelapoupeeparis.com.
Open Tuesday to Sunday 10am to 6pm.
Closed Mondays and public holidays.
Entrance fee.

Address book

The place for a rendezvous

The Majesty
35 rue de Rivoli, 4th.
Open Monday to Friday 7am to midnight, and from 9.30am on Saturdays.
Tel.: 01-49-96-58-75.

Shopping

A Mariage Frères
Teas from around the world. There is a small museum upstairs and a restaurant to sample the teas.
30 rue du Bourg-Tibourg, 4th.
Tel.: 01-42-72-28-11.
www.mariagefreres.com

B Les Touristes
Colourful flowers adorn everything from tablecloths to bags, material and cushions.
17 rue des Blancs-Manteaux, 4th. Tel.: 01-42-72-10-84.
www.lestouristes.eu

Restaurant

C Les Marronniers
They even serve a burger named after a French environmental activist, José Bové. Dine in the restaurant, sitting on high stools at the bar or on the terrace. A must on the gay circuit. Main courses €10–20.
18 rue des Archives, 4th.
Tel.: 01-40-27-87-72.

SAINT-PAUL

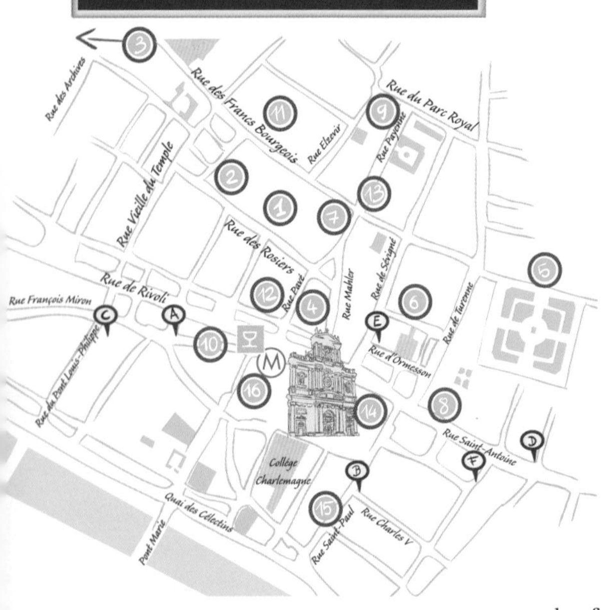

History

This station takes its name from the luxurious medieval royal residence built and adorned by Charles V. His son Charles VI, known as the Mad, also lived there. The 'Hôtel Saint-Pol', called after a missionary who preached his message as far away as the Orient, included a church where kings and their heirs were baptised. All that remains of this church is a wall at the corner of rue Saint-Paul and rue Neuve Saint-Pierre. The impressive Church of Saint-Paul-Saint-Louis, built in the 18th century by order of Louis XIII, stands right next to the station. Its architectural style is typical of French-Italian baroque, with its flamboyant, three-storey facade. It was inspired by the Church of the Gesù in Rome. At the station exit there is an example of a 'Val d'Osne' metro totem, named after the place where they were forged. They were made in the 1920s and feature a luminous opaline globe that stands 20 metres (22 yards) high. They are very rare on the metro system nowadays. Intricate wrought ironwork surrounds the word 'metro'.

SIGHTSEEING

A walk round the Jewish Quarter

1 *Rue des Rosiers:* the street has now been taken over by fashion shops but was once full of rose bushes. The Jewish community was first welcomed here, then banished and forbidden to carry out so-called noble tasks. It returned in the 20th century.

The Yellow Shop/Sacha Finkelsztajn: a focal point for Jewish life in the area from 1946. You can buy bread, cakes, bagels, pretzels and macaroons for Passover.

27 rue des Rosiers, 4th.
Tel.: 01-42-72-78-91.
finkelsztajn.com

Musée d'Art et d'Histoire du Judaïsme: Paris's Jewish museum is housed in the beautiful Hôtel de Saint-Aignan. You can see liturgical objects and Hebrew manuscripts, as well as quality exhibitions on art and culture.

71 rue du Temple, 3rd.
Tel.: 01-53-01-86-53. www.mahj.org
Entrance fee.

Synagogue: built in 1913, this is a fine example of Art Nouveau by Hector Guimard, who designed the iconic metro entrances.

10 rue Pavée, 4th.

Squares to visit

Place des Vosges: formerly Place Royale, it began as a town-planning project under Henri IV and was inaugurated under Louis XIII. A rare well-preserved example of Renaissance architecture. Each side measures 108 metres (118 yards). Houses and walkways have roofs of slate. In the centre is a replica of a bronze statue of Louis XIII. The original was melted down during the Revolution. The Vosges *département* was the first to pay its taxes from 1800, which earned it a Parisian square in its name.

6 **Place du marché Sainte-Catherine:** a lovely little square built in the 17th century on the ruins of the Sainte-Catherine church.

Grand town houses

7 **Hôtel d'Angoulême Lamoignon:** Renaissance-style town house built for Diane de France from 1584. Guillaume de Lamoignon, the first President of the Parliament of Paris, lived here. Later some of the greatest minds of the time, like Racine and Bourdaloue, who preached at nearby Church of Saint-Paul,

would be received here. Novelist Alphonse Daudet also stayed here. Savour the many architectural features that reveal Diane de France's love of hunting, such as arrows.

24 rue Pavée, 4th.
View from the outside, no visits.

8 **Hôtel de Béthune-Sully:** building began in 1625 on this town house, a fine example of Louis XIII style. Maximilien de Béthune, Duke of Sully (1559–1641), Henri IV's finance minister, lived here. There is a sundial on the south facade at the far end of the orangery in the second courtyard.

62 rue Saint-Antoine, 4th.
No visits allowed.

9 **Hôtel de Marle (Swedish Cultural Centre):** originally built in the 16th century, it was transformed for Hector de Marle, advisor to the Parliament of Paris. His initials can be seen in the remarkable beamed ceiling on the first floor. The town house was beautifully restored and was bought by the Swedish government in 1965. It now houses the Swedish Institute and a very nice Swedish café, open Tuesday to Sunday from noon to 6pm. Terrace open in fine weather.

11 rue Payenne, 3rd.
Tel.: 01-44-78-80-20.
Open Tuesday to Friday 10am to 1pm and 2pm to 5.30pm, weekends noon to 6pm.

10 **Hôtel de Beauvais:** 17th century town house designed by Antoine Le Pautre, the royal architect. The main building overlooks the street, which is unusual, since that was where common people would be. This architectural choice can be explained by the lack of space. A beautiful oval courtyard with Ionic columns and pilasters. Mozart also lived here. Nowadays the building houses the Paris Administrative Appeals Court.

68 rue François-Miron, 4th.
No visits allowed.

11 **Rue des Francs-Bourgeois:** some of the finest town houses in the area are to be found on this street, including the Hôtel d'Albret at no. 31. Note the tympanum over its superb door. Take time to explore this street with its ancient facades, which now house trendy boutiques.

Architectural curiosities

2 Rue Pavée: the first paved street in Paris in the 15th century. There used to be prisons here.

3 5 rue Payenne: this was a Positivist temple. Its unusual facade is decorated with a bust of philosopher Auguste Comte, the founder of positivism.

4 Église Saint-Paul-Saint-Louis: on the second pillar on the right as you enter an inscription remaining from the Paris Commune reads *La République ou la Mort!* ('The Republic or death!').

Leisure

15 Musée de la Magie et de la Curiosité: this museum recounts the history of magic and conjuring under its 17th century vaulting, through a variety of objects.

11 rue Saint-Paul, 4th.
Tel.: 01-42-72-13-26.
www.museedelamagie.com
Entrance fee.

16 Further reading: for French speakers, see *Rendez-vous au métro Saint-Paul* by Cyrille Fleischmann (Éditions Le Dilettante, 1992).

Address book

The place for a rendezvous

Les Chimères
133 rue Saint-Antoine, 4th.
Open every day 8am to 2am..
Tel.: 01-42-72-71-97.

Shopping

A Galerie Sentou
Designer furniture and objects.
29 rue François Miron, 4th.
Tel.: 01-42-78-50-60.
Open Tuesday to Saturday 10am to 7pm.

B Épicerie Thanksgiving
A store with American specialities. Its restaurant serves Louisiana cuisine.
20 rue Saint-Paul, 4th.
Tel.: 01-42-77-68-29.
www.thanksgivingparis.com

C Izraël
An Aladdin's cave with scents and spices from around the world, from traditional ones

to unusual ones, and some expensive ones.
30 rue François Miron, 4th.
Tel.: 01-42-72-66-23.
Open Tuesday to Friday 9.30am to 1pm and 2.30pm to 7pm and Saturday 9am to 7pm.

D Miyakodori
This shop is hidden behind an electric blue facade. You can stock up on Japanese objects. Ideal for gifts.
1 impasse Guéménée, 4th.
Tel.: 01-42-78-23-11.
www.miyakodori.fr

Out on the town

E Le Double Fond
A café and theatre specialising in magic and conjuring. Quality shows.
1 place du Marché Sainte-Catherine, 4th.
Tel.: 01-42-71-40-20.
www.doublefond.com

Restaurant

F Au Vin des Pyrénées
Bistro atmosphere, interesting food, located in a former wine merchant's shop. Main courses €12–18.
25 rue Beautreillis, 4th.
Tel.: 01-42-72-64-94.
Open Monday to Sunday noon to 2.30pm and 8pm to 11.30pm, bar open until 2am.

BASTILLE

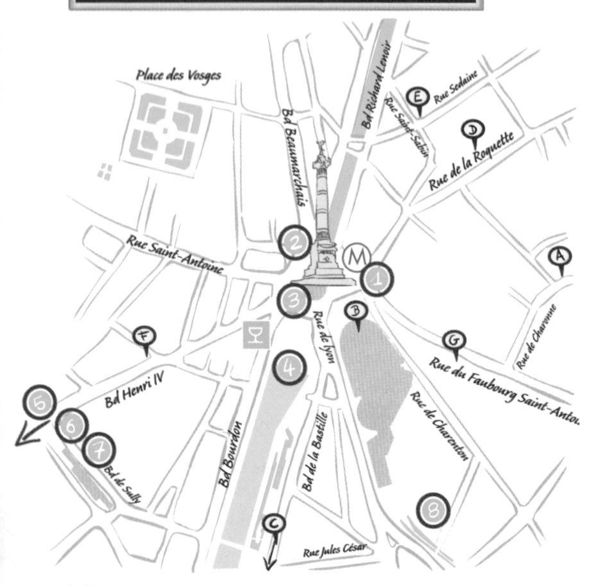

History

A most historic station. The Bastille was a medieval fortress with eight towers 20 metres (22 yards) high, built 1370–1383 under Charles V. It became a prison under Cardinal Richelieu. The station is named after the prison, whose inmates included Voltaire, the Marquis de Sade and Nicolas Fouquet. At the time of the Revolution, the Bastille prison symbolised arbitrary royal power. With the storming of the Bastille on July 14 1789, the people threw off the yoke of the monarchy and heralded the start of the French Revolution. Its destruction would begin on 16 July. Ceramic murals depicting this, some in relief, can be seen inside the station near the Boulevard Bourdon exit. They are the work of Liliane Bélembert and Odile Jacquot. The prison's exterior walls were unearthed in 1905 when building line 5 north towards Bobigny-Pablo Picasso, and these have been preserved. The fortress's outlines have been re-created on the platforms using stainless steel bands. Another feature here is the variety of entrances, illustrating how they have evolved from 1900 to 1970. There is the Art Nouveau Guimard entrance on Boulevard Beaumarchais, and at other exits there are Dervaux signposts with the 'Metro' sign and the yellow 'M' from the 1960s, which took the same colour as the metro ticket of the time. Finally, at boulevard Henri IV, there is a mast-antenna with 'Metro' written in blue inside concentric circles.

SIGHTSEEING

walk through history

Remains of the Bastille: before leaving the station on line 5 from Bobigny, some stones of the former prison are visible.

The July Column: the column that dominates Place de la Bastille commemorates the three-day uprising known as the *Trois Glorieuses* on 27, 28 and 29 July 1830 against the monarchy and Charles IX, and for a Republic. Main features are the lion heads and the statue *The Spirit of Freedom* balancing on the top, over 47 metres (51 yards) from the ground.

3 **The former Bastille towers:** mind the traffic for this walk, and take it slowly—if you can—if you use a bike or a car. You will see darker, round cobblestones amid the cobbles of the Place de la Bastille, which follow the original outline of the former fortress.

4 **Port de l'Arsenal:** timber cargos used to arrive here for the various furniture makers and sellers on rue du Faubourg Saint-Antoine. A few of them are still there. Cruises leave from Port de l'Arsenal.

http://www.parisinfo.com/visite-paris/excursions-1/en-bateau/

5 **Square Henri-Galli :** on boulevard Henri-IV, just before the Seine, you can see the stone remains of one of the towers, 'La Tour Liberté', which were discovered while the station was being built in 1899.

6 Pavillon de l'Arsenal: built in 1879 by architect Clément on the site of a gunpowder factory ('*arsenal*') to exhibit a timber magnate's paintings. It was once used by La Samaritaine department store as a workshop. Nowadays you can discover Paris's urban development and planning with models and temporary exhibitions. On the ground floor there is a complete picture of Paris showing how the city and its habitat have changed.

21 boulevard Morland, 4th.
Tel.: 01-42-76-33-97.
Open Tuesday to Saturday 10.30am to 6.30pm and Sundays 11am to 7pm.
www.pavillon-arsenal.com
Admission free.

7 Bibliothèque de l'Arsenal: one of the finest libraries in Paris, located in the former residence of the artillery masters from the neighbouring Arsenal. In the 18th century, one of them, Antoine-René d'Argenson, Marquis of Paulmy, assembled a collection of the books available to scholars of the time.

1 rue de Sully, 4th.
Tel.: 01-53-79-39-39.
Open Monday to Friday 10am to 6pm and Saturdays 10am to 5pm.
Admission free.

A walk in the park

8 Promenade Plantée: stroll amid greenery from Bastille to the Bois de Vincennes woods along a former railway line. Forget about the city on this walk of over 4.5 km (2.8 miles).

Address book

The place for a rendezvous

Bistrot La Cavetière
41 boulevard Bourdon, 4th.
Open Monday to Saturday noon to 2am.
Tel.: 01-42-76-09-94.

Out of the ordinary

A Mum & Babe
A novel idea in Paris: how to get your hair done without leaving your kids alone. You take them with you, of course. An unusual place offering lots of activities for children while their mothers are being pampered.
3 rue Keller, 11th.
Tel.: 01-43-38-83-55.
www.mumandbabe.fr
Open Tuesday to Saturday 9.30am to 6.30pm.

Culture

B Opéra Bastille
Opened in 1989, conceived by Canadian-Uruguayan architect Carlos Ott, it features transparent facades, walls in blue granite from Lannelin in Brittany, pear wood from China and a glass ceil-

ing. The main auditorium can accommodate 2,700 people. Seats are sometimes available a few hours before the performance. Ticket office on-site.
67 rue de Lyon, 12th.
Tel.: 01-43-47-13-22.
www.operadeparis.fr

Ⓒ La Maison Rouge

Avant-garde exhibitions by the Antoine de Galbert Foundation. And as a bonus, delicious sweet and savoury goodies from the Rose Bakery (open Wednesday to Sunday 11am to 7pm, brunch on weekends, early dinner on Thursdays).
10 boulevard de la Bastille, 12th.
Tel.: 01-40-01-08-81.
www.lamaisonrouge.fr
Entrance fee.

Out on the town

Ⓓ Rue de la Roquette

A wide selection of bistros for eating, drinking and all kinds of music.

Restaurants

Ⓔ Café de l'Industrie

This bistro with colonial decor has three addresses on both sides of the street. Inside there is intimate lighting from small lamps, black and white photographs and worn, red leather sofas. Crowded for Sunday brunch. Typical *brasserie* fare.
Main courses €15–19.
16 rue Saint-Sabin (the largest, our favourite), 11th.
Tel.: 01-47-00-13-53.
Open all week 8.30am to 2am.

Ⓕ Le Réveil Bastille

Mounted Republican Guards from their nearby base pass regularly, to the joy of restaurant-goers. Meat from Salers, egg mayonnaise and pleasant wines. An authentic Parisian bistro. Very nice terrace. Main courses €12–15.
29 boulevard Henri IV, 4th.
Tel. 01-42-72-73-26.
Open Tuesday to Saturday 7.30am to 11pm, until 8pm on Mondays.

Ⓖ Barrio Latino

Vast restaurant on four floors. The wrought iron staircase is also spectacular: it was designed by Gustave Eiffel. A little piece of Havana in the heart of Paris. Tapas, salsa and *caliente* atmosphere guaranteed.
Cocktails around €15.
46 rue du Faubourg-Saint-Antoine, 12th.
Tel.: 01-55-78-84-75.
Open all week 10am to 2am and until 3am on Saturdays, brunch Sundays noon to 4pm, with salsa lessons and activities for children.

Next stations

GARE DE LYON

See line 14, p 358

REUILLY-DIDEROT

Brasserie Diderot, 118 boulevard Diderot, 12th.

NATION

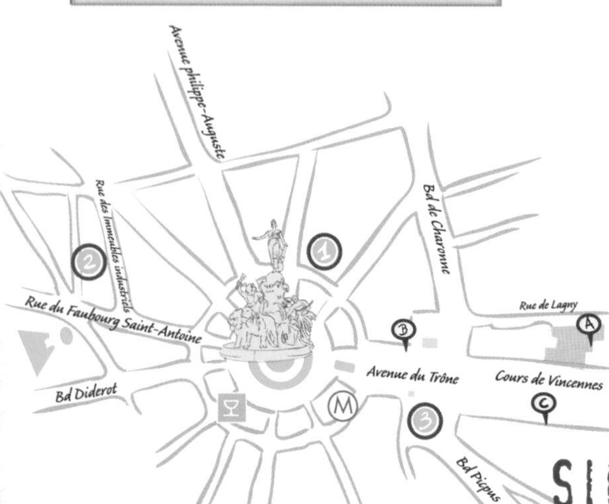

History

The square was once called 'Place du Trône', or 'Throne Square', in honour of King Louis XIV on his return from Reims with Maria Thérèse of Austria, after his coronation. The guillotine was kept here during the Revolution because residents near Concorde had complained about the noise and smell from the convoys of convicts. It was renamed 'Place de la Nation' in 1880 to commemorate *'La Fête Nationale'* or Bastille Day. Another name can be seen on line 9: 'Place des Antilles', with the coats of arms of Guadeloupe and Martinique.

SIGHTSEEING

Architecture

1 **Place de la Nation:** right in the middle is *The Triumph of the Republic* by sculptor Aimé Jules-Dalou. The vast, ornate bronze of a symbolic figure of the Republic standing aloft on her chariot was commissioned by the City of Paris in 1879. You can also see symbolic figures for Genius, Freedom, Justice and Abundance.

2 **Rue des Immeubles industriels:** an interesting side street just beyond the square runs between rue du Faubourg Saint-Antoine (numbers 307–309) and Boulevard Voltaire

(numbers 262–264). It was built in 1873, and one of its planners, Émile Leménil, constructed a group of 20 identical buildings designed to be functional and for industrial use, particularly for furniture makers. This initiative was typical of 19th century utopianism and drew on philosopher Charles Fourier's ideas. The buildings had large picture windows, which have survived to this day. They were revolutionary, conceived for industrial activities in the basement and on the ground floor and employee housing on the upper floors. Other remains of this industrial past can be seen at the following addresses: 76 rue de Montreuil; 262–266 boulevard Voltaire (11th); 307–309 rue du Faubourg Saint-Antoine (12th).

Colonnes d'Octroi: in 1788, architect Claude Nicolas Ledoux had two Doric columns erected, each with a statue on top, one of Philippe Auguste and the other of Saint Louis. The statues are still there. The columns mark the 'frontier' where *octroi*, a tax, became payable.

Address book

The place for a rendezvous

Café Le Triomphe
6 place de la Nation, 12th. Open daily 6am to 2am.
Tel.: 01-43-43-22-36.

Cooking classes

Ⓐ L'Atelier des Chefs Paris Printemps Nation
It is advisable to book for these classes at the Nation branch of Printemps department store. You learn tricks from the great chefs. Seasonal themes, varied approaches and menus.
21 cours de Vincennes (4th floor), 20th.
Tel. 01-49-70-97-50.
atelierdeschefs.fr
Open Tuesday to Saturday 10am to 7pm.

Restaurant

Ⓑ Chez Prosper
Popular *brasserie* right next to one of the square's statues. Lively bistro atmosphere and a remarkable Auvergne-style burger. They also serve a Nutella tiramisu. Main courses €12–17.

7 avenue Trône, 11th.
Tel.: 01-43-73-08-51.
Open Monday to Saturday 7am to 2am, Sunday 8am to 2am.

Shopping

Ⓒ Market
A very nice market along Cours de Vincennes.
Wednesday 7am to 2.30pm and Saturday 7am to 3pm.

Next stations

PORTE DE VINCENNES

L'Europe, 87 cours de Vincennes, 20th.

SAINT-MANDÉ

La Tourelle, 1 avenue Foch, 94160 Saint-Mandé.

BÉRAULT

Au Corner, 14 rue Victor-Basch, 94300 Vincennes.

CHÂTEAU DE VINCENNES

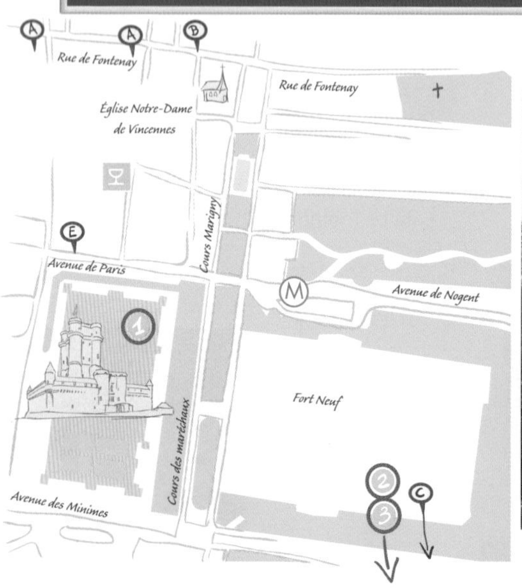

History

This station is located at the eastern end of line 1. It was inaugurated in 1934 when the metro's first line was extended. It has six exits, and the main one, *sortie 2*, leads to one of the most symbolic places of the French monarchy, the famous Château de Vincennes. There are many remnants of this royal history in the vicinity of the station. The Château was a manor under the Capetians and became a royal residence between the 16th and 17th centuries. Kings were born and died here, like Charles V. Louis XIV had residences built in the grounds. In the 18th century the site became a state prison. The Duke of Enghien was executed here in 1804, and the spot is marked with a plaque.

SIGHTSEEING

A walk through history

1. **Château de Vincennes:** the tallest medieval fortress in Europe with a keep 50 metres (55 yards) high. Within its walls were Charles V's dungeon, a holy chapel, and two residences built for Louis XIV by architect Louis Le Vau. A good example of the medieval art of fortification, its outer walls measure 378 metres (413 yards) by 175 metres (191 yards).
Avenue de Paris, 94300 Vincennes.
Tel.: 01-48-08-31-20.
www.chateau-vincennes.fr. Open daily

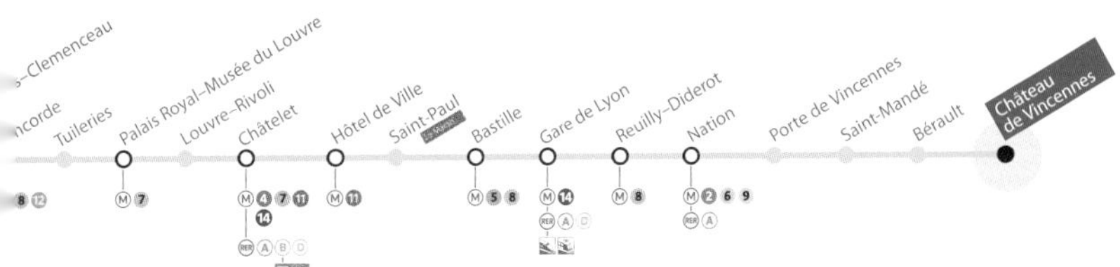

10am to 6pm from May to August and 10am to 5pm from September to April. Closed on public holidays. Entrance fee.

t of the ordinary

Evenings at the Vincennes Hippodrome: you can watch horse races here with friends and family most Tuesdays and Fridays 7pm to 11pm.

2 route de la Ferme, 12th.
Tel.: 01-49-77-14-70.
www.hippodrome-vincennes.com
Entrance fee.

A walk in the park

3 **Parc Floral:** on the edge of the Bois de Vincennes woods, the Parc Floral de Paris is famous for its horticultural presentations, exhibitions and theme gardens. It was officially recognised as a botanical garden in 1998 and has a unique collection of plants that will delight all lovers of floral art and botany.

Admission free September to June, entrance fee Wednesdays, Saturdays and Sundays June 6 to September 21.

Address book

The place for a rendezvous

Le Saint Louis
1 avenue du Château, 94300 Vincennes. Open Tuesday to Friday 7am to 11pm and to 8pm on Saturdays. Tel.: 01-43-98-19-95.

Shopping

A Librairie Millepages
Lively bookstore situated on a courtyard. Good book selection. Also stocks CDs. Often holds events with authors.
91 and 174 rue de Fontenay, 94300 Vincennes.
Tel.: 01-43-28-04-15 and 01-43-28-84-30.
www.millepages.fr
Open all week 9.30am to 7.30pm except Monday mornings, Sundays 10.30am to 1pm.

B Market
On Sunday mornings stalls take up the whole of rue de Fontenay as well as some surrounding streets.

Culture

C Cartoucherie de Vincennes
A unique theatre venue in a former barracks. Home to several avant-garde theatre companies including Théâtre du Soleil, founded by Ariane Mnouchkine, and Théâtre de la Tempête, and also to American choreographer Carolyn Carlson.
On the same road as the hippodrome, bus stop 'Cartoucherie', 94300 Vincennes.
Tel.: 01-43-74-24-08.
www.cartoucherie.fr

D Festival America
Biennial festival putting the spotlight on North American literature and culture, usually held end of September in even-numbered years.
Tel.: 01-43-98-65-09.
www.festival-america.org

Restaurant

E Don Bartolomeo
A pizza place worth visiting just for its cuisine, but also for its pleasant indoor terrace. Peaceful, and often sunny too. And there's a parrot called Kiwi. Main courses €9–15.
22 avenue de Paris, 94300 Vincennes.
Tel.: 01-43-65-00-73.
Open daily noon to 3pm and 6.30pm to midnight.

line 2

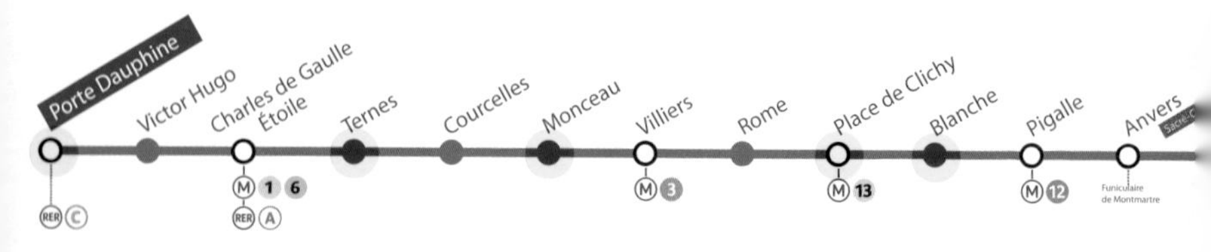

History

Opened on 13 December 1900, the first section of the line connected Étoile station (now called Charles de Gaulle – Étoile) to Porte Dauphine station. The addition, between 1902 and 1903, of several stations as far as Nation enabled one to reach the northeast of the city. The line was then known as 'line 2 North' before definitively becoming 'line 2' in 1907.
To serve the northeast of the capital, part of the line was constructed on a viaduct. Thus it runs overhead for over two kilometres (2,2 yards) passing through four stations: Barbès-Rochechouart, La Chapelle, Stalingrad and Jaurès, even running above the railway tracks of Gare du Nord and Gare de l'Est. The metal girders supporting the metro vary in length between 19.48 and 75.25 metres (63.91 and 246.88 feet), the longest being those over the railway tracks. Line 2 was marked by one of the metro's most tragic accidents 'the Couronnes tragedy' in 1903. More than 80 people died after fire broke out in a train carriage, at the time largely made of wood. Different, safer carriages were made after this sad episode, the celebrated Sprague-Thomson carriages.

Porte Dauphine / Nation

PORTE DAUPHINE

History

This station was named after Marie-Antoinette. Still very young, residing at the Château de la Muette, the *dauphine* decided to open the Porte de la Faisanderie. The nobility passed by here to reach Longchamp. Today, the metro station principally serves the Bois de Boulogne. The station is remarkable because of the well-preserved entrance, designed by Hector Guimard (place des Généraux du Trentinian), which still has its fan-shape glass awning. The station also has its original 30-metre (98-feet) diameter turning loop. Note also the brown-coloured ceramic tiles, an early trial subsequently abandoned in favour of the famous bevelled white tiles.

SIGHTSEEING

A walk in the park

1 **Bois de Boulogne:** this former hunting ground, part of the 13th-century royal estate, takes its name from the tiny chapel built by Philip the Fair in 1301, following a pilgrimage to Boulogne-sur-Mer. Louis XVI opened the site to the public, then the Bois de Boulogne progressively became a place for strolling and canoodling. During the Belle Époque, at Napoleon III's request, the engineer Jean-Charles Alphand laid out the terrain. Lakes, gardens, alleyways and, above all, the racetrack were built.

Off the beaten track

2 **Frieze from the Pavillon Perse, 1889 Exposition Universelle:** ceramicist Émile Müller and sculptor Charles

Louis Lesueur conceived the glazed earthenware panels for the Persian Pavilion at the 1889 World Fair, inspired by the archers on the Palace of Darius (c.500 BC) at Susa in Iran, now in the Louvre.

11 rue des Sablons, 16th.
Private cul-de-sac, open during the week. Admission free.

Jardin Shakespeare: an open-air theatre in the heart of the woods, near to the Pré Catelan restaurant. Plays have been performed here in summer since 1953, notably works by Shakespeare. One of the curiosities of the garden is that it is 'decorated' according to works by the English playwright: moorland heather from *Macbeth*, species of tree from the Forest of Arden in *As You Like It*, and even the little stream, so fatal for Ophelia, evoked in *Hamlet*.

Route de la Reine-Marguerite, 16th.
Tel.: 01-44-14-41-14

Address Book

The place for a rendezvous

Le Régent
148 rue de la Pompe, 16th.
Open Monday to Friday 7.30am to 8pm.
Tel.: 01-47-27-51-91.

Sleep in a gypsy caravan

A Camping de Paris-Bois de Boulogne
One hardly expects to be able to sleep in a gypsy caravan in the middle of a Parisian park. Yet it is possible in the freshly renovated campsite. From €80 the night.

2 allée du Bord-de-l'Eau, 16th.
Tel.: 01-45-24-30-00.

Restaurant

B Le Pré Catelan
Renowned gastronomic restaurant. With a Napoleon III decor, friezes by 19th-century satirical cartoonist Caran d'Ache and the cuisine of chef Frédéric Anton. Above all, fine ingredients are celebrated here (notably fish and shellfish). Beware, the prices match the majesty of the setting. Around €80 – 120.
Route de Suresnes, 16th.
Tel.: 01-44-14-41-00.
www.precatelanparis.com
Services Tuesday to Saturday at noon and 7.30pm.

Next stations

VICTOR HUGO

Café Victor Hugo
4 place Victor-Hugo, 16th.

CHARLES DE GAULLE – ÉTOILE

See line 1, page 16

TERNES

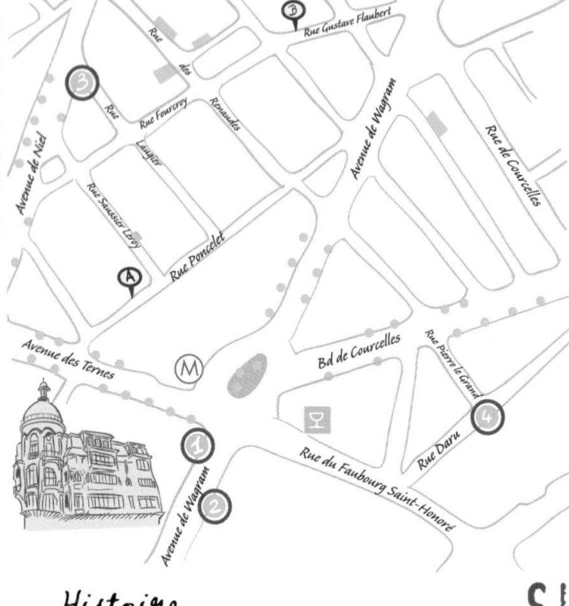

Histoire

'Ternes' is a corruption of 'Villa Externa', the farm belonging to the Bishop of Paris in the Middle Ages. It became 'Estern' and then 'Ternes', as opposed to the 'Villa Episcopa', the bishop's palace itself. In 1860, the land was joined to Paris. One used to stop here on the way to Saint-Germain-en-Laye for a spot of fresh air. The central strip where flowers are sold today was formerly home to fruit and vegetable sellers. This neighbourhood used to have a holiday air. The historian Pierre Miquel even recalls that a clinic used to practice hydrotherapy here during the Second Empire. Later the construction of large apartment buildings buried this bucolic mood—and the arrival of the metro in 1902 even more so.

SIGHTSEEING

Off the beaten track

1. **Cercle Wagram:** poker addicts won't want to miss these renowned gaming rooms.
47 avenue de Wagram, 17th.
Tel.: 01-43-80-65-13.
www.cerclewagram.com.
Smart dress and ID essential.

Architecture

2. **Hôtel Élysées Ceramic:** an Art Nouveau building (especially its balconies and railings) built in 1904 by the architect Jules Lavirotte, with a facade covered in glazed earthenware floral decoration.
34 avenue de Wagram, 8th.

Magasin Fnac: you can certainly make your cultural purchases at this music, book and electronic goods store, but we recommend this address above all for the 1912 building, conceived by Marcel Oudin. Originally, the exposed concrete and visible structure seemed (too?) modern. The dome was subsequently covered in slate, which has given it a more bourgeois appearance.

28 avenue Niel, 17th.
Open Monday to Saturday 10am to 8pm, until 9pm on Thursday.

Next station

COURCELLES

Le Courcelles
94 boulevard de Courcelles, 17th.

A walk in the Russian Quarter

4 **Cathédrale Alexandre Nevski:** Russian Orthodox cathedral consecrated in 1861. Alexander Nevsky, a 13th-century Russian saint and hero, succeeded in pushing back the Swedes at the battle of the Neva. Several churches and cathedrals are dedicated to him. This one follows a traditional Byzantine style on a Greek cross plan with remarkable five onion domes and a 50 metres (164 feet) high spire. For the anecdote, Picasso was married here to Russian dancer, Olga Khokhlova. Don't miss the Russian restaurants on rue Daru, here you are in Paris's Russian quarter!

12 rue Daru, 8th. Admission free.

Address book

The place for a rendezvous

Les 4 Saisons
268 rue du Faubourg-Saint-Honoré, 8th.
Open Tuesday to Sunday 7am to 9pm.
Tel.: 01-42-12-99-15.

Shopping

A Le Stübli
This tea room and food shop has a good choice of German patisseries, such as *apfelstrudel*.
11 rue Poncelet, 17th.

Restaurants

B Bistrot d'à côté Flaubert
One of star chef Michel Rostang's offshoot bistros, or 'father and daughters', as they like to emphasise. One comes here not just for the food (*andouillette* from Bobosse, Bresse hen…), but also for the bistro decor and the collection of mugs and tankards. Main courses €25–35.
10 rue Gustave-Flaubert, 17th.
Tel.: 01-42-67-05-81.
Closed Saturday lunch, Sunday and Monday.

MONCEAU

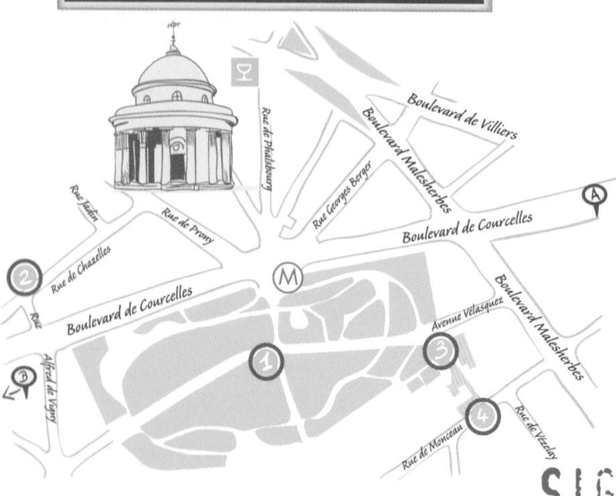

SIGHTSEEING

A walk in the park

History

The station owes its name to a little town on the western edge of Paris, already known as Mousseaux in 1300. At the beginning, one went hunting in the area. It took the Duc de Chartres to develop a pretty park around his château, conceived in the spirit of an English garden and reshaped under the Second Empire. In the 19th and 20th centuries, Monceau became one of the most prized addresses in Paris. Numerous town houses were constructed, in particular encroaching on the park. The Rothschild family, a rich banking family, lived here as did the heirs to Menier chocolate. In the end, it's rather strange to have a metro station in a district where everyone had their own chauffeur! Adorned with its Guimard entrance, it opened nonetheless on 7 October 1902.

1 **Parc Monceau:** the Duc d'Orléans's private park, acquired at the end of the 1770s. Writer, painter and architect Louis Carrogis Carmontelle imagined for him a place reuniting different epochs and places. Thus you might come across an Egyptian pyramid dedicated to Isis, Greek columns or an 18th century Japanese lan-

tern, offered by the city of Tokyo as a sign of friendship in 1982. One equally finds a rotunda composed of 16 columns. It is one of the tax pavilions of the old Mur des Fermiers Généraux, designed by Claude Nicolas Ledoux. The iron park gates are by Gabriel Davioud.

Boulevard de Courcelles, 8th.
Open daily 7am to 10pm in summer, 7am to 8pm in winter.

ff the beaten track

25 rue de Chazelles: the Statue of Liberty was born here in the Gaget et Gauthier metal foundry. 'One could believe one is in a fairytale land, in the factory where dwarves were manufacturing a giant in metal' enthused an anonymous chronicler in the *Journal Illustré* in 1883.

ulture

Musée Cernuschi: this is the former residence of Henri Cernuschi, who was passionate about antique Asian bronzes. You will find here the monumental Buddha from Meguro, a Japanese bronze from the end of the 18th century, vases, ceramics, terracottas and other Asian treasures.

7 avenue Vélasquez, 8th.
Tel.: 01-53-96-21-50.
www.cernuschi.paris.fr
Admission free.

4 **Musée Nissim de Camondo:** Moïse Camondo, an avid collector of 18th century decorative arts, left his splendid *hôtel particulier* (town house) built overlooking the park in 1871 to the Arts Décoratifs. Splendid interiors (library, kitchens...) have been left in their original state according to the wishes of its former owners. Remarkable pieces.

63 rue de Monceau, 8th.
Tel.: 01-53-89-06-50.
www.lesartsdecoratifs.fr
Entrance fee.

Address book

The place for a rendezvous

L'Iris
9 rue Logelbach, 17th.
Open Monday to Friday 7am to 6pm.
Tel.: 01-47-63-77-10.

Shopping

A La Petite Rose
Pastry chef Miyuki Watanabe trained with the greats and this Japanese-run patisserie-cum-tea room is a treat between football sessions in the Parc Monceau. Outdoor terrace.
11 boulevard de Courcelles, 8th.
Tel.: 01-45-22-07-27.
Open Thursday to Tuesday 10.30am to 7.30pm.

B Thierry Rozet
A jeweller creating original, modern designs.
110 boulevard de Courcelles, 17th.
Tel.: 01-53-34-06-95.
www.thierryrozet.com
Open Tuesday to Saturday 10am to 7pm.

Next stations

VILLIERS

Dôme de Villiers
4 avenue de Villiers, 17th.

ROME

Le Paris Rome
62 boulevard des Batignolles, 17th.

PLACE DE CLICHY

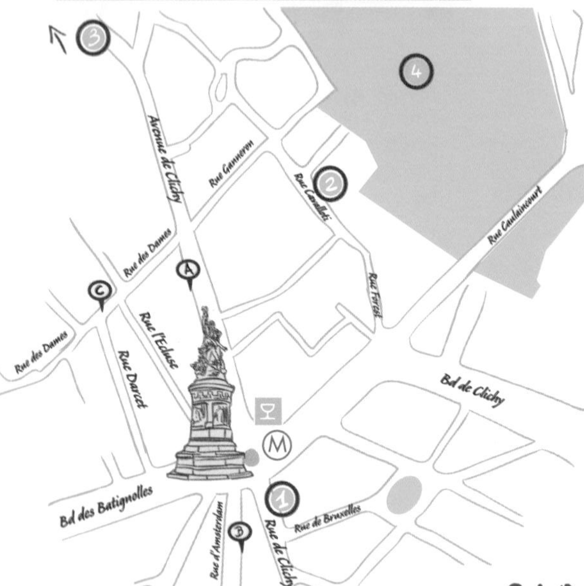

History

In the centre of the square on leaving the station is a statue of Marshal Moncey (1754–1842). At 8 metres (26 feet) high, it recalls the bravura of this man at the head of the Garde Nationale in 1814, when the Napoleonic downfall was already underway. With his men, he held out against the troops of Cossack soldiers led by the 'traitor' Langeron, at the Clichy gate. The square, formerly delineated by one of Ledoux's tax pavilions, served as a boundary for the *octroi* goods tax.

SIGHTSEEING

Off the beaten track

1. **Cercle Clichy Montmartre:** this popular gaming hall opened in the premises of an old *bouillon* dining hall in 1947. Poker and billiards are played here. The first official French billiards championship was even held here in 1990.
84 rue de Clichy, 9th.

2. **Rue Cavalotti:** in the evening when everyone has gone home and the shops are closed, take a stroll along this street where the closed shutters have been painted by artists. A true open-air gallery.

3. **Cité des Fleurs:** this little residential enclave was built in 1847. Each resident was obliged to plant at least three flower-

ing trees. A village atmosphere right in the heart of Paris!

59 rue de La Jonquière or 154 avenue de Clichy, 17th.

Address book

The place for a rendezvous

Au Petit Poucet
5 place de Clichy, 17th.
Open daily 7.30am to 2am.
Tel.: 01-45-22-36-76.

Shopping

A Guerrisol
A cult address for vintage fans, a sort of Ali Baba's cave where one can always unearth inexpensive, good-quality clothes. Shoes, jackets, trousers, dresses, you can find everything here!
19 avenue de Clichy, 17th.
Tel.: 01-40-08-03-00.
Open Monday to Saturday 10am to 7pm.

Out on the town

B Hammam Club
Dance the night away to Oriental rhythms. Varied programme of DJs and musicians.

Monument

4 Cimetière de Montmartre: extending over 11 hectares (27 acres), it opened in 1825 on the site of the Montmartre gypsum quarries. Among the tombs are those of filmmaker François Truffaut, singer Dalida, writer Alfred de Vigny, composer Jacques Offenbach, dancer Vatslav Nijinsky portrayed as Petrouchka and Margaret Kelly Leibovici, founder of the Bluebell Girls at the Lido cabaret.

20 avenue Rachel, 18th.
Tel.: 01-53-42-36-30 or 01-40-71-75-23 (guided tours). Admission free.

94 rue d'Amsterdam, 9th.
Tel.: 01-55-07-80-00. www.hammamclub.com
Nightclub open Thursday to Sunday 11.30pm to dawn.

Restaurant

C Le Bistro des Dames
A well-hidden secret for French cuisine with Mediterranean touches. There's a lovely calm terrace and even a hotel if you want. Main courses €15–18.
18 rue des Dames, 17th.
Tel.: 01-45-22-13-42.
Open Monday to Friday noon to 3pm, 7pm to 2am, Saturday and Sunday 12.30pm to 10.30pm.

BLANCHE

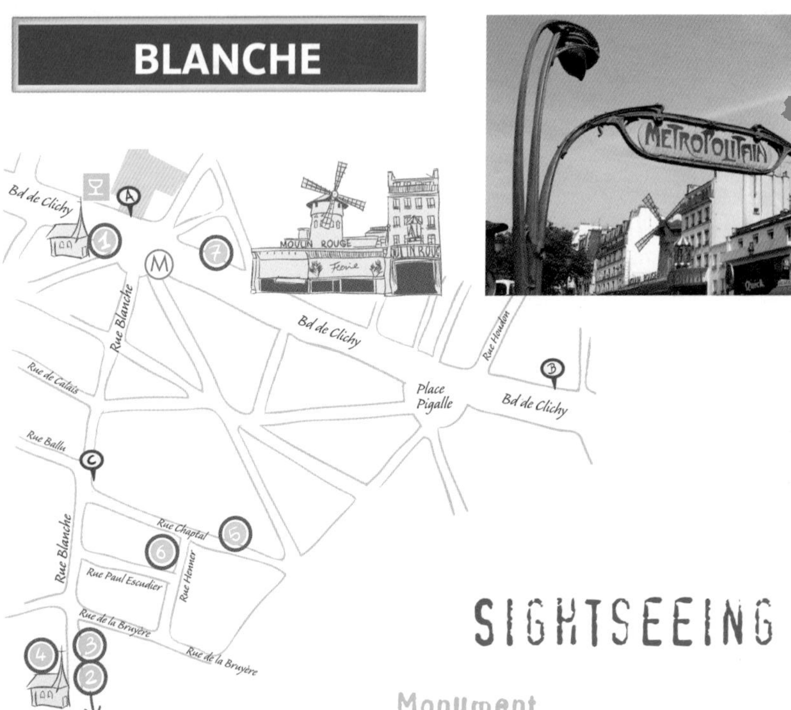

SIGHTSEEING

Monument

1. **Chapelle Sainte-Rita:** this very simple building contains a chapel dedicated to the patron saint of lost causes, also the patron saint of prostitutes. Lovely stained glass of the saint with roses.
65 boulevard de Clichy, 9th.

Not-to-be-missed facades

2. **19 rue Blanche:** imposing building. Raise your head to admire the Corinthian pilasters framing a modern iron window.

3. **21 rue Blanche:** unusual construction by Girault (1901) with a glass awning, wrought-iron balconies and curved windows on the 1st floor. What style !

4. **25 rue Blanche:** German evangelical church.

History

This station gets its name from rue Blanche ('white street') so called because of the whiteness of the gypsum from the Montmartre quarries. The heavily laden carts and wagons that took this route left some traces behind them: all the houses were white from plaster, hence the name. It leads to a monument of Parisian nightlife, the famous Moulin-Rouge, and to the Montmartre district. The Art Nouveau entrance is the work of Hector Guimard and is a listed historic monument.

10 rue Chaptal: but isn't that Beethoven on the facade of the former building of the SACEM (Society of Authors, Composers and Music Publishers)?

13 rue Henner: finish the promenade with a Louis-Philippe-style building, once the home of poet Guillaume Apollinaire.

Out of the ordinary

Musée de l'Érotisme: the history of eroticism through works of art, from religious art to contemporary art via folk art. Educational and original.

72 boulevard de Clichy, 18th.
Tel.: 01-42-58-28-73.
www.musee-erotisme.com

Address book

The place for a rendezvous

O'Sullivans Pub Montmartre
92 boulevard de Clichy, 18th.
Open daily noon to 5am.
Tel.: 01-53-09-25-21.

Out on the town

A Le Moulin-Rouge
This temple of cabaret has been open since 1889. It is still perfect for mixing with the riff raff today, with a dinner-show to the sound of the French cancan.
82 boulevard de Clichy, 18th.
Tel.: 01-53-09-82-82.
www.moulinrouge.fr

B Les Trois Baudets
Now a concert venue, this former theatre has a beautiful art deco facade. Regular concerts of 'new French music' are ideal for discovering up-and-coming talents of French *chanson*.
64 boulevard de Clichy, 18th.
Tel.: 01-42-62-33-33.
www.lestroisbaudets.com.
Concerts all week 6.30pm to 1.30am.

Restaurant

C Le Dit-Vin
The Dit-Vin (or 'divine') restaurant gives pride of place to the divine bottle. Wine bar, wine merchant with well-prepared dishes and wines by the glass, it's divine. Main courses €12–15.
68, rue Blanche, 9th.
Tel.: 01-45-26-27-37.
Open Monday to Friday 10am to 3pm, and 6pm to midnight.

Next stations

PIGALLE
See line 12, page 304

ANVERS
Le Post Café, 70 boulevard de Rochechouart, 18th.

BARBÈS-ROCHECHOUART
See line 4, page 95

LA CHAPELLE
Le Danton, 22 place de la Chapelle, 18th.

STALINGRAD

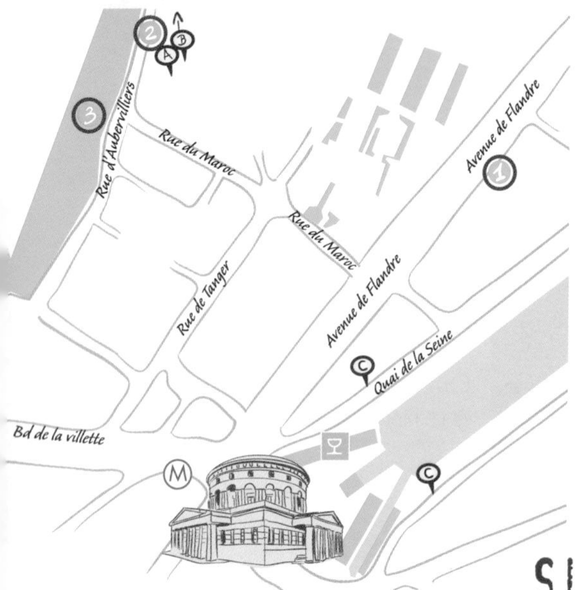

History

Stalingrad evokes an episode in the Second World War. After a long and bloody conflict, Russian troops at last got the better of the German army of the Third Reich on 2 February 1943. On the square is Claude Nicolas Ledoux's Rotonde de la Villette, which was built in the 18th century to survey the goods tax gate. Symbol of absolutism par excellence, it was spared destruction during the Revolution. A square charged with history! The station, inaugurated in 1903, was originally called Aubervilliers–Boulevard de la Villette, before being renamed in 1946 following the Russians' battle victory.

SIGHTSEEING

A walk through history

1. **Cimetière Juif Portugais:** it was created at the end of the 18th century and dedicated to the Portuguese Jewish community. Occupying a little under 500 square metres (5,382 square feet), with just a handful of tombs, it was previously outside the city wall, behind the Mur des Fermiers Généraux. It closed in the 19th century when a Jewish section was opened in the Père-Lachaise cemetery.
44 avenue de Flandre, 19th.
Admission free.

Culture

2. **Le Centquatre:** an original art space in the totally renovated former buildings of the municipal undertaker, with a superb

central nave in iron, glass and concrete. There's nothing deadly here any more, rather, musical events (concerts, performances, dance) and a host of other artistic projects from the artists in residence. A true celebration of culture.

104 rue d'Aubervilliers or 5 rue Curial, 19th. Tel.: 01-53-35-50-00. www.104.fr

Open Tuesday to Sunday 11am to 8pm, open late during events.

walk in the park

Jardin d'Éole: a pleasant park spread over more than four hectares (around 10 acres), dedicated to the god of wind. Nearly 1,000 trees and bushes, plants of all sorts, are spread over little mounds and hills, providing a breath of fresh air in the urban atmosphere of the district. Lawns open to the public and several playgrounds for children.

Rue du Département, 18th.

Open 8am to 9.30pm in summer, until 5.45pm in winter.

Admission free.

Address book

The place for a rendezvous

Coté Canal

5 quai de Seine, 19th.
Open daily 8am to midnight.
Tel.: 01-40-36-92-49.

Restaurants

A Le Café Caché

It's 50s style at this café-*brasserie* designed by Sébastien Wierinck, one of the designers of the Centquatre, with metal lamps, old armchairs with geometrical lines, and wooden seats. Breakfast, brunch and light snacks (salads, sandwiches) are served. Main courses €10–15.

104 rue d'Aubervilliers or 5 rue Curial, 19th. Tel.: 01-42-05-38-40. www.cafecache.fr Open Monday to Saturday noon to 3pm, 7.30pm to 10pm, Sunday noon to 5pm, 6.30pm to 10pm.

B La Baraque à Pizzas

For an ice cream or a gourmet pause. The place recalls memories of childhood holidays. A perfect timewarp. Less than €15.

104 rue d'Aubervilliers or 5 rue Curial, 19th. Open Tuesday to Sunday 11am to 8pm.

C Cinémas

MK2 Quai de Seine and MK2 Quai de Loire benefit from unusual architecture maximising light and transparency. Agreeable auditoriums.

14 quai de la Seine, 19th.
Tel.: 08-92-69-84-84.
7 quai de la Loire, 19th.
Tel.: 08- 92-69-84-84.

Next stations

JAURÈS

See line 5, page 130

COLONEL FABIEN

Le Longchamp

2 rue de Meaux, 19th.

BELLEVILLE

The station is at the lower end of rue de Belleville, whose summit is one of the highest points in Paris (128 metres/420 feet). Today, this neighbourhood is one of the most cosmopolitan parts of the capital.

History

For once, the metro station is actually named after the district it serves. Belleville is also a street and an avenue! Long a rural district, over time, Belleville became one of the working-class districts on the fringes of the capital. It was only in 1860 that the town became part of Paris. During the 1830 and 1848 revolutions and, above all, the Paris Commune in 1871, workers, weapons in hand, made their voice heard to the State and above all their wish to become a republic at the price of blood and struggle. It was also a district with *guinguette* dance halls where Parisians came for entertainment.

SIGHTSEEING

Out of the ordinary

1 ***Il faut se méfier des mots (Don't trust words):*** above the cradle with its labourer hard at work, one finds this work by Ben, alias Benjamin Vautier (born 1935). This artist's works are recognisable from his loopy

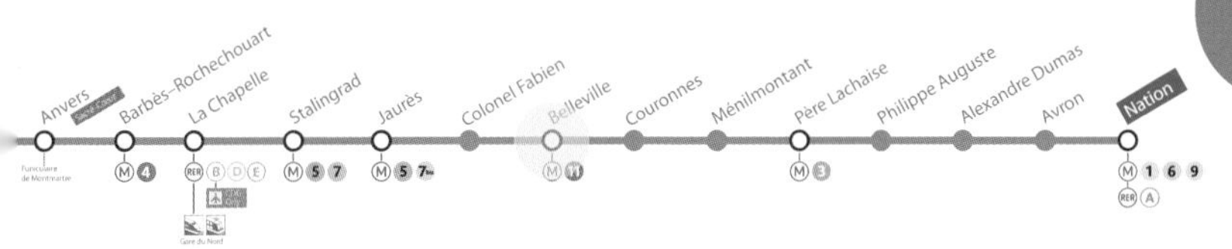

handwriting and his aphorisms with double meanings. But, in this case, should one only mistrust words? In the area are other works, such as *Le Rendez-vous,* at the corner of rue de Belleville and rue Julien Lacroix, a work by Jean Le Gac (born 1952).

Place Fréhel, 20th.

Belleville Windmills: one visits this street for its superb view over the capital. But one also comes here for its windmills of a new type on the top of the Maison de l'Air. Here there are no blades humming in the wind, but two sort of resonating boxes. Between them they produce enough electricity a year for four average households.

At the top of the Parc de Belleville, rue Piat entrance. Free access.

Regard Saint-Martin: here one collects spring water. And it still functions! Access at the bottom of rue des Cascades. Also worth a look, at 44 rue des Cascades, two glass blowers in the well-hidden house where Jean Becker filmed *Casque d'Or*.

Next station

COURONNES

Le Malgache

2 boulevard de Ménilmontant, 20th.

4 **Cimetière de Belleville:** there are more than 3,000 concessions in this cemetery but one tomb in particular drew our attention: that of Jules Caillaux (1849 – 1916). The condoleances come from the 'flowers and feathers' assurance company!

Corner of rue de Belleville and rue du Télégraphe. Admission free.

5 **40 rue du Télégraphe:** a plaque indicates that this is the highest point in Paris (128.50 metres/422 feet).

Address book

The place for a rendezvous

La Vielleuse

2 rue de Belleville, 20th.
Open daily 6am to midnight.
Tel.:43-58-06-38.

Shopping

A Maison Safraoui

Tablewares from Nabeul, henna and other Tunisian products.

31 boulevard de la Villette, 10th.
Tel.: 01-42-40-91-12.

B Le Caire Belleville

An Ali Baba's cave of spices from around the globe.

63 rue de Belleville, 19th.
Tel.: 01-42-06-06-01.
Open Tuesday to Saturday 10am to 10pm.

Restaurant

C Chapeau Melon

The bowler hat is a wine bar specialising in biodynamic wines. Seasonally inspired dishes focus on quality ingredients. Main courses around €25.

92 rue Rébeval, 19th.
Tel.: 01-42-02-68-60.
Open Monday to Friday 11am to 1pm, 5pm to 10pm, Saturday 11am to 8pm.

Street market

D A popular street market known for exotic produce and low prices.

Boulevard de Belleville, 11th.
Tuesday and Friday 7am to 2.30pm.

MÉNILMONTANT

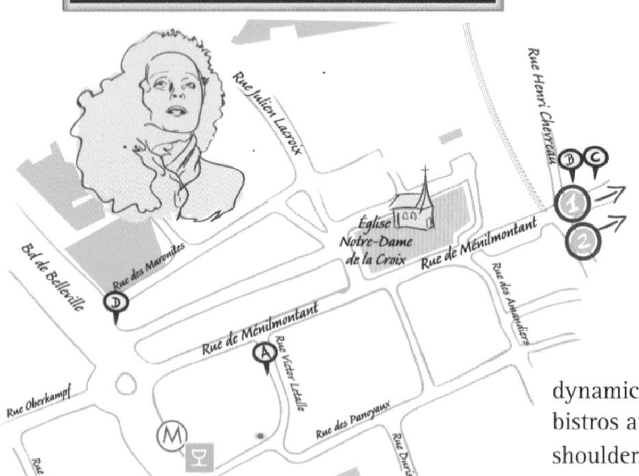

History

The district perhaps gets its name from *mesnil* (a small farm) and *mauvais temps* (bad weather) or from *mesnil montant*, from the hilly landscape. It was in this district previously outside the Mur des Fermiers Généraux, and therefore not subject to taxes on produce, that one used to come to drink a glass of wine during a promenade. It was only in 1860 that the district was definitively integrated within Paris, following a decision by Baron Haussmann. It is also the district of utopians, Saint-Simonians, future industrialists and politicians or new squatters, in passing by one of the neighbourhood's iconic figures, Edith Piaf. Today it is one of Paris's most dynamic neighbourhoods where bistros and fashion boutiques rub shoulders in a trendy atmosphere.

SIGHTSEEING

Off the beaten track

1 **Squat de la Miroiterie:** the oldest artists' squat in Paris has in its time been threatened, closed and transformed into an exhibition space and concert venue. It was a place of in-

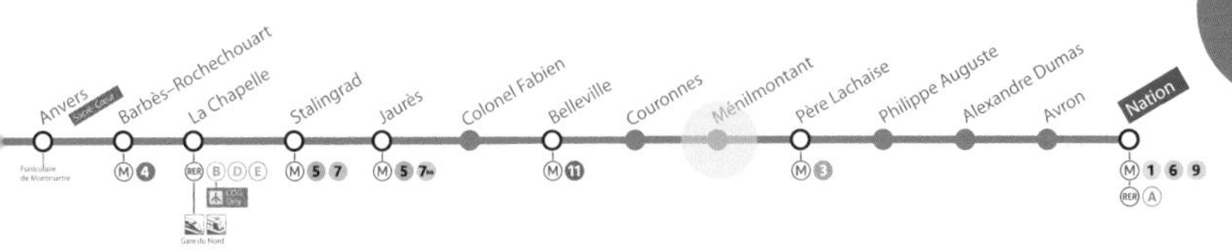

tense artistic experimentation. From punk to capoeira and Indian dance, it is open to forms of expression from all over the world.

88 rue de Ménilmontant, 20th.
Gallery open Wednesday to Sunday.

145 rue de Ménilmontant: there's no longer much to see historically at this address. However, it is here that the Saint-Simonians used to gather in 1832 under the leadership of Barthélemy Prosper Enfantin to imagine an alternative society, essentially industrial, at the moment when cholera ravaged Paris. They even proposed an 'industrial coup d'état'.

lture

Musée Édith Piaf: dedicated fans of Piaf flock to this pocket-sized museum where one finds objects that belonged to the star of French *chanson*. Among them, her famous little black dress, soft toys and Marcel Cerdan's boxing gloves.

5, rue Crespin-du-Gast, 11th.
Tel.: 01-43-55-52-72.
Open (only by appointment) Monday to Wednesday 1pm to 6pm, Thursday 10am to noon. Admission free.

Address book

The place for a rendezvous

Brasserie du Soleil
136 boulevard de Ménilmontant, 20th.
Open daily 8am to 2am.
Tel.: 01-46-36-47-44.

Out on the town

A La Féline
One of the most rocking bars in the area. A haunt of young Parisians, no bigger than a pocket handkerchief. Frequent concerts and inexpensive drinks.
6 rue Victor-Letalle, 20th.
Tel.: 01-40-33-08-66.
Open Wednesday to Sunday 6pm to 2am.

B La Maroquinerie
This former leather workshop has become a concert space for up to date bands. There's also an attractive restaurant for eating out with friends.
Festive atmosphere.
23 rue Boyer, 20th.
Tel.: 01-40-33-35-04.
www.lamaroquinerie.fr
Open daily 7.30pm to 11.30pm.

C La Bellevilloise
A hotspot of Parisian nightlife. A former workers' cooperative converted into a concert venue that is very much of today. Jazz brunch at the weekend.
19–21 rue Boyer, 20th.
Tel.: 01-46-36-07-07.
www.labellevilloise.fr

Opening times depend on the programme.

Restaurant

D Chez Max
Caribbean specialities. Amid pretty tablecloths in creole checks, try pork colombo or creole black pudding. The chef also proposes some items to take away. Main courses €10–15.
16 boulevard de Belleville, 20th.
Tel.: 01-43-58-31-30.
Open Tuesday to Saturday noon to 3pm, Friday and Saturday 8pm to 11pm.

PÈRE LACHAISE

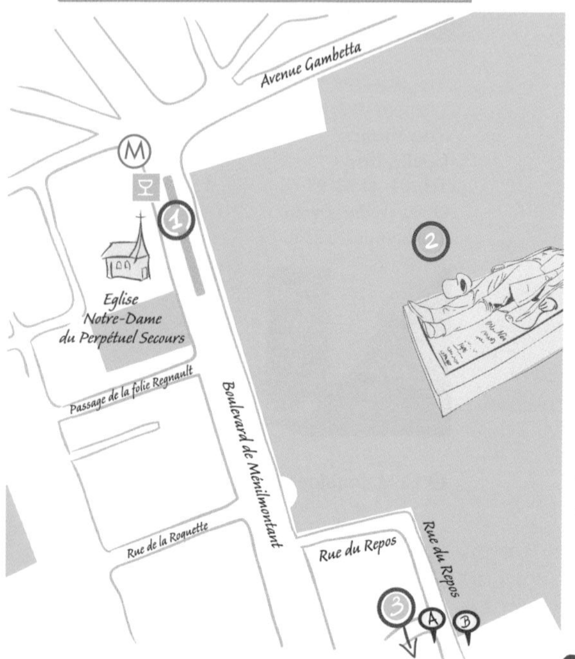

History

So who was this Father Lachaise?
A Jesuit property in the 17th century, it was a place dedicated to convalescence. François d'Aix de La Chaise (1624–1709), known as 'Père La Chaise', Louis XIV's confessor, retired there. Later, the domaine was bought by the Préfet de la Seine, when Napoleon, then a Consul, proclaimed 'the right of each citizen to be buried whatever their race or religion'. With Montmartre in the north and Montparnasse in the south, only a cemetery in the east was lacking. The architect Alexandre Théodore Brongniart was charged with its construction in 1803. It is a real city within the city. Don't hesitate to ask for a map or to look at the internet site before visiting. As to the metro station, it was the first to have an escalator, as early as 1909. You will soon understand why!

SIGHTSEEING

Out of the ordinary

1 **La Roulotte du Père-Lachaise:** Altiz, tarot messenger and wise man of French fairgrounds, had observed that the art of tarot had almost disappeared. He decided to keep up the tradition. Consul-

tations by appointment for tarot, dowsing (pendulum) and other uses of the occult sciences.

61 boulevard de Ménilmontant, 11th.
Tel.: 06-03-99-10-11.

numents

Cimetière du Père-Lachaise: the largest cemetery in Paris at over 44 hectares (109 acres). There are several footpaths—but, beware, it climbs and descends. One finds, among others: Jim Morrison (zone 6), Frederick Chopin (zone 11), Yves Montand and Simone Signoret (zone 44) and Victor Noir (zone 92). A real personality! The lifesize effigy of the journalist, who was killed by a cousin of Napoleon III, has a protuding bulge in his trousers that is said to have powers of fertility for anyone who touches it.

16 rue du Repos, 20th. Tel. 01-55-25-82-10. www.pere-lachaise.com. Admission free.

3 **Villa Riberolle:** here you have the impression of being in a different era. A forgotten alleyway, with its old cobblestones, workshops, artists and garage…

35, rue de Bagnolet, 20th.

Address book

The place for a rendezvous

Café Analdaro
65 boulevard de Ménilmontant, 11th.
Open Monday to Friday 6.30am to 11pm.
Tel.: 01-40-21-13-35.

Shopping

A Le Bateau de Safran
A real Indian palace hidden at the end of an alleyway from another era. Find your fill of Indian furniture, objects, shawls and sarees.
9 villa Riberolle, 20th. Tel.: 01-44-93-90-32. www.lebateaudesafran.com. Open mornings by appointment.

Restaurant

B Mama Shelter
You come here for many reasons. The decoration, first of all, by Philippe Starck, dark, with its blackboard on the ceiling. And for the affordable gastronomic cuisine, conceived by the chef Alain Senderens. A hotel, it also offers a very trendy bar, fashionable brunch and pizzas.
The place to be in the 20th arrondissement !
Main courses €10–20.
109 rue de Bagnolet, 20th. Tel.: 01-43-48-45-45. Open Monday to Saturday noon to 3pm and 7pm to midnight.

Next stations

PHILIPPE AUGUSTE
Le Père La Chaise
15 boulevard de Ménilmontant, 11th.

ALEXANDRE DUMAS
Le Saint René
148 boulevard Charonne, 20th.

AVRON
Usine de Charonne
1 rue Avron, 20th.

NATION
See line 1, page 44

line 3

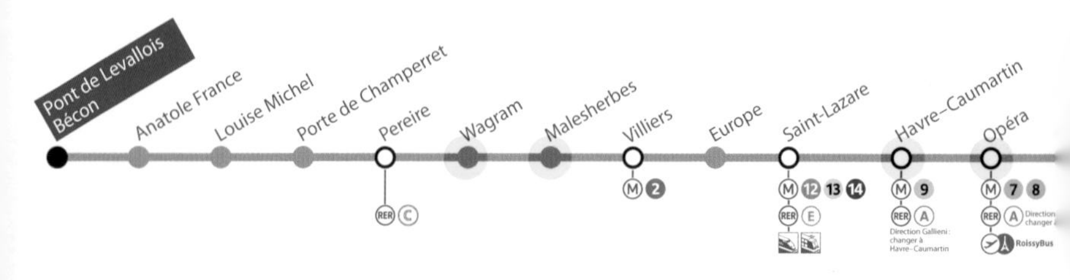

History

Line 3 links Pont de Levallois – Bécon (Levallois-Perret) to Galliéni (Bagnolet). Curiously, it was not the third line to be opened but the fifth! The line was put into service in sections: from Villiers to Père Lachaise on 19 October 1904, from Père Lachaise to Gambetta on 25 January 1905, from Villiers to Pereire on 23 May 1910 and, finally, from Pereire to Porte de Champerret on 15 February 1911. In 1921, its extension between Gambetta and Porte des Lilas improved services to the east of the capital, while remaining on the Right Bank. In 1937, the Porte de Champerret terminus was extended as far as Pont de Levallois. To this line 3, a line 3bis was added in 1971, from Gambetta station. To do this improvements were carried out, involving the disappearance of the Martin Nadaud station. Line 3 thus has two terminuses in the east, at Galliéni and Porte des Lilas.
Line 3 was the first in the network to have iron rails MF 67, still in place today. Line 3bis has one of Paris's best known ghost stations, called Haxo, on the link line between Porte des Lilas and Place des Fêtes. Built in 1921, it has never been opened to the public.

Pont de Levallois – Bécon / Galliéni

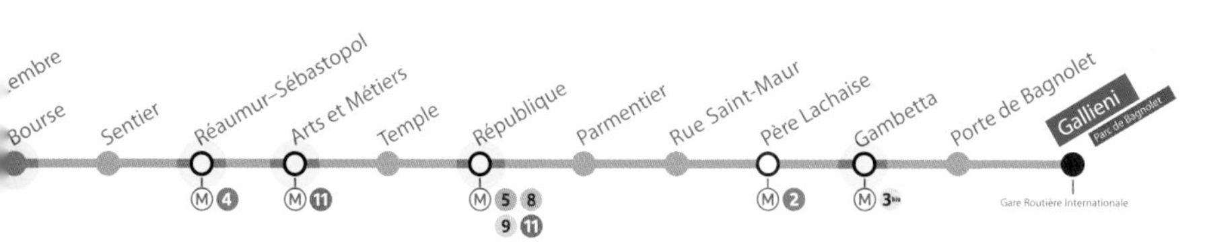

WAGRAM

History

The metro station gets its name from the eponymous avenue. The Battle of Wagram is one of the most glorious episodes of the Napoleonic era. On 5 and 6 July 1809, Napoleon and his troops pushed back the Austrian army, commanded by the Archduke Charles, northeast of Vienna. Fielding off Austrian counter-attacks, Napoleon launched a massive offensive using most of his troops and won the battle. The station awning was designed by Hector Guimard.

SIGHTSEEING

Architecture

1 **Rue Fortuny:** this street named after a Spanish painter contains some architectural treats. At no. 8, pause a moment before this building with medieval flour-

ishes, with pretty statues at the corners of the windows. Note also the latticework on the walls and the sculpted columns around the doors. At no. 22, admire the grimacing characters above the door. At no. 27, vibrant colours range from red brick to turquoise

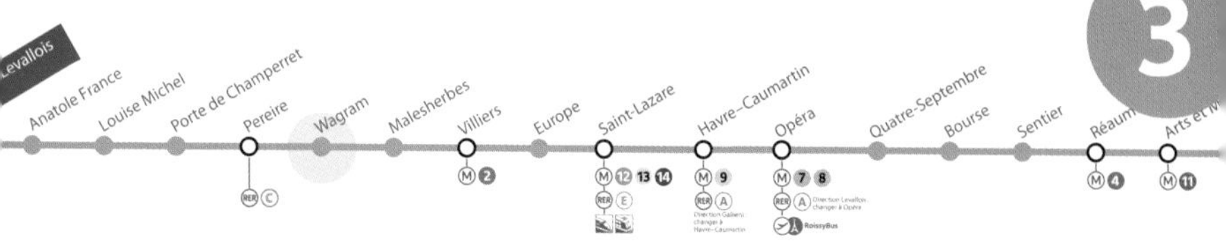

faïence via black (see photo opposite). At no. 35, you can quite simply see rats (in stone, don't worry) running over the facade. Finally, take in the finesse of the doorknob in the form of a mermaid at no. 46.

134 avenue de Villiers: the facade of this building has a fine example of a stepped gable.

Address book

The place for a rendezvous

Le Central
65 rue Prony, 17th.
Open Monday to Saturday 6.30am to 9pm.
Tel.: 01-47-66-74-51.

Shopping

A Cap Hispania
If you dream of Rioja wines, Iberico Bellota ham or *turron*, hurry to this delicious Spanish deli.
23 rue Jouffroy-d'Abbans, 17th.
Tel.: 01-46-22-11-60.
www.caphispania.fr
Open Monday 4pm to 7pm, Tuesday to Saturday 10am to 2pm, 4pm to 7.30pm.

B Les Poupées Retrouvées
This is more than just an antique shop but a return to childhood, as ancient dolls and toys find a new life.
90 rue Jouffroy-d'Abbans, 17th.
Tel.: 01-48-88-98-77.
www.lespoupees-retrouvees.com
Open Monday to Friday 2pm to 7pm.

Restaurants

C L'Ampère
A vintage setting and bistro atmosphere. The northern French chef knows how to update yesterday's dishes for today's tastes. Friendly service. Around €20.
1 rue Ampère, 17th.
Tel.: 01-47-63-72-05.
www.lampere.fr
Open Monday to Friday until 10.30pm.

D Agapé
A gastronomic restaurant in a very elegant setting. High-quality ingredients both landwards (meat from butcher Hugo Desnoyers) and seawards. Main courses around €45.
51 rue Jouffroy d'Abbans, 17th.
Tel. : 01-42-27-20-18.
www.agape-paris.fr
Open Monday to Friday noon to 2.30pm, 8pm to 10.30pm.

Previous stations

PONT DE LEVALLOIS – BÉCON
Le Narval
120 rue Anatole-France,
92300 Levallois-Perret.

ANATOLE FRANCE
Café de France
75 rue Anatole-France,
92300 Levallois-Perret.

LOUISE MICHEL
Le Comptoir
28 rue Carnot,
92300 Levallois-Perret.

PORTE DE CHAMPERRET
Brasserie Royal Villiers
4 place de Champerret, 17th.

PEREIRE
Bistrot le Royal Pereire
1 place de Maréchal-Juin, 17th.

MALESHERBES

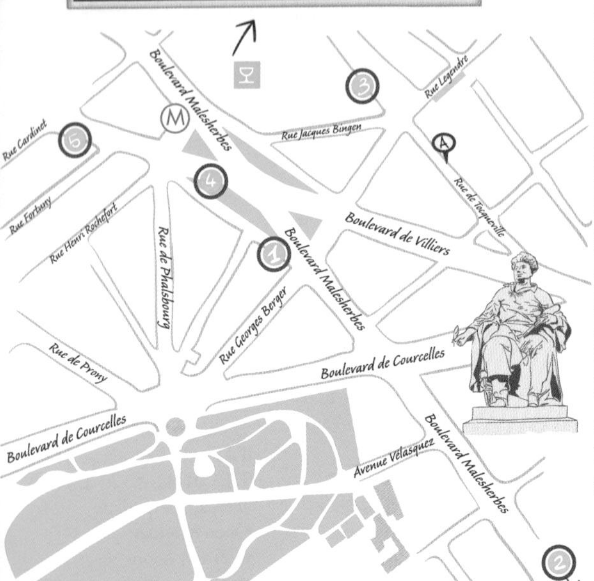

History

The exception proves the rule: unusually, this station honours a great personality from French history. Chrétien Guillaume de Lamoignon de Malesherbes (1721–1794) came from a noble family. Politician and Procureur Général of the Parlement de Paris, he became director of the royal library in 1750. He defended the *Encyclopédistes*. He even had Diderot's writings sent to his own home to protect them from censorship. Passionate about botany, he became a member of the Académie des Sciences in 1750 and the Académie Française in 1775. During the trial of Louis XVI, under the Convention in 1792, he defended the king, which led to him being guillotined in his turn during the Terror.

SIGHTSEEING

Architecture

1 ***Hôtel Gaillard (Banque de France):*** this strange Renaissance-style brick residence, which now belongs to the Banque de France, was commissioned by

Émile Gaillard from architect Jules Février and constructed between 1878 and 1884. The architect found his inspiration in the Château de Blois (Louis XII wing) and Château de Gien. The original owner had a fine collection of faïence and tapestries. The interiors and panelling date from the 15th century.

1 place du Général-Catroux, 17th.
Admission free.

Beaux-Arts doorway in the Hôtel Sédille: behind a heavy wooden doorway, in the interior courtyard, is the well-preserved doorway from the Pavillon des Beaux-Arts at the 1878 World Fair.

28 boulevard Malesherbes, 8th.
Admission free.

Art nouveau building by Charles Plumet: don't miss the facade of this building built for a Monsieur van Loyen, with its covered balcony, open loggia and arcatures. Inside, the superb hallway has faïence decoration by Émile Müller. There is burgeoning ironwork around the lift.

36 rue de Tocqueville, 17th.
Admission free.

Place du Général-Catroux: this square contains statues of the novelist Alexandre Dumas *Père* and actress Sarah Bernhardt. It was laid out in 1862, but renamed in 1977 after one of the generals who joined Charles de Gaulle during the Second World War.

Culture

5 Musée Jean-Jacques Henner

Portraits by the Alsatian artist Jean-Jacques Henner (1829–1905). A pretty museum housed in the studio of the painter Dubufe (1853–1909).

43 avenue de Villiers, 17th.
www.musee-henner.fr
Closed some public holidays.
Entrance fee.

Address book

The place for a rendezvous

Le Saint Fleuret
87 rue Cardinet, 17th.
Open Monday to Friday 7am to 8pm.
Tel.: 01-46-22-90-83.

Restaurant

A Chez Karl et Érick
Two brothers, one in the dining room, the other in the kitchen. Meticulously-prepared original dishes are served in a refined bistro setting.
Around €30.
20 rue de Tocqueville, 17th.
Tel.: 01-42-27-03-71.
Open Monday to Saturday noon to 2pm, 7.30pm to 10.30pm.

Next stations

VILLIERS

See line 2, page 55

EUROPE

Paris-Europe
51 rue de Rome, 8th.

SAINT-LAZARE

See line 12, page 310

HAVRE-CAUMARTIN

1970s orange ceramic tiles (after those at Mouton-Duvernet station) were used in this station but they were abandoned shortly afterwards, as they proved too dark in practice.

History

This metro station is dedicated to the town of Le Havre, through the street it serves. It is true that the neighbouring Gare Saint-Lazare train station provides the chance to part for a trip to this lively port on the Normandy coast, founded by François Ier in 1517. Caumartin refers to the family from Ponthieu, or more precisely Antoine-Louis Lefebvre de Caumartin, Marquis de Saint-Ange and Prevost of the Paris Merchants, who contributed to the transformation of Paris between 1778 and 1784—notably this street, which still bears his name. The style 'Mouton'

SIGHTSEEING

Monuments

1. **Église Saint-Louis-d'Antin:** it's almost possible to walk past this church without noticing it. In this district dedicated to the god of shopping, it appears rather incongruous. Built by Alexandre Théodore Brongniart, architect of the Bourse, it was originally the chapel of a Capucine monastery (now Lycée Condorcet). Inside, there is stained glass by Édouard-Amédée Didron and an organ by Cavaillé-Coll.
63 rue Caumartin or 4 rue du Havre, 9th.

2. **Hôtel Le Péra:** worth a look for its facade designed by architects Michel Proux and Jean-Michel Demones in 1982. The stone creates a continuity with the neigh-

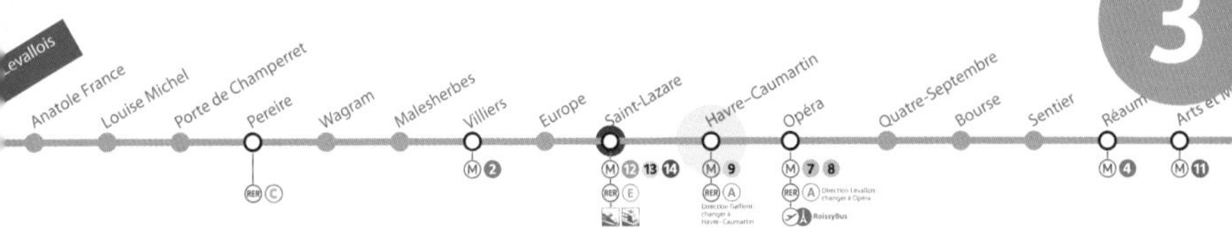

bouring buildings, while the glass of the arcade gives an impression of modernity.

17 rue de Caumartin, 9th.
Tel.: 01-53-43-54-00. Admission free.

L'Heure pour Tous by Arman: an accumulation of clocks (no longer too on time...) in the form of a totem (1989). Unusual, though a little stressful for a train station hinterland! Surely a question of ensuring day trippers don't miss their train.

Parvis of Gare Saint-Lazare.

partment stores

Galeries Lafayette: built between 1908 and 1912 by Georges Chedanne and Ferdinand Chanut, the store is worthwhile not only for its choice of goods (clothes, housewares, perfumes, jewellery...) but also for its 33-metre (108-feet) high stained glass dome, supported by ten metal columns, inspired by Byzantine architecture. In December, a giant Christmas tree sits in the middle.

40 boulevard Haussmann, 9th.
Tel.: 01-42-82-34-56.
www.galerieslafayette.com
Late-night shopping Thursday until 9pm.

5 **Printemps:** the Printemps stores were founded in 1865. The buildings have undergone numerous modifcations. The dome on the 6th floor of Printemps de la Mode, constructed in 1923 by master glassmaker Brière, now contains a *brasserie*. At the end of the year, the Christmas window displays are always a huge success!

64 boulevard Haussmann, 9th.
Tel.: 01-42-82-50-00.
www.printemps.com
Late-night shopping Thursday until 10pm.

Address book

The place for a rendezvous

Le Clos Bourguignon
39 rue Caumartin, 9th.
Open Monday to Saturday 7am to midnight.
Tel.: 01-47-42-56-60.

Restaurant

A Le Déli-cieux
For making the most of the view and admiring Paris from above. Snacks and hot dishes. Main courses €15.
9th-floor terrace of Printemps de la maison. Non-stop service Monday to Saturday 11am to 9pm.

OPÉRA

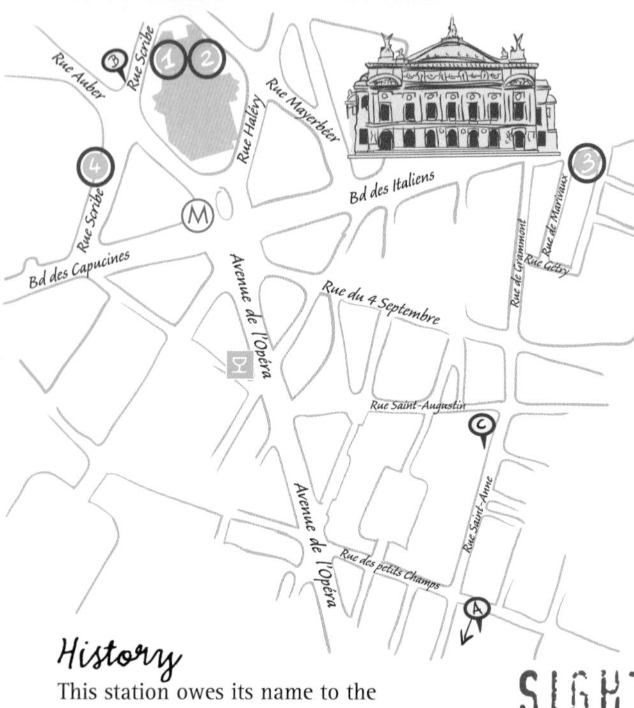

History

This station owes its name to the building dedicated to the arts, with its facade crowned by sculptures. Constructed by Charles Garnier, whose name it took at the end of the 19th century, the opera was commissioned by Napoleon III. After surviving an assassination attempt at another nearby opera (since demolished), he wanted an access ramp from adjoining rue Scribe that was hidden from the public. It was done. Today, the metro station is a hub of transport connections reunited in a deep well. The signage is in 'Parisine', a typeface created in the 1980s by Jean-François Porchez and adopted by the whole network. In 2010, the station was even redecorated for the needs of an IKEA advertisement with sofas in place of the usual seats.

SIGHTSEEING

Architecture

1 **Opéra Garnier:** built by the architect Charles Garnier in 1874 in 'Napoleon III' style, as Garnier himself would say or, rather, a mixture of Baroque and neo-Renaissance styles, with its grand staircase and its salamander, symbol of perpetual regeneration. The painted ceiling by Chagall dates from 1964. Used for both ballet and opera, the opera house can seat only 1,971 spectators, in some 11,000 square metres (118,403 square feet) of space. A statue of Garnier as Apollo stands near a window in the grand foyer.
At the exit of the metro station.
Tel.: 0892-89-90-90. www.operadeparis.fr

The grand staircase, the foyers, museum, temporary exhibition gallery and the auditorium (when not closed for artistic or technical reasons) are open for visits daily 10am to 5pm (until 6pm from 16 July to 5 September). Entrance fee.

...t of the ordinary

Opéra Garnier Beehives: former stagehand, John Paucton, has set up beehives on the roof of the opera. It's not open to visitors, but one can buy the celebrated Opéra de Paris honey at Fauchon on place de la Madeleine.

...lture

Opéra-Comique: a theatre founded under Louis XIV from travelling fairground troupes. The repertoire, largely consisting of opera adaptations, was enriched by plays and light opera. The initial opera house burned down in 1838 but was rebuilt. From 1840, the Opéra-Comique was a success, notably with pieces by Georges Bizet. Today the opera house, dating from the Belle Époque after a second fire, is directed by Jérôme Deschamps, with a programme particularly known for reviving rarely performed operas.
5 rue Favart, 2nd.
Tel.: 01-42-44-45-40.
www.opera-comique.com

4 **Musée de la Parfumerie Fragonard**
The perfume museum is housed in a fine Napoleon III-style town house, built in1860 by the architect Lesoufaché, a pupil of Charles Garnier.
9 rue Scribe, 9th. Tel.: 01-47-42-04-56. www.fragonard.com. Admission free.

Address book

The place for a rendezvous

Café du Cadran
1 rue Daunou, 2nd.
Open daily 6.30am to 2am.
Tel.: 01-42-61-72-41.

Shopping

A K-mart
A Japanese supermarket where you can find Japanese produce and everything necessary to make sushi and sashimi. Useful practical tools that are often unfindable elsewhere!
8 rue Sainte-Anne, 1st.
Tel.: 01-58-62-49-09.

B Uniqlo
Trendy good-value clothes from the leading Japanese brand spread over 2,150 square metres (23,142 square feet).
17 rue Scribe, 9th.
Tel.: 01-58-18-30-55.

Restaurants

C Rue Sainte-Anne
This street contains numerous Korean, Chinese, Japanese and Thai restaurants.

Next station

QUATRE-SEPTEMBRE

Le Gaillon, 2 rue de la Michodière, 2nd.

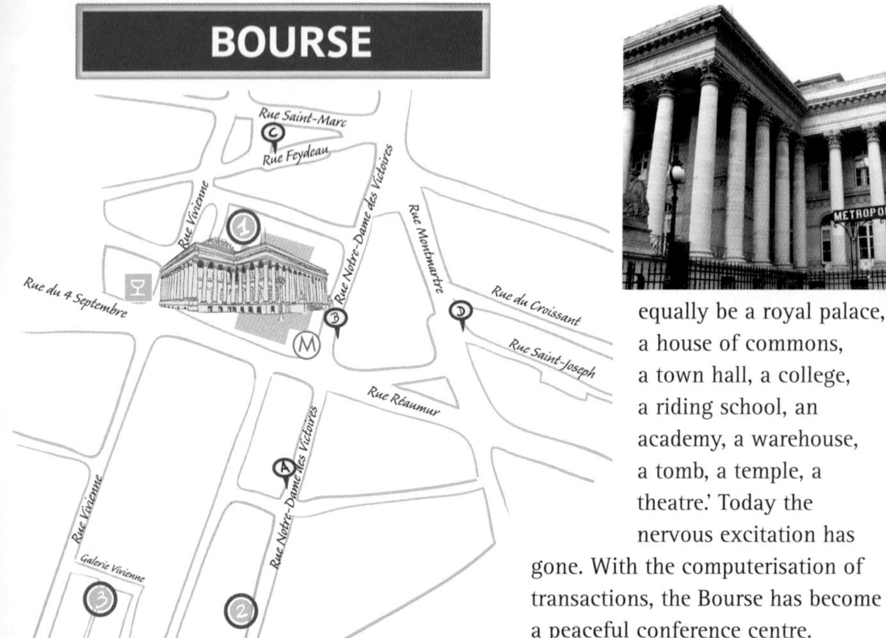

History

This station's name after the Paris stock exchange is unequivocal. However, you have to go back a little in time to imagine the effervescence and the mood of 'luxe and lucre' that once reigned in this temple of finance. On leaving the metro, passers-by will discover the colonnades of this palace that aroused the amused irony of Victor Hugo: 'Greek by its colonnades, Romanesque by the arches of its doors and windows, Renaissance by its grand urban vaults. One can hardly marvel too much at a monument that might equally be a royal palace, a house of commons, a town hall, a college, a riding school, an academy, a warehouse, a tomb, a temple, a theatre.' Today the nervous excitation has gone. With the computerisation of transactions, the Bourse has become a peaceful conference centre.

Monuments

1 **Palais Brongniart:** ringed by a peristyle of Corinthian columns, the antique-style stock exchange used to be a true 'temple to money'. In 1808, the architect Alexandre Théodore Brongniart was charged with constructing the edifice. Inside, the main hall has a glass dome, which soars 25 metres (82 feet) above the ground, surrounded by arcaded galleries. Adorned by statues of Commerce and Industry, sculpted by Dumont and Duret, the building has been calm since 1987. However, in the 'pit', until that year, a frenzied crowd of men used to vibrate to the rhythm of the

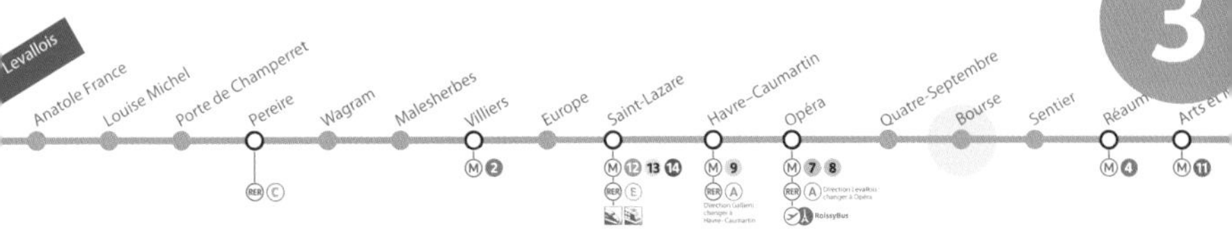

fluctuations of the stock exchange. Today computers have replaced the throng of traders drunk on adrenalin.
28 place de la Bourse, 2nd.
www.palaisbrongniart.com

Basilique Notre-Dame-des-Victoires: the last relic of an Augustinian monastery of which it was the chapel, it was inaugurated with great pomp by Louis XIII in 1629. Its name recalls the victorious siege of La Rochelle. At the time the town was a stronghold of Protestantism in France. Supported

by the English, keen to undermine the power of their rival, it was the last bastion of the Huguenots. When the clergy fled with the Revolution, the church became the seat of the national lottery and, later, a stock exchange during the Directoire. It returned to a religious use in 1802. Today it is a place of pilgrimage. Some 37,000 ex votos on the walls reveal the fervour of the pilgrims, among them, Saint Thérèse of Lisieux.

A romantic walk

3 Galeries Vivienne and Colbert

Surrealist poet Louis Aragon called them 'human aquariums'. The poetic and mysterious covered passages still cast their spell today. Galerie Vivienne was built in 1823 according to designs by the architect

Delannoy. Caduceus, anchors and horns of abundance decorate the half-moon windows. Goddesses and nymphs people the rotunda. Its style is Pompeiian neoclassical. It is crowned by an elegant glass roof and decorated with mosaics, paintings and sculptures. As to the Galerie Colbert, located at 6 rue des Petits-Champs, it was conceived by Billaud in 1826. At the centre is a vast rotunda, illuminated by a glass dome. A majestic bronze candelabra bearing a crown of seven crystal globes, nicknamed the 'luminous egg cosy', occupies the space, along with an 1822 bronze by Nanteuil representing Eurydice bitten by a snake.

The place for a rendezvous

Brasserie Le Vaudeville
29 rue Vivienne, 2nd.
Open daily 7am to 1am.
Tel.: 01-40-20-04-62.

Shopping

Ⓐ Elvis My Happiness
Fans of the King won't believe their eyes. Collectors' discs, glittery stage costumes, figurines and even Elvis motif china, nothing is missing from this shrine to the son of a seamstress and a Mississippi farmworker, who was propulsed in just a few years to the status of a worldwide star worshipped by millions. The shop's kitsch is deliberate—we love it!
9 rue Notre-Dame-des-Victoires, 2nd.
Tel.: 01-49-27-08-43.
Open Monday to Saturday 10.30am to 1pm, 2.30pm to 7pm.

Restaurant

Ⓑ Brasserie Gallopin
This grand old lady has reigned over the district since 1876, celebrating its 135 years of existence in 2011. You will be blown away by the beauty of the interior, adorned by Victorian-style wood panelling. Its sumptuous mahogany bar, sparking chandeliers and gorgeous glass skylight made for the 1900 World Fair take you back to the dawn of the 20th century. Add to that the waiters' Belle Époque garb and the ceaseless ballet of silver dishes and brass platters, and you will feel decidedly in another era. On the menu, shellfish rivals with roast pork with thyme:

players, place your bets, *rien ne va plus,* choose! Set menus €23 – 36. Reservation essential.
40 rue Notre-Dame-des-Victoires, 2nd.
Tel.: 01-42-36-45-38.
www.brasseriegallopin.com
Open daily noon to midnight.

Out on the town

Ⓒ Le Truskel

In a rock and roll ambience, ordering a pint at the bar turns out to be a journey through modernity. Le Truskel is a hybrid: all at once British pub, rock venue and improvised nightclub. Until 5 in the morning the atmosphere mounts under the combined effects of music and vodka. The Strokes and Franz Ferdinand have done after shows here, Jarvis Cocker and Nigel Godrich have pretty much set up residence. Noctambules are not mistaken, Le Truskel has become an indissociable element of Parisian all-nighters.
12 rue Feydau, 2nd.
Tel.: 01-40-26-59-97.
Open Tuesday to Saturday 8pm to 5am, Thursday from 7pm.

Ⓓ Le Social Club

This Parisian temple of electronic music has gained an international reputation. The building once housed the printworks that produced *L'Aurore* (meaning dawn), the daily newspaper in which Georges Clemenceau published Emile Zola's celebrated letter *J'accuse* defending Dreyfus in 1898. The Social Club is far from that past, but it will surely be dawn when you leave.
142 rue Montmartre, 2nd.
Tel.: 01-40-28-05-55.
www.parissocialclub.com
Open Tuesday to Saturday 11pm to 6am.

Next station

SENTIER

Brasserie des Petits Carreaux
17 rue des Petits-Carreaux, 2nd.

RÉAUMUR – SÉBASTOPOL

SIGHTSEEING

History

The former Rue Saint-Denis station was renamed in 1907 by associating two hitherto unconnected names. René-Antoine Ferchault de Réaumur (1683–1757) was a French physicist, who doubled as a researcher in all fields. We can credit him with the invention of the alcohol thermometer and an opaque white devitrified glass. Sébastopol is a town in the Ukraine that recalls an episode in the Crimean War. Today, the platforms of line 3 have the distinction of being decorated with the front pages of French newspapers related to the Second World War.

Architecture

1 **Former Félix Potin shop:** built in

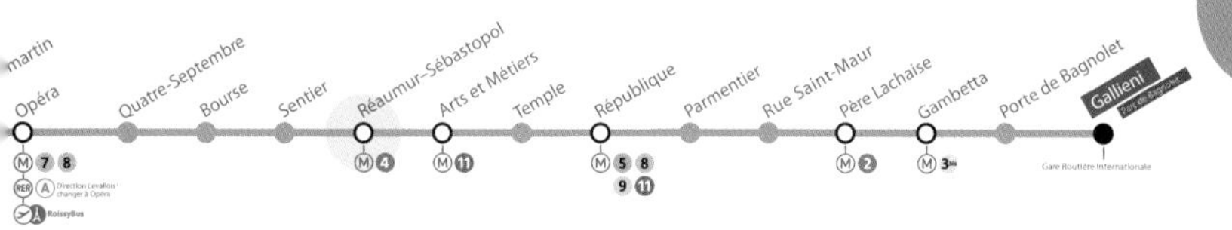

1910 by the architect Charles-Henri Le Maresquier, it is neo-Baroque in style, with a rotonda at its prow, polychrome decoration and bees as a symbol of plenty. This former outlet of the Félix Potin food stores is now a Monoprix supermarket.

51 rue Réaumur, 3rd.

(Corner of rues Réaumur and Sébastopol).

2 **Passage de la Trinité:** opened in 1827 in place of the Hospice des Enfants Bleus, for orphans abandoned at the Hôpital de la Trinité, hence its name.

21 rue de Palestro

or 164 rue Saint-Denis, 2nd.

3 **Église Saint-Nicolas-des-Champs**

This church has evolved through the ages as its eclectic styles show. A chapel in the 12th century, it later gained a Gothic facade and belfry. The nave and the south doorway are Renaissance and, in the 18th century, columns and other antique marvels appeared. The Revolution caused its closure and itt was only in 1802 that it because a place of worship again.

254, rue Saint-Martin

or 49 rue de Turbigo, 3rd.

Tel.: 01-42-72-92-54.

4 **Maison de Nicolas Flamel**

This house was built in 1407, although its facade is later (18th century). Nicolas Flamel, an academic, put up needy labourers. Their rent? To say prayers for the dying. On the second and fifth pillars one can spot the initials N and F. He was also known as an alchemist—as Harry Potter remembers very well! His house is often considered to be the oldest in Paris. Today it houses the Auberge de Nicolas Flamel restaurant.

51 rue de Montmorency, 3rd.

Address book

The place for a rendezvous

Café Le Capitole
105 boulevard de Sébastopol, 2nd.
Open Monday to Saturday 6am to 11pm.
Tel.: 01-42-33-96-54.

Out on the town

A Gaîté Lyrique
Concerts and exhibitions in a theatre dating from 1862. An innovative venue dedicated to current and contemporary music and digital culture.
3 bis rue Papin, 3rd.
Tel.: 01-53-01-51-51.
www.lagaitelyrique.com
Open Tuesday to Saturday 2pm to 8pm, Sunday 2pm to 6pm.

Restaurant

B 404
The bar-restaurant of Momo, a genuine star, who has also opened annexes in London, Beirut and Dubai. Sun-filled North African cuisine includes lentil salad, fish tagine, couscous and sweet *pastillas*. Refined decor. A voyage for the senses and flavours in the heart of Paris. Average €30 – 40.
69 rue des Gravilliers, 3rd.
Tel.: 01-42-74-57-81.
Open daily noon to 2.30pm, 7.30pm to 11.30pm.

ARTS ET MÉTIERS

History

This metro station was totally renovated in 1994 for the bicentenery of the Musée des Arts et Métiers, which it serves. The impression of being in Jules Verne's Nautilus submarine is guaranteed with this design by François Schuiten. The Belgian graphic artist has worked on comic strips, notably *Les Cités Obscures.* The profusion of copper accentuates the submarine atmosphere. On the ceiling, machinery spurs on the imagination and portholes here and there complete the intended illusion of a bubble cut off from the world for the length of a journey. It's a great invitation to discover the history of machines of yesterday and today at the neighbouring museum. This station is one of the last in the network to still have escalators with wooden slats.

SIGHTSEEING

Out of the ordinary

1 **Musée des Arts et Métiers:** in 1794, the Abbé Grégoire decided to create a Conservatoire National des Arts et Métiers in order to conserve and highlight recently invented machines and tools. The collection was installed in the former Abbaye Saint-Martin-des-Champs, which had lost its religious function at the Revolution. One can, however, still visit the church, where cars and planes are now displayed. The museum is divided into seven sections, with demonstrations in each: scientific instruments, materials, construction, communications, energy, mechanics and transport. Perfect for understanding the how and the why of everyday life through the 8,000 objects in the museum.
60 rue Réaumur, 3rd.

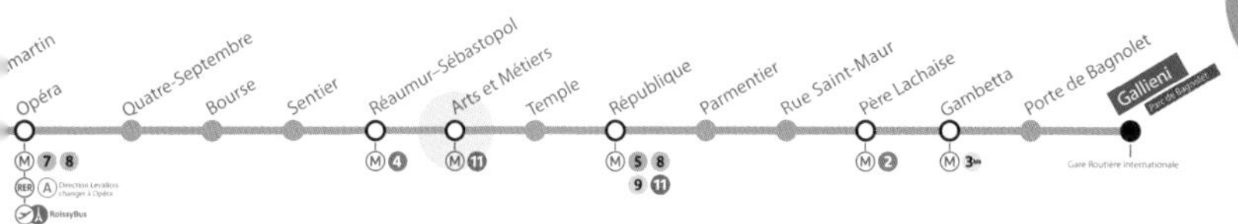

Tel.: 01-53-01-82-00.
www.arts-et-metiers.net.
Open Tuesday to Sunday 10am to 6pm.
Closed 25 December and 1 May.
Entrance fee. Guided tours available.

chitecture

Rue Volta: a rather sombre street to be named in tribute to Alexandre Volta, inventor of the electric battery. The half-timbered house at No.3 was long believed to date from the late 13th century, but is probably early 17th century. Below are the shops and counters, upstairs, not very high (less than 2 metres/6 feet), the accommodation.

Address book

The place for a rendezvous

Le Royal Beaubourg
105 rue Beaubourg, 3rd.
Open Monday to Saturday 7am to 10pm.
Tel.: 01-42-72-37-30.

Shopping

A Comme un Roman
A two-storey bookshop with an original selection of books.
39 rue de Bretagne, 3rd.
Tel.: 01-42-77-56-20.
www.comme-un-roman.com
Open Tuesday to Saturday 10am to 7.45pm, Sunday 10am to 1.30pm.

B Popelini
The choux pastry specialist! There are numerous flavours (dark chocolate, coffee, Madagascar vanilla, lemon, pistachio and morello cherry, rose and raspberry and plenty of other varieties depending on the chef's mood!) and it's possible to buy a single cream puff to take away for tea.
29 rue Debelleyme, 3rd.
Tel. : 01-44-61-31-44.
www.popelini.com
Open Tuesday to Saturday 11am to 7.30pm, Sunday 10am to 3pm.

C Marché des Enfants Rouges
A bit of a timewarp. This covered market (one of around a dozen in Paris alone) replaced a historic orphanage, where the children were dressed in red (hence the name 'red children'). Today, you'll find fruit and vegetable sellers, a florist, and a few tables for eating a tasty couscous. Very busy at weekends. A welcome pause.
39 rue de Bretagne, 3rd.
Open Tuesday to Saturday 8.30am to 1pm, 4pm to 7.30pm, Sunday 8.30am to 2pm.

Culture

D Galerie Christian Berst
One of the rare Paris galleries specialising in Art Brut. Occasional temporary exhibitions.
3–5 passage des Gravilliers, 3rd.
Tel.: 01-53-33-01-70.
Open Wednesday to Saturday 2pm to 7pm or by appointment.

E Galerie Éric Dupont
Shows both emerging and confirmed artists, often visible in art fairs all over the globe.
13 rue Chapon, 3rd.
Tel.: 01-44-45-04-14.
www.eric-dupont.com
Open Tuesday to Saturday 11am to 7pm or by appointment.

Next station

TEMPLE

Café À la tour du Temple
160 bis rue du Temple, 3rd.

RÉPUBLIQUE

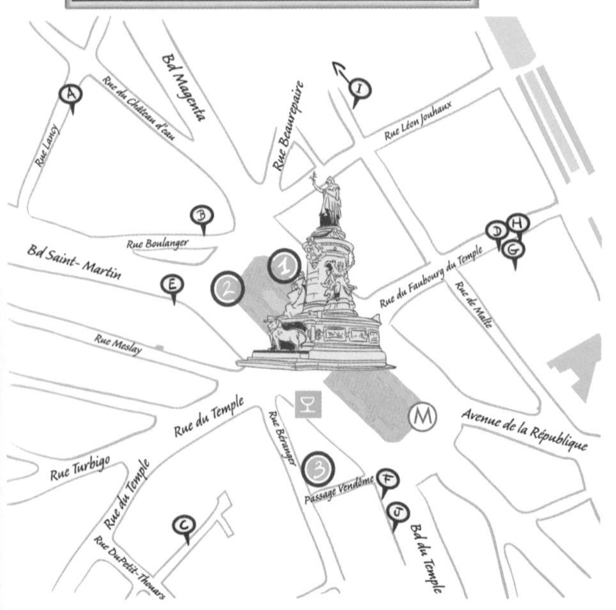

History

This station is at the heart of the metro network. It holds a record: with five interchanges it is, along with Châtelet, the station with the most interchanges in the network. It serves the square of the same name, originally the Temple gateway in Charles V's city wall, then Place du Château-d'Eau. In 1811, a first fountain by Pierre-Simon Girard adorned its centre. A second fountain with bronze lions designed by Gabriel Davioud, commissioned by Baron Haussmann, replaced it in 1867.
In 1880, the fountain was moved to place Félix-Éboué, where it can still be seen and is particularly striking at night. With the arrival of Socialists and Radicals in the Paris City Council in 1878, this square was chosen to celebrate the Republic. A competition was launched. The project by the Morice brothers was selected: Charles for the plinth, Léopold for the statue.
The group was inaugurated–of course–on 14 July 1883. The statue on the top of the structure is almost 10 metres (33 feet) high, with a 15.5-metres (51-feet) base. A similar project was conceived by Jules Dalou. Entitled *Le Triomphe de la République*, it stands at the centre of place de la Nation (see page 44).
In 2010, a project for the renovation of the square was voted. It plans

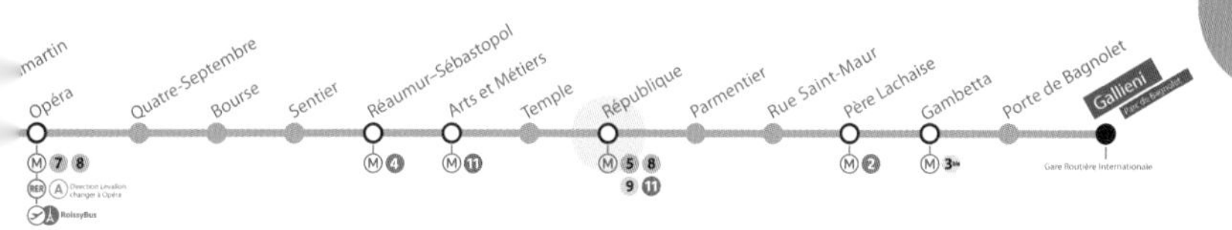

to pedestrianise the centre and to move road traffic to a single side. The square remains nonetheless the starting or finishing place of numerous demonstrations.

SIGHTSEEING

chitecture

Place de la République: pause a while to study the statuary of the monument dedicated to the Republic made by the Morice brothers in 1883. The Republic is dressed in a toga, like people in Antiquity. She holds an olive branch in her right hand and places her left hand on the law tablets. The mention 'Rights of Man' was added later. She is wearing the traditional Phrygian bonnet, symbol of the Revolution. At her feet are the three allegorical figures of the French national motto: Liberty, a flame in hand on broken iron chains; Equality holds a tricolore flag, as well as a pair of scales; Fraternity ensures the happiness of the children around her and the good harvests of those she protects. Note also the 12 bronze bas-reliefs, like 12 crucial steps in the Republic from 1789 to 1880. Pell-mell among them are the Tennis Court Oath and the abolition of privileges. The lion, with his urn and military attributes, symbolises universal suffrage.

② ***Fountains on Place de la République:*** the strange dolphin-shaped fountains hardly seem to be having a ball! They are also the work of the Morice brothers and were installed in 1883.

③ ***Passage Vendôme:*** one of the survivors of Paris's celebrated covered arcades. Initially, especially in the 19th century, they were constructed to protect passers by from rain—and to facilitate their purchases. This passage is 57 metres (62 yards) long and was created in 1827, later restored, transformed and modified. Originally, it connected Boulevard du Temple to the Couvent des Filles-Saint-Sauveur. This passage is named after Philippe de Vendôme, Grand Prior of the Temple, who sold some of his land to the city of Paris in the 17th century.

Place de République
or 16–18 rue Béranger, 3rd.
Admission free.

Address book

The place for a rendezvous

Le Royal République
9, place de la République, 3rd.
Open Monday to Sunday 7.30am to 1am.
Tel.: 01-42-72-31-44.

Shopping

Ⓐ Thanx God I'm a VIP
A vintage clothes shop run by Sylvie Chategnier. The organiser of the TGV parties in the 1990s has succeeded in transmitting her love of clothes and designer accessories to her clubbing friends at reasonable prices. Become part of the VIP family!
12 rue Lancry, 10th.
Tel.: 01-42-03-02-09.
www.thanxgod.com
Open Tuesday to Sunday 2pm to 8pm.

Culture

Ⓑ Galerie Octobre
Specialises in contemporary art.
24 rue René-Boulanger, 10th.
Tel.: 06-08-05-34-06.
www.octobre.org
Open Tuesday to Thursday 2pm to 7pm and by appointment on Monday and Friday.

Leisure

Ⓒ Ateliers Terre et Feu
Drawing and sculpture courses for adults and children. Perfect for finding inspiration.
8 cité Dupetit-

Thouars, 3rd.
Tel.: 01-45-77-10-10.
http://paris.terre-et-feu.com

Out on the town

Ⓓ Théâtre le Temple

A theatre since 1792 which today programmes comedy shows.

18 rue du Faubourg-du-Temple, 11th.
Tel.: 0892-350-015.
www.theatreletemple.com

Ⓔ Caveau de la République

This café-*théâtre* opened in 1901 showcases satirists treating current events. Raymond Souplex, Pierre Dax and Laurent Ruquier cut their teeth here.
23 place de la République or 1 boulevard Saint-Martin, 3rd.
Tel.: 01-42-78-44-45.
www.caveau.fr

Ⓕ Théâtre Dejazet

Inaugurated in 1851 on the site of a former real tennis court. Initially used for music hall and operetta, it then belonged to the actress Virginie Dejazet until 1870. In the 1970 and 80s, it hosted both the comedian Coluche and singer Juliette Gréco. Comedy acts and singers still perform here.
41 boulevard du Temple, 3rd.
Tel.: 01-48-87-52-55.
www.dejazet.com

Ⓖ Le Gibus

A mythic nightclub and concert venue that exists since 1967. The Police and the Sex Pistols both performed here. Today, DJs give pride of place to electronic music, rock and other pounding beats.
18 rue du Faubourg-du-Temple, 11th.
Tel.: 01-47-00-78-88.
www.gibus.fr

Ⓗ Favela Chic

Here it's all about letting your hair down to Brazilian music and devilish rhythms. It is also a restaurant with a menu of Brazilian specialities (*paes de queijo, feijoada, muqueca,* etc.).
18 rue du Faubourg-du-Temple, 11th.
No street sign, entrance in the galerie under the porch.
Tel.: 01-40-21-38-14.
Open Tuesday to Saturday 8pm to midnight.

Ⓘ Le Nouvel Alhambra

Inaugurated in 2008 after being totally rebuilt and modernised, this former cinema has quickly become a cult address for the latest music sounds.
21 rue Yves-Toudic, 10th.
Tel.: 01-40-20-40-25.

Restaurant

Ⓙ Chez Jenny

The temple of Alsatian gastronomy. If you dream of a good *choucroute*, this is the place to take refuge! The setting is a 1930s brasserie with panelling by Alsatian artist, Spindler. Main courses €20–30.
39 boulevard du Temple, 3rd.
Tel.: 01-44-54-39-00.
www.chez-jenny.com
Open daily noon to midnight.

Next stations

PARMENTIER

Les Anémones
41 avenue de la République, 11th.

RUE SAINT-MAUR

Café Lafreco
63 rue Saint-Maur, 11th.

PÈRE LACHAISE

See line 2, page 66

GAMBETTA

History

French statesman Léon Gambetta was born in Cahors in 1838 and died in Sèvres in 1882. Place Gambetta, in front of the 20th arrondissement Town Hall, with the metro station at its feet, today honours this former mayor of the arrondissement. He was minister of the interior during the Government of National Defense during the Franco-Prussian War and proclaimed the Third Republic at the Hôtel de Ville in 1870. He became president of the Assemblée Nationale and then President of the Council from 1881 to 1882. On 11 November 1920, his heart was transferred to the Panthéon. The diffused lighting of this station gives it a strange and original atmosphere. This fast-evolving district is the new stronghold of trendy Parisians.

SIGHTSEEING

Architecture

1 **Fountain on Place Gambetta:** three people are behind this work from 1992: architect Alfred Gindre, artist Jean-Louis Rousselet and master glassmaker J. Dixmier. The shards of glass seem to rise towards the sky in a disorderly manner, yet the ensemble remains harmonious. The water flows from the edge towards the centre. Also to be admired at nightfall.

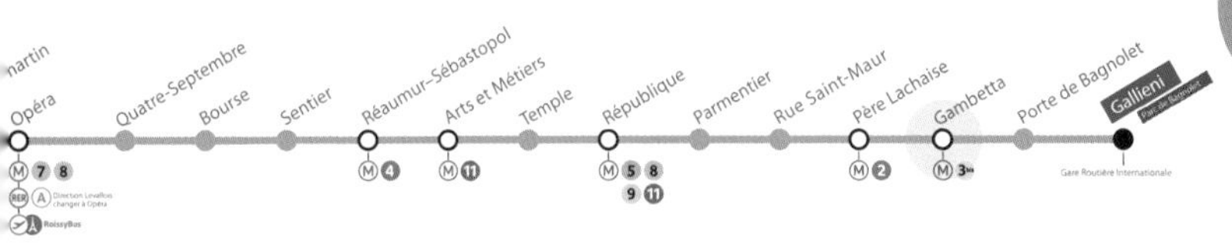

t of the ordinary

Corner of rues Pelleport and Belgrand: a cheerful distortion on the walls of an RATP warehouse. Rather than the habitual 'LOI DU 29 JUILLET 1881' and 'DÉFENSE D'AFFICHER'—billsticking prohibited—one can actually read 'LOI DU 29 JUILLET 1881' and further on 'DÉFENSE D'ÉLÉPHANT'. You do a double take but this neat graffiti makes one smile.

Address book

The place for a rendezvous

Bar du Métro
10 place Gambetta, 20th.
Open daily 5.30am to 2am.
Tel.: 01-46-36-95-10

Leisure

A MK2 Gambetta
This cinema is a local fixture with a programme that is both popular and demanding. programmation.
6 rue Belgrand, 20th.
Tel.: 01-46-36-34-69.

Shopping

B La Campagne à Paris
An old-fashioned grocer that doesn't appear to have changed for years. Attentive service, well-selected products (*charcuterie*, chocolates, etc.) and an excellent wine cellar.
210 rue des Pyrénées, 20th.
Tel.: 01-46-36-88-57.

C La Girafe et la Lune
A halfway house between toyshop and children's bookshop (comic books, mangas, etc.). It is very well stocked, with adorable soft toys waiting to be adopted.
16 rue de Cambodge, 20th.
Tel.: 01-46-36-80-47.
Open Tuesday to Saturday 10am to 7.30pm.

D L'Arbre à Plumes
A disorderly treasure trove of lamps, stickers, tablewares, jewels, pouffes and beautiful objects. You're sure to find something you love.
89–91 rue Pelleport, 20th.

Out on the town

E Chez Betty
A tiny cheerful wine bar and bistro.

The atmosphere is surely due to Betty's generous welcome and perfect advice. Exhibitions of local artists. Menus €32–42.
14 avenue du Père-Lachaise, 20th.
Tel.: 01-46-36-06-07.
Open Tuesday to Saturday 6.30pm to midnight.

Culture

F Théâtre National de la Colline
Since 1993, this address a few steps from place Gambetta has been dedicated to theatre. Today, the Théâtre National de la Colline presents a panorama of 20th century and contemporary drama.
15 rue Malte-Brun, 20th.
Tel.: 01-44-62-52-52.
www.colline.fr

line 4

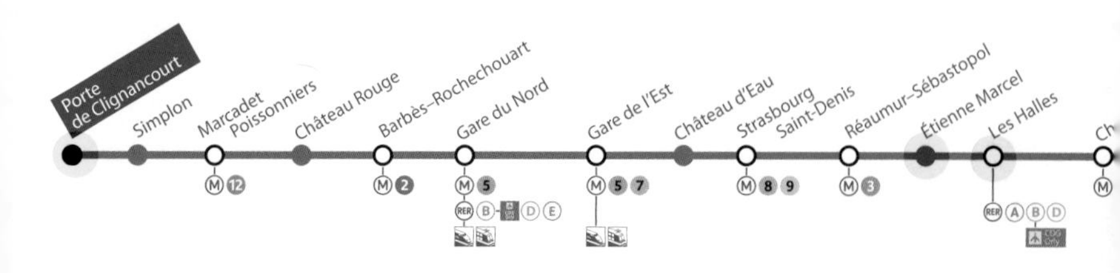

History

This line connects the north of Paris with the south, from Porte de Clignancourt to Porte d'Orléans. It opened up gradually, first serving Porte de Clignancourt – Châtelet in 1908, and then Porte d'Orléans – Raspail in 1909. The two sections joined up in 1910. The main difficulty encountered during the construction of this north-south line was the tunnelling under the Seine. The soft mud on the embankment was so difficult to dig that it had to be artificially frozen beforehand. Nor were the residents happy with the route and they protested vigorously, especially the academics from the Institut de France, who did not want to be interrupted by vibrations from the underground train. The route therefore had to be altered to suit them via Châtelet and Île de la Cité. In the 1960s, to improve profitability on this already very busy line, trains with rubber tyres were put into service and the stations were enlarged. In 1977 a further extension enabled the Les Halles station to be built just 30 metres (98 feet) to the east of the existing station, to cater to the RER passengers. In 2012, line 4 will be extended to the south as far as Mairie de Montrouge (the Montrouge town hall).

rte de Clignancourt / Porte d'Orléans

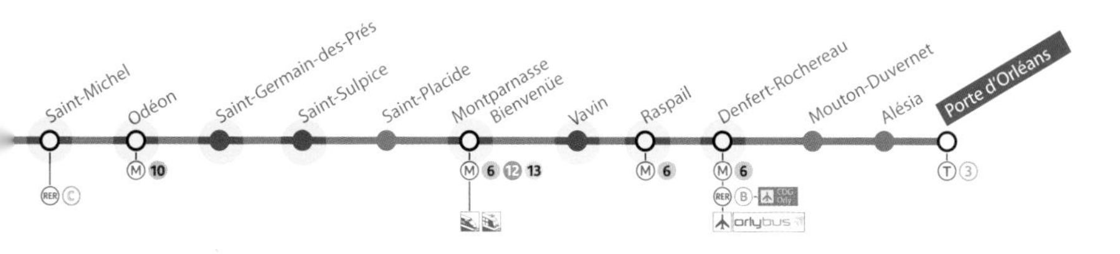

PORTE DE CLIGNANCOURT

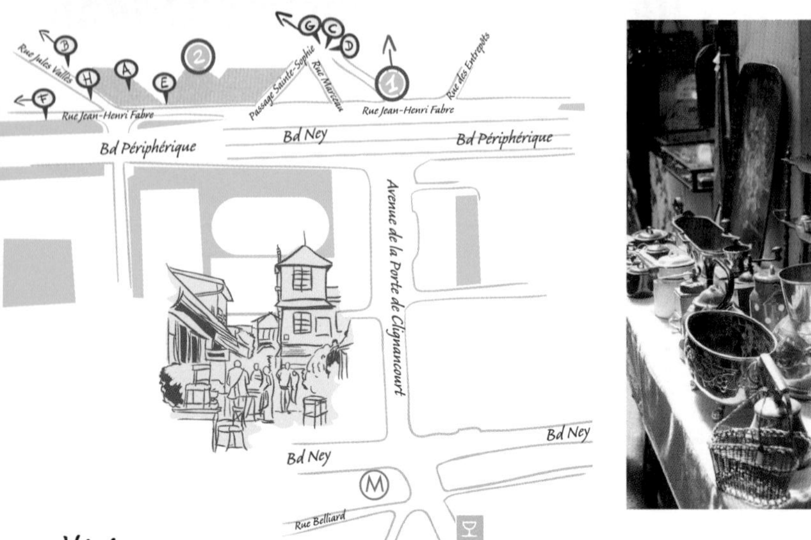

History

Clignancourt was a hamlet near the gates of Paris that was attached to the capital in 1860. It originally belonged to the Abbey of Saint-Denis before ownership was transferred to the Liget family. It was later acquired by the Brisard family, and finally by the Abbey of Montmartre. It became a working class area, since it was outside the Paris gates and therefore cheaper for the workers in the nearby factories to live there. The Saint-Ouen flea market set up by the so-called Thiers Walls (named after the Prime Minister) that surrounded Paris at the time. These walls disappeared at the end of the 20th century but the market grew better organised and remained. It is still very popular today, mostly at the weekend.

SIGHTSEEING

A walk in the city

1. **Cimetière de Saint-Ouen:** the tombs of the writer Alphonse Allais and the painter Suzanne Valadon are in this cemetery.
   69 avenue Michelet, 93400 Saint-Ouen. Open 8am to 5pm.

2. **Marché aux Puces de Saint-Ouen:** the Saint-Ouen flea market is the main reason for coming to Clignancourt! Be warned, there are several markets within the market, each with its own speciality, so you can spend hours here. Apparently this is where the term 'flea market' originated, when a visitor stood on the city wall and catching sight of all the stallholders swarming around below, exclaimed, '*Mais*

c'est un vrai marché aux puces!' (it's a real market of fleas), and the expression stuck.

Porte de Clignancourt.
Open Saturday to Monday 10am to 5.30pm.
Reservations required for the guided tours: 01-40-11-77-36.

Address book

The place for a rendezvous

Brasserie Royal Clignancourt
82 boulevard d'Ornano, 18th.
Open daily 6am to 9pm.
Tel.: 01-42-55-49-58.

Shopping

A Marché Malik
A market specialised in clothing. The name comes from the Albanian owner of Le Picolo bistro.
53 rue Jules-Vallès or rue Jean-Henri-Fabre.

B Marché Jules Vallès
Two covered arcades full of all kinds of nick-knacks. This is really what a flea market is all about!
7–9 rue Jules-Vallès.

C Marché Vernaison
A market with several hundred stands and one of the ones that really marks the identity of this flea market. You will find a little bit of everything here—but you will have to rummage around for it!
99, rue des Rosiers or 136, avenue Michelet.

D Marché Biron
Specialised in 19th century furniture and 1950s design.
85 rue des Rosiers or 118 avenue Michelet.

E Marché Dauphine
The most modern of all the markets here, with lots of paintings from different periods.
132–140, rue des Rosiers.

F Librairie de l'Avenue
This is the largest second hand bookshop in the Paris region. It was opened in 1959 and has more than 150,000 books.
31 rue Lécuyer, 93400 Saint-Ouen.
Tel.: 01-40-11-95-85.
www.librairie-avenue.com
Open Monday to Saturday 9am to 6pm.

Restaurants

G Chez Louisette
This former *guinguette* or dance hall has been open for business since 1930. It has a festive atmosphere and someone is usually up for singing a ditty or two. Regional French cooking.
130 avenue Michelet, 93400 Saint-Ouen, in the middle of Marché Vernaison.
Tel.: 01-40-12-10-14.

H Le Picolo
The authentic flea market bistro. People have been coming here since 1919, when the rag-and-bone men and rag merchants would pop in for a glass of white wine (known as a *'piccolo'*) between sales.
58 rue Jules-Vallès, 93400 Saint-Ouen.

Next stations

SIMPLON

Le Ouest Bar
64 boulevard d'Ornano, 18th.

MARCADET-POISSONNIERS

Bistrot Marcadet
79 boulevard Barbès, 18th.

BARBÈS-ROCHECHOUART

Au Petit Mignon Café
36 rue de Clignancourt, 18th.

ÉTIENNE MARCEL

Étienne Marcel succeeded in forming a *Conseil de Tutelle*, or regulatory body.

History

This station lies on the border between the 1st and 2nd arrondissements. It was opened in 1908 and takes its name from the neighbouring rue Étienne-Marcel. Étienne Marcel himself was a provost of merchants under Jean le Bon (John the Good). He was born in 1315 and died in 1358. He was a rich draper and headed the Third Estate in the 1356 and 1357 Estates General, where he stood against royal power, and especially the Dauphin, the future Charles V.
At a time when the country was at war (the famous Hundred Years' War against England), the plague was rife and King John II was captured at Poitiers,

SIGHTSEEING

Architecture

1 **L'Arbre à Liège:** the remnants of a shop sign from the Middle Ages is still visible on the façade.
10 rue Tiquetonne, 2nd.

2 **Tour de Jean-sans-Peur :** Jean Sans Peur was the Duke of Burgundy. He arranged for the assassination of his enemy, Louis d'Orléans, brother of King Charles VI, and fearful of reprisals fortified his home, the Hôtel de Bourgogne. Original parts of the building can be seen in the Salle de Conseil (board room).
20 rue Étienne-Marcel, 2nd.
Tel.: 01-40-26-20-28. Entrance fee.

Passage du Bourg-l'Abbé: this is a famous Parisian covered arcade that was built in 1827. The two caryatids at the entrance are by Aimé Millet, the one on the left representing crafts, and the one on the right representing commerce. There is pretty arched glass dome in the middle.

120 rue Saint-Denis, 2nd. Open Monday to Saturday 7.30am to 7.30pm.

Passage du Grand Cerf: this elegant arcade has a beautiful glass ceiling and metal beams. It is 113 meters (370 feet) long and the ceilings are more than 12 meters (39 feet) high. It is full of boutiques and one of the biggest Parisian arcades. It used to be the place where the stagecoaches from eastern France ended their journey. The arcade is neoclassical in style.

145 rue Saint-Denis, 2nd.
Open Monday to Saturday 8.30am to 8pm.

Address book

The place for a rendezvous

Café Étienne
14 rue Turbigo, 1st.
Open 8am to 2am.
Tel.: 01-42-36-79-46..

Shopping

Ⓐ Pâtisserie Stöhrer
This pastry shop has specialised in rum babas since 1730! Nicolas Stöhrer was pastry maker to King Leopold of Poland,

and invented the cake specially for him. Even the Queen of England has come here to taste one!
51 rue Montorgueil, 1st.
Tel.: 01-42-33-38-20.
www.stohrer.fr
Open all week 7.30am to 8.30pm.

Leisure

Ⓑ Spa Nuxe
If you feel like pampering yourself, this elegant place decorated in stone and dark wood, is just the place. You might also obtain some good advice from John Nollet, hairdresser to the stars, who was designed Audrey Tatou's hairstyle for the film *Amélie*.
32 rue Montorgueil, 1st.
Tel.: 01-55-80-71-40.
www.nuxe.com
Open Monday to Friday 9.30am to 9pm, Saturday 9.30am to 7.30pm.

Restaurant

Ⓒ DEPUR (Drôle d'Endroit Pour Une Rencontre)
Meaning 'funny place to meet up', it is in fact a cosy and friendly restaurant with an outside terrace. The food is both stimulating and affordable and there is also a bar. Hamburgers and cheesecake galore. About €15–25.
4 bis rue Saint-Sauveur, 2nd.
Tel.: 01-40-26-69-66.
www.droledendroit.com
Breakfast daily 8am to noon. Sunday brunch 12am to 5pm.

Previous stations

GARE DU NORD

See line 5, page 132

GARE DE L'EST

See line 7, page 168

CHÂTEAU D'EAU

Café Château d'Eau,
55 rue du Château-d'eau, 10th.

STRASBOURG SAINT-DENIS

See line 8, page 224

RÉAUMUR SÉBASTOPOL

See line 3, page 82

LES HALLES

Histoire

This area of Paris has often been called the '*ventre de Paris*' ('the city's stomach') because Les Halles (meaning covered market) was where the food market stood since the time of Philippe Auguste. In 1851, Napoleon III asked the architect Baltard to design a covered market using steel girders. When completed it housed all the different segments of the wholesale food market. However, as Paris grew, it proved to be inadequate and in 1969 the wholesale market moved to Rungis, a larger site outside Paris. Les Halles was then transformed into a shopping centre called Forum des Halles in 1977, so it is still dedicated to commerce but not specifically to food. A project is underway to inject a new lease of life into this concrete monster by extending the esplanade into a large walkway-cum-garden with a transparent roof.

SIGHTSEEING

Architecture

1 ***Église Saint-Eustache:*** the curious church, built between 1532 and 1667, has a gothic exterior and a Renaissance interior, complete with pilasters and columns, and a classic detail that was re-worked in the 18th century. Eustace is the patron saint of hunters because his divine revelation occurred when he was hunting a stag. Louis XIV took his first communion in this

church. There is a very moving painting of the Martyrdom of Saint-Eustache by Simon Vouet above the rue du Jour doorway.

2 impasse Saint-Eustache, 1st.

Fontaine des Innocents: this Renaissance period fountain by Jean Goujon (see photo opposite), was the model for the famous Wallace fountains.

At the corner of rue Saint-Denis and rue Berger, 1st.

...t of the ordinary

L'Écoute: called *Listening* this sandstone statue was made in 1986 by Henri de Miller (1953–1999). The head is resting on one hand and appears to be listening to the ground. A very soothing work.

Place René-Cassin, opposite Saint-Eustache church.

Address book

The place for a rendezvous

Le Saint-Eustache
14 rue de Montmartre, 1st.
Open daily 6am to 8pm.
Tel.: 01-42-36-08-93.

Shopping

A La Droguerie
A trendy haberdasher's and a Mecca for buttons, ribbons, and every possible thing you could need for making dresses, bags, hats and other accessories. You will get excellent advice into the bargain.
9–11 rue du Jour, 1st.
Tel.: 01-45-08-93-27.
www.ladroguerie.com
Open Monday 2pm to 6.45pm, and Tuesday to Saturday 10.30am to 6.45pm.

B Dehillerin
Here you will find every kind of kitchen utensils that any master chef could possibly require—and even some you never knew existed!
18 and 20 rue Coquillière;
51 rue Jean-Jacques-Rousseau, 1st.
Tel.: 01-42-36-53-13.
www.e-dehillerin.fr
Open Monday 9am to 12.30pm and 2pm to 6pm, Tuesday to Saturday 9am to 6pm.

C El Paso Booty
The perfect boutique for anyone looking for a pair of cowboy boots! All sorts of American accessories can be found here from bandanas to cowboy hats, including hipflasks and Zippo lighters.
79 rue Saint-Denis, 1st.
Tel.: 01-42-33-42-07.
www.elpaso-booty.fr
Open Monday to Saturday 10.30am to 7.30pm.

D Forum des Halles
Worth a detour for the stores and especially the young designer boutiques. If you enjoy exhibitions, books, and films, the newly renovated Forum des Images is worth visiting, just by the Sainte-Eustache exit.
Tel.: 01-44-76-96-56.
www.forumdeshalles.com
Open all week 10am to 8pm.

Restaurant

E Dans le Noir
A strange experience, worth trying out once in a lifetime. In this restaurant you will eat and drink in total darkness. Expect plenty of strange sensations! The menu is, of course, a surprise. About €35–47. The tasting menu (€72) includes three different wines and a cocktail.
51 rue Quincampoix, 4th.
Tel.: 01-42-77-98-04.
www.danslenoir.com
Two sittings every evening at 7.45pm and 10pm. Lunch only on Saturday and Sunday.

Next station

CHÂTELET

See line1, page 32

CITÉ

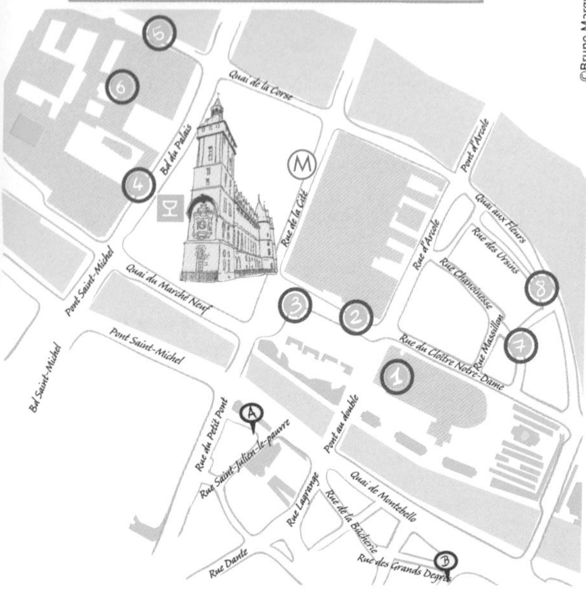

©Bruno Marguerite/RATP

History

Cité station gets its name from Île de la Cité, which it serves. The metro line was originally meant to pass under the Institut de France, a French academic institute that groups several academies together, but the learned academicians fought against it and managed to get the route of changed so as not to disturb their lofty thoughts. As a result the station was only opened in 1910, a year after the line became operational. Building the station required all the engineering expertise of the time. The island (Île de la Cité) has served as a stopover from one bank of the Seine to another since the Gallo-Roman period and was home to the Parisii tribe more than 2,000 years ago. There was even a Roman temple to Jupiter here once. You will notice the riveted metal sheets just inside the metro. The platforms and rails, stairs and lift are all contained in two metal caissons, 19 metres (62 feet) below ground. The lift was among the first to be installed in the underground network in 1911, along with the one in République station. The entire platform area is underneath the Seine. Since the ground was far too muddy to dig, it was decided to 'simply' freeze it to -25°C (-13°F) with special refrigeration machines and brine. The work advanced very slowly, at a pace of just one metre per month during the year it took to build. One cannot help being impressed by the engineering work this construction entailed, down to the sharp incline of the steps (more than

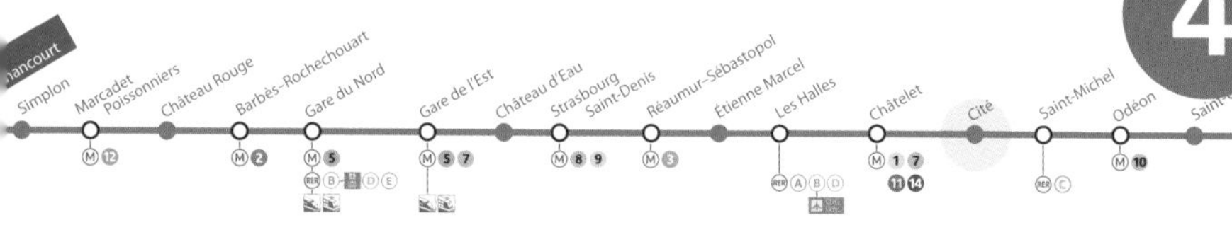

13 meters, or 42 feet). The station has a very characteristic look, notably because of its green lighting.

SIGHTSEEING

numents

Cathédrale Notre-Dame: Notre-Dame Cathedral is a masterpiece of medieval art built between the 12th and the 14th centuries. It was extensively restored by Viollet-le-Duc in the 19th century and his face was reproduced on one of the apostles on the spire. The magnificent doors show the Last Judgement, with hell to the left of Christ and paradise to the right. Inside, the nave is spectacular, as is the rose window above the King's Gallery, which is more than 10 metres (32 feet) wide. It is also worth stopping at the Trésor or treasury house (a fee is charged) to see the purported relics of the Passion, namely the crown of thorns, a piece of the holy cross and one of the nails used in the crucifixion. *Place Jean-Paul-II, parvis de Notre-Dame-de-Paris, 4th.*

The cathedral is open daily 8am to 6.45pm. (7.15pm on Saturday and Sunday). If you want to go up to the towers, be warned that you will have to climb 387 steps!
Tel.: 01-53-10-07-00. The towers are open daily 10am to 6.30pm from April to September (late nights until 11pm on Saturday and Sunday in June, July, and August) and 10am to 5.30pm from October to March.

2 **Parvis Notre-Dame:** you will have a superb view of the cathedral from Notre-Dame Square, recently renamed Jean-Paul-II Square. If you look down at your feet will see the outline of where the old buildings once stood before Baron Haussmann pulled them down. They are

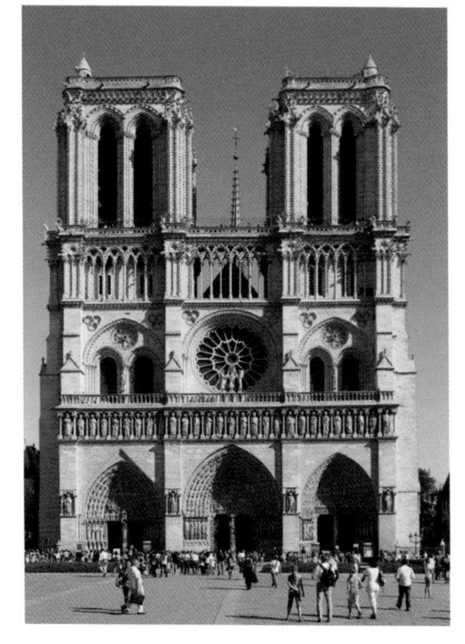

marked out on the ground in lighter colour stone. Also on the ground, facing the cathedral doors, is 'ground zero' for all the roads of France, placed here in 1924. This is the point from which all the roads of France are measured.

③ **Crypte Archéologique du Parvis Notre-Dame:** the archaeological crypt is the place to go if you want to understand how the city developed over its long history, as revealed through many years of excavations. From the Lutetia of antiquity and the vestiges of a 4th century wall that surrounded the town, to the remains of Baron Haussmann's sewage system, to mention just a few discoveries.

7 parvis Notre-Dame, place Jean-Paul-II, 4th.
Tel.: 01-55-42-50-10. Open Tuesday to Sunday 10am to 6pm.
Closed on public holidays. Entrance fee.

④ **Sainte-Chapelle:** a masterpiece of flamboyant gothic architecture built by Saint Louis to house some Passion relics. To really appreciate the beauty of the light, you should see the stained glass windows in the upper chapel by daylight—and a sunny day if possible.

4 boulevard du Palais, 1st.
Tel.: 01-53-73-78-51. Open daily 9.30am to 6pm from March to October and 10am to 5pm from November to February. Late night on Wednesday until 9pm from 15 May to 15 September. Entrance fee.

⑤ **Conciergerie:** the former palace, Palais de la Cité, was built during the Capetian dynasty. This was the first royal residence before the kings moved to the Louvre, but it was converted into a prison during the Revolution. The beautiful towers date to the 14th century, including the Tour de l'Horloge (clock tower), which was the first public clock in France. It was placed there by order of Charles V and still has its original dial. Inside the Conciergerie is one of the largest Gothic halls in Europe with beautiful cross arches.

2 boulevard du Palais, 1st.
Tel.: 01-53-40-60-80.
Open daily from 9.30am to 6pm.
Entrance fee.

Palais de Justice: this was once part of the royal palace before it was turned into the 'palace of justice', and it is still a law court today. Built under the Capetian kings in around 1000, it was later modified by both Saint Louis and Philippe le Bel. Charles V was the last king to occupy the premises, and left principally because of the numerous rioters who found it too easy to access the building—first and foremost being Étienne Marcel! From then on the kings lived in the Louvre because it was better protected. To give you an idea of the size, here are few numbers: the palace covers a surface area of 4 hectares (9 acres), has 24 kilometres (15 miles) of corridors, 7,000 doors and 3,150 windows!

4 boulevard du Palais, 1st.
Tel: 0892-683-000. Court cases are open to the public in the afternoon.

Off the beaten track

10 rue Chanoinesse: this is where two of the world's most famous lovers met, Abélard and Héloïse, in the house of Héloïse's Uncle Fubert.

1 rue des Ursins: stop in front of this medieval house for a few minutes and look closely. In fact it is really a pastiche of a medieval house that was built in the 1960s.

Address book

The place for a rendezvous

🍸 Brasserie Les Deux Palais

3 boulevard du Palais, 4th.
Open all week 6.30am to 9.30pm.
Tel.: 01-43-54-20-86.

Shopping

Ⓐ Shakespeare & Co

An English language bookshop opened by George Whitman in 1951 when he came to improve his French at the Sorbonne. At the time it was possible to borrow books as well as buy them. It is still a hive of activity today with an excellent selection of books.

37 rue de la Bûcherie, 5th.
Tel.: 01-43-25-40-93.
www.shakespeareand-company.com
Open Monday to Friday 10am to 11pm, Saturday and Sunday 11am to 11pm.

Restaurant

Ⓑ L'Atelier Maître Albert

Sober but welcoming décor. This is Guy Savoy's *rôtisserie,* where he keeps up the tradition of spit-roasting meat and fish. Enjoy the techniques of a Michelin star chef at a reasonable price. Relaxed and friendly service. About €35.

1 rue Maître-Albert, 5th.
Tel.: 01-56-81-30-01.
www.ateliermaitreal-bert.com
Daily noon to 2.30pm and 6.30pm to 11.30pm. Only open for dinner on Sunday.

SAINT-MICHEL

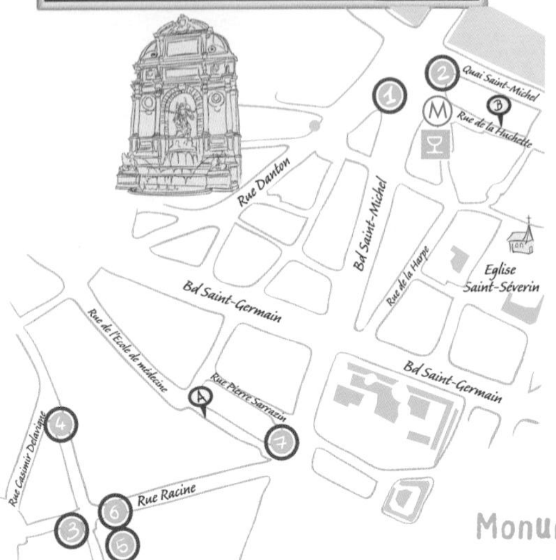

History

In the Bible Saint Michael is often the bearer of good news and he is represented fighting Satan or demons, as it is the case with the statue of Saint Michael by Gabriel Davioud that stands on Place Saint-Michel, at the crossroad of Quai des Grands-Augustins, Quai Saint-Michel and Boulevard Saint-Michel. Saint-
Michel metro station was named after the boulevard it served when it was opened in 1910, but it was the bridge that gave its name to the neighbouring roads and station, in reference to a chapel belonging to King Louis VII. The bridge was originally built in wood, and was rebuilt by Napoleon III, hence the 'N' on the bridge aprons.

SIGHTSEEING

Monument

1 **Fontaine Saint-Michel:** the fountain was commissioned by Baron Haussmann, who was displeased with the view of Boulevard Saint-Michel from Île de la Cité To fill the corner he asked Gabriel Davioud

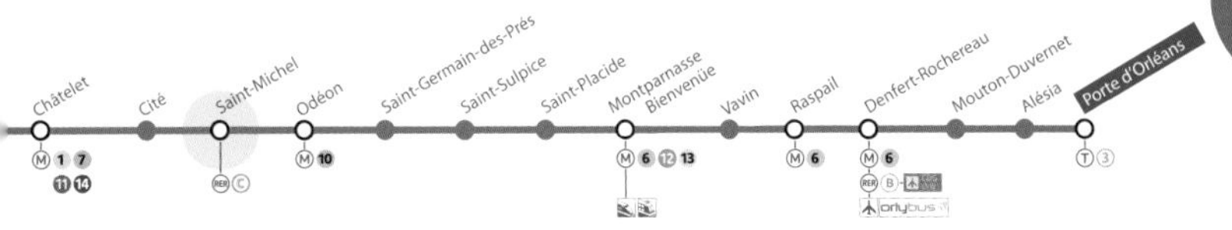

o draw up some designs for a fountain. ˉhe fountain was inaugurated in 1860 and :onsists of four basins topped by a cul-de-our niche in the middle of which Saint ·Aichael is striking down a dragon. He is surounded by four statues representing pru-lence, strength, justice and temperance. Vater pours from the mouths of winged lragons into the basins. This is *the* meeting ɔlace in the neighbourhood.

iterary walk

Gibert Jeune: there are eight Gibert ·eune bookshops on Place Saint-Michel alone, each with its own specialty: social sciences and religion, literature, law, management, sciences, medicine and well-being. You can also sell old books here.
Place Saint-Michel, 6th. www.gibertjeune.fr. Open Monday to Saturday 9.30am to 7.30pm.

Le Dilettante: this book shop belongs to Dominique Gautier, Anna Gavalda's publisher, who maintains the old tradition of publisher's book shops and sells both new and second hand books. Most works are 20th century.
19 rue Racine, 6th. Tel.: 01-43-37-98-98. www.ledilettante.com. Open Monday to Saturday 10.30am to 7.30pm.

Librairie de l'Escalier: carefully selected works on the history of social sciences and Asia. The charming owner lived through the tumultuous events of May 1968 in this very bookstore!
12 rue Monsieur-le-Prince, 6th. Tel.: 01-43-54-39-89. Open Monday to Saturday 10am to 7pm.

5 **Librairie Samuelian:** orientalist bookshop.
51 rue Monsieur-le-Prince, 6th. Tel.: 01-43-26-88-65. Open Tuesday to Saturday 2pm to 6.30pm.

6 **You Feng:** Asian bookshop.
45 rue Monsieur-le-Prince, 6th. Tel.: 01-43-25-89-98. www.you-feng.com Open Monday to Saturday 9.30am to 7pm.

7 **Gibert Joseph:** the other big bookstore for new and second-hand books.
26–34 boulevard Saint-Michel, 6th. Tel.: 01-44-41-88-88. Open Monday to Saturday 10am to 8pm.

Address book

The place for a rendezvous

Le Rive Gauche
6 place Saint-Michel, 6th.
Open all week 6.30am to midnight.
Tel.: 01-40-51-06-28.

Shopping

A Pâtisserie Viennoise
You would sell your soul for one of their *apfelstrudel* or little plum-filled cakes. A small tearoom with very few tables but a wide selection of tarts to eat on the go.
8 rue de l'École-de-Médecine, 6th. Tel.: 01-43-26-60-48. Open Monday to Friday 8.30am to 7.30pm.

Culture

B Théâtre de la Huchette
Ionesco's *La Cantatrice Chauve* (The Bald Soprano) has been staged here at 7pm every day since 1957!
To date there have been more than 17,000 performances.
23 rue de la Huchette, 5th. Tel.: 01-43-26-38-99. theatre-huchette.com

ODÉON

History

Since antiquity, the odeon was a small theatre and in ancient Greece there were at least four in Athens alone. The odeons were mainly for singing and had a smaller capacity than the traditional theatres. In Paris, the construction of the Théâtre-Français, or French theatre as it was originally called (and which still stands in the same place today) began in 1779. King Louis XVI bought the gardens of the Hôtel de Condé and gave it to the city of Paris, which erected a neoclassical building there for the Théâtre-Français troupe. The narrow streets on either side of the odeon were covered. Those roofs have now disappeared but at the time they kept theatregoers out of the rain while they waited for the performance. The theatre only came to be called Théâtre de l'Odéon in 1797. It burnt down in 1799 and was destroyed again in 1818. It was rebuilt yet again but no longer had the same prestige as its rival, the Comédie-Française. During the events of May 1968, it was occupied by the students. The metro station was opened in 1910. While named after the theatre, it also celebrates a neighbourhood hero, Danton. Inside the station, on the platform for the line heading north to Porte de Clignancourt, you will see a showcase containing Danton's bust and there is a statue of him outside the station that marks a place where he lived before the French Revolution. It is a real landmark for Parisians.

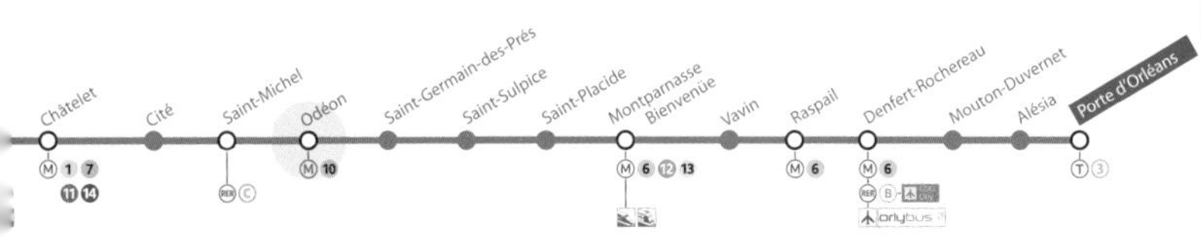

SIGHTSEEING

chitecture

Fish La Boissonnerie: lovely mosaics of fish in this former fishmonger-turned-'drinksmonger', as the name implies (fishmonger = *poissonnerie* and drinks = *boisson*). You can eat here too, and not just fish.

69 rue de Seine, 6th.

Cour de Rohan: 'Rohan' from the town of Rouen, as in the nearby Hôtel de l'Archevêque de Rouen (the Archbishop of Rouen's town house). This is a succession of quiet and little-known courtyards. In the 16th century Henri II built a house here for his favourite mistress, Diane de Poitiers, and in the 20th century the painter Balthus had his workshop here. There is even a tower from Philippe Auguste's old city walls, so Parisian history is really concentrated in this small area. In the second courtyard, note the *'pas de mule'* tripod that was used for climbing onto one's horse.

Access through rue du Jardinet or Cour du Commerce-Saint-André, 6th.

3 **Cour du Commerce-Saint-André**
This would be a logical continuation for your walk. The 18th century houses replaced Philippe Auguste Paris walls. During the Revolution, Jean-Paul Marat published his newspaper, *L'Ami du Peuple* at no. 8, while the notorious Mr Guillotin worked on his invention, the guillotine, at no. 9.

Access through Boulevard Saint-Germain.

4 **Danton's statue:** opposite the metro entrance you will see Danton's statue. This is a popular meeting place for Parisians and stands where George Danton used to live during the French Revolution.

A medieval walk

5 **Rue Séguier, rue Gît-le-coeur and rue Suger:** hunt around these streets to discover the Paris of the Middle Ages. The low houses and narrow streets narrow seem almost unchanged.

A 'medical' walk

6 Musée Dupuytren: this unusual museum was opened in 1835 in the former Couvent des Cordeliers (Cordeliers' convent) thanks to a legacy from a certain Doctor Dupuytren, Professor of Medicine. Since the museum is devoted to pathology and medicine, there are quite a few unnerving exhibits. While many items are models, there are also plenty of real anatomical parts in jars, so if you are squeamish forget it!

15 rue de l'École-de-Médecine, 6th. Tel.: 01-42-34-68-60. Open Monday to Friday 2pm to 5pm. Admission free.

7 Musée d'Histoire de la Médecine
The history of Medicine museum has a few key exhibits from French medical history such as the stethoscope invented by Laennec and the instrument case that belonged to Doctor Antommarchi, which he used to perform the autopsy on Napoleon in Sainte-Hélène. Not to mention a knife that belonged to Louis XVI's surgeon, which he used to operate on a fistula.

12 rue de l'École-de-Médecine, 6th. Tel.: 01-76-53-16-93. Open Monday to Wednesday, Friday and Saturday 2pm to 5.30pm from October to mid-July, and from mid-July to the end of August open Monday to Friday 2pm to 5.30pm. Entrance fee.

Culture

8 Odéon Théâtre de l'Europe: the building work on the theatre began in 1779. It is surrounded by arcades and was originally destined for the troupe of players from the Théâtre-Français, who were short of space in the Jeu de Paume. The theatre is Italian in style, with a cubic stage and the seating in a semi-circle. Today the theatre puts on plays by contemporary playwrights that make a lively break from the conven-

tional theatrical tradition. Behind the theatre, on Place Paul-Claudel, you will still see bullet holes above the arch that came from the liberation of Paris during the Second World War.

Place de l'Odéon, 6th. Tel.: 01-44-85-40-40. www.theatre-odeon.fr Performances at 8pm Tuesday to Saturday and a 3pm matinee performance on Sunday.

9 Théâtre Érotique ChoChotte
Left bank eroticism! The women get very close to the spectators when they elegantly perform their striptease, so there's plenty to get excited about right here in the heart of the Latin Quarter! The décor resembles a private old-fashioned boudoir, and performances have several different themes.

34 rue Saint-André-des-Arts, 6th. Tel.: 01-43-54-97-82. www.theatre-chochotte.com Entrance fee (€50 for men and €30 for women).

Address book

The place for a rendezvous

Le Danton
103 boulevard Saint-Germain, 6th.
Open all week 7am to 2am.
Tel.: 01-43-54-65-38..

Shopping

A Cire Trudon
Trudon has kept the secret of its manufacturing process since 1643. All the wax candles are made from a plant base and the scents

blend in perfectly. The candles last between 50–70 hours and each one recalls a period or episode in history, in France or elsewhere.
78 rue de Seine, 6th.
Tel.: 01-43-26-46-50.
www.ciretrudon.com
Open Monday to Saturday 10am to 7pm..

B Jérôme Dreyfuss

A leatherworker and bag maker, famous for his use of soft leather and original shapes (how many women still do not own a 'Billy'?). A classic!
1 rue Jacob, 6th.
Tel.: 01-43-54-71-63.
www.jerome-dreyfuss.com.
Open Monday and Tuesday 11am to 2pm and 3pm to 7pm. Wednesday to Friday non stop.

C Maison Georges Larnicol

This pastry and chocolate maker from Quimper in Brittany obtained the 'Meilleur Ouvrier de France' (best craftsman in France) award in 1993 and now has a shop in Paris. He sells macaroons, a Breton specialty called *kouignettes*, biscuits from churned butter, and *sorchettes*, cakes that were specially made for the surfers in La Torche, also in Brittany. Any of these will give you the energy you need to continue your shopping in the area.
132 boulevard Saint-Germain, 6th.
Tel.: 01-43-26-39-38.
chocolaterielarnicol.fr
Open Sunday to Thursday 9am to 10pm, and 11.30pm Friday, midnight Saturday.

Out on the town

D Café de l'Odéon

Inside the foyer of the theatre all year round, but on the square from May to October, when you can make the most of the lovely big terrace to sit out it. A perfect place for a snack or just a drink.
Place de l'Odéon, 6th.
Tel.: 01-44-85-41-30.
www.cafedelodeon.com
Open Tuesday to Friday noon to 3pm and 7pm to midnight.

Restaurants

E KGB (Kitchen Gallery Bis)

William Ledeuil has succeeded in creating the perfect fusion of French dishes and Asian flavours. He has a lightness of touch and surprising explosive tastes. This is a real gastronomic miracle against a streamlined backdrop with impeccable service. KGB is the annexe of Ze Kitchen Gallery, its rather more formal sister restaurant. About €60.

25 rue des Grands-Augustins, 6th.
Tel.: 01-46-33-00-85. Open Tuesday to Saturday 12.15pm to 2.30pm and 7pm to 10.30pm.

F Le Comptoir du Relais

Just a handful of tables, and even fewer outside, so you may have to wait in line unless you come early at opening time. 'Masterchef' Yves Camdeborde, will tickle your taste buds with simple but excellent food. About €40.
9 carrefour de l'Odéon, 6th.
Tel.: 01-43-29-12-05.
Open Monday to Friday noon to 6pm and from 8.30pm for dinner, reservations required. Saturday and Sunday noon to 11pm without reservations.

SAINT-GERMAIN-DES-PRÉS

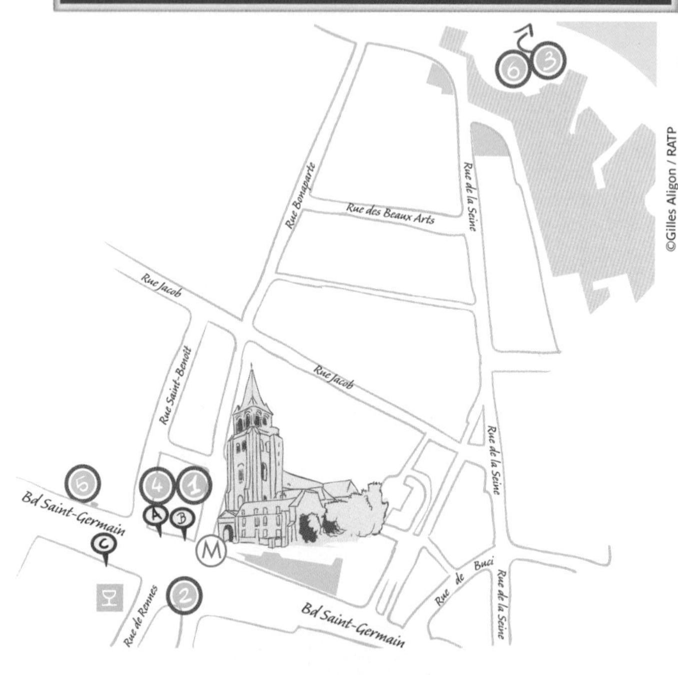

©Gilles Aligon / RATP

History

This neighbourhood has been famous for its church since 555, when Germain founded the first abbey here. It housed the sacred relics brought back by Clovis' son, Childebert. The abbey was constantly improved and enlarged over the years and many pilgrims flocked to the church (which was then in the middle of the fields). From the 8th century until the 13th century, it was a centre of French intellectual life. Three church towers were added in around the year 1000. During the Revolution the church was turned into a prison. Two church towers wer destroyed in 1821 being insalubrious and now only the portal with the clo tower remains. The French poet, Nicol Boileau rests in on of the aisles. In the metro station, ther is a bronze statue by Gualtiero Busat called *Les Messagers* (the messengers) and a mosaic by André Ropion depicting the printer Gutenberg. Literary works are projected onto the platform ceilings.

SIGHTSEEING

Monuments

1. ***Statue:*** the statue on Place Saint-Germain-des-Prés is by Ossip Zadkine (1890–1967).

2. ***Fontaine en bronze:*** the strange bronze fountain on Place du Québec at the corner of rue de Rennes and rue Bonaparte (opposite the Cartier boutique) is by

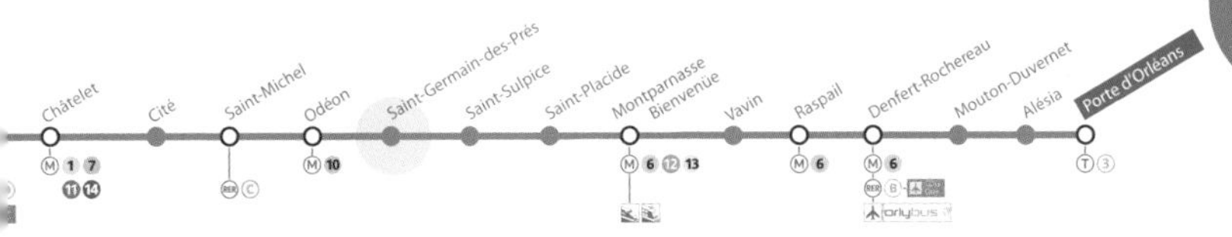

Gindre and Daudelin. It was a present from the city of Quebec to France in 1984 and symbolises ice breaking.

Pont des Arts: this was the first iron bridge in Paris (1801). Lovers come to place padlocks with their initials here for life. Very romantic.

Literary walk

La Hune: a bookshop open practically until midnight during the week, it is a perfect haunt for booklovers. Upstairs you will find a selection on art and design. On the rue Saint-Benoît side is a stencilled graffiti by Miss Tic, a quotation from (and a tribute to) Marguerite Duras, who used to live in this street. It says *'Faire d'un mot le bel amant d'une phrase'*, which roughly translates as 'turn a word into the lovely lover of a phrase'
170 boulevard Saint-Germain, 6th.
Tel.: 01-45-48-35-85. Open Monday to Saturday 10am to 11.40pm, and Sunday 11am to 8pm.

L'écume des Pages: one of the most famous bookshops in Paris, and a benchmark for book lovers. Open late.
174 boulevard Saint-Germain, 6th.
Tel.: 01-45-48-54-48. Open Monday to Saturday 10am to midnight, Sunday 11am to 10pm.

Institut de France: built by Louis Le Vau in 1663, the Institute is worth a visit for its spectacular Coupole des Quatre-Nations (cupola of the four nations). The best students from those four regions once studied here, but now the building houses five academies, including the prestigious Académie Française.
23 quai Conti, 6th.

Address book

The place for a rendezvous

Emporio Caffe
149, boulevard Saint-Germain, 6th.
Open daily from noon to midnight.
Tel.: 01-45-48-62-15.

Restaurants

A Café de Flore
This famous café has stood here since 1887, having acquired its name from a nearby statue. The surrealists used to frequent the café, along with such famous people as Simone de Beauvoir and Jean-Paul Sartre, Juliette Gréco, and Brigitte Bardot. You will still see quite a few personalities there today. Superb terrace.
About €40.
172 boulevard Saint-Germain, 6th.
Tel.: 01-45-48-55-26.
www.cafedeflore.fr
Open daily 7am to 2am.

B Les Deux Magots
Open since 1887 in a former novelty store, this was a liquor seller that catered to Verlaine and Rimbaud. Picasso used to come here in its present *brasserie* form, and today it is popular with the media and fashion world.
About €25–30.
6 place Saint-Germain-des-Prés, 6th.
Tel.: 01-45-48-55-25.
www.lesdeuxmagots.fr
Open all week 7am to 1am, meals served from 7pm.

C Chez Lipp
Léonard Lipp established this *brasserie* in 1880 and it immediately became popular with literary, political and artistic circles. It has a polished mahogany façade and the décor is 1900, with wall ceramics by Léon Fargues and a painted ceiling by Charly Garrey.
About €40.
151 boulevard Saint-Germain, 6th. Tel.: 01-45-48-53-91. Open all week 11.30am to 1am.

SAINT-SULPICE

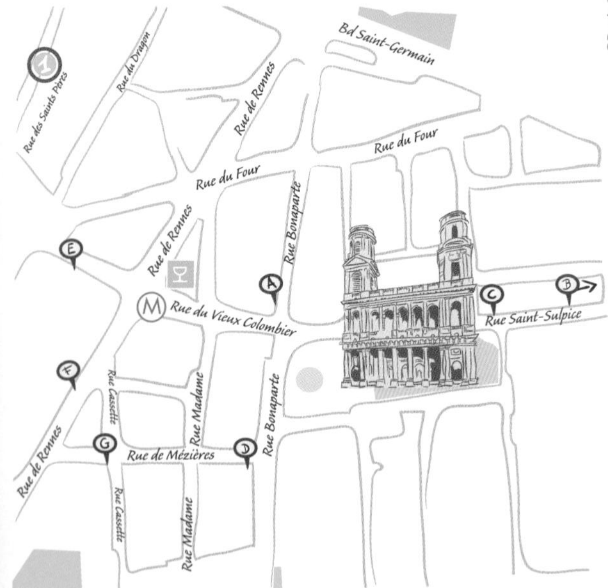

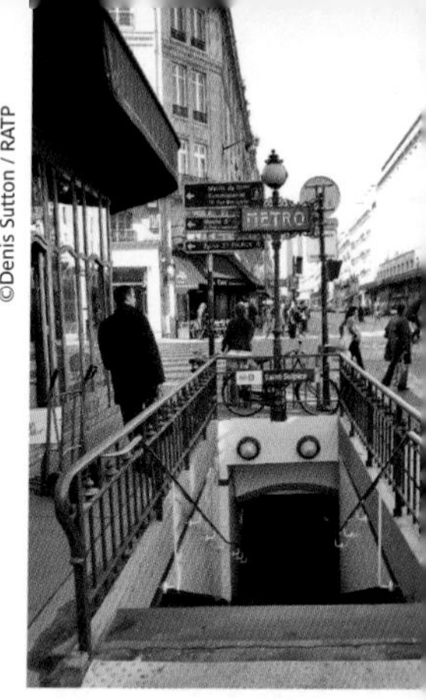

©Denis Sutton / RATP

History

The station's name refers to Sulpice the Pious (576–647), who was the Bishop of Bourges from 621 and chaplain to Clotaire II. The church was built in 1211, and then rebuilt and enlarged in 1646 by the architect Christophe Gamard. There are some lovely Delacroix paintings inside as well as the intriguing brass line that serves as a meridian to the gnomon. *Da Vinci Code* fans will remember that! The church's façade is in two architectural styles. You can amuse yourself by observing the differences from the steps of the Fontaine des Orateurs Sacrés, or fountain of sacred orators, namely Fénelon, Bossuet, Fléchier and Massilon. The metro station opened in 1910.

SIGHTSEEING

Off the beaten track

1 ***Hôtel des Saints-Pères:*** those people lucky enough to stay in this historic hotel are fortunate indeed! Each room is decorated in a different style. The building's façade was designed by Daniel Gittard, Louis 14th's architect, in 1658. Room no. 100 has a 300 year-old fresco on the ceiling by an artist from the Versailles school. Occupants can sleep peacefully under the protection of Leda and the Swan.

65 rue des Saints-Pères, 6th.
Tel.: 01-45-44-50-00. The starting price for the room with the fresco is €315.

Address book

The place for a rendezvous

Le Café du Métro
67 rue de Rennes, 6th.
Tel.: 01-45-48-58-56.
Open Monday to Saturday 7.30am to midnight.

Shopping

A Pierre Hermé
The Master of Macaroons hardly needs an introduction. This pastry maker has won acclaim for daring and delicious variations of these soft and yet crispy delicacies.
72 rue Bonaparte, 6th.
Tel.: 01-43-54-47-77.
www.pierreherme.com
Open Sunday to Thursday 10am to 7pm (19.30pm on Friday), Saturday 10am to 8pm.

B Liwan
A boutique that stands at the crossroads of the Silk Route and the Orient, and celebrates oriental scents and incense. You will find Aleppo soap and numerous oriental cosmetics products, amongst other things. A sensual experience if ever there was one!
8 rue Saint-Sulpice, 6th.
Tel.: 01-43-26-07-40.
Open Monday 2pm to 7pm, Tuesday to Saturday 10.30am to 7pm.

C Muji
The name is an abbreviation of *mujirushi ryohin*, which means 'no brand'. Every day items to use from the minute you get up to when you go to bed at night.
27 rue Saint-Sulpice, 6th.
Tel.: 01-46-34-01-10.
www.muji.fr
Open Monday to Friday 10am to 7.30pm, and 8pm on Saturday.

D Librairie La Procure
A bookshop specialised in religious literature. I also has books on general topics and an excellent history section.
3 rue de Mézières, 6th.
Tel.: 01-45-48-20-25.
www.laprocure.com
Open Monday to Saturday 9.30am to 7.30pm.

Entertainment

E Théâtre du Vieux Colombier
Open since 1913 in the former Théâtre de l'Athénée-Saint-Germain, the theatre was founded by the literary critic Jacques Copeau, who was also the co-director of *La Nouvelle Revue Française*. Louis Jouvet played in this innovative theatre. Today it is managed by the Comédie-Française.
21 rue du Vieux-Colombier, 6th.
Tel.: 01-44-39-87-00.
www.vieux.colombier.free.fr

F Cinéma L'Arlequin
Originally this site was earmarked to be an electric power plant! Fortunately that project failed and Jacques Tati later had the building transformed into this quality cinema with three auditoriums providing a rich and varied programme. A well-known cinema show on French TV hosted by Claude Jean Philippe, used to be recorded here on Sunday mornings.
76 rue de Rennes, 6th.
Tel.: 01-45-44-28-80.

Restaurant

G Pizza Chic
A well-lit pizzeria with large bay windows and cosy little lamps in the evening. The delicious pizzas somehow manage to be soft and chewy at the same time. Good quality for €15–20.
13 rue de Mézières, 6th.
Tel.: 01-45-48-30-38.
Open for lunch from Monday to Friday 12.30am to 2.30pm, Saturday 12.30pm to 3pm, and Sunday noon to 3pm. Open for dinner Monday to Thursday 7.30pm to 11pm, Friday and Saturday 7.30pm to 11.30pm, and Sunday 7pm to 10pm.

Next station

SAINT-PLACIDE

Café Saint Placide
127 rue de Rennes, 6th.

MONTPARNASSE-BIENVENÜE

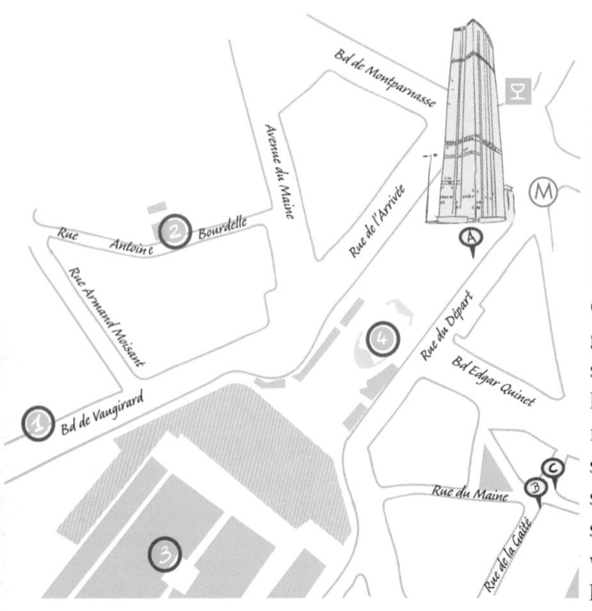

History

Mont Parnasse, or Mount Parnassus, was the nickname given to this former rubbish-strewn hill by the Fermiers Généraux tax wall that surrounded Paris. The students from the Latin Quarter would come here to seek inspiration, to flirt and make the most of the wine, which was cheaper being beyond the tax barrier. The hill was levelled in 1760. This metro station also pays tribute to the engineer who invented the *Métropolitain* (metro), Fulgence Bienvenüe. A graduate of the prestigious École Polytechnique, he started working on the railways, designed Buttes-Chaumont Park and began the construction of the underground railway in 1896. The station was originally called Maine on line 5. The engineer's name was added to the station name while he was still alive, in 1933. Today it serves Montparnasse station, which was designed by Jean-Marie Duthilleul in 1987.

SIGHTSEEING

Culture

1 Musée L'Adresse Musée de La Poste

One of our favourite Parisian museums. You will learn everything there is to know about transport and other means of communication, as well as the origins of the expression 'seven league boots' and the French nursery rhyme *'À dada sur mon bidet'*.

34 boulevard de Vaugirard, 15th.
Tel.: 01-42-79-24-24.
www.ladressemuseedelaposte.com
Open Monday to Saturday 10am to 6pm. Closed on public holidays. Entrance fee.

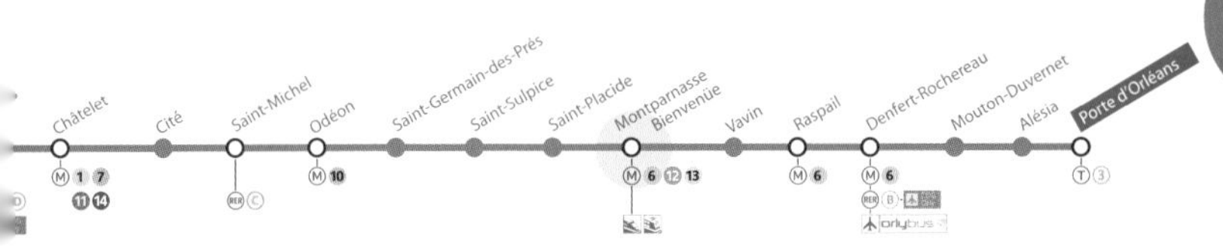

Musée Bourdelle: the museum is located in Antoine Bourdelle's former workshop. Bourdelle was a sculptor and a former student of Rodin who lived here from 1885 to 1929. The museum was recently extended by the architect Christian de Portzamparc. Almost the first thing you see is a magnificent statue of Heracles the archer.

18 rue Antoine-Bourdelle, 15th.
Tel.: 01-49-54-73-73. www.bourdelle.paris.fr
Open Tuesday to Sunday 10am to 6pm.
Admission free.

walk in the park

Jardin de l'Atlantique: this is really an outdoor waiting room! The garden was set up on the station roof in 1995 and is shaped rather like large steamer.
Admission free.

onument

Tour Montparnasse: the Montparnasse tower was built in 1973. This urban totem pole is 210 metres (689 feet) high, with 59 stories on an almond-shaped base. It has 25 lifts, one of which takes you from the ground floor to the 56th floor in 38 seconds. There is a marvellous panoramic view of Paris from the top.
Parvis de la tour Montparnasse.
Tel.: 01-45-38-52-56.
www.tourmontparnasse56.com
Open daily 9.30am to 11.30pm from April to September, and Sunday to Thursday 9.30am to 10.30pm, Friday and Saturday 9.30am to 11pm.from October to March.
Entrance fee.

Address book

The place for a rendezvous

Café Montparnasse
Place du 18-juin-1940, 6th.
Open daily 8am to 2am.
Tel.: 01-45-48-99-34.

Shopping

Ⓐ Western Heritage
You would think yourself in Texas in this boutique! Everything you need for an all-American outfit.
10 rue du Départ, 15th.
Tel.: 01-45-38-73-73.
western-heritage.fr
Open Monday to Friday 10.30am to 7.30pm, Saturday 10am to 7.30pm.

Out on the town

Ⓑ Le Tournesol
A trendy little bar, amusingly decorated and with a pleasant terrace for sunny days.
9 rue de la Gaîté, 14th.
10am to 2am.

Restaurant

Ⓒ Le Plomb du Cantal
A place to go to for specialties from the Auvergne region, including *truffade* and *aligot*, two delicious potato dishes! Excellent meat and decent table wines. €25–40.
3 rue de la Gaîté, 14th.
Tel.: 01-43-35-16-92.
Open daily 7am to midnight.

VAVIN

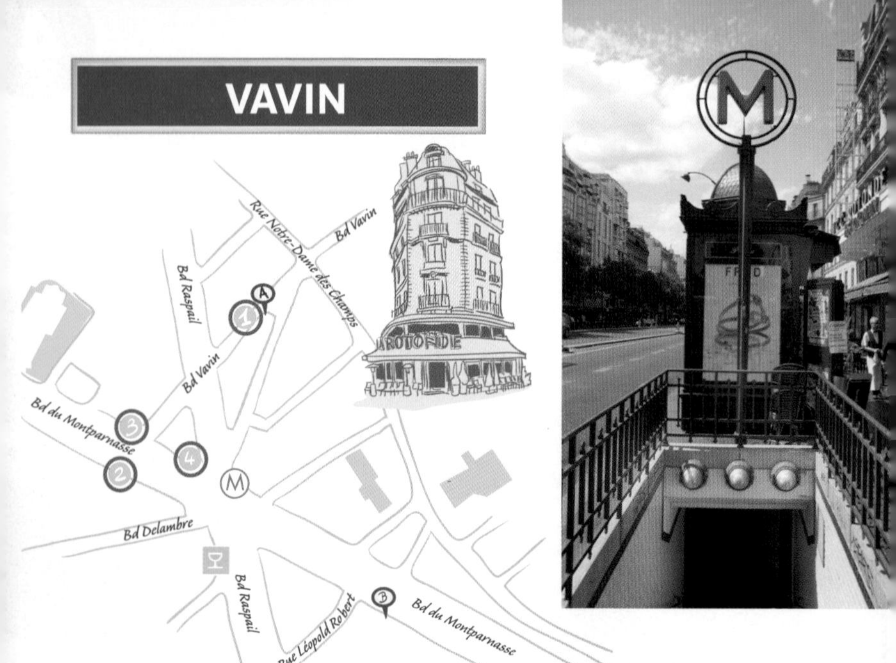

History

Alexis Vavin was an 18th century notary and royalist politician. He was born in Paris in 1792 and owned several properties in what is now the 6th arrondissement. He was elected Deputy for Paris on 2 March 1839 and was a member of the constituent and later the legislative assemblies. He did not approve of the coup d'état against Napoleon III, and supported the monarchists. Known for his integrity and his desire for justice, he was respected by colleagues in his own party as well as by the opposition. He died in Paris in 1863 and is buried in the Père-Lachaise cemetery. The street is named after him, as is the metro station, which opened in 1910.

SIGHTSEEING

Architecture

1 **Façade:** don't miss the terraced building designed by the French architect Henri Sauvage in 1912, notable for its white sandstone tiled walls.
26 rue Vavin, 6th.

Spirit of the 50s

2 **La Coupole:** an iconic Montparnasse *brasserie*. This was a former wood and coal warehouse before being transformed into a *brasserie* in 1927. In the 1950s all the great artists of the time came here, including Hemingway, Kessel, Simone de Beauvoir, Picasso, and Dalí to name but a few. The 33 painted pillars are a reminder of that time,

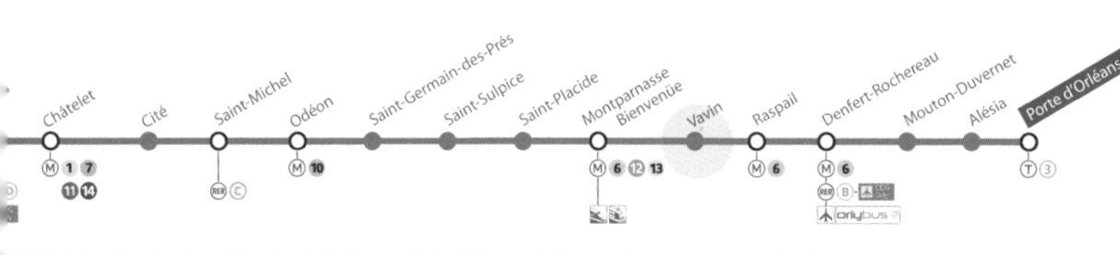

each one decorated in the spirit of those illustrious patrons. Today customers flock to La Coupole for the lamb curry and to discover the Art Deco interior. In the old days there was a dance floor as well, but unfortunately that has now closed. €45 – 50.

102 boulevard du Montparnasse, 14th. Tel.: 01-43-20-14-20. Open Sunday to Wednesday 8am to midnight, and 1am from Thursday to Saturday.

Le Select: nothing appears to have changed in this so-called 'American' bar. Artists of all kinds have flocked here for almost a century! €15 – 20.

99 boulevard du Montparnasse, 6th. Tel.: 01-45-48-38-24. Open Monday to Friday 7am to 2am, closes at 3am weekends.

La Rotonde: painters, film makers, journalists and publishers have been eating at this *brasserie* since 1911. There is a smaller alcove in addition to the main brasserie part. The lunchtime menu is very reasonable. €15 – 20.

105 boulevard du Montparnasse, 6th. Tel.: 01-43-26-48-26. www.rotondemontparnasse.com. Open daily 7.15am to 1am.

Address book

The place for a rendezvous

Le Petit Broc
206 boulevard Raspail, 14th. Tel.: 01-40-47-74-83. Open Monday to Friday 7.30am to 10.30pm and 9am to 11pm on Saturday and Sunday.

Shopping

A Marie Papier
A high-end paper shop with a broad selection including albums, loose sheets, notebooks and boxes in a variety of colours and weights.

26 rue Vavin, 6th. Tel.: 01-43-26-46-44. Open Monday 2pm to 7pm, Tuesday to Saturday 10am to 1pm and 2.30pm to 6.45pm.

B Tschann
A general-interest bookstore that has been here since 1929 and played a part in the cultural life of Montparnasse. Samuel Beckett was one of the main beneficiaries, Marie-Madeleine Tschann being a great fan!

125 boulevard du Montparnasse, 6th. Tel.: 01-43-35-42-05. Open Monday to Saturday 10am to 10pm.

RASPAIL

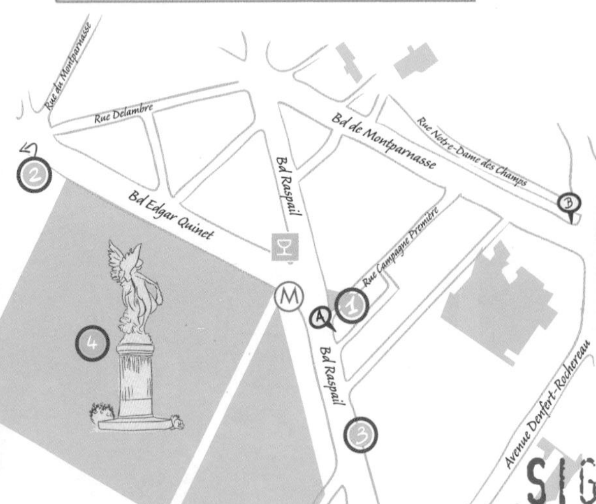

History

François-Vincent Raspail was born in the city of Carpentras on 29 January 1794. He became a chemist and made numerous discoveries about microbes. He thought of using camphor to fight bacteria. He was also a politician and staunch republican. He took part in the Trois Glorieuses in 1830 (see page 40) and was imprisoned several times. He was a deputy for the Bouches-du-Rhône, and stood in the 1848 presidential elections but obtained less than 1% of the votes. The station named after him was opened in 1906.

SIGHTSEEING

Architecture

1 **Façade Arfvidson (1911) :** a building with a blend of Art Deco, Art Nouveau and international styles. Worth seeing for the polychrome sandstone tiles by Alexandre Bigot and the ochre and beige garlands. *31 rue Campagne-Première, 14th.*

2 **Place de la Catalogne (1985) :** this row of buildings was designed by the Catalan architect Ricardo Bofill., who wanted to blend the antique classicism with contem-

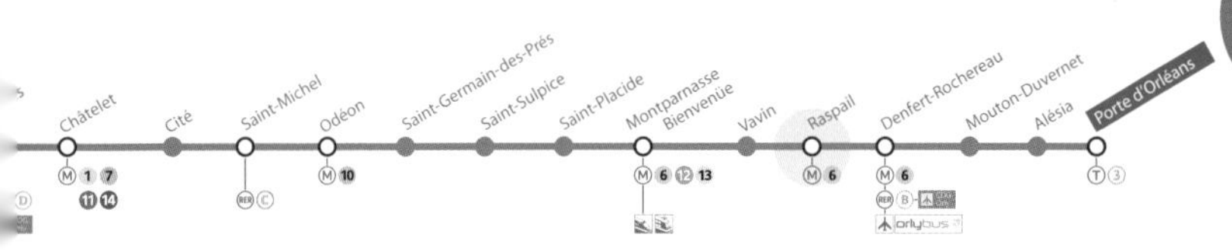

porary and even futurist forms. He certainly succeeded. The leaning fountain in the centre is by Shamaï Haber.

...lture

Fondation Cartier: since 1984, this foundation has been devoted to assisting contemporary artistic creation by disseminating it as broadly as possible. The foundation moved to this glass building designed by Jean Nouvel in 1994, which still has a cedar of Lebanon planted by Chateaubriand in 1823. Under the foundation's president, Alain Dominique Perrin, this exhibition space displays graphic arts, videos and dance performances. A rich and varied programme.

261 boulevard Raspail, 14th.
Tel.: 01-42-18-56-50. fondation.cartier.com
Open Tuesday to Sunday 11am to 8pm.
Late night on Tuesday to 10pm. Entrance fee.

Cimetière du Montparnasse: this cemetery has stood here since 1824. Among its 'inhabitants' are Serge Gainsbourg (1), Jean-Paul Sartre and Simone de Beauvoir (14) in their pebble-covered grave, Baudelaire (26), Kessel, Philippe Noiret (3) and Jean Carmet (22). Don't miss the cubist statue by Brancusi (22).

3 boulevard Edgard Quinet, 14th.
From 6 November to 15 March open Monday to Friday 8am to 5.30pm, Saturday 8.30am to 5.30pm, and Sunday and public holidays 9am to 5.30pm.
From 16 March to 5 November open Monday to Friday 8am to 6pm, Saturday 8.30am to 6pm, and Sunday and public holidays 9am to 6pm. Admission free.

Address book

The place for a rendezvous

Café des Arts
234 boulevard Raspail, 14th.
Open Monday to Saturday 6.30am to 9pm.
Tel.: 01-43-21-20-56.

Restaurants

A Le Duc
One of the best fish restaurants in Paris but not exactly cheap. Valet parking service.
About €70 – 80.
243, boulevard Raspail, 14th.
Tel.: 01-43-22-59-59.
Open Tuesday to Friday noon to 2pm and 8pm to 10.45pm and Saturday evening.

B La Closerie des Lilas
This former post-house on the Fontainebleau road later became an open-air dance hall where people could mix with the riffraff in a delightful lilac-filled garden, usually for a drink before or after a ball. The many artists and writers who frequented the place include Paul Cézanne, Théophile Gautier, Paul Verlaine and Apollinaire. The Tuesday Discussions drew many poets and writers and the surrealists also held lively debates here. The Closerie des Lilas still has an artistic air about it today and you will frequently see celebrities. It is the perfect place for a romantic dinner.
About €30.
171 boulevard du Montparnasse, 6th.
Tel.: 01-40-51-34-50.
www.closeriedeslilas.fr
Open daily noon to 2.30pm and 7pm to 11.30pm.

DENFERT-ROCHEREAU

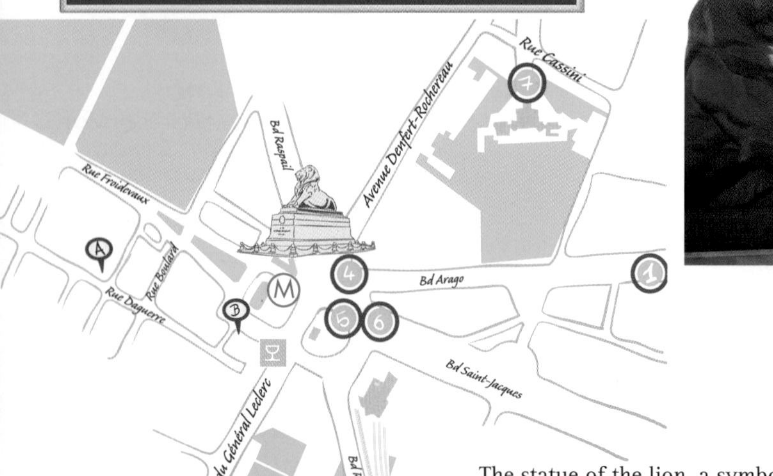

History

The square used to mark the boundary between the upper road (the present rue Saint-Jacques) and the lower road. From 'lower' to 'hell' is just one step, and people started calling the gate in the Fermiers Généraux tax wall '*Barrière d'Enfer*', the tollgates of hell, which later became 'Denfert'. Claude Nicolas Ledoux, architect at the time of Louis XVI, built the pavilions for collecting the city toll, and they still stand today. There was therefore a phonetic, if not an historic logic in naming the square in honour of Pierre Philippe-Aristide Denfert-Rochereau (1823–1878), who fought the Prussians in Belfort in 1870. The statue of the lion, a symbol of his town in Franche-Comté, recalls that 'hell' from which he emerged victorious, but that's where any connection ends! The metro station is still equipped with the original Guimard public lavatories, and was one of the first stations to acquire an escalator.

SIGHTSEEING

Off the beaten track

1. ***The urinal in front of the Santé prison:*** this old green urinal was for (male!) passers-by but also served the policemen during their rounds. Useful! *Boulevard Arago, 14th.*

2. ***Villa Adrienne:*** these lovely brick houses have an English air about them. *19 avenue du Général-Leclerc, 14th.*

Châtelet · Cité · Saint-Michel · Odéon · Saint-Germain-des-Prés · Saint-Sulpice · Saint-Placide · Montparnasse Bienvenüe · Vavin · Raspail · Denfert-Rochereau · Mouton-Duvernet · Alésia · Porte d'Orléans

Villa Hallé: a small semi-circular street that makes you feel you are in a small country town.
Rue Hallé, 14th.

Lion de Belfort: this lion is a reproduction of the lagnificent lion at the foot of the citadel in the town of Belfort (Franche-Comté). In 1879 Frédéric-Auguste Bartholdi made this statue in honour of his compatriots who withheld the siege in the 1870 war against the Prussians. That explains the inscription at the base, 'To the defence of the nation 1870–1871'.
Place Denfert-Rochereau, 14th.

Pavillons Ledoux: a reminder of the 'gates of hell', this is where the city poll was paid before entering Paris. Today it is the entrance to the catacombs.

Catacombs: thrills guaranteed for anyone wanting to visit this 18th century ossuary. You will have to brave 130 steps in a temperature of 14°C (57°F), and the skulls and other human bones (from some 6 million corpses) are all yours. They were brought together here in the former limestone quarries that were used to build Paris. Nothing is wasted!
1 avenue du Colonel-Henri-Rol-Tanguy, 14th.
Tel.: 01-43-22-47-63.
www.catacombes-de-paris.fr
Open Tuesday to Sunday 10am to 5pm. The ticket office closes at 4pm. Closed on public holidays. Entrance fee.

7 **Observatoire:** the observatory was founded by Colbert in 1667 and is in a building by Claude Perrault. It is the centre for astronomic research in France today.
77 avenue Denfert-Rochereau, 14th.
Tel.: 01-40-51-22-21. www.obspm.fr
Opening hours are changeable, so check beforehand.

Address book

The place for a rendezvous

Le Rendez-Vous Denfert
2 avenue du Général-Leclerc, 14th.
Open all week 6am to 2am.
Tel: 01-43-21-34-05.

Shopping

A Rue Daguerre
You will find everything you could possibly need for your food shopping in this street among the marvellous butchers, cheese shops, delicatessens, and greengrocers.

Restaurant

B Swann et Vincent
restaurant specialised in Italian food and a welcome resting place in the square. About €30.
22 place Denfert-Rochereau, 14th.
Tel.: 01-43-21-22-59.
www.swann-vincent.fr
Open all week noon to 2.30pm and 7pm to 11.30pm.

ext stations

MOUTON-DUVERNET

Café d'Orléans, 43 avenue Général-Leclerc, 14th.

ALÉSIA

Le Zeyer, 234 avenue du Maine, 14th.

PORTE D'ORLÉANS

Café le Paris Orléans 129 avenue du Général-Leclerc, 14th.

line 5

History

Historically, line 5 was the first north-south route in the capital, opened well before line 4. It links the prefecture of Seine-Saint-Denis from Bobigny – Pablo Picasso to Place d'Italie in the 13th arrondissement. The line was originally intended to connect the Gare d'Austerlitz (then called Gare d'Orléans-Austerlitz) to the Gare de l'Est via Gare de Lyon, but the project was abandoned because of technical difficulties (notably the incline and crossing the Seine). The Austerlitz viaduct, which traverses the dramatic glass roof of the train station, was built between 1903 and 1904, but it was the more spectacular, helicoidal Quai de la Rapée viaduct, with a sharp bend, that took the most work and time (1903 – 1906). Further on, the line was next extended as far as Jacques Bonsergent station (then called Lancry) from 1906, as well as towards Place d'Italie. From October 1907, line 5 absorbed the trace of the line known as '2 South' between Place d'Italie and Étoile, was then extended as far as Gare du Nord. Thus eastern Paris was served from 1929. From 1942, line 5 having become too long, the 'Étoile – Place d'Italie' section became line 6. The new line 5 terminus at Bobigny was inaugurated in 1985.

obigny – Pablo Picasso / Place d'Italie

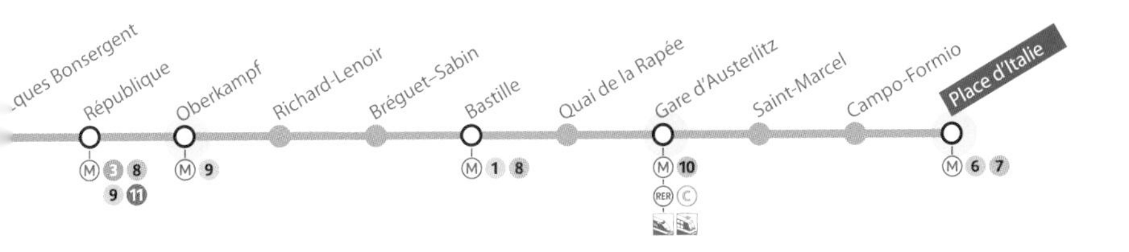

PORTE DE PANTIN

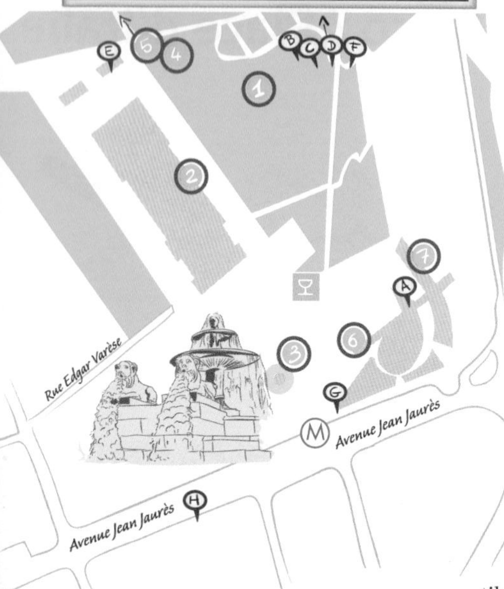

History

At the gates of this former village, once behind the Paris fortifications, is one of Paris's most architecturally interesting districts. Since the end of the 1970s, the former meat and poultry market has been totally restructured. In 1983, Swiss architect Bernard Tschumi's rehabilitation project brought life back to the former market hall built by a pupil of Baltard. It was the time for the building to be completely renovated and the starting point for the huge project that one can now enjoy. In Pantin, one hitherto found the houses and wooden shacks of refugees come to France to seek their fortune. It was the seat of numerous industries, such as tobacco factories. Today, one discovers brand new constructions there.

The station opened only in 1942. Until 1907, the most northerly stop on line 5 was Gare du Nord, although the necessity of expanding to the Paris gates and beyond had appeared evident as early as the 1920s. Inside the station, yellow ceramic tiles represent musical notes, which is perfectly logical just steps from the 'music city'.

SIGHTSEEING

Architecture

1 **Parc de la Villette:** the park extends over more than 55 hectares (136 acres) on the site of a former livestock market and abattoirs. The last beast died here in 1977. Since then a harmonious ensemble has emerged from the ground, although it looks a little surreal nonetheless when you come out of the station. The largest park in Paris was conceived by Bernard Tschumi according to a system of lines and intersections, punctuated by monuments and old-style

'*folies*'. A real construction game. Assorted buildings are spread over the park, as well as a Bamboo Garden (with more than 30 varieties of bamboo), vines, blue spruce and the Garden of Childhood Fears. At night, thanks to clever lighting, scare yourself in the Garden of Islands or the Garden of Shadows, next to the Zénith concert venue. Boo!
211 avenue Jean-Jaurès, 19th.
Tel.: 01-40-03-75-75.
www.villette.com. Admission free.

Grande Halle de la Villette: the livestock market's former cattle and poultry hall was built in the 19th century by Jules de Mérindol, a pupil of Victor Baltard (architect of the now demolished covered market at

Les Halles) at the request of Napoleon III. It is now used for large exhibitions.
211 avenue Jean-Jaurès, 19th.
Tel.: 01-40-03-75-75.
Admission free.

3 Fontaine aux Lions de Nubie

Made in 1811 to adorn what is now Place de la République, the fountain served during the market era as a trough for freshly arrived animals. Now, everyone dips their feet in it in hot weather.
Outside the Grande Halle.

④ Cité des Sciences et de l'Industrie

A kid's dream on several floors, the endless corridors are just made for getting lost in. Activities at every corner are an accessible way to understand science. For small (the excellent Cité des Enfants) and big. The building was designed by architect Adrien Fainsilber.

30 avenue Corentin-Cariou, 19th.
Tel.: 01-40-05-70-00 and 01-40-05-80-00.
www.cite-sciences.fr
Open Tuesday to Saturday 10am to 6pm, Sunday 10am to 7pm. Entrance fee.

⑤ La Géode: a giant steel ball in which one can see oneself! Inside, a huge 1,000-square metre (10,764-square feet) screen for watching films at 180°. One way to get to the heart of things! Innovative and instructive.

26 avenue Corentin-Cariou, 19th.
Tel.: 0892-684-540 or 01-40-05-79-99.
www.lageode.fr
Open Tuesday to Sunday, screenings 10.30am to 8.30pm, except during special programmes; times vary on Monday. Entrance fee.

⑥ Cité de la Musique: Christian de Portzamparc's architecture is composed of curves and straight lines. Simply walking around it is a spatial voyage. Classical and world music concerts take place in the main concert hall and the amphitheatre. Excellent acoustics.

221 avenue Jean-Jaurès, 19th.
Tel.: 01-44-84-44-84.
www.cite-musique.fr
Bookings Tuesday to Saturday noon to 6pm, Sunday 10am to 6pm.

⑦ Musée de la Musique: a clear playful way to discover four centuries of music in the West. Thus one follows five themes spanning the birth of opera, music during the Enlightenment, Romantic Europe, the acceleration of history and World music. It is rich and educational, and never boring. Some fine musical instruments. Musicians perform every afternoon.

Inside the Cité de la Musique, 221 avenue Jean-Jaurès, 19th.
Tel.: 01-44-84-44-84.
Open Tuesday to Saturday noon to 6pm, Sunday 10am to 6pm. Entrance fee.

Address book

The place for a rendezvous

Café de la Musique
Place de la Fontaine-aux-Lions, 19th.
Open daily 9am to 1am. Tel.: 01-48-03-15-91.

Shopping

Ⓐ Harmonia Mundi
Thousands of CDs and DVDs devoted to music. Inside the Cité de la Musique.
Tel. : 01-53-19-90-23.
Open noon to 6pm, until 8pm on concert evenings.

Culture

Ⓑ Festival du Cinéma en Plein Air de Paris
Take rugs, deckchairs and settle down on the lawn to appreciate both old and recent films. A summer treat for Parisians and tourists alike.
Prairie du Triangle, Parc de la Villette, 19th.
Tel.: 01-40-03-75-75.

Out on the town

Ⓒ Le Zénith
One of the city's biggest concert venues.
211 avenue Jean-Jaurès, 19th.
Tel.: 0890-710-207.
www.zenith-paris.com

Ⓓ Le Cabaret Sauvage
Dance, music, theatre, concerts and all facets of the cabaret spirit. Eclectic, varied programme.
59 avenue Macdonald, 19th.
Tel.: 01-42-09-03-09.
www.cabaretsauvage.com

Ⓔ Tarmac
Theatre, dance, music, puppets and tales from around the world privilege the French language and French creations.
Behind the Grande Halle, place du Charolais, 19th.
Tel.: 01-40-03-93-95.
www.letarmac.fr

Ⓕ Trabendo
Hosts contemporary (Manu Chao, Rita Mitsouko or Charlotte Gainsbourg) and electronic (Yuksek) music talents.
Behind the Cité de la Musique, 211 avenue Jean-Jaurès, 19th.
Tel.: 01-42-01-12-12.
www.trabendo.fr

Restaurants

Ⓖ Café-brasserie de la Musique
Beautiful terrace outdoors in fine weather and relaxed mood indoors. Main courses around €17.
213 avenue Jean-Jaurès, 19th.
Tel.: 01-48-03-15-91.
Open Sunday and Monday 9am to midnight, Tuesday to Thursday 9am to 1am, Friday and Saturday 9am to 2am.

Ⓗ Le Bœuf Couronné
This temple to meat, near the former meat market, has the atmosphere of a rather chic bistro of yesteryear. Set menus €32 – 45.
188 avenue Jean-Jaurès, 19th.
Tel.: 01-42-39-44- 44.
Open daily noon to 3pm, 7pm to midnight.

Previous stations

BOBIGNY – PABLO PICASSO

Espace Farmento, 4 rue Maria Callas, 93000 Bobigny.

BOBIGNY – PANTIN RAYMOND QUENEAU

La Source
7 rue de Paris, 93000 Bobigny.

ÉGLISE DE PANTIN

Le Paris Est
111 avenue Jean-Lolive, 93500 Pantin.

HOCHE

Au Général Hoche
60 avenue Jean-Lolive, 93500 Pantin.

OURCQ

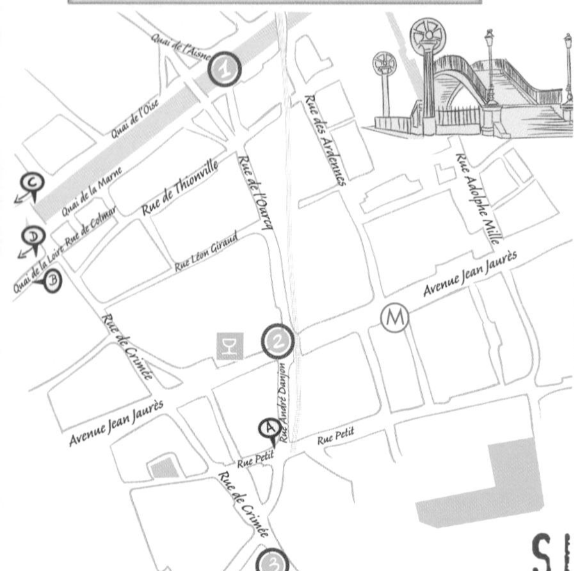

©Jean-François Mauboussin / RATP

History

The Canal de l'Ourcq was constructed in the 19th century and was completed in 1821. It initially served to supply Paris with water from the Aisne départe-ment via the Bassin de la Villette and the Seine. The canal also allowed the transport of goods for more than 110 kilometres (68 miles).
The disappearance of factories from central Paris and the modernisation of the district contributed to the canal finding other uses, more oriented towards leisure. The station opened in 1947. On the Bobigny direction platform is a limewood statue by artist Thierry Grave.

SIGHTSEEING

A walk along the canal

1. **Canal de l'Ourcq:** one can walk or cy-cle alongside the canal (as far as Meaux) or navigate on it (various trips are possible). A true 'immersion' in eastern Paris. Change of scenery assured.
Information on boat trips: Paris Canal, Bassin de la Villette, 21 quai de la Loire, 19th. Tel.: 01-42-40-96-97. A fee is charged.

…chitecture

161 avenue Jean Jaurès: this is the headquarters of the Federation of Companions of the Building Trades and a glance at the facade shows that they know what they are doing. More precisely, it contains a hostel where companions can stay during their apprenticeship. The three statues depict the legendary founders of the companions: Master Soubise, on the left, then King Solomon, recalling the passage in the Bible (1 Kings 5:13-18) where Solomon sends workers to Lebanon to construct the Ark of the Covenant, and last, on the right, Master Jacques. Inside are some of the spectacular 'master pieces' made by the companions.
161 avenue Jean-Jaurès, 19th.
Tel.: 01-42-40-53-18.

Église Saint-Serge-de-Radogène
This former Protestant church from 1861 became a Russian Orthodox church in 1924. There is superb painted wood inside.
93 rue de Crimée, 19th.
Tel.: 06-98-46-32-81.

Next station

LAUMIÈRE

L'Avenue
41 avenue de Laumière, 19th.

Address book

The place for a rendezvous

L'Escale
133 avenue Jean-Jaurès, 19th.
Open daily 7am to 2am.
Tel.: 01-42-01-43-80.

Leisure

A Hammam Medina Centre
Turkish bath and sauna, heated stones, swimming pool in basement. On the ground floor, Oriental *pâtisseries* and mint tea are perfect for de-stressing. For being pampered according to the rules of the art.
43, rue Petit, 19th.
Tel.: 01-42-02-31-05.
hammam-medina.com
Open Monday to Friday 11am to 10pm, Saturday and public holidays 10am to 9pm, Sunday 9am to 7pm. Entrance fee.

Out on the town

B Cafézoïde
The first café for children from 0 to 16 (and their parents) has lots of learning workshops and numerous other activities. No alcohol or cigarettes, evidently.
92 bis quai de la Loire, 19th.
Tel.: 01-42-38-26-37.
cafezoide.asso.fr
Open Wednesday to Sunday 10am to 6pm.

C Antipode
For tea on a barge. A nice bar with an alternative feel. Also puts on concerts.
Facing 55 quai de Seine, 19th.
Tel.: 01-40-36-89-52.
www.abricadabra.fr
Open Monday to Friday 4pm to 1.30am, Saturday and Sunday 10am to 1.30am.

D Bar Ourcq
A bar where you'll find folk music and, above all, *pétanque* balls available for a game at apéritif time.
68 quai de Loire, 19th.
Tel.: 01-42-40-12-26.
Open Friday 3pm to midnight, Saturday 3pm to 2am.

JAURÈS

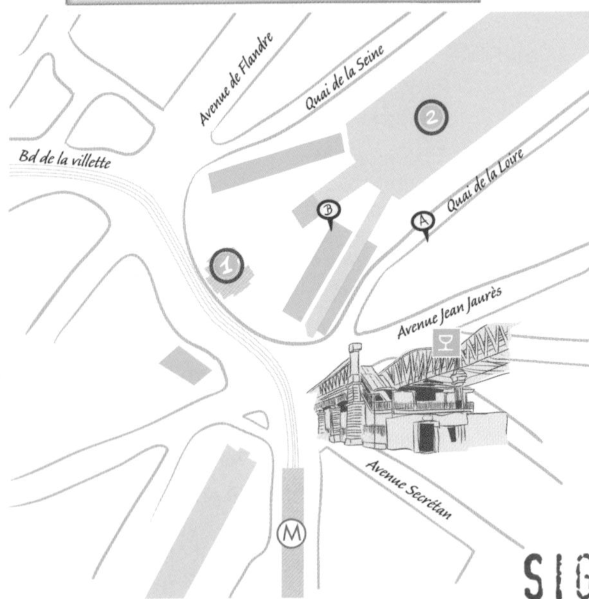

History

The history of this station is intimately linked to France's martial past. Opened in 1903, it was then called 'Rue d'Allemagne'. Trains in a hurry used to go through it without stopping. It was renamed on the eve of the declaration of war on 3 August 1914: out went references to the nation that was going to be France's enemy. Socialist politician Jean Jaurès had just been assassinated by a nationalist student on 31 July, as he left the headquarters of his daily paper, *L'Humanité*, founded in 1904. The authorities of the time decided to pay him homage, in naming the station that served Paris's poorest neighbourhoods after the flamboyant Socialist and pacifist, opposed to the rise of this world conflict, an 'athlete of ideas' as Trotsky liked to present him.

SIGHTSEEING

Beside the water

1 **Rotonde de la Villette:** near to Paris's 'little Venice', the Rotonde is unanimously agreed to be the most majestic of the four tax pavilions of the Mur des Fermiers Généraux built by Claude Nicolas Ledoux in 1784. Completed on the eve of the French

Revolution, it was thus only in use for a very short time. Facing it on the spacious esplanade, passers-by can listen to the sound of the fountain before settling down in the sun to regard the ripples of the water. The Rotonde has recently been restored and now contains a restaurant.

Place de la Bataille-de-Stalingrad, 19th.

Bassin de la Villette: this broad pool was one of the grand urbanisation projects desired by Napoleon I when he undertook the digging of the Canal de l'Ourcq to link it to the Canal Saint-Martin—and thus the Seine—in order to supply Paris with drinking water and merchandise. It was inaugurated in 1808, on the anniversary of Napoleon's coronation as emperor on 2 December 1804. An enchanting place for promenading and boating, the Bassin used to be surrounded by colourful bistros where the banter of the sailors come to unload coal or sugar rivalled that of the talkative bar owners.

Quai de Seine and quai de la Loire, 19th.

Address book

The place for a rendezvous

Le Conservatoire
10 avenue Jean-Jaurès, 19th.
Open daily 6am to midnight.
Tel.: 01-42-08-57-76.

Restaurants

A Au Rendez-Vous de la Marine
In this former *bougnat* (bar-cum-coal depot), you will contemplate the film stars whose portraits are pinned on the wall like rare butterflies. This timewarp bistro used to be the meeting place of the sailors who unloaded their coal or wood on the quaysides of the Ourcq and Villette canals.
À la carte around €25.
14 quai de la Loire, 19th.
Tel.: 01-42-49-33-40.
Open Tuesday to Saturday noon to 2pm, 7.30pm to 10.30pm.

B 25° Est
How agreeable it is to have a drink beside the sunny Bassin or on the roof terrace of this restaurant, far from urban agitation. The designer decor makes it a destination of choice for the artists who exhibit here and for you if you come here to eat. Set menus from €11.80.
10 place de la Bataille-de-Stalingrad, 19th.
Tel.: 01-42-09-66-74.
www.25est.com
Open Tuesday to Sunday 11am to 2am.

Next station
STALINGRAD
See line 2, page 60

GARE DU NORD

©Gilles Aligon / RATP

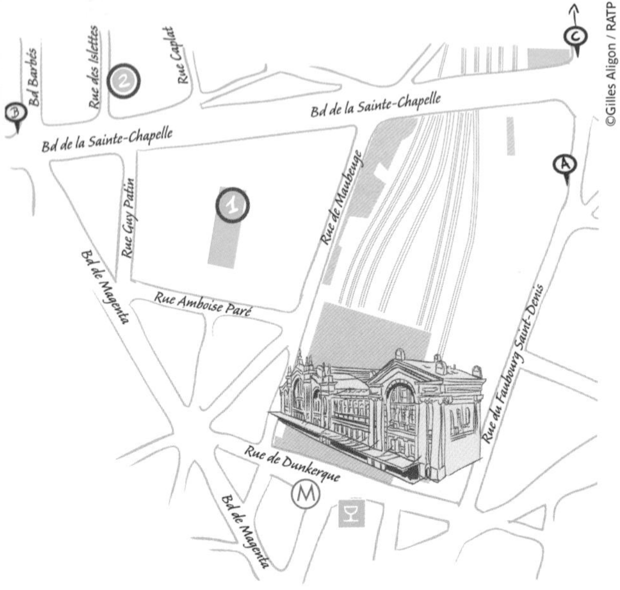

History

The construction of Gare du Nord train station began in 1842 and was completed in 1865 by Jacques-Ignace Hittorf. The architect of the Cirque d'Hiver thus finished the work begun by his colleague Léonce Reynaud. The facade shows the influence of Roman baths. From the place Napoleon III, just in front, if you raise your head you can see nine statues. These represent different towns and regions of the north of France served by trains from this station. The station was inaugurated in 1846 by Baron James de Rothschild. It was the first rail network of the Louis-Philippe era. Since 1994, the station has acquired another dimension with the Eurostar trains arriving from London. The metro station opened in 1907, still shows traces of a former cloister (at the line 4 level) and adopted the Andreu-Mott style of white bevelled tile in the 1970s.

SIGHTSEEING

Monument

1 ***Hôpital Lariboisière:*** this is hardly a place where you would go spontaneously, but this hospital, constructed from 1846 by the architect Pierre Gauthier, met the new hygiene rules of the epoch, following the cholera epidemics at the beginning of the century. Built in neo-Renaissance style with three pavilions for women and three for men arranged symmetrically either side of a courtyard, it is thus known as 'Pavilion style'. On the front of the chapel are statues representing Faith, Hope and Charity.
2 rue Ambroise Paré, 10th.
Tel.: 01-49-95-65-65. Admission free.

n exotic walk

La Goutte d'Or and Barbès-Rochechouart: a lively district. 'La Goutte d'Or' or drop of gold was the simple white wine that once ran in the glasses of these hills. Today, the district, with its street of the same name, is where African, Asian and European communities have chosen to live. Come here preferably on a Saturday, when there is plenty of atmosphere.

Address book

The place for a rendezvous

Brasserie Terminus Nord
23 rue de Dunkerque, 10th. Open daily 7.30am to 12.30am (Friday and Saturday until 1am). Tel.: 01-42-85-05-15 www.terminusnord.com

Shopping

Ⓐ VS Compagnie
A food store where you find spices from India, Sri Lanka, Réunion and Mauritius to add fire to your dishes.
197 rue du Faubourg Saint-Denis,10th. Tel.: 01-40-34-71-65. Open Tuesday to Saturday 9am to 9pm.

Ⓑ Magasins Tati
A visit to this budget store is essential. Here you can find practically everything necessary for everyday life, but our favourite department remains the wedding dresses.
4 boulevard de Rochechouart, 18th. Tel.: 01-55-29-52-20. www.tati.fr Open Monday to Friday 10am to 7pm, Saturday 9.30am to 7pm.

Restaurant

Ⓒ Dishny
Paneer tikka (Indian cheese kebabs with vegetables), royal fried rice with chicken, prawns and squid, savoury *dosa* pancakes and other Indian and Sri Lankan specialities for low prices. A feast. Around €10–15.
25 rue Cail, 10th. Tel.: 01-42-05-44-04. http://dishny.fr Open daily noon to 11.30pm.

Next stations

GARE DE L'EST

See line 7, page 168

JACQUES BONSERGENT

Café le Bonsergent
6 place Jacques-Bonsergent, 10th.

RÉPUBLIQUE

See line 3, page 86

OBERKAMPF

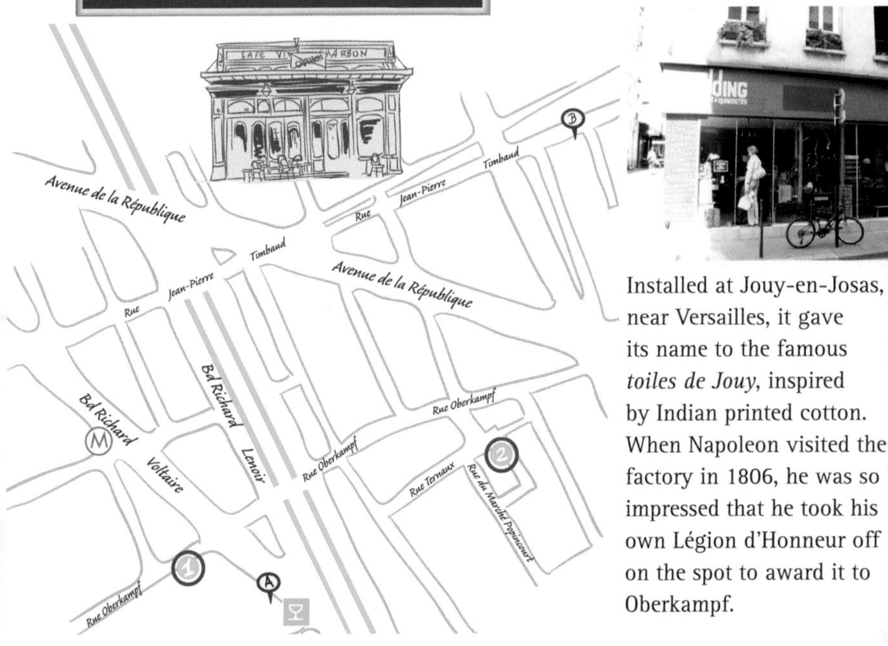

History

Both the station and the nearby street are named after industrialist Christophe Philippe Oberkampf (1738–1815). Descended from a family of Bavarian dyers, Oberkampf had an extraordinary destiny. He first worked as an engraver in Mulhouse, before becoming a colourer at the factory of the Arsenal in Paris. He owes his renown to the creation of the first factory to produce printed cotton using engraved copper plates, in 1759. He acquired French nationality in 1770 and his factory had the privilege of becoming one of the royal factories. Installed at Jouy-en-Josas, near Versailles, it gave its name to the famous *toiles de Jouy*, inspired by Indian printed cotton. When Napoleon visited the factory in 1806, he was so impressed that he took his own Légion d'Honneur off on the spot to award it to Oberkampf.

SIGHTSEEING

A trendy walk

① **Rue Oberkampf:** over the years, pretty one-storey cottages gave way to courtyards and alleyways bordered by workshops busy with craftsmen specialising in tools. Little by little the physiognomy of the district has been transformed: art galleries and architectural practices, artists and designers have replaced small shops. Since the 1990s, the street has mutated into a trendy hangout

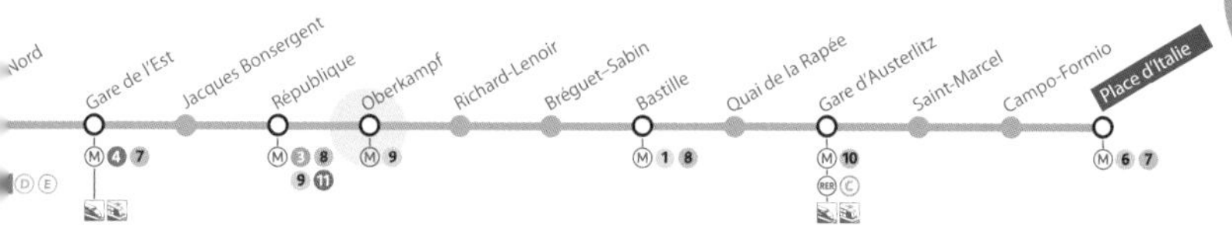

f Parisian youth. At nightfall young people ıvade the cafés and restaurants, nightclubs nd music venues to have fun into the early ours.

ue du Marché-Popincourt: you'll be harmed by the villagey atmosphere of this animated street. The names of the second-hand hops La Garçonnière, Alasinglinglin, Belle urette… are like a daydream. From faded film osters and old dinner services to Scandinaian design or crazy 60s objects, you're sure to nearth something in these boutiques overowing with forgotten treasures.

ue du Marché-Popincourt, 11th.

Address book

The place for a rendezvous

Café Bataclan
50 boulevard Voltaire, 11th.
Open daily 8am to 1am.
Tel.: 01-49-23-96-33.

Out on the town

A Le Bataclan
This concert venue, which was originally a grand café-concert, is name after one of Offenbach's operettas, *Ba-Ta-Clan*. Designed by the architect Charles Duval in 1864, the building was then topped by a Chinese pagoda roof. The café and the theatre were on the ground floor with a huge dancefloor. All the music greats have appeared in this legendary concert hall, making its century-old foundations resonate.

50 boulevard Voltaire, 11th.
Tel.: 01-43-14-00-30.
www.bataclan.fr

B L'Alimentation Générale
Despite the name, this is not a food store but a charming bar putting on an astonishing music programme that will get you dancing to its frenzied rhythms. Concerts on Wednesday, Thursday and Sunday. Entrance fee at weekends after midnight.
64 rue Jean-Pierre-Timbaud, 11th.
Tel.: 01-43-55-42-50.
Open Wednesday to Sunday 6pm to 2am (Friday and Saturday until 2am, Sunday until midnight).

ext stations

RICHARD-LENOIR
Le Rush Bar,
rue Saint-Sébastien,
th.

BRÉGUET-SABIN
Le Bloody Mary
41 rue Amelot, 11th.

BASTILLE
See line 1, page 40

QUAI DE LA RAPÉE
Café Barjot
18 avenue Ledru-Rollin, 12th.

GARE D'AUSTERLITZ

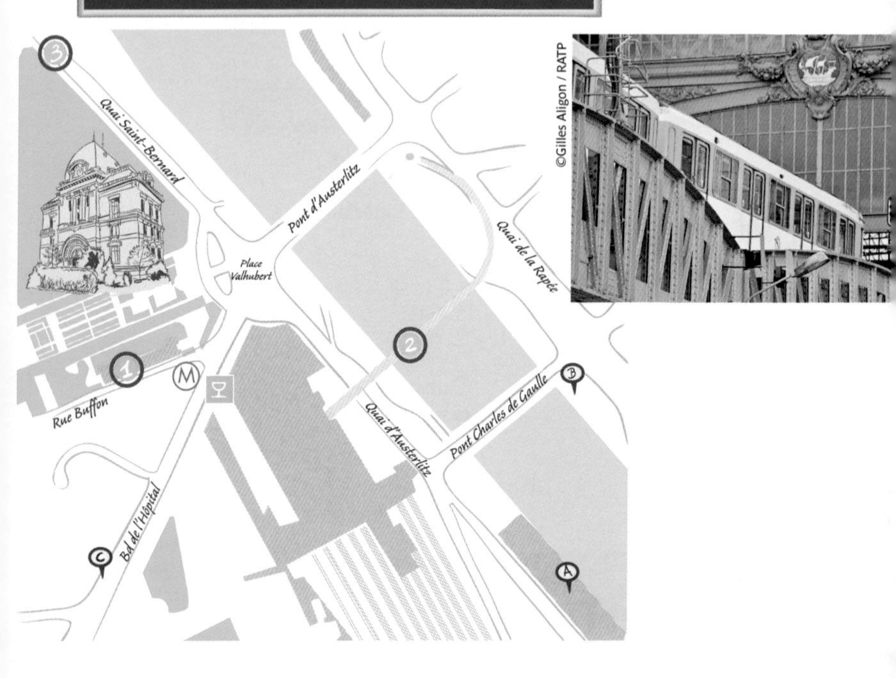

History

This station bears the name of the train station that celebrates one of the most epic conflicts of the Napoleonic era, that of Austerlitz—also dubbed the 'Battle of the Three Emperors'. It took place on 1805 in southern Moravia. After nine hours of fearsome combat, Napoleon's Grand Army defeated the Austro-Russian forces of Emperor Francis I of Austria and Tzar Alexander I. The station is served by metro lines 5 and 10. If there really is one spectacular line, it is certainly the overhead line 5: it runs under the immense glass and steel roof of Gare d'Austerlitz, under which are the train station platforms. This laminated-steel structure, in a 50 metre (164 feet) span, elevates the line to cross the Seine on the metal Austerlitz viaduct. The line 10 route is much more simple: it terminates at Gare d'Austerlitz. The station was originally called Gare d'Orléans, and then renamed Gare d'Orléans-Austerlitz in 1930, which you can still see inscribed on the walls of line 10. Gare d'Austerlitz station was formerly the end stop of the Paris-Orléans rail company, one of ix private rail companies that were ıationalised and amalgamated in 1938 o become the SNCF, national rail :ompany. The district used to be known ıs Austerlitz and in 1985 the station ıdopted the same name.

SIGHTSEEING

of the ordinary

Galerie de Paléontologie et 'Anatomie comparée du Jardin es Plantes: opened in 1898 in prepaation for the Paris World Fair of 1900, the ;allery of Paleontology and Comparative .natomy was born from the desire of emient professors Gaudry and Pouchet. The wo scientists wanted to make this place a museum for sharing collections that had reviously been inaccessible to the public.

The imposing red brick facade is decorated with nature-inspired sculptures. Its large windows allow one to imagine the interior bathed with light. And it is the case. The remarkable gallery in stone and metal built after plans by architect Ferdinand Dutert extends for nearly 80 metres (262 feet). On the second floor, visitors are hypnotised by the skeletons of prehistoric monsters. Resting their elbows on the wrought-iron railing that runs the length of the gallery, they dream in front of the collections brought back from voyages in the 18th and 19th centuries. Fossils of vertebrates, scary dinosaurs and unlikely invertebrates populate the gallery. Luc Besson came here to shoot some of his film *Adèle Blanc-Sec*, adapted from Tardi's strip cartoon. As cinephiles will tell you, in it one sees a Pterosaurus egg hatch, whose occupant escapes through the window.

57 rue Cuvier, 5th.
Open Monday to Friday 10am to 5pm, Saturday, Sunday and public holidays 10am to 6pm.

2 **Viaduc d'Austerlitz:** the viaduct connects the line 5 station, situated within the canopy of the train station —so large that under the Commune, during the Siege of Paris, it was used as a workshop for manufacturing hot air balloons— to Quai de la Rapée metro station. So as to not disturb navigation on the Seine, the project chosen consisted of putting in place two parabolic arches, supported on either side of the river by two stone pillars, without any intermediate support. The viaduct was built between November 1903 and December 1904. Its decoration by Formigé makes numerous maritime al-

lusions: fish, rowing boats, anchors and tridents are prettily engraved on the metal. At the base of the arches, the majestic arms of the City of Paris sign this work in metal.
Metros Gare d'Austerlitz and Quai de la Rapée.

Culture

3 **Quai Saint-Bernard and Musée de la Sculpture en Plein Air:** the Quai Saint-Bernard, once the old path to Ivry, got its name from the nearby Couvent des Bernardins and to the Porte Saint-Bernard, which once stood at the end of Pont Sully. In the 17th and 18th centuries, bathers used to frequent this spot. Legend has it that Henri IV came here himself to bathe his son, the future Louis XIII. Today, the quaysides are invaded by promenaders curious to discover the museum of open-air sculpture. Installed on the banks of the Seine, square Tino-Rossi it opened to the public in 1980. Works by César, Brancusi, Gilioli, Zadkine and Schöffer take the air, in this place dedicated to art and relaxation.
Quai Saint-Bernard, 5th.
Admission free.

Address book

The place for
a rendezvous

Austerlitz Café
4 boulevard de l'Hôpital, 5th.
Open daily 7am to midnight.
Tel.: 01-45-87-29-83.

Culture

Ⓐ Cité de la Mode et du Design

The industrial buildings were designed in 1907 by Morin-Goustiaux as the Magasins Généraux warehouses. They are constructed in reinforced concrete and have a modular structure that was totally avant-garde at the period. For the rehabilitation, the French and New Zealand architects Jakob et MacFarlane were chosen for their daring approach, which echoes that of their illustrious predecessor. The new site houses the Institut Français de la Mode fashion school, an events space, as well as eventually shops and restaurants beside the Seine. Although only partially open, its bright green structure merits the detour.

34 quai d'Austerlitz, 13th.

Luxury

Ⓑ Le VIP Paris

The VIP Paris is a magnificent yacht, which marries charm and luxury to provide an alternative vision of Paris. At nightfall it sets off for a cruise on the Seine, accompanied by a candlelit dinner, and then offers the possibility of spending the night in one of its cabins, entirely fitted out in mahogany. Breakfast is provided the next morning to help recover from the emotion of the evening. Around €160–200 per person. Reservation essential.

Port de la Rapée, 12th.
Tel.: 01-48-84-45-30.
www.le-vip-paris.com
Welcome on board from 6pm, breakfast 9am to noon.

Restaurant

Ⓒ Le Bibimbap

Bibambap is nothing to do with bebop but is an authentic Korean dish prepared in a cooking pot. Based around rice, melting courgettes, crisp grated carrots and bean sprouts, it will awaken your tastebuds to these flavours from elsewhere. Egg adds a sunny touch and fine slivers of beef seasoned with sesame oil complete the palette of flavours. Discretely located under the foliage of boulevard de l'Hôpital, the Bibimbap seduces with its inventive and refined take on Korean cuisine. Menus from €9.80 (lunch).

32 boulevard de l'Hôpital, 5th.
Tel.: 01-43-31-27-42.
www.bibimbap.fr
Open daily noon to 2.30pm, 7.30pm to 10.30pm.

Next stations

SAINT-MARCEL

Le Sancerre
2 boulevard Saint-Marcel, 5th.

COMPO-FORMIO

L'Alliance
115 boulevard de l'Hôpital, 13th.

PLACE D'ITALIE

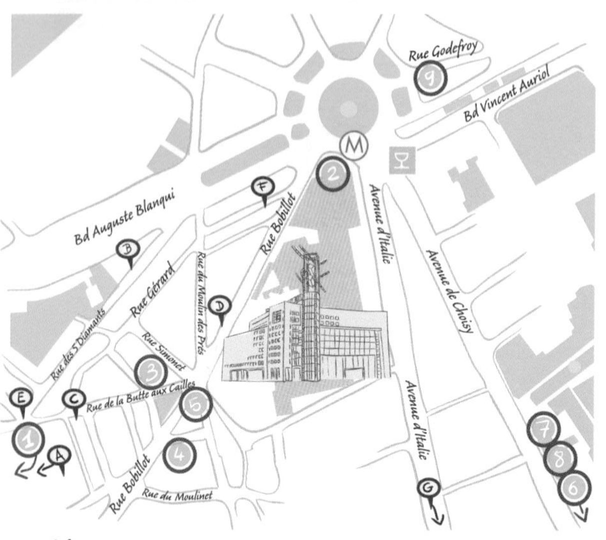

History

Place d'Italie is a reminder that this used to be the entry point of the Roman road from Lyon. It was also the tax barrier until the 19th century, which separated Paris from Gentilly. Claude Nicolas Ledoux had constructed two pavilions here (as at Denfert-Rochereau). They were set on fire during the Revolution and demolished a few years later. Its most notable episode came when Louis Eugène Cavaignac, head of the government, tried to put down revolting workers in 1848. One of his men, General Bréa de Ludre, was assassinated nearby after having been hit and insulted. Another, Mangin, was killed with an axe. The revolt was far from under control...

Today, place d'Italie is a busy crossroads between south and east Paris. In the centre is a monument to Marshal Alphonse Juin inaugurated in 1983. On the square in front of the 13th arrondissement town hall, Zadkine's sculpture *The Return of the Prodigal Son* accompanies the married couples coming out of the town hall. The metro line serving this arrondissement and square opened in 1906. It later underwent numerous alterations with the enlargement and extension of the various lines.

SIGHTSEEING

Architecture

1 **Temple Antoiniste:** the strange building on a small square at the junction of several streets is a sort of church for the Antoiniste religious movement. The founder of the

movement, Louis Antoine (1846–1912), used his talent as a medium to try to cure the sick.

34 rue Vergniaud, 13th.

Centre Commercial Italie-2: you can't miss this shopping centre on leaving the metro. With its very futuristic, curved glass facade, architect Kenzo Tange sought to create a link between the traditional neighbourhood in stone around rue Bobillot and the numerous tower blocks in the south of the arrondissement. The campanile on the parvis houses the lift shaft. Finally, the sculpture at the top is a work by Thierry Vidé.

30 avenue Italie, 13th.
Tel.: 01-53-80-17-03.

3 **Butte aux Cailles:** a villagey atmosphere reigns on this hill. Pause at 10 rue Daviel, with its little half-timbered houses, and in the war widows' area, towards rue du Moulin-des-Prés. Up the hill, on Passage Boiton or rue Barrault, old paving stones, rampant weeds and little bistros give a happy impression of being in another age.

4 **Piscine de la Butte-aux-Cailles**

This is one of the oldest swimming pools in Paris, built in 1924 by the architects Louis Bonnier and François Hennebique, and was the first to have footbaths and showers. The swimming pool is fed by an artesian well, providing iron-rich water at 28°C. Its architecture in red brick recalls that of northern France. The interior has an impressive vault and arches.

5 place Paul-Verlaine, 13th.
Tel.: 01-45-89-60-05.

5 Artesian Well on Place Paul-Verlaine: if you see people arriving at this kind of fountain bearing empty bottles, it's quite normal. This is pure water from an artesian well hollowed out 582 metres (1,909 feet) underground. Exploited from 1863, the well was made available to Parisians from 1904. Today, a fountain explains the story of this water. Instructive and refreshing!

Place Paul-Verlaine, opposite the swimming pool.

A Chinatown walk

6 Supermarché Tang Frères: this Asian and Chinese supermarket is a local institution for fruit, vegetables, sauces and innumerable preparations unavailable elsewhere. And even some craft items.

48 avenue d'Ivry, 13th.
Open Tuesday to Friday 9am to 7.30pm, Saturday 8.30am to 7.30pm, Sunday morning only.

7 Chinese McDonalds: this branch of the famous fast-food chain follows the style of the Paris Chinatown. A red pagoda with green tiles is almost believable. Inside, however, the service is the same as elsewhere.

1 avenue de Choisy, 13th.
Tel.: 01-53-79-26-11.

8 Église Notre-Dame-de-Chine A recently consecrated church intended for the Catholics of the Chinese district. Very modern, it was conceived by François Payen, along a very unusual plan because the church is not centred but spirals around the altar. Note the frescoes painted by local residents to the right of the door.

27 avenue de Choisy, 13th.
Tel.: 01-45-86-28-68.

9 17 rue Godefroy: a commemorative plaque recalls that former Chinese premier Zhou Enlai lived in a hotel on this site.

Address book

The place for a rendezvous

Café de la Place
194 avenue de Choisy, 13th.
Open daily 6am to 2am, Saturday and Sunday from 7am.

Shopping

A Boulangerie-Pâtisserie Laurent Duchêne
Discover the cakes of a *meilleur ouvrier de France* (best artisan of France). Some of the

creations have Asian touches. Satisfy your hunger pangs with desserts, cakes and a savoury corner.

2 rue Wurtz, 13th.
Tel.: 01-45-65-00-77.
Open Monday to Saturday 7.30am to 8pm.

Out on the town

B Théâtre des Cinq Diamants

Revisited classics and modern creations.

10 rue des Cinq-Diamants, 13th.
Tel.: 09-50-99-97-58. www.theatre-5-diamants.fr

C Le Merle Moqueur

This bar is a haunt of nightbirds and other local regulars. Atmosphere guaranteed. Some very original house rums.

11 rue de la Butte-aux-Cailles, 13th.
Tel.: 01-45-65-12-43.
Open daily 5pm to 2am.

Restaurants

D L'Avant-Goût

Christophe Beaufront has fun preparing dishes that combine French tradition with gastronomic and Asian accents, such as his *pot-au-feu* with spices. The pared-back little dining room is attractively decorated with works of art. Attentive service and tempting wine list (a good selection from the Touraine). The more impatient can go to the wine shop across the street and take away some dishes. Around €40, inexpensive menu at lunch.

26 rue Bobillot, 13th.
Tel.: 01-53-80-24-00.
www.lavantgout.com
Open Tuesday to Saturday noon to 2pm, 7.30pm to 10pm.

E Les Cailloux

Exquisite Italian specialities, such as *linguine, trofie* and *pennete*, are served along with delicious meat and fish. At the heart of the Butte, liveliness guaranteed in a chic bistro setting. €20–30.

58 rue des Cinq-Diamants, 13th.
Tel.: 01-45-80-15-08. www.lescailloux.fr
Open daily 10am to midnight.

F Sukhothai

One of our favourite Thai restaurants in the area. A few steps from bustling place d'Italie, refined setting and traditional dishes, such as *pad thaï*. €15–25.

12 rue Père-Guérin, 13th.
Tel.: 01-45-81-55-88.
Open Monday to Friday noon to 2.30pm, 6pm to 10.30pm, closes at 11pm on Saturday and Sunday.

G Lao Thai

This little restaurant doesn't look much but its dishes are an explosion of flavours. Quite spicy. Try the sliced beef with basil, a true feast. €15–25.

128 rue de Tolbiac, 13th.
Tel.: 01-44-24-28-10.
Open Thursday to Monday noon to 2pm, 7pm to 11pm.

line 6

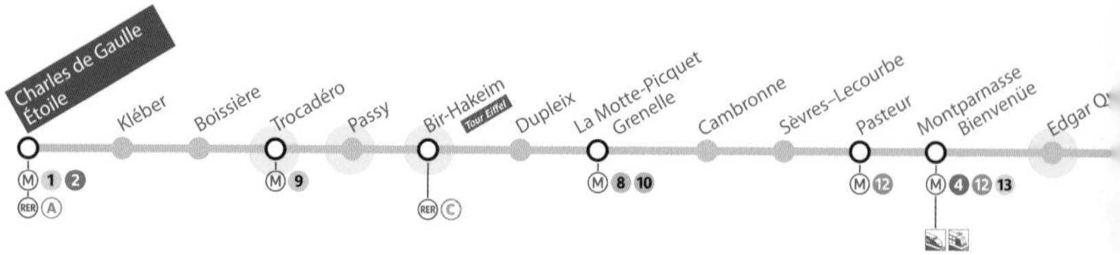

Charles de Gaulle Étoile — Kléber — Boissière — Trocadéro — Passy — Bir-Hakeim (Tour Eiffel) — Dupleix — La Motte-Picquet Grenelle — Cambronne — Sèvres-Lecourbe — Pasteur — Montparnasse Bienvenüe — Edgar Q

History

This line follows a semi-circular route in the southern part of Paris between Charles de Gaulle – Étoile to the west and Nation to the east, along the former external boulevards. The line was opened between 1900 and 1906 between Étoile and Place d'Italie, and was first called line 2 South or 'Circulaire Sud'(south circular) before becoming part of line 5, but the Place d'Italie to Nation segment that opened in 1909 was immediately called line 6. The line is 13.6 kilometres (8.5 miles) long, but 45% of the track is above ground (6.1 kilometres or 3.8 miles). The trains have been equipped with rubber tyres since 1974.

This is one of the most pleasant lines to take on the Paris Metro because of its many outstanding views of some of the capital's great monuments and landscapes. Generally speaking, most of the Paris metro stations are below ground and only 26 stations are above ground, but most of these are on lines 2 and 6. The viaducts built to carry the train lines above street level were designed by the architect Jean-Baptiste Formigé, and made it possible to avoid digging a large number of tunnels by following the routes of the boulevards. The viaducts were made of brick and freestone with Gustave Eiffel-type metal structures.

Charles de Gaulle – Étoile / Nation

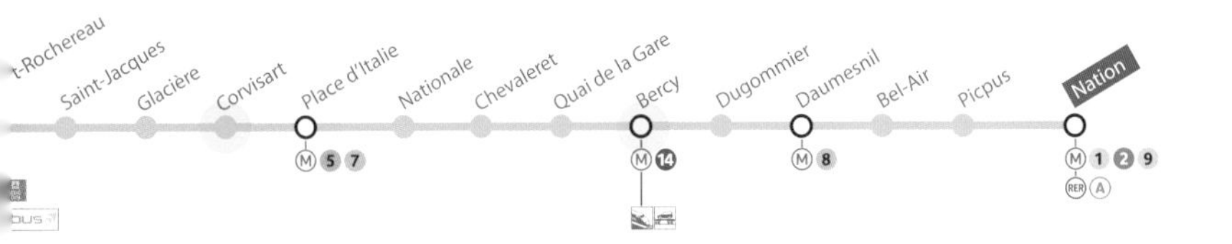

TROCADÉRO

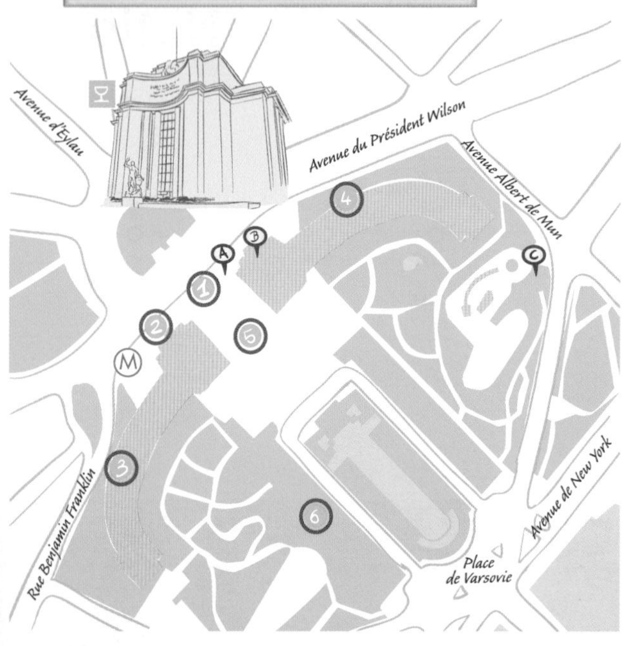

History

Trocadéro is the name of the square, the esplanade that overlooks the Eiffel Tower, and the sloping gardens that go right up to the Seine. Until the Second Empire, Chaillot was a quiet country village, the name being derived from *caillou*, meaning stone, in reference to the soil on the hill on which the village was perched. The fate of the village changed when Napoleon I decided to build a palace for his son, the King of Rome, on this spot, in the antique Roman style. That gave rise to property speculation on the hill, where a number of buildings were built. The project was abandoned when the Empire fell and later a Moorish style palace, inspired by the Giralda minaret in Seville, was built there for the Universal Exhibition of 1878. It was named the Palais du Trocadéro in remembrance of a battle won on 31 August 1823 by the French expeditionary corps, which took the fort of Trocadero, near Cadiz in Spain, which re-established King Ferdinand VII on his throne. For nearly 50 years, the Trocadero palace housed the French Monuments Museum as well as the first Museum of Ethnology in Paris, before the Musée de l'Homme (Museum of Mankind). The Trocadero gardens were created during the same period. However, the palace was not appreciated by Parisians and in 1937 it was pulled

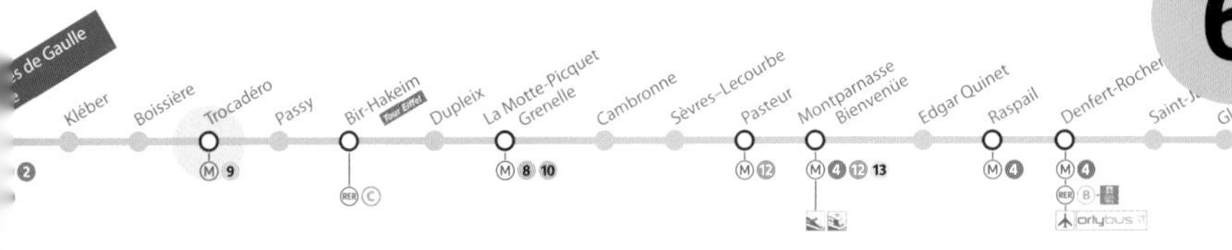

down and replaced by the current Palais de Chaillot, which kept most of the original framework with the addition of an esplanade. It was here in the Palais de Chaillot that the Universal Declaration of Human Rights was signed on 10 December 1948. In 1985, on a suggestion by the then President of the French Republic, François Mitterrand, the esplanade was named Parvis des Droits de l'Homme (Human Rights' Square).

SIGHTSEEING

onument

Palais de Chaillot: this vast building was made for the 1937 Universal Exhibition by Jacques Carlu (who obtained the Prix de Rome award), together with Hippolyte Boileau and Léon Azéma in the neoclassical style that was characteristic of the 1930s. More than 70 artists worked on the decoration. The Chaillot palace houses several museums including the Musée de l'Homme (ethnology), the Musée de la Marine (navy), and the Cité de l'Architecture et du Patrimoine (a complex devoted to architecture and architectural heritage that includes the French Monuments Museum, the École de Chaillot School of Architecture and the Institut Français d'Architecture). Palais de Chaillot also houses the Théâtre National de Chaillot.
17 place du Trocadéro, 16th.
Tel.: 01-44-05-39-10.
Open Monday to Saturday 11am to 7pm, Sunday 1pm to 5pm.

Culture

2 **Musée de l'Homme:** the museum is closed for renovation until 2012, but is still holds a number of temporary exhibitions on anthropology and ethnology.
Place du Trocadéro, 16th.
Tel.: 01-44-05-72-72.
www.museedelhomme.fr
Open Wednesday to Monday 10am to 5pm. Closed on public holidays.
Entrance fee

3 **Musée de la Marine:** the navy museum and has a permanent collection of marvellous models and paintings in addition to holding temporary exhibitions..

Place du Trocadéro, 16th.
Tel.: 01-53-65-69-69.
www.musee-marine.fr. Entrance fee.

4 **Cité de l'Architecturee et du Patrimoine:** established in 2007, this 'architecture and architectural heritage complex' holds exhibitions, conferences and workshops on those themes in France and worldwide.

Place du Trocadéro, 16th.

Tel.: 01-58-51-52-00.
www.citechaillot.fr. Open Wednesday to Monday 11am to 7pm. Late night on Thursday to 9pm. Entrance fee.

Off the beaten track

5 **Esplanade du Trocadéro:** the Trocadero Esplanade (renamed Human Rights Square), lies between the two wings of the Chaillot Palace. From up

here you get a unique and marvellous wide-angle view of the Eiffel Tower.
Free access.

A walk in the park

6 **Jardins du Trocadéro:** the Trocadero Gardens extend from the Chaillot Palace to the Seine and provide a backdrop to a very pleasant walk. This is a very popular place to go for the 14 July fireworks display.
Place du Trocadéro, 16th.

Address book

The place for a rendezvous

Café Le Malakoff
6 place du Trocadéro, 16th.
Open daily 7.30am to 1am.
Tel.: 01-45-53-75-27.

Restaurant

A Café Carlu
You will get a marvellous view of the Eiffel Tower from this café-cum-restaurant right in the heart of the Palais de Chaillot. Menus €25–30.
1 place du Trocadéro, 16th.
Tel.: 01-53-70-96-65.
Open Wednesday to Monday 11am to 7pm, and to 9pm on Thursday.

Leisure

B Théâtre National de Chaillot
A mecca for modern ballet in Paris.
1 place du Trocadéro, 16th.
Tel.: 01 53 65 30 00.
www.theatre-chaillot.fr

C CinéAqua Paris
The Trocadero Aquarium contains some 500 different aquatic species in impressive displays, as well as a shark tunnel. There are also cinemas for films, and workshops for children.
2 avenue des Nations-Unies, 16th.
Tel.: 01-40-69-23-23. www.cineaqua.com
Open daily 10am to 7pm. Entrance fee.

Previous stations

CHARLES DE GAULLE – ÉTOILE

See line 1, page 16

KLÉBER

Café Brassac
37 avenue Kléber, 16th.

BOISSIÈRE

Le Kléber
80 avenue Kléber, 16th.

PASSY

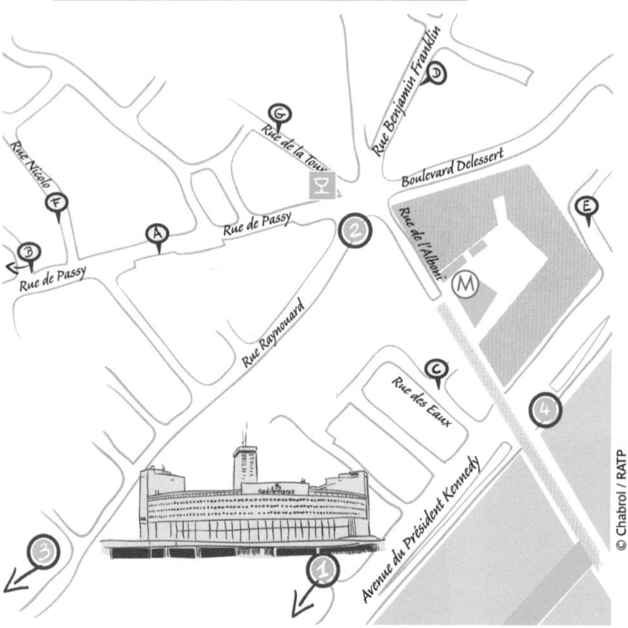

© Chabrol / RATP

History

The station was named after the old village of Passy, which was one of three communes that stretched along the right bank of the Seine, together with Chaillot and Auteuil. In the 18th century the village grew rapidly because of its spring water sources (the first had been discovered in 1650), which drew crowds of people in search of thermal cures. Under Napoleon III and because of Baron Haussmann's town planning, the villages of Passy, Auteuil and Chaillot were merged into greater Paris in 1860. The station opened in 1903 and part of it is above ground because of the sharp incline of the hill, and part at street level. When it opened it was the final station on line 2 South. The viaduct was built between 1903 and 1906, making it possible to connect the left bank of the Seine to the station known today as Bir-Hakeim.

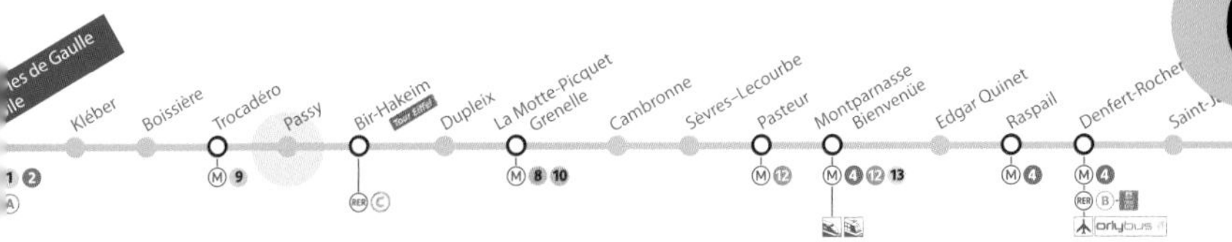

SIGHTSEEING

onument

Maison de Radio France: this building was designed by the architect Henry Bernard to house the French Public Radio and Television Corporation. It was inaugurated in 1963 by the then president Charles de Gaulle, who initiated the project. It is a circular construction with a circumference of 500 metres (1,640 feet) and a 70 metre-high (230 feet) tower in the centre. The building is symbolic of the development of the French media and contains more than 60 recording studios. All the major French public radio stations have their headquarters here: France Info, France Musique, France Culture, France Inter and France Bleu. A tour of the building is a good way to learn about the history of the media, since the tours include a visit to the radio museum that traces the history of information transmission from Roman times and displays some landmark inventions such as the optical telegraph created by the Chappe brothers (1793), the Morse telegraph (1832), Bell's telephone (1876), and the first telegram sent from the Eiffel Tower to the Pantheon in 1898. There is also a reconstruction of a TV studio from the 1930s. In addition, visitors may attend the classical and contemporary music concerts held in the Maison de Radio France, usually for a very reasonable price.

116 avenue du Président-Kennedy, 16th. Tel.: 01-42-30-57-02. www.radiofrance.fr.

Open Monday to Saturday 10.30am to 4.30pm. Closed on public holidays.

Entrance fee (the ticket includes the visit to the museum as well as the tour of Maison de Radio France and the recording studios, which you can see through the large glass partitions).

A walk through history

2 **Passy:** when you leave from the Passy station exit, you can enjoy getting lost in the magnificent streets, marked with the history of Passy village. Take the rue des Eaux, a reminder of Passy's thermal vocation, and then turn off into rue Raynouard, where the buildings straddle the hillside overlooking the Seine. At number 47 you will see Balzac's house, one of this neighbourhood's illustrious inhabitants. Maupassant also lived (and died) here, as did Benjamin Franklin. Meander through these pleasant streets, es-

pecially rue Berton, a picturesque little paved road, where Balzac used to stroll, take a look at the Ranelagh theatre, which is a classified monument, and go up to the Muette crossroads where a royal castle stood before the Revolution, but has since disappeared.

③ ***Rue Berton:*** a picturesque little paved road, where Balzac used to stroll.

④ ***The view:*** if you want a stunning view of the Eiffel Tower, simply take the metro between Passy and Bir-Hakeim stations.

Address book

The place for a rendezvous

Café Le Passy
2 rue de Passy, 16th.
Open Monday to Saturday 7am to 1am, Sunday 9am to 7pm.
Tel.: 01-42-88-31-02.

Ⓐ Rue de Passy
This is a very chic street, well known for its elegant boutiques and frequented by the local fashionistas.

Ⓑ Franck et Fils
The 16th arrondissement needed one department store worthy of the name,

and this is it! Franck et Fils is part of the Bon Marché group and is rather like that store's little sister. It prides itself on having all the brands that combine luxury and fashion.
80 rue de Passy, 16th.
Tel.: 01-44-14-38-00.
www.francketfils.fr
Open Monday to Friday 10am to 7pm, Saturday 10am to 8pm.

Culture

Ⓒ Musée du Vin
The wine Museum will take you on a journey through the wine universe, with its many tasks and tools as well as the product itself. Established in a former limestone quarry, visitors go underground to visit the museum, attend conferences or go to wine tastings. This is an

excellent opportunity to taste excellent AOC classified wines (*Appellation d'Origine Controlée*) or even some great grand cru ones. If that should make you hungry, there is a restaurant in the vaulted cellar that once served as a storeroom for the Passy abbey.
5 square Charles-Dickens, 16th.
Tel.: 01-45-25-63-26.
www.museeduvinparis.com
Open Tuesday to Sunday 10am to 6pm. Entrance fee.

D Musée Clemenceau

This is where the French Prime Minister Georges Clemenceau lived for 35 years until his death on 24 November 1929. The garden-level three-room

apartment with a view of the Eiffel Tower has been transformed into a museum devoted to him and the place is exactly as it was when the man known as 'the tiger' lived there. A visit to his private apartment provides another view of the man, who was a great art lover. A room on the first floor traces Clemenceau's life and work though various items such as portraits, photos, books, newspapers and manuscripts. You will also see the famous coat and gaiters he wore when inspecting the front during the First World War.
8 rue Benjamin-Franklin, 16th.
Tel.: 01-45-20-53-41.
www.musee-clemenceau.fr
Open Tuesday to Saturday 2pm to 5.30pm. Closed on public holidays and in August. Entrance fee.

Restaurants

E L'Astrance

If you would like to savour dishes prepared by the three-star Michelin chef, Pascal Barbot, you will need to book three months ahead! À la carte lunchtime menu €70–120, evening menu €190.
4 rue Beethoven, 16th.
Tel.: 01-40-50-84-40.
Open Tuesday to Friday.

F Akasaka

This tiny Japanese restaurant only has about 20 covers, but is greatly prized by visiting Japanese as well as showbiz celebrities. You will find excellent Japanese cuisine, delicate maki, grilled meat, algae and cucumber salads. À la carte lunchtime menu about €20, and €50 in the evening.
9 rue Nicolo, 16th.
Tel.: 01-42-88-77-86.
Open Tuesday to Saturday noon to 2pm and 7pm to 10pm.

G Comme des poissons

Another good Japanese address in this neighbourhood. It is known for its excellent sushi, but also for its service, which leaves something to be desired. Judge for yourself! About €70.
24 rue de la Tour, 16th.
Tel.: 01-45-20-70-37.
Open Tuesday to Saturday noon to 2.30pm and 5.30pm to 10pm as well as for lunch on Sunday.

BIR-HAKEIM

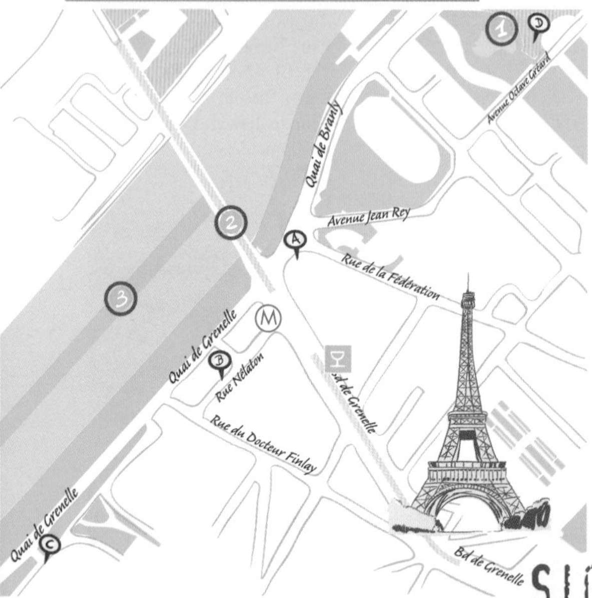

History

This is one of the stations above ground. It opened on 24 April 1906 when it was called Grenelle (from the eponymous neighbourhood and boulevard). In 1949, the name was changed to Bir-Hakeim in honour of the battle that took place in May and June 1942 around the oasis of that name in the Libyan desert. This is the closest metro station to the Eiffel Tower and consequently much frequented by tourists.

SIGHTSEEING

Monuments

1 **Tour Eiffel:** designed by Gustave Eiffel for the 1889 Universal Exhibition, the 320 metre (1,050 feet) tower was the highest man-made structure in the world at the time, after the Cheops Pyramid. Long denigrated as being too modern, the 'Iron Maiden' has since won acclaim and become the very symbol of Paris for the entire world. It is the most visited monument in the capital. Don't miss the nightly light show from nightfall to 1am (2am in the summer) when the tower sparkles for a few minutes every hour on the hour.

Champs de Mars, 7th.
Tel.: 0892-701-239. www.tour-eiffel.fr
Open daily 9am to midnight from 17 June to 28 August, and 9.30am to 11pm the rest of the year. Entrance fee.

Pont de Bir-Hakeim: if you have a feeling of *déjà-vu* when you see the Bir-Hakeim bridge and viaduct, there is a reason. The bridge has served as a backdrop to numerous films, including *Peur sur la ville*, *The Last Tango in Paris*, and *Inception*. The Passy bridge, predecessor to the Bir-Hakeim bridge, was built for the 1878 Universal Exhibition, and was a metal pedestrian bridge. In 1905 it was rebuilt on two levels, one for pedestrians and cars, and a viaduct above for the metro's line 6. It was renamed in 1848 in remembrance of the battle of Bir-Hakeim and was listed an historic monument in 1986.

Access via the Quai de Grenelle on the Left Bank, or Avenue du Président-Kennedy on the Right Bank.

walk in the park

Île aux Cygnes: there is a long tree-lined promenade called l'Allée des Cygnes (Swan Alley) on this artificial island on the Seine. A small replica of the Statue of Liberty was placed at one end of the island in 1889. It is by Frédéric Auguste Bartholdi and was a gift to France from French citizens living in the United States.

Take the steps at Bir-Hakeim bridge level.

Address book

The place for a rendezvous

L'Atome

29 boulevard de Grenelle, 15th.
Open Monday to Saturday 6am to midnight.
Tel.: 01-45-78-72-66.

Culture

A Maison de la Culture du Japon

This Japanese cultural centre was inaugurated in 1997. It is devoted to traditional and contemporary Japanese culture and hosts exhibitions, shows and conferences. It is also a place to study the Japanese language and gastronomy as well as the tea ceremony, calligraphy, *ikebana* (flower arrangement), origami, manga, and other Japanese arts.

101 bis quai Branly, 15th.
Tel.: 01-44-37-95-01.
www.mcjp.fr

Restaurants

B Le Concert de Cuisine

The name of this restaurant, 'kitchen concert', says it all! The ingredients dance on the griddle in full view of the hungry clients (which include former President Jacques Chirac and his wife). Evening menu €40–57.

14 rue Nélaton, 15th.
Tel.: 01-40-58-10-15.

C Le Benkay

This restaurant on the 4th floor of the former Hotel Nikko (now a Novotel) is reputed to be the best Japanese restaurant in Paris. The idea is to enjoy excellent Japanese *teppanyaki* cuisine in a calm atmosphere with a marvellous panoramic view of the Seine. Lunchtime menu €42, à la carte €90–120.

61 quai de Grenelle, 15th.
Tel.: 01-40-58-21-26.
www.restaurant-benkay.fr

D Le Jules Verne

Located on the 2nd floor of the Eiffel Tower, 125 metres (410 feet) above ground, this restaurant is a gastronomic adventure, orchestrated by two great chefs Alain Ducasse and Pascal Feraud. Lunch on weekdays €85, and €165–200 at weekends, dinner €200.

Eiffel Tower (access from the south pillar), avenue Gustave-Eiffel, 7th.
Tel.: 01-45-55-61-44.
www.lejulesverne-paris.com

EDGAR QUINET

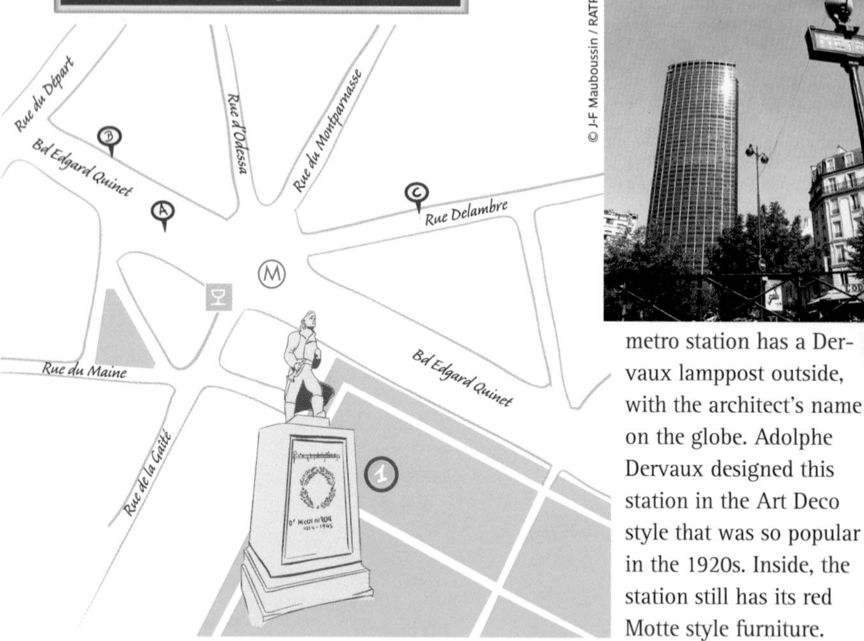

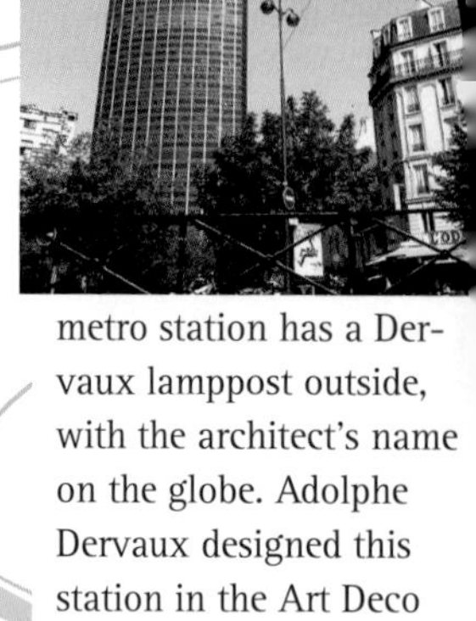
© J-F Mauboussin / RATP

History

This station opened in 1906, and the name is a tribute to the 19th century French intellectual Edgar Quinet (1803–1875), who combined a long academic career with a lifelong political commitment. A firm republican, he was elected deputy in 1848 but had to go into exile in 1851 because of his political opinions. He was elected deputy again after he returned to France in 1871. Among the works he published are *Révolutions d'Italie* (revolutions of Italy) in 1852 and '*Esprit Nouveau*' (the new spirit) in 1874. The Edgar Quinet metro station has a Dervaux lamppost outside, with the architect's name on the globe. Adolphe Dervaux designed this station in the Art Deco style that was so popular in the 1920s. Inside, the station still has its red Motte style furniture.

SIGHTSEEING

A walk in the cemetery

1 Cimetière du Montparnasse: Montparnasse Cemetery is a 19 hectare (47 acre) island of greenery in the 14th arrondissement. It was created in the early 19th century on a similar model to the Passy, Montmartre and Père-Lachaise cemeteries, on sites of former farms. A large number of artists, sculptors, and men and women of letters have been laid to rest here, including Raymond Aron, Charles Baudelaire, Simone de Beauvoir, Samuel Beckett, Antoine Bourdelle, Constantin Brancusi, and Eugène Ionesco. Perhaps the most popular star

buried here recently is singer and composer Serge Gainsbourg. It is worth strolling around this cemetery for the sheer enjoyment of the trees and greenery, if nothing else.
3 boulevard Edgar-Quinet, 14th. Tel.: 01-44-10-86-50. Open Monday to Friday 8am to 5.30pm, Saturday 8.30am to 5.30pm, and Sunday and public holidays 9am to 5.30pm. Closes at 6pm from 5 March to 5 November. Admission free.

Address book

The place for a rendezvous

Le Café de la Liberté
1 rue de la Gaîté, 14th.
Tel.: 01-43-20-94-56.
Open Monday to Friday 7am to midnight, Saturday and Sunday until 2am.

Shopping

A Marché de la Création Paris Montparnasse
The Montparnasse district used to be a hive of artistic activity in the 20th century and a group of artists, called the 'Montparnasse hoard' began to exhibit their works on the pavements. As a result this open-air art market came to be nicknamed *Marché aux navets*, or rubbish market! It is still held every Sunday from 10am to nightfall all along Boulevard Edgar-Quinet. You will not find rubbish here, but plenty of works by painters, sculptors, ceramicists, and other artists at 'direct' workshop prices.
www.marchecreation.com

Restaurants

B La Cerisaie
A tiny restaurant specialising in regional cooking from southwest France, but don't be deceived by its size! The small dining room has a selective menu of great Basque country classics beautifully executed by the chef, including duck casserole, little ravioli with foie gras, Salers free-range beef and baby lamb.
Menus at €23 and €32.
70 boulevard Edgar-Quinet, 14th.
Tel. : 01-43-20-98-98.

C Ti Jos
You can't miss this *crêperie*, or French pancake restaurant, which dates to the 1930s.
It is considered a Mecca of Breton culture in Paris and is located in the heart of a Breton district. You will find crêpes and buckwheat pancakes as well as other regional specialties. When you have finished enjoying these, you can go downstairs to the Breton pub for a drink and some music. À la carte from €15, menu at €7.60 at lunchtime.
30 rue Delambre, 14th.
Tel.: 01-43-22-57-69.

Previous stations

DUPLEIX
Le Bistrot Dupleix
62 boulevard de Grenelle, 15th.

LA MOTTE-PICQUET GRENELLE
See line 8, page 202

CAMBRONNE
L'Eiffel Café
4 boulevard de Grenelle, 15th.

SÈVRES – LECOURBE
Okafé
2 boulevard Pasteur, 15th.

PASTEUR
Café Le Pasteur
35 boulevard Pasteur, 15th.

MONTPARNASSE-BIENVENÜE
See line 4, page 114

CORVISART

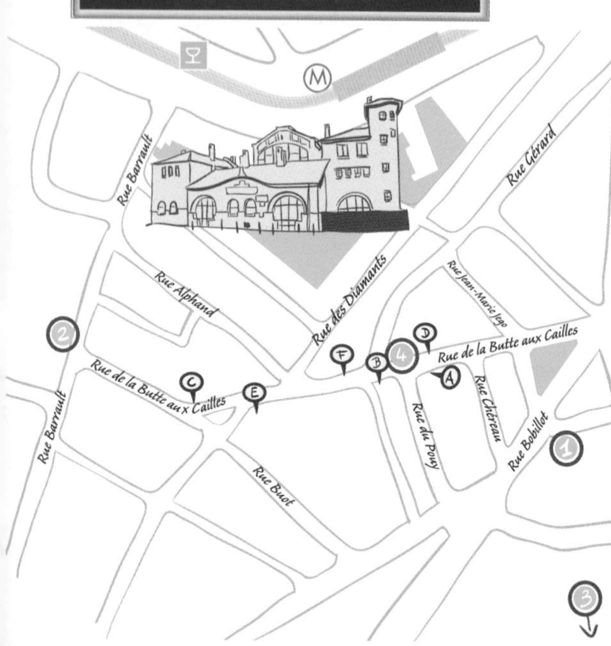

History

The station opened in 1906 and took its name from nearby rue Corvisart, a tribute to Napoleon I's personal physician Jean-Nicolas Corvisart (1755–1821). He was a heart and lung specialist with the grand title of Prime Physician to the Emperor. This is the station you need if you want to visit the Butte-aux-Cailles neighbourhood, a picturesque enclave in the heart of the 13th arrondissement. Butte-aux-Cailles was once a woody, grass-covered hill with a number of windmills on it, overlooking the river Bièvre. The name came from a certain Pierre Caille, who bought the land in 1543 at the same time as a hillside vineyard. It became a poor part of Gentilly, and was annexed to the capital in 1860. It played an important role in the Paris Commune. Later the river Bièvre was covered over and the *butte* or hillock, by then a working class suburb and one of the highest point in Paris, had changed appearance. However, it was impossible to build large heavy buildings here because of the limestone quarries. That proved to be a blessing, for today Butte-aux-Cailles still looks like a picturesque village. It is a popular place to stroll around in and to enjoy the bars and cafés.

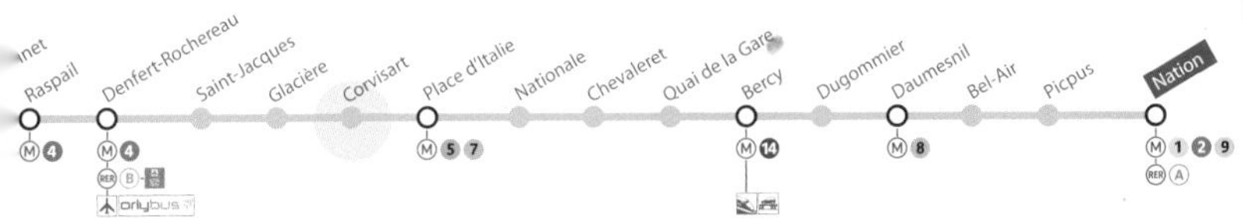

SIGHTSEEING

Monument

1 *Piscine de la Butte-aux-Cailles*
The Butte-aux-Cailles swimming pool was build in 1924, and is one of the oldest in Paris. It has a red brick Art Nouveau façade and a very modernist interior with concrete arches. It also has a solarium and a pubic bath house. It has been a listed historic monument since 31 July 1990, one of only two swimming pools in Paris with that classification.

5 place Paul-Verlaine, 13th.
Tel.: 01-45-89-60-05. Variable opening hours depending on school holidays. Check the opening hours on the municipal website at http://www.mairie13.paris.fr/mairie13/jsp/site/Portal.jsp?page_id=602. Entrance fee.

A walk in the city

2 *Working Class Housing (Petite Russie, Petite Alsace)* : when you leave the metro station take rue Bobillot and then rue Simonet to join rue des Cinq-Diamants which is the main street in the neighbourhood. You can take the streets that meander around the northern part of rue de la Butte-aux-Cailles, and stop in Square Brassaï. From the entrance to Passage Sigaud, you will see a row of houses known as Petite Russie (little Russia) that were built in 1920 to house Russians fleeing the Bolshevik revolution. Continue along rue Barrault until you reach another row of houses known as Petite Alsace (little Alsace) on rue Daviel. These pretty beamed houses were built as social housing in the 1910s. Opposite is Villa Daviel a private street with pretty brick houses and gardens.

3 *Garden Cities around the Butte-aux-Cailles:* on the other side of rue de Tolbiac, the bucolic Butte-aux-Cailles enclave continues in the middle of the rather dour 13th arrondissement. Follow rue du Moulin des Prés until you reach Square des Peupliers, and then walk along the pretty millstone houses along rue Henri-Pape. If you then join rue Dieulafoy you will find yourself in one of the garden cities, a utopic 1920s concept by the architect Jean Walter, who dreamed of reconciling the city with the countryside. Linger here a while before heading west to another of these called Cité Florale, where you will find a maze of streets with plant names, such as rue des Glycines (wisteria street), rue des Liserons (bindweed street) and so on.

4 *Rue de la Butte-aux-Cailles*
The windmills that used to stand here have long gone, but the charm remains. Lined with low buildings and criss-crossed with small streets, this area is full of neighbourhood bars and restaurants. The fountain on Place Paul-Verlaine still provides the inhabitants with excellent spring water today.

Address book

The place for a rendezvous

Havane Café
70 bis boulevard Auguste-Blanqui, 13th.
Open daily 6.30am to midnight.
Tel.: 01-43-37-48-64.

Shopping

A Mon Œil
An original neighbourhood needs to be viewed through original eyewear! This unique and unusual optician sells retro, stylised, classic and vintage spectacle frames.
7 rue de la Butte-aux-Cailles, 13th.
Tel.: 01-45-65-29-19.
Open Monday 5pm to 8pm, Tuesday to Friday 10.30am to 2pm and 3.30pm to 8pm, Saturday 10.30am to 1.30pm and 2.30pm to 8pm.

Out on the town

B Le Merle moqueur
You don't need to be an expert to recognize an institution when you see one! Locals and others wanting a drink flock to this warm and lively bar with its exotic décor and 1980s music.
11 rue de la Butte-aux-Cailles, 13th.

C La Folie en Tête
This popular neighbourhood bar is a traditional stopping point. Away from the capital's trendy hotspots, regulars come to

enjoy the good-natured atmosphere, world music, rock and jazz, and drinks that don't make too big a dent in your purse. The barman's specialty is a 'Caïpi-Fresh' rum punch with fresh fruit.
33 rue de la Butte-aux-Cailles, 13th.
Tel.: 01-45-80-65-99.
Open Monday to Saturday 5pm to 2am, Sunday 6pm to midnight.

Restaurants

D Le Temps des Cerises

This is pure Paris of yesteryear, a world without mobile phones, reminiscent of workers solidarity and good, simple nosh! Le Temps des Cerises reflects the neighbourhood it stands in: no-nonsense and dashed good. An informal restaurant where you can clink glasses around good basic French fare. About €15–25.
18 rue de la Butte-aux-Cailles, 13th.
Tel.: 01-45-89-69-48.
Open Monday to Friday noon to 2.30pm and 7pm to 11.45pm.

E Les Cailloux

Lovers of Italian food living on the Butte are well set up with Les Cailloux. The owner and his family never skimp on good, authentic products, straight from Italy. The restaurant specialises in northern Italian cooking, mostly from Florence, in a sober and elegant setting. À la carte €45-50, lunch menus as €13.50 and €17.50.
58 rue des Cinq Diamants, 13th.
Tel.: 01-45-80-15-08.

F Chez Paul

It anyone mentions gastronomy in the Butte-aux-Cailles neighbourhood, this is what they mean! Whether the delicious *pot-au-feu* (boiled beef and vegetables), or home-roasted suckling pig with sage, the food here is good and copious and there is plenty of atmosphere to boot. It you feel like it, try out the 'happy hour' as French grandmothers once knew it, with the *apéritifs* of the time, such as the wine drink mixed with Lillet, a plant and spice-based drink called Claquescin, Anis (made from aniseed) and Port. Cheers! À la carte €25–50.
22 rue de la Butte-aux-Cailles, 13th.
Tel.: 01-45-89-22-11.
Open daily from noon to 2.30pm and 7.30pm to 11pm, Sunday noon to 3pm.

Previous stations

RASPAIL

See line 4, page 118

DENFERT-ROCHEREAU

See line 4, page 120

SAINT-JACQUES

Café Caramel
41 boulevard Saint-Jacques, 14th.

GLACIÈRE

Les Échos du Monde
9 rue Vulpian, 13th.

Next stations

PLACE D'ITALIE

See line 5, page 140

NATIONALE

À la Halte des Taxis
132 boulevard Vincent-Auriol, 13th.

CHEVALERET

La Nouvelle Gare
49 boulevard Vincent-Auriol, 13th.

QUAI DE LA GARE

Le Café Gourmand
190 avenue de France, 13th.

BERCY

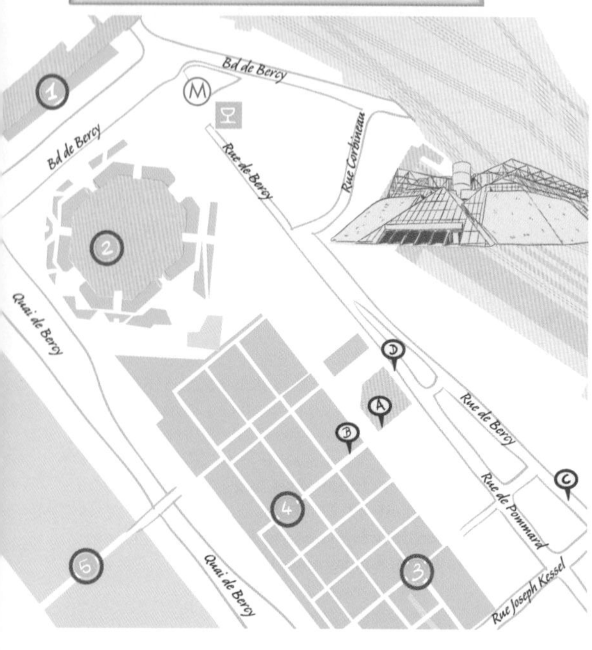

© Gilles Alligon / RATP

History

Bercy station is right in the heart of the Bercy neighbourhood, from which it gets its name. A small hamlet in the Middle Ages, Bercy became a fiefdom over the years and acquired a magnificent chateau in a vast estate. The commune of Bercy was attached to Paris 1860 and the chateau destroyed soon after. The metro station opened in 1909 on the right bank of the Seine, next to a stone bridge built in 1864. The bridge was widened to bear the load of the metro and the 171 metre (561 feet) long metro viaduct was reinforced with a metal roadway and decorated with 41 arches to reflect its original style. Since the bridge was enlarged again in the early 1990s, the metro viaduct is now in the centre of the wider bridge. Bercy station was connected to line 14 when the line opened on 15 October 1998.

SIGHTSEEING

Architecture

❶ ***Ministère de l'Économie et des Finances:*** the Ministry of Economy and Finance was housed in the Richelieu wing of the Louvre palace until 1988, when it moved to this new building designed by Paul Chemetov and Borja Hui-

dobro. This gigantic complex with a surface area of 230,000 m^2 (2,475,699 square feet) has set the tone for the new Bercy neighbourhood. Inspired by the nearby Bercy viaduct, the two architects designed two 72 metre (236 feet) high arches, the one plunging into the Seine above Quai de Bercy (the Bercy embankment) and the other above rue de Bercy, and connected by a succession of 32 metre (105 feet) arches. The buildings were designed to give rise to a new district and are arranged around a number of streets, galleries, terraces, patios, fountains and gardens.
139 rue de Bercy, 12th.

2 Palais Omnisport de Bercy: this sport stadium was inaugurated on 3 February 1984 by Jacques Chirac, then Mayor of Paris, and marked the beginning of the development of eastern Paris. It is an enormous covered area of 55,000 m^2 (592,015 square feet), and the name *'omnisport'* is only part of it, since it is known as much

for it massive concerts as for its sporting events. The space is flexible and can seat between 3,500 and 17,000 people. The outside resembles a lawn-covered pyramid.
8 boulevard de Bercy, 12th.
Tel.: 01-40-02-60-60.

A walk in the park

3 Parc de Bercy: for some people Bercy Park is a sports ground, and for others a place to rest and stroll. Either way, these 14 hectares (35 acres) of greenery count among the great Parisian parks. There are three connected gardens with different atmospheres. The Jardin Romantique or romantic garden, which has ponds with goldfish and lotuses, is by Bercy-Village and is the most bucolic of the three. The Parterres (flower-beds) Garden is accessed by a footbridge, and devoted to plants and gardening, with an educational kitchen gardens for school children, trimmed hedges, flowers, etc. The Prairies close to the Palais Omnisport stadium comprises tree-lined stretches of grass for the more athletic members of the public.

4 **Jardins Yitzhak Rabin:** if you feel like a little peace and quiet, take a few minutes to stroll around these gardens devoted to the memory of Yitzhak Rabin, the Israeli Prime Minister and peace advocate, who was assassinated in 1995. Fruit trees, water features and vines grow peacefully in this area between rue Paul-Belmondo, rue Joseph-Kessel and Place Leonard-Bernstein.

5 **Passerelle Simone de Beauvoir**
Inaugurated in 2006, the footbridge that connects Bercy Park with the Grande Bibliothèque (the big library) is very different from the other footbridges in Paris. This is the 37th Parisian bridge and its contemporary and poetic design is by the Austrian architect Dietmar Feichtinger. It is reserved for 'soft' means of transport, meaning pedestrians and cyclists, and is located between the Bercy and Tolbiac bridges.

Access on the Right Bank via Quai de Bercy and on the Left Bank via Quai de la Gare.

Address book

The place for a rendezvous

Le Bercy
118 rue de Bercy, 12th.
Open Monday to Friday 6am to midnight, and from 7pm on Saturday and Sunday.
Tel.: 01-43-43-44-29.

Leisure

A Cinémathèque
This building with its daring architecture lies to the northeast of Bercy Park. It is the French Cinémathèque and houses the film archives. It was designed by the world famous architect, Frank O. Gehry, who built the Guggenheim

Museum in Bilbao (Spain) and the Walt Disney Concert Hall in Los Angeles, amongst other things. In this Canadian architect's signature manner, space is broken up and dislocated, while volume and materials are imbricated. The new Cinémathèque was inaugurated in the autumn of 2005, having previously been housed in the Palais de Chaillot, and is very important place for the history of French and World Cinema. You can explore the great themes of cinema history by visiting the collections and exhibitions, and view the great silver screen classics in its film theatres.

51 rue de Bercy, 12th. Tel.: 01-71-19-33-33. www.cinematheque.fr

Films and conferences from Wednesday to Monday. Entrance fee.

Musée de la Cinémathèque: The Cinémathèque Museum is open Monday, and from Wednesday to Saturday noon to 7pm and Sunday 10am to 8pm. Entrance fee. Architectural walking tours are organised at 2pm on the first Sunday of the month to explore the building and the park around it.

Ⓑ Maison du Jardinage

In the middle of the Parterres Garden in Bercy Park, surrounded by fruits, flowers and plants, the Maison du Jardinage (gardening house) provides a haven for all would-be-gardeners. Numerous horticultural workshops are organised all year round, and there is also an exhibition area and a library with works on gardening and the ecology, in addition to workshops for children every Wednesday.

41 rue Paul-Belmondo, 12th. Tel.: 01-53-46-19-19.

Restaurants

Ⓒ Le Café Cartouche

You have to go down a few steps to get to this café, ensconced between Bercy and Cours Saint-Émilion. It is a good old-fashioned neighbourhood bistro, with a very authentic menu that is easy on the purse. Lunch menus at €14 or €17, à la carte €20–30.

4 rue de Bercy, 12th. Tel.: 01-40-19-09-95.

Ⓓ Le 51

The restaurant in the Cinémathèque plays with shapes and concepts around giant picnic tables both inside and outside on the pleasant terrace. It is a playful, trendy designer restaurant that is part *rôtisserie* part barbecue. Quality take-away food too. À la carte €16–35.

51 rue de Bercy, 12th. Tel.: 01-58-51-10-91.

Next stations

DUGOMMIER

Café le Croq Soleil
3 boulevard de Reuilly, 12th.

DAUMESNIL

Au Va-et-Vient
6 place Félix-Éboué, 12th.

BEL-AIR

Le Bar des Amis
20 rue Louis-Braille, 12th.

PICPUS

Le Rendez-Vous
70 rue du Rendez-Vous, 12th.

NATION

See line 1, page 44

line 7

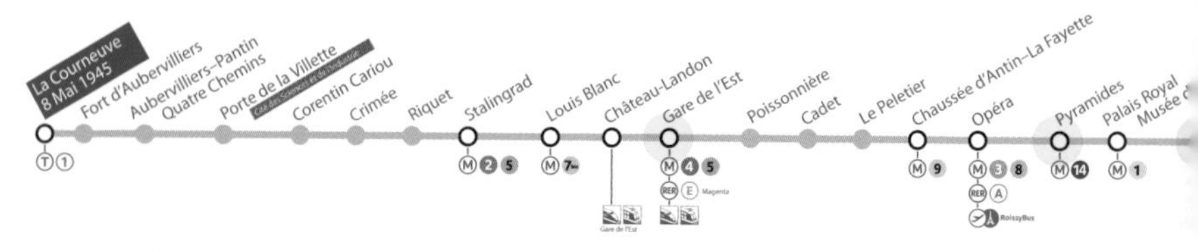

History

Rome wasn't built in a day, and nor were the 18.594 kilometres (11.55 miles) of this line, which took 70 years to complete. Line 7 curves across the capital from the north-east to the south-east, with 38 stops on its sinuous route—a record. In 1910 the first section from Porte de la Villette to Opéra came into service. Six years later, during the First World War, the line was extended from Opéra to Palais Royal. The station was given a simple surface coating since earthenware tiles were in short supply because of the war. The line was only extended south-east to Pont Marie in 1926, and this section had to be made more sinuous than the rest so as to go around the Louvre. In 1931 the line crossed the Seine, a technical and human achievement, and was extended all the way to Porte d'Ivry. Like line 13, line 7 had a branch line at Louis Blanc, but this was closed in 1967 and replaced by an autonomous line 7bis that runs from Louis Blanc to Pré Saint-Gervais. In 1982 a decision was taken to build a second branch line in the southern part of the line, from Maison Blanche to the inner suburbs beyond.

La Courneuve / Mairie d'Ivry / Villejuif – Louis Aragon

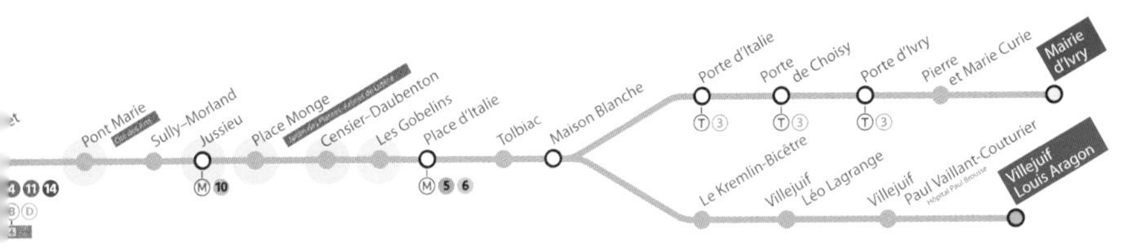

GARE DE L'EST

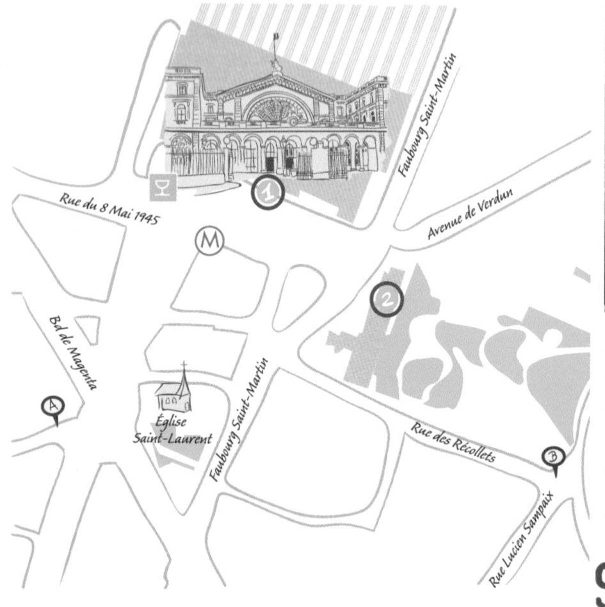

History

This metro station was dug under Gare de l'Est, so it has almost the same name–Gare-de-l'Est-Verdun. The industrial, working class neighbourhood around it used to house noisy tanning and paper-making workshops next to the Saint-Martin Canal. Nowadays people come to stroll alongside the canal and in the neighbouring streets with their car-unfriendly speed bumps. A major renovation of Gare de l'Est and its metro station to spruce them up for passengers arriving on the new TGV Est, the high-speed train line east to Strasbourg and Germany, was completed in 2007. On the platforms of both line 5 and line 7, orange tiles were replaced with white tiles, and Parisine typography, created for the RATP in 1996 by graphic artist Jean François Porchez, replaced the previous Motte typography.

SIGHTSEEIN

A walk through history

1 **Gare de l'Est:** at the top of the ornate western facade is a remarkable statue by sculptor Philippe Joseph Henri Lemaire that symbolises the town of Strasbourg. The eastern end of the station has a statue by sculptor Varenne personifying Verdun. The Alsace-style *brasseries* around the station show that this is the first refuge for travellers arriving from the east of France. The station was nicknamed the *'Château des courants d'air'* ('drafty palace') by poet Jacques Réda. In its icy but majestic hall with its immense glass roof you can see a fresco by American painter Albert Herter (1926) depicting conscripts leaving for the front during the First World War. .

Rue du 8-mai-1945, 10th.

Couvent des Récollets: dating from the 17th and 18th centuries, the building has served as a convent, a barracks and an austere hospice, and Napoléon III requisitioned it for a military hospital. Located near both Gare de l'Est and Gare du Nord on Canal Saint-Martin, it was put to heavy use during both World Wars. Nowadays it is an international residence for artists and researchers, with over 160 artists and authors from more than 80 countries using it as a base. Inquisitive visitors can wander in the splendid cloister. When you leave, look up to see the commemorative plates on the walls. Nearby, between rue de Paradis and rue de la Fidélité, runs the aptly-named Passage du Désir.
148 rue du Faubourg-Saint-Martin, 10th.

Address book

The place for a rendezvous

Brasserie Flo
4 rue du 8-mai-1945, 10th
Open daily 6.30am to 11.30pm.
Tel: 01-42-05-79-54.

Restaurants

Ⓐ La Fidélité
This restaurant has become an essential haunt for Parisian night owls. You will love its magic feel. It has an incredibly high ceiling with mouldings, a *fin-de-siècle* immaculate white decor, red leather benches and a basement with a vaulted ceiling and subdued lighting. À la carte, simple and classical dishes straight out of a guide to French bistro gastronomy.
Menus €26–34.
12 rue de la Fidélité, 10th.
Tel.: 01-47-70-19-34.
Open Monday to Saturday 8pm to 1am.

Ⓑ L'Atmosphère
You will love the intimate atmosphere of this little corner café opposite Canal Saint-Martin. The Hôtel du Nord of the eponymous 1938 film with actress Arletty is just nearby. The restaurant takes its name from Arletty's famous line: 'Atmosphere, atmosphere, do I look like I do atmosphere?'.
Main courses €11.
49 rue des Sampaix, 10th.
Tel.: 01-40-38-09-21.
Open daily 9.30am to 2am, restaurant open noon to 3.30pm and 7pm to 11pm.

Previous stations

STALINGRAD
See line 2, page 60

LOUIS BLANC
Café Le Cristal
35 rue Louis-Blanc, 10th.

CHÂTEAU-LANDON
Le Château-Landon
185 rue du Fbg-Saint-Martin, 10th.

PYRAMIDES

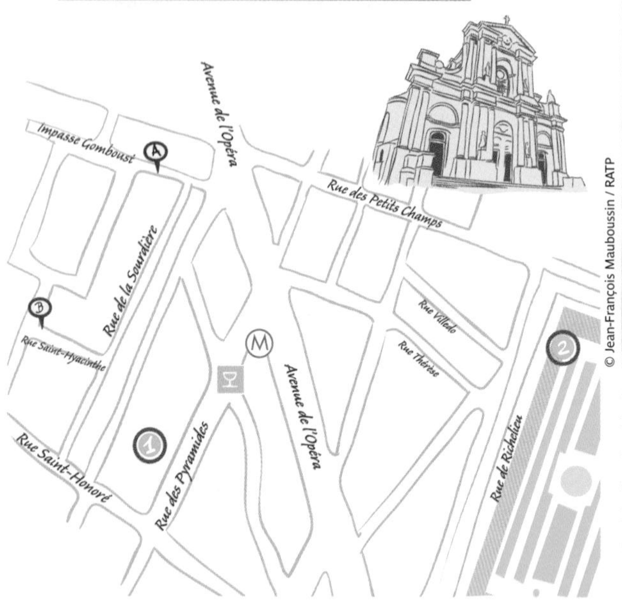

© Jean-François Mauboussin / RATP

History

The station, which opened in 1916, is named after the Battle of the Pyramids in which Napoléon Bonaparte's Army of the Orient beat back Mourad Bey's Mameluks in 1798. This opened the Cairo road to Bonaparte, and he arrived there on July 24, a young, impetuous general who wanted to unravel the mystery of this desert empire. He ordered archaeological investigations and set up the venerable French Institute in Cairo. Both Egyptian and rail references can be seen in a piece of artwork by artist Jacques Tissinier on the platform of line 14 called *Tissignalisation n°14*. It is made of 1,000 steel discs, each with a sheet of coloured papyrus in red, white, blue and orange.

SIGHTSEEING

Architecture

1 **Église Saint-Roch:** Louis XIV and Anne of Austria in 1653 laid the first stone for this vast religious edifice designed by architect and engineer Jacques Le Mercier. There were many bitter fights in its forecourt during the Royalist insurrection of 1795, and its walls still bear the scars of these conflicts—they are full of holes. The Church of Saint-Roch, the parish for artists, is famous for its unparalleled acoustics. Tragedian Pierre Corneille, landscape architect André Le Nôtre and philosopher Denis Diderot were buried here.
296 rue Saint-Honoré, 1st.

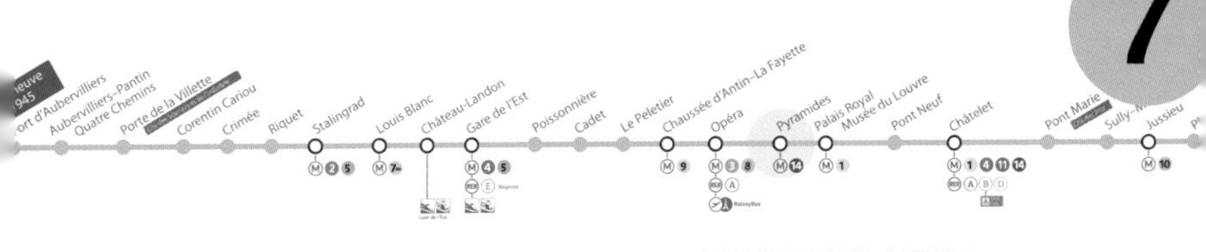

Théâtre du Palais-Royal: Molière and his theatre company played in this theatre, which was built for Cardinal Richelieu, from 1662 to 1673. When Molière died, his friend, the composer Jean-Baptiste Lully, sent the company away and took over the theatre for his own Royal Academy of Music. Paul Sédille, known for his design for rebuilding Printemps department store, also designed the theatre's spectacular outdoor stairway, which is made of iron covered with mosaics and dates from 1880. Go inside to savour the carmine red and gilt decor and a sculpture by Jules Dalou.
38 rue de Montpensier, 1st.

Address book

The place for a rendezvous

Bistrot Pyramide
20 rue des Pyramides, 1st.
Open Monday to Friday 8am to 2am, and from noon on weekends.
Tel.: 01-42-60-47-66.

Restaurants

Ⓐ Le Bistrot Saint-Honoré
Take a stroll in the Marché Saint-Honoré area to see the impressive glass building designed by Richard Bofill for bank BNP Paribas's offices there. Then you will be ready to sit down in this cute little bistro with its delicious Burgundy cuisine.
Menus €29–35.
10 rue Gomboust, 1st.
Tel.: 01-42-61-77-78.

Ⓑ Le Rubis
This place is an institution that takes you back in time to a long lost Paris. Give in to the charm of its tiled interior and boisterous atmosphere and plunge into the past with a seat at the zinc bar and a glass of Bordeaux.
Dish of the day from €11.
10 rue du Marché-Saint-Honoré, 1st.
Tel.: 01-42-61-03-34.

Previous stations

CHAUSSÉE D'ANTIN – LA FAYETTE
See line 9, page 258

OPÉRA
See line 3, page 76

Next station

PALAIS ROYAL – MUSÉE DU LOUVRE
See line 1, page 26

PONT NEUF

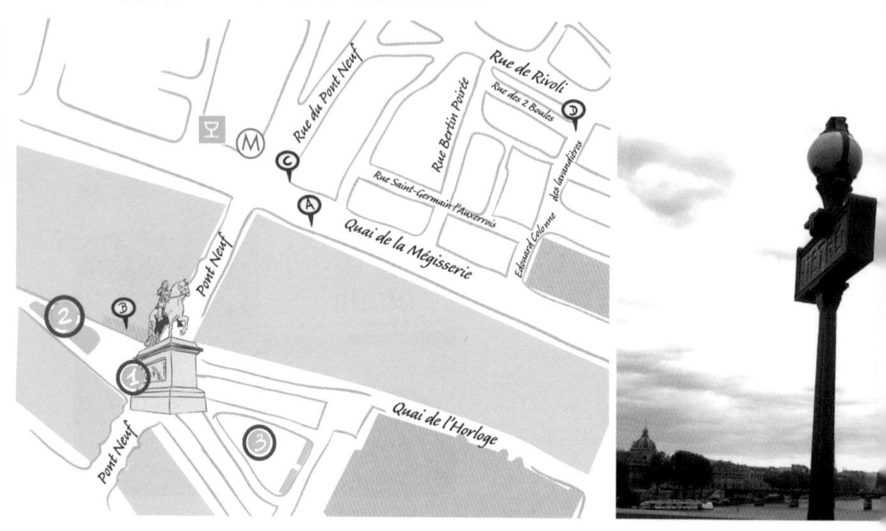

History

This station is right next to the bridge of the same name and was opened in 1926. It is also next to La Samaritaine department store, named after one of the bridge's water pumps, which has a curious interior decoration–there are coins stuck on its walls in a reference to the neoclassical Hôtel de la Monnaie, headquarters of the National Mint, which faces it from the Left Bank.
The station is practically a museum in its own right, with its two showcases exhibiting real coins. Outdoors, second-hand booksellers still set up shop on the pavement, as they have since just after the bridge was completed in 1607. Although its name means 'brand new bridge', it is in fact the oldest bridge in Paris. During the ceremony for the start of building work in 1578, Henri III was weeping openly, as he was in mourning for his two favourites who had just killed each other in a duel. As a result it was called the Pont des Pleurs, or the Bridge of Tears, for some time afterwards. It was a lively, bustling thoroughfare where people would gather to see the street vendors and players performing songs or eating fire. It has distinctive half-moon recesses designed by Pierre Desilles and Androuet du Cerceau, and was the first Paris bridge to be built without houses. Now it serves as a base for some of the river cruises along the Seine.

SIGHTSEEING

walk through history

Equestrian statue of Henri IV

The king's wife, Marie de Médicis, commissioned the original statue from sculptor Giambologna in 1604. It was cast in Italy, but the boat carrying it was shipwrecked off Sardinia, and the statue had to be recovered from the depths. It only arrived in Paris in 1614, and Henri IV had died in 1610. It was destroyed during the Revolution, but Louis XVIII, who reigned from 1814 to 1824, commissioned François Frédéric Lemot to make a bronze replica. The replica was so heavy that horses and oxen were unable to erect it, and the common people combined their efforts to erect the statue. Victor Hugo wrote of this episode: 'Dragged by a thousand arms, this heavy colossus rolls on [...], an entire people has dedicated this bronze to your memory [...].' But the story of the statue does not stop there. Tradition demands that boxes containing a written account of the event, the list of subscribers and a few of the main achievements of the person depicted be inserted in any statue. So there should have been four cedar boxes in Henri IV's horse. But when the statue was restored in 2004, seven boxes were discovered. They included a magnificent work in blue Moroccan leather trimmed with lace called *'La Henriade'*, which Voltaire wrote as a tribute to the king. .

Place du Pont-Neuf, 1st.

② **Square du Vert-Galant:** Henri IV was nicknamed the *'Vert-Galant'*, meaning a ladies' man, because of his active love-life even into his advanced years. The equestrian statue of the king stares down from the bridge over the square's lawns. First there was a bathhouse under the square's willows and linden trees, then a café where concerts were held. Today lovers walk hand in hand along its pathways. It has one of the best views of the Hôtel de la Monnaie and the Louvre.

③ **Place Dauphine:** In 1584 Henri III decided to divide the land at the tip of Île de la Cité into plots to raise money to build the Pont-Neuf. Three islands had to be made into one. When Henri IV took over the project in 1601, he established a triangular space called 'Dauphine', in honour of the Dauphin or heir to the throne, the future King Louis XIII. Then he sold the land to the president of the Paris Parliament, Achille de Harlay, who was given the task of building a group of residences in the style of Place Royale. De Harlay did exactly that. The land was sold in 12 lots and 32 identical residences and arcades were laid out around the triangular, enclosed space, each in white stone and brick with slate roofs. The two surviving corner houses at the apex of the triangle are worth a look.

Address book

The place for a rendezvous

Café du Pont Neuf
14 quai du Louvre, 1st.
Ouvert tous les jours, de 7h30 à minuit.
Tel.: 01-42-33-32-37.

Shopping

Ⓐ Booksellers

They came to ply their wares on Quai de la Mégisserie as soon as the Pont-Neuf was finished. At the time books were only accessible to the elite and cost a fortune, but gradually the business of selling second-hand books developed. The concentration of booksellers here allowed the authorities to ensure that no illicit writings were being sold when censorship was still in force. The booksellers gradually took over from the tanners whose trade used to dominate here. There are 217 booksellers along the Seine today, on both the Left and Right Banks.

Quai de la Mégisserie, 1st.

Out on the river

Ⓑ Bateaux-Vedettes du Pont-Neuf

How about a ride on a *bateau-mouche*, the famous Paris sightseeing river boats? It may be a bit clichéd but can also be romantic. This trip on the river will take you back in time into Paris's unique magic. Price €13 (€6 for children under 6).

Embarcadère du square du Vert-Galant, 1st.
Tel: 01-46-33-98-38.
www.vedettesdupontneuf.fr

Restaurants

Ⓒ Kong

This restaurant spread over two floors was decorated by designer Philippe Starck and is known for its trendy atmosphere and affordable prices. On the menu are French dishes given an Asian slant. Its Plexiglas chairs and fluorescent bar with wicked cocktails transport you to places like New York, Hong-Kong or some other great international metropolis. But there is a wonderful view over the Seine to remind you that you are in fact in Paris, the City of Light. À la carte €35 – 60.

1 rue du Pont-Neuf, 1st.
Tel.: 01-40-39-09-00.
www.kong.fr

Ⓓ Au Vieux Comptoir

Situated at the 'Sainte-Opportune' exit from Châtelet station, this bistro is reputed for its friendly, convivial atmosphere and the simple but delicious dishes it serves.

A useful stop for shopaholics visiting the shops on rue de Rivoli to rest their feet. Midday menu €13.

17 rue des Lavandières, 1st.
Tel.: 01-45-08-53-08.
www.au-vieux-comptoir.com

Next station

CHÂTELET

See line 1, page 32

PONT MARIE

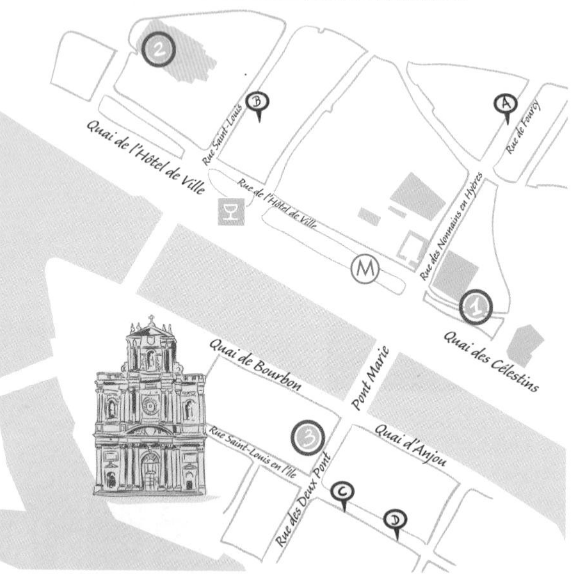

© Denis Sutton / RATP

History

This station opened in 1926 and was named after the bridge where it is located. Pont Marie itself, which links the Right Bank at Hôtel de Ville to Île Saint-Louis, is named after Christophe Marie, the engineer who designed it. Building began in 1614 and was completed in 1635. Initially houses were built on the bridge, but in 1788 the authorities outlawed this because of the danger to life and limb. There had been numerous fatal accidents, as in 1658, when nearly 20 houses were swept away when the river broke its banks, killing dozens of people. The bridge is situated on Quai des Célestins in the Saint-Gervais quarter. The roads twist and turn here, leaving no doubt as to their medieval origins. In 1254 Saint Louis established a Carmelite priory, and the monks were nicknamed '*les barrés*' because of their habits' black and white stripes. The Carmelites later wanted to be closer to the university and so they moved to the Left Bank, near the present-day Place Maubert, selling the priory on the Right Bank in 1319. In 1352 the buyer's son donated the priory to the Célestins, a Benedictine order founded by Pierre de Morrone, a hermit who took the name Célestin V when he became pope in 1294. Paris owes far more than this bridge to Christophe Marie. He initiated all the

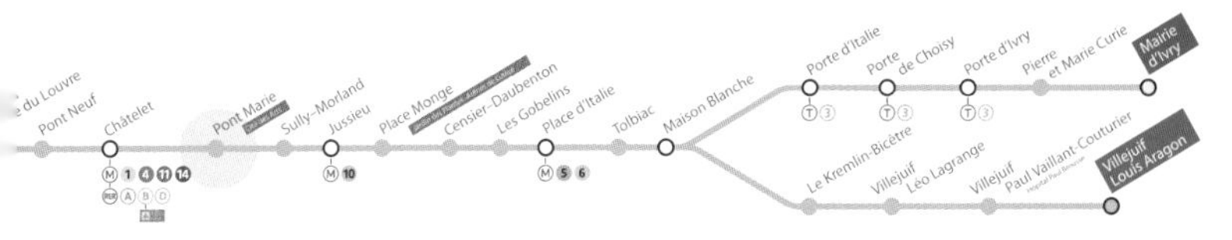

work on the Île Saint-Louis, including giving it two stone bridges to facilitate access to the island, and magnificent riverside thoroughfares. To this day, Île Saint-Louis represents the embryonic Paris from which the City of Light grew in the minds of Parisians. It is a timeless place, both accessible yet distant, a magnificent island that has kept all its historical charm.

SIGHTSEEING

chitecture

Hôtel de Sens: this former fortress is a rare remnant of medieval Paris, as can be seen in its corner turrets with corbelling, its flamboyant porch and its dungeon whose gatehouse has a machicolation, a floor opening allowing people inside to drop stones on attackers. This was where Cardinal Antoine Duprat held the meeting of the Council of Sens in 1528 which designated Lutherian theology as a heresy. Queen Margot, the ex-wife of Henri IV known for her eccentricity and lavish tastes, came to live here a few years after she was repudiated by the king. The building was used as an office for stagecoaches from Franche-Comté in the 18th century and a factory making Saint-James jams in the 19th century. In 1940 it was given a neoclassical look by architect Charles Halley. Today it houses a library dedicated to the decorative arts.

1 rue du Figuier, 4th.

2 **Église Saint-Gervais-Saint-protais:** the church was erected on the site of a 6th century chapel which had

served as a refuge for a small village of fishermen and boatmen, its walls protecting them from Viking invasions. Building of the church began towards the end of the 15th century, and it ended up as a remarkable mix of artistic styles. The delicate Gothic style of the nave, built by kings' architect Pierre Chambiges, is a curious contrast with the bold classical façade designed by 17th century architect Salomon de Brosse. Inside, 16th century stained-glass windows depict *The Wisdom of Solomon*, while in the centre of the Chapel of the Virgin is a remarkable, ornate keystone. The organs date from 1628 and are the oldest in Paris. A musical dynasty, the Couperins, were organists here from father to son for eight generations.
Place Saint-Gervais, 4th.

3 **Île Saint-Louis:** it would take pages to describe all the splendours of this island. Originally it was a verdant pasture which was regularly flooded by the river. In 1614, Christophe Marie was given the task of meticulously converting the island into a fashionable enclave for Parisians. Its grand town houses are splendid in bold cut stone, and on rue Saint-Louis-en-l'Île, the facades adorned in places with delicate sculptures. The Hôtel de Lauzun at 17 quai d'Anjou has wrought-iron balconies and ornate drainpipes. It was the headquarters of the Club des Haschischins, or the Hashish Club, which was dedicated to drug-induced experiments and counted Baudelaire, Balzac and Gautier among its regulars. On Quai de Bourbon a bargeman's cabaret would delight the crowd at the Franc-Pinot bar, now a jazz club. The immaculate white interior of the baroque church of Saint-Louis-en-l'Île sets off the gilded angels that adorn it.

Address book

The place for a rendezvous

Brasserie du Pont Louis-Philippe
66 quai de l'Hôtel-de-Ville, 4th.
Open daily 10.30am to 2am.
Tel.: 01-42-72-29-42.

Culture

A Maison Européenne de la Photographie
The permanent photographic exhibition in this grand 18th century town house contains

20,000 works, including by Raymond Depardon, William Klein and Sebastião Salgado. There are also temporary exhibitions of old or contemporary photographs. There is also a charming café where you can relax.

5-7 rue de Fourcy, 4th.
Tel.: 01-44-78-75-00.
www.mep-fr.org
Open Wednesday to Sunday 11am to 8pm.
Entrance fee, except on Wednesdays after 5pm.

Ⓑ Mémorial de la Shoah

The Holocaust Memorial serves as a museum, a resource centre and a meeting place. The 'Wall of Names' in its courtyard carries the surnames of 76,000 Jews who were deported from France to the Nazi concentration camps. There is also a 'Wall of the Just' which pays tribute to those who courageously saved Jews during the Nazi occupation of France. This is Europe's biggest research centre on the Holocaust thanks to its library and its archives, including Gestapo documents.

17 rue Geoffroy-l'Asnier, 4th.
Tel.: 01-42-77-44-72.
www.memorialdelashoah.org
Open Sunday to Friday 10am to 6pm and until 10pm on Thursdays.

Shopping

Ⓒ Berthillon

Cross the river on Pont Marie to explore the Île Saint-Louis with its numerous town houses, and taste the delicious ice-cream made using the recipes of its founder, Monsieur Berthillon. The owner of a *café-hôtel,* he embarked on making ice cream in 1954. The Maison Berthillon has become an institution in Paris.

31 rue Saint-Louis-en-l'Île, 4th.
Tel.: 01-43-54-31-61. www.berthillon.fr
Open Wednesday to Sunday 10am to 8pm.

Ⓓ La Charlotte de l'Isle

This wonderful place is both a tea room and a chocolate shop. It's an ideal place to discover your inner child. You can choose from many kinds of tea—sweet, sour, light, bitter, smoked or scented—and enjoy them in peace. Or you can give in to the tempting odour of hot chocolate, under the gaze of the witches on broomsticks which form part of its eccentric decor.

24 rue Saint-Louis-en-l'Île, 4th.
Tel.: 01-43-54-25-83.
www.lacharlottedelisle.fr.
Open Thursday to Sunday 2.30pm to 7.30pm.

Next station

SULLY-MORLAND

Le Sully
6 boulevard Henri-IV, 4th.

JUSSIEU

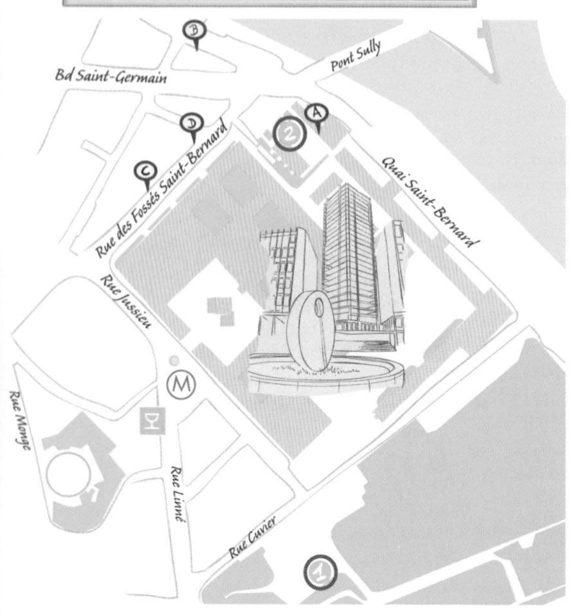

© Denis Sutton / RATP

History

This station opened in 1931 with the name Jussieu-Halle-aux-Vins because of the wine market set up by Napoleon Bonaparte here. This was shortened to simply Jussieu once the market had disappeared. When it was set up in 1622, alcohol consumption was growing in the capital, and the market was to meet this rising demand. But despite its impressive storage capacity, it soon became too small. It has to be said that during the 19th century, there was a phenomenal increase in the volume of wine transported by sea, river and rail from all over France and later from Algeria. The Jussieu university campus was built in 1957 on the site of the old wine market. Its main feature is the Zamansky tower, which was closed during the last decade for asbestos removal. Its design is often the butt of ironic comments from professors and students alike because of the unlikely choices made by its architect, Edouard Albert. The campus is named after the illustrious de Jussieu family which produced several renowned botanists from the 17th to 19th century. Of particular note are the three Jussieu brothers Antoine (1686–1758), Bernard (1699–1776) and Joseph (1704–1799), sons of a pharmacist in Lyon. Antoine took over as director of the Jardin des Plantes from Joseph Pitton de Tournefort and set up the Muséum National d'Histoire Naturelle, the Natural History Museum, in collaboration with his brother Bernard. The youngest, Joseph, went on expeditions to South America.

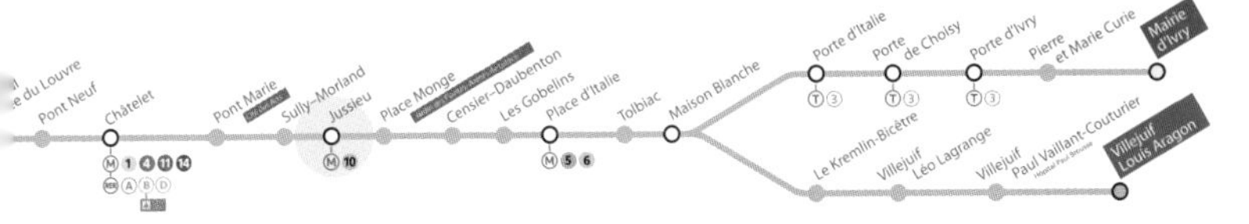

SIGHTSEEING

botanical walk

Jardin des Plantes: Louis XIII decided to create a 'royal garden of medicinal herbs' here in 1633. At first it was used to teach medical students, but was opened to the public in 1640. The Jussieu brothers, both botanists, and naturalist Louis Jean-Marie Daubenton presided over its expansion, and it became a renowned place of science. In 1793, the government during the French Revolution, the National Convention, established it as a national museum. Its galleries were built over the 19th and 20th centuries, and it has exceptional botanical collections. Dahlias are displayed in a French-style garden, a rose garden and an iris garden. There is also an ecological garden inspired by English gardening traditions, and a labyrinth was built in 1640 on an artificial hill for the amusement of visitors. You will see a column a little further along marking Daubenton's sepulchre. The greenhouses were built in 1834 by architect Charles Rohault de Fleury in a perfect harmony of glass and metal, like cathedrals for the plant kingdom. And you must not miss the menagerie, set up here during the Revolution after the royal menagerie was confiscated. Nowadays it has snakes, crocodiles and various colourful animals. Paris was under siege during the Commune of Paris and its people were starving. So they ate the animals, and exotic dishes were served in the capital's smartest restaurants at Christmas. It is worth going to see the orang-utans, they love mimicking people. A good indication that that Man is descended from apes! If you have any doubt about this, visit the Grande Galerie de l'Évolution here.

57 rue Cuvier; 2 rue Buffon;
36 rue Geoffroy-Saint-Hilaire;
place Valhubert, 5th.
www.jardindesplantes.net

Monument

❷ ***L'Institut du Monde Arabe:*** the Arab World Institute is a standard-bearer in Paris for the magnificence of Arab culture. It was built at the initiative of France and 22 Arab countries. Its mission is to promote Arab-Muslim culture and disseminate information about it. Two architects, Jean Nouvel and Pierre Soria, took on the difficult task of creating an edifice to represent the mixing of Western and Oriental cultures. The northern side, facing the centre of Paris, symbolises the West, while the southern face represents the exuberance and voluptuousness of the Orient. It has 240 motor-controlled *moucharabiehs*, machrabiyas, Arabic latticed windows, which open and close in relation to the light falling on them. The 'Tour des Livres' or Book Tower has the spiral shape of the ancient minarets of the East. The place functions as a centre for cultural exchanges. There are temporary exhibitions, a shop and in particular, a bookshop, where you can wander at will. Do not miss the museum either, for the richness of this culture with one-thousand-and-one facets.

1 rue des Fossés-Saint-Bernard, 5th.
www.imarabe.org

Address book

The place for a rendezvous

Le Relais Jussieu
37 rue Linné, 5th.
Open Monday to Friday
7am to 9pm.
Tel.: 01-43-31-61-51.

Restaurants

Ⓐ Le Ziryab

The Arab World Institute's restaurant perched on the rooftops of Paris. You can overlook the capital in an elegant and refined oriental atmosphere. It serves Lebanese specialities delivered by Noura, the Lebanese restaurant chain. A glass of mint tea and a few pastries should get you back on your feet for more sightseeing. À la carte €15 – 30.

1 rue des Fossés-Saint-Bernard, place Mohammet-V, 5th. Tel. : 01-55-42-55-42.

Ⓑ La Tour d'argent

Through the wrought iron gate you can discover this restaurant's version of French luxury and sensuality. It claims to have been founded in 1582 by Rourteau, which would make it the oldest restaurant in France. It offers a magical view over the Seine, Notre-Dame-de-Paris and Île de la Cité. This charm is enhanced by an elegant wood decor, a mind-blowing wine menu and refined dishes. One of these, the restaurant's speciality, is *canard au sang*, or pressed duck, following a recipe devised in the 19th century by its then owner, Frédéric Delair. You will understand why this restaurant has become a symbol of French gastronomy over the centuries. *Dégustation* menu about €160.

15 quai de la Tournelle, 5th.
Tel.: 01-43-54-23-31.
www.latourdargent.com

Ⓒ Moissonnier

The area opposite the Arab World Institute tends to be quiet at night, which is a shame, as you could easily miss the restaurant hidden behind curtained windows. The generosity of the cooking is matched only by the warm welcome from the owners. One you are sitting comfortably on the red bench, you will be served from a trolley of salad dishes from Lyon. Follow this with traditional *quenelles de brochet* (pike dumplings in a creamy sauce) and a light wine for a most pleasant evening. There is a whole army of regulars, so don't be the last in. Menu €20.

28 rue des Fossés-Saint-Bernard, 5th.
Tel.: 01-43-29-87-65.

Ⓓ L'AOC

A colourful bistro using only strictly controlled ingredients from the French countryside. The stars of the place are the terrines and rib of beef near the roasting spit. It's just like traditional family lunches at grandmother's place, a journey down memory lane for some. Menu €21.

14 rue des Fossés-Saint-Bernard, 5th.
Tel.: 01-43-54-22-52.
www.restoaoc.com

PLACE MONGE

© Denis Sutton / RATP

History

The station at Place Monge was opened on 15 February 1930 when line 10 was extended to Place d'Italie, and it became a stop on line 7 a year later. The square after which it is named is dedicated to Gaspard Monge (1746–1818), mathematician and a figure in the French Revolution. He was a specialist in infinitesimal analysis and one of the founders of the elite French schools École Normale Supérieure and École Polytechnique. He was close to Robespierre and was appointed to the Provisional Executive Committee in 1792 with Danton and was minister for the Navy. The painter and poet Charles André Wolf lived at number 4 on this leafy square. On Wednesdays, Fridays and Sundays there is a colourful market here. Opposite it is the Caserne Monge gendarmerie, which is built on the site of a former convent of the Religious Hospitallers of Notre-Dame-de-la-Miséricorde (Our Lady of Mercy). The convent was first set up in the village of Chantilly by Jacques Le Prévost, Lord of Herbelay, north-west of Paris. In February 1656 it was given permission to move to a suburb of Paris on condition that its revenue be used only

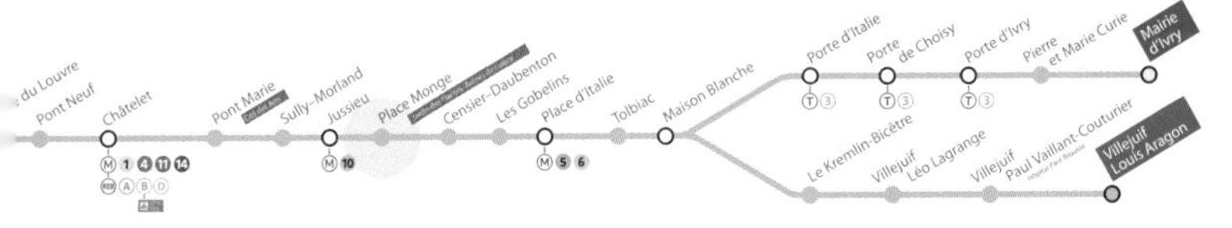

to feed and keep poor and sick women and girls. The convent was closed during the Revolution and it became the headquarters of the 6th company of royal gendarmes in 1821. The building was then renovated in 1840 to house the Municipal Guard, and then the Republican Guard, which carries out missions of honour and security.

SIGHTSEEING

walk through history

Arènes de Lutèce: these remains are to be found in a public square. They date from the end of the 1st century when Paris was called Lutetia, and were discovered while digging a road in 1869. This Gallo-Roman amphitheatre could hold 10,000 people. Fierce battles between gladiators and lions took place here. Much later, there was also a fierce battle to preserve the amphitheatre. It was first saved by a public fund-raising effort in 1917 and again in 1980 by a campaign for defending ancient Paris.

Access at 49 rue Monge, rue des Arènes and square Capitan, 5th.

2 **Rue Mouffetard:** 'as if moored to Mount Sainte-Geneviève, the land of Mouffetard forms a steep, refracting reef against which the powerful waves of the new Paris come and break. I love rue Mouffetard. [...] It is encrusted in the city like a plump parasite. It does not scorn the rest of the globe: it merely ignores it.' It seems author Georges Duhamel (1884–1966) was right. Even though store chains are methodically ousting the small local shops, the area still retains its village spirit. This steep road still follows its medieval route down the side of the hill to the Saint-Médard church. It evokes the memory of a Paris that no longer exists with adjoining street names

like rue de l'Épée-de-Bois, rue du Puits-de-l'Ermite, rue Gracieuse, rue de la Clef or rue Quatrefages. Known affectionately as *'La Mouff'*, the road owes its name to the overpowering smell from the tanneries on the banks of the adjacent Bièvre river, a tributary of the Seine. You can pick out the ancient buildings from their picturesque signs denoting the activity that went on there. For instance, in Place de la Contrescarpe, which was built in 1852, a low relief of two oxen dating from the 18th century can be seen at number 6, which was once a butcher's shop. The Cabaret de la Pomme de Pin has been located at the site of number 1 since the Middle Ages. At 122 rue Mouffetard, the sign *'Bonne Source'* is a reminder that there was a well here dating from the time of Henri IV. Look up at number 134 to see the arabesques of plants and animals on this classified facade from the 17th century. But these are not the only surprises on rue Mouffetard. A real-life treasure was discovered when the building at number 53 was demolished. Louis Nivelle, a king's horseman, advisor and secretary, had buried 3,351 gold coins bearing the head of Louis XV. Legend has it that Henri IV granted permission for the market here as thanks for the crowd saving him when his steed galloped out of control. Follow the flow of passers-by and take this road, keeping your eyes open for fleeting signs of its distant past.

Address book

The place for a rendezvous

Le Bistrot du Marché
75bis rue Monge, 5th.
Open daily 6.30am to 2am.
Tel.: 01-43-31-04-81.

Culture

Ⓐ Théâtre de la Vieille Grille
This is an intimate setting with an interior in padded dark red velvet, run by Anne Quesemand and Laurent Berman. It is a *café-théâtre* located in a former grocery and wine shop on the road that used to lead to the former wine market on Quai des Bernardins. A splendid black-and-gold Bacchus watched over the entrance like a look-out. Famous French performers like singer Jacques Higelin began their careers here.
9 rue Larrey, 5th.
Tel.: 01-47-07-22-11.
www.vieillegrille.fr

Restaurants

Ⓑ Chez Léna et Mimile
This restaurant gets its charm from its terrace, which overlooks a pretty fountain just near the bustling rue Mouffetard. A mixture of French gastronomy and modern molecular cuisine in a bistro decor. Desserts by famous pastry chef Pierre Hermé will delight gourmets. And just listening to the sound of the fountain will make you think just briefly that you must have left Paris. À la carte €25–30.
32 rue Tournefort, 5th.
Tel.: 01-47-07-72-47.
www.chezlenaetmimile.fr.

Ⓒ Le Jardin d'Ivy

A secret garden where lovely flowers decorate a quiet, beautiful courtyard. This adorable restaurant came was born from a love story between an Australian woman and a man from Auvergne. They decided to open a restaurant serving traditional French cuisine. She is a painter, he cooks, and their partnership has created a haven of peace a stone's throw from the incessant hubbub of rue Mouffetard. Decorative candle-holders, subdued lighting, with a soft, elusive atmosphere in the evening. So romantic. Menu from €14.
75 rue Mouffetard, 5th.
Tel.: 01-47-07-19-29.
www.lejardindivy.com

Ⓓ Le Requin Chagrin
This is one of the rare places to have survived the invasion of barbaric bar-lounges on rue Mouffetard. A pleasant bar near Place de la Contrescarpe, it owes its name to a West Indian restaurant that used to be here. In Creole, the term *'requin chagrin'* (literally 'sad shark') designates ladies of the night who are no longer as young as they used to be. You can enjoy 'happy hour' here at the magnificent wooden counter and choose from 11 types of beer.
10 rue Mouffetard, 5th.
Tel.: 01-44-07-23-24.

CENSIER – DAUBENTON

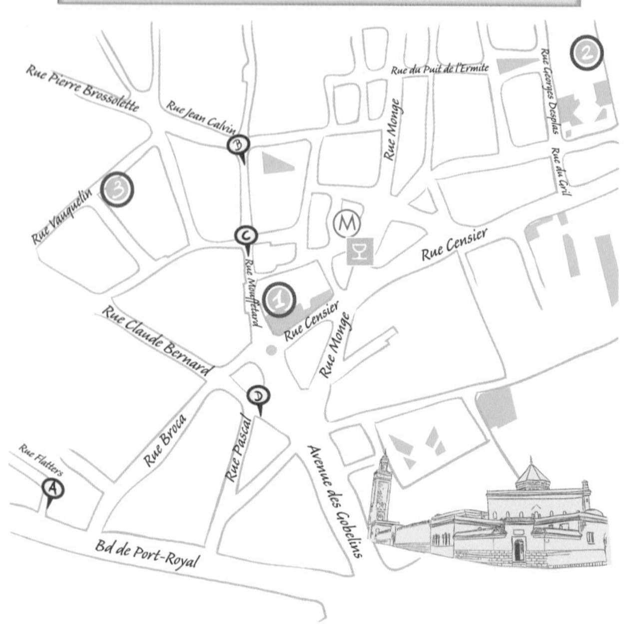

History

This station has been used for an ecological experiment since April 2010. It is the first place in the world to be lit using diodes. It was opened on 15 February 1930 with the lengthy name 'Censier Daubenton Halle-aux-Cuir', which was kept until 1965. The name refers to nearby rue Censier and rue Daubenton, and also to the tanners' market that used to exist along the banks of the nearby river Bièvre. Louis Jean-Marie Daubenton (1716–1800), was appointed keeper and demonstrator of the king's cabinet and became the first director of the Museum of Natural History that was built nearby. A naturalist and doctor, he worked with Georges Louis Leclerc de Buffon on a multi-volume work on natural history in which he detailed nearly 200 species of quadrupeds. His extremely precise descriptions can be considered as the beginning of comparative anatomy. However, he had had to hide his interest in the subject for a long time. His father, Jean Daubenton, sent him to Paris to study theology. When his father died in 1736, he became free to choose his own career, qualified as a medical doctor in 1741 and returned to his native Dijon to practice. But Buffon, a childhood friend, arranged for him to be summoned to become his deputy in the king's garden in 1742. He died on New Year's Eve in 1799 and is buried next to the labyrinth in the Jardin des Plantes.

SIGHTSEEING

walk through history

Église Saint-Médard: this church was built on the site of a chapel during the Wars of Religion in the 15th century, which was a dangerous undertaking. During an outbreak of violence between Catholics and Protestants in 1561 known as 'the tumult of Saint-Médard' it was pillaged by Protestants. In 1784 it was given a Grecian look, which was fashionable at the time. Architect Louis-François Petit-Radel re-carved its columns in a Doric style. During the revolutionary period, Father Dubois, the parish priest, became one of the first religious figures in Paris to swear allegiance during the Civil Constitution of the Clergy in 1790. In the 18th century it was decided to close its cemetery because there had been episodes of collective hysteria at the grave of a Jansenist (a follower of a Christian theological movement) known for his healing powers. A piece of graffiti from the time reads: 'By order of the King, God is forbidden to perform miracles in this place.'

141 rue Mouffetard, 5th.

2 **Mosquée de Paris:** at the inauguration ceremony for building the Paris mosque in 1922, Marshall Hubert Lyautey, former military governor then resident-general of French Morocco, began his speech with these words: 'When the minaret you are about to built is erected, one more prayer will rise towards the beautiful skies of Île-de-France, and the Catholic steeples of Notre-Dame will certainly not be jealous.' The first strokes of the pickaxe rang out and the *mihrab*, the niche that indicates the direction of Mecca, was installed. The mosque was built in memory of Muslims who fell in the trenches of the First World War. Dur-

austere facade built by Albert Philibert Aldroph, an architect for the Paris municipal authority, in 1881. Photographer Eugène Atget immortalised the Jewish village on rue Mouffetard around the beginning of the 20th century, with its Yiddish feel and its caftan-clad pedlars from Poland. This community's peaceable existence was annihilated by the Nazis. Its sanctuary was looted and orphans who had sought refuge in the school grounds were arrested and taken to the camp at Drancy. The scrolls of the Torah were only saved because Paul Langevin, director of ESPCI, who was among the first resistance fighters, took them to safety on the other side of the street. 9 rue Vauquelin, 5th.

ing the Second World War it provided a refuge for hundreds of Jews during the Nazi occupation. Its splendid interior courtyard and patios adorned with mosaics, square-shaped minaret and Hispano-Moresque (Moorish) style make it a peaceful haven and a symbol of fraternity.

2bis place du Puits-de-l'ermite, 5th.

3 **Synagogue de la rue Vauquelin:** this is a short road with no less than three prestigious institutions—symbols of rationality, irrationality and spirituality. At number 10 is a temple to science, the École de Physique et de Chimie Industrielles de la Ville de Paris (ESPCI, Paris School of Industrial Physics and Chemistry), which produced five Nobel Prize winners including Pierre and Marie Curie. At number 15 is the Bibliothèque Sigmund-Freud (Sigmund Freud Library) founded by Princess Marie Bonaparte. And at number 9 is the École Rabbinique de Paris (Paris Rabbinical School), with an

Address book

The place for a rendezvous

Le Comptoir des Arts
100 rue Monge, 5th.
Open daily 7am to 2am.
Tel.: 01-45-35-28-34.

Culture

A Le Petit Musée des Éclairages Anciens
This small museum of ancient lighting is the work of Mr Ara who brings oil lamps,

paraffin lamps and gas lamps back to life in his workshop. A gallery of ancient lamps, flames and butterfly stoves sit beside fringed lamp shades. You will have a magical time here between light and shade, amid the crystal paraffin lamps and ornate ceiling lights from the beginning of the 20th century. Some lamps that have been perfectly renovated are for sale with their original fuel: oil, paraffin or alcohol.

4 rue Flatters, 5th.
Tel.: 01-47-07-63-47.
Admission free.

Ⓑ L'Épée de Bois

This is one of the last art cinemas in the capital, which means its seats are somewhat rickety and you can hear the projector whirring. But that is exactly what puts the soul in this timeless place.

100 rue Mouffetard, 5th.
Tel.: 0892-68-07-52.
www.cinema-epee-de-bois.fr

Out on the town

Ⓒ Le Verre à Pied

You will love this authentic, charming bistro that has not changed since 1914. It is a far cry from the bar-lounges that disfigure rue Mouffetard. A cast-iron stove, cracked tiles and cramped counter give it a warm and welcoming feel. It is more than just a neighbourhood bar, it also holds exhibitions.
Lunch menu €13.50.

118bis rue Mouffetard, 5th.
Tel.: 01-43-31-15-72.

Ⓓ Le Café Léa

With its large picture windows and intimate decor, the atmosphere in this café is friendly, young and female. Café Léa is above all a neighbourhood meeting place where locals and students gather for light salad lunches or a dinner of red mullet in coconut sauce. It's also nice to go there on Sundays for its brunch at €18.

5 rue Claude-Bernard, 5th.
Tel.: 01-43-31-46-30.

LES GOBELINS

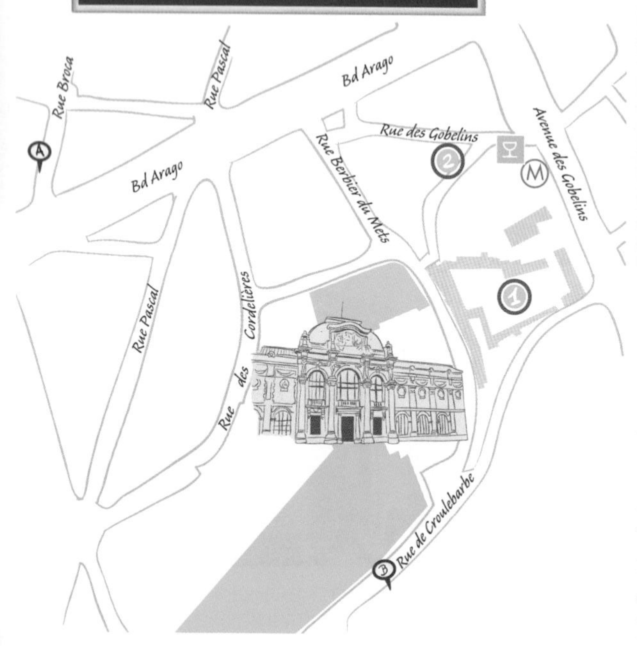

History

This station opened the same day as Censier-Daubenton in 1930 and stands on the border between the 5th and 13th arrondissements. It is named after a factory that has existed since the 15th century on the banks of the Bièvre river, and is near Square René-Le-Gall, which is also known as Jardin des Gobelins. It has a neoclassical style and was built in 1938 by architect Jean-Charles Moreux on the site of a tiny island, the Île aux Singes (Monkey Island), in the middle of the Bièvre. Nowadays a stream runs through the area, and in olden times there were *guinguettes*, popular restaurants and dance halls, and other types of *brasserie* that the factory workers would go to. The square took the name of resistance fighter René Le Gall a short while after the liberation of Paris.

SIGHTSEEING

A walk through history

1 ***La Manufacture des Gobelins:*** in the 15th century, before the Bièvre was covered over, Gilles Gobelin, a dyer by trade, invented a bright red dye made from cochineal. It made him a rich man. Then, in 1662, Jean-Baptiste Colbert, Louis XIV's finance minister, set up a royal factory on the site which had previously only housed a mill. Painters, engravers, cabinet makers and foundry men worked there. Nowadays the factory makes magnificent carpets and tapestries for the palaces of the French Re-

public. La Manufacture des Gobelins acts as a catalyst for know-how and tradition. Some models, however, were designed by contemporary artists like Picasso, and Jean Lurçat, who was instrumental in the revival of contemporary tapestry.

42 avenue des Gobelins, 13th.

Château de la Reine-Blanche

You can see an octagonal tower belonging to a dilapidated 16th century edifice if you look from rue Gustave-Geffroy. There is argument about the origin of its name, as no queen called Blanche ever stayed here. Its existence was unknown for a long time. Legend has it that this is where the 'Bal des Ardents', or the Ball of the Burning Men, took place in 1393. It is said that during the ball, Charles VI lost what little mental capacity he had.

4 rue Gustave-Geffroy, 13th.

Address book

The place for a rendezvous

Café Canon des Gobelins
25 avenue des Gobelins, 13th.
Open daily 7am to 2am.
Tel.: 01-43-36-58-34.

Restaurants

A L'Ourcine
Hidden away on rue Broca, this restaurant has a new menu every day. The chef who runs it formerly worked at gourmet restaurant La Régalade. Unusual dishes include whelks in a mayonnaise sauce, curry with apples, cod roasted with conserved garlic, puréed fennel and saffron potatoes, rice in coconut milk, sesame *tuiles* and Espelette pepper jelly.
Lunch menu €26.
92 rue Broca, 13th.
Tel.: 01-47-07-13-65.

B L'Etchegorry
This Basque restaurant is nearly 80 years old. Its predecessor, Le Cabaret de la Mère Grégoire, was praised by Victor Hugo and Chateaubriand also went there. It is situated near Square René-Le-Gall and is full of provincial charm. Dishes like escalope of foie gras with piperade leave no doubt as to its origins in South-West France.
Lunch menu €18.
41 rue Croulebarbe, 13th.
Tel.: 01-44-08-83-51.
www.etchegorry.com
Open Tuesday to Saturday noon to 2pm and 7pm to 10.30pm.

Next stations

PLACE D'ITALIE
See line 5, page 140

TOLBIAC
Le Canon de Tolbiac
151 rue de Tolbiac, 13th.

MAISON BLANCHE
Le Gandon
19 rue Philibert-Lucot, 13th.

METRO

line 8

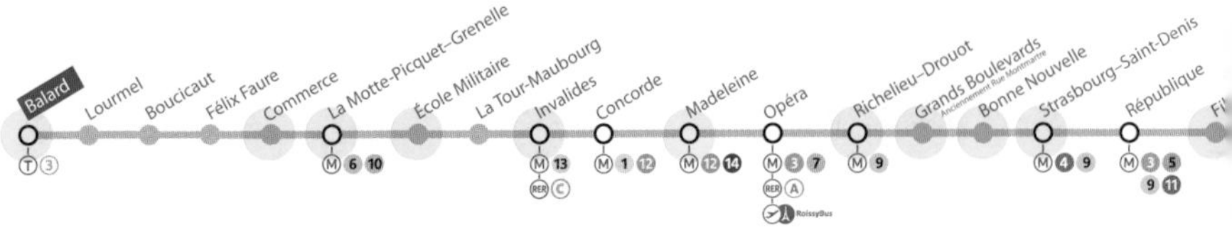

Balard
Lourmel
Boucicaut
Félix Faure
Commerce
La Motte-Picquet–Grenelle
École Militaire
La Tour-Maubourg
Invalides
Concorde
Madeleine
Opéra
Richelieu–Drouot
Grands Boulevards
Anciennement Rue Montmartre
Bonne Nouvelle
Strasbourg-Saint-Denis
République

History

Line 8 of the Paris Metro connects Balard station in the southwest with Créteil–Préfecture in the southeast, crossing the right bank of the Seine on a similar route to line 9. It was the last line to be built under the 1898 concession, its main vocation being to link up Porte d'Auteuil and Opéra. The first section opened in December 1913. The route was altered in the 1930s since the western section was being covered by line 10. Today the line goes right up to suburban Créteil, the main city of one of the more recent Île-de-France departments. One of its special features is that it crosses two rivers: the Seine underground between Concorde and Madeleine, and the Marne above ground between Charenton – Écoles and École Vétérinaire de Maisons-Alfort.

Balard / Créteil – Préfecture

Bastille
Ledru-Rollin
Faidherbe–Chaligny
Reuilly–Diderot
Montgallet
Daumesnil
Michel Bizot
Porte Dorée
Porte de Charenton
Liberté
Charenton–Écoles
École Vétérinaire de Maisons-Alfort
Maisons-Alfort–Stade
Maisons-Alfort–Les Juilliottes
Créteil–L'Échat
Créteil–Université
Créteil–Préfecture
M 1 5
M 1
M 6

A.T.
INVALIDES
A.T.
065

BALARD

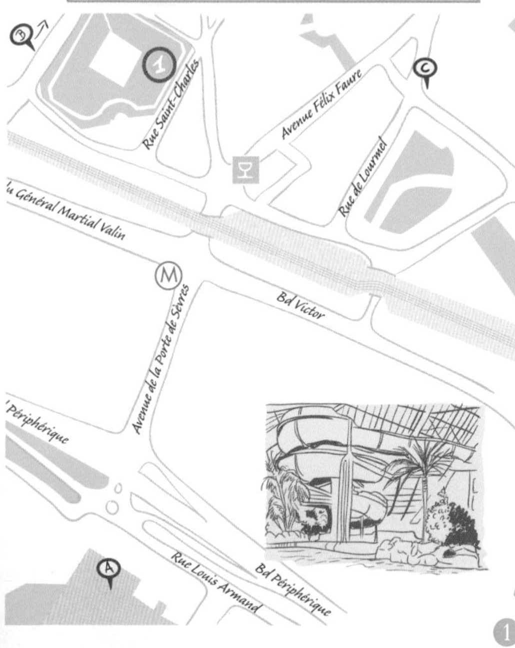

History

Balard station opened in 1937, taking its name from the street and the square both named after the chemist Antoine Jérôme Balard (1802–1876). The station's architecture, both inside and out, is fairly plain. The only point of interest is the entrances, which are decorated with Dervaux signposts. These are in Art Deco style with the word 'Metro' set against a red background, which so often tower over the wrought iron balustrades or freestone surrounds. Balard is located in the south of the 15th arrondissement, by the *Périphérique* (Paris ring road).

SIGHTSEEING

A walk in the Park

1 **Parc André-Citroën:** opened i 1992, this is one of the largest recer parks in Paris, covering 14 hectares (3 acres) along the banks of the Seine an providing a great view of the former Ci roën car factory. This is a very innovativ park, structured around several differer areas with water as the common them including a canal and fountains. The vas lawn provides a pleasant resting spot fc visitors. The more curious among ther can admire the exotic plants in the vas greenhouses or walk in the thematic ga dens, which include a white and blac garden, in addition to six 'serial' garden created by landscape gardener Gilles Clé ment.

56 rue Balard, quai André-Citroën. Open 8am in the week and 9am on weekends, closes at sunset.

Address book

The place for a rendezvous

Café Le Balard
3 place Balard, 15th.
Open daily 6am to 10pm.
Tel.: 01-45-54-19-31.

Leisure

A Aquaboulevard
A perfect place if you enjoy crowds or giant waterslides! This is the largest water sports centre in Europe (7,000 square metres) with a multitude of water activities for children of all ages.
4 rue Louis-Armand, 15th.
Tel.: 01-40-60-10-00.
Open from Monday to Thursday 9am to 11pm, Fridays 9am to midnight, Saturdays 8am to midnight and Sundays 8am to 11pm.
Entrance fee.

B Paris Air Balloon
If you want a 360-degree view of the capital, there's no better way than 150 meters above ground in a fixed gas balloon. This has been a feature in the centre of the André-Citroën park since 1999, but the balloon is more than just a tourist attraction. Since 2008 it has been measuring air quality in partnership with Airparif, the official air monitoring body in France. The balloon changes colour according to the quality of Paris air, ranging from green (good), to orange (poor) and red (bad).
Parc André-Citroën, 15th.
Tel.: 01-44-26-20-00.
www.ballondeparis.com
Open daily 9am until 40 minutes before the park closes, depending on the weather conditions.
A fee is charged.

Restaurant

C La Cave de l'Os à Moelle
A brick-walled cellar with a large common table and a set menu served on an odd assortment of plates. The atmosphere is very much that of a country inn. The set menu includes soup, pâté, the dish of the day, a selection of cheeses and unlimited deserts. The lunch menu is at €22.50 and the dinner one €25.
181 rue de Lourmel, 15th.
Tel.: 01-45-57-28-28.
Open from Tuesday to Sunday noon to 3pm, with two evening sittings at 7.30pm and 9.30pm.

Next stations

LOURMEL
Le Boyard
117 avenue Félix-Faure, 15th.

BOUCICAUT
Le Bistrot 12
22 avenue Félix-Faure, 15th.

FÉLIX FAURE
À la Tour Eiffel
96 rue du Commerce, 15th.

COMMERCE

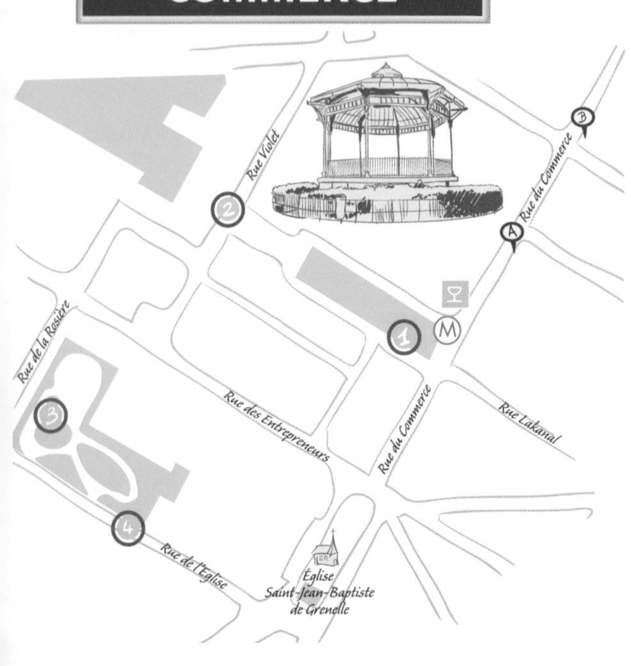

History

Commerce station was so called after the street and square of the same name, served by that station. Because the street is so narrow, the two platforms are not in line, rather like Liège station on line 13. The station gives onto what was once the village of Grenelle, planned by Jean-Léonard Violet and Alphonse Letellier in 1824, bordering the then-Vaugirard village, which Haussmann annexed to Paris in 1860.

SIGHTSEEING

A walk in the city

1. **Place du Commerce:** this long rectangular esplanade stretches out in the shade of the large chestnut trees, reminiscent of the village that once surrounded it. Children, nannies, mothers and walkers share the space with *pétanque* players. Take a look at the façade of the former town hall, in Louis-Philippe style.

2. **Rue Violet:** follow the street to the square. At no. 6 place Violet, you will see a fire station with a neoclassical façade, built in 1824 and a now a protected regional building.

Square Violet: opened up in 1876, the square has a large shady lawn with an attractive bandstand where concerts are held in the summer.

Rue de l'Église: there are several architectural gems on and around rue de l'Église, such as the 1905 Art Nouveau building on the corner with place Étienne-Pernet, and the neoclassical Saint-Jean-Baptise-de-Grenelle church (no. 23).

Address book

The place for a rendezvous

Le Commerce
80 rue du Commerce, 15th.
Open daily
6am to 11pm.
Tel: 01-48-28-77-01.

Shopping

A Rue du Commerce
This is a high street in the Grenelle neighbourhood that the locals like to frequent for their daily food shopping, but you will also find shops and boutiques selling perfume, clothes, lingerie and décor.

Restaurant

B Café du Commerce
This three-storey restaurant has played a part in the neighbourhood history. It was originally a fabric shop but in 1921 it became a restaurant called 'Aux Mille Couverts', providing workers from the nearby Javel-Grenelle car factory with cheap means from a set menu. It was modelled on the other Parisian *bouillon* restaurants in the 19th century, which were inexpensive eateries where workers could eat boiled beef, hence the name *bouillon*, meaning stock. Today the Café du Commerce is a good and attractive Parisian *brasserie* that offers simple food from good and carefully-selected ingredients. Approximately €30.
51 rue du Commerce, 15th.
Tel.: 01-45-75-03-27.
www.lecafeducommerce.com
Open daily noon to 5pm and 7pm to midnight.

LA MOTTE-PIQUET – GRENELLE

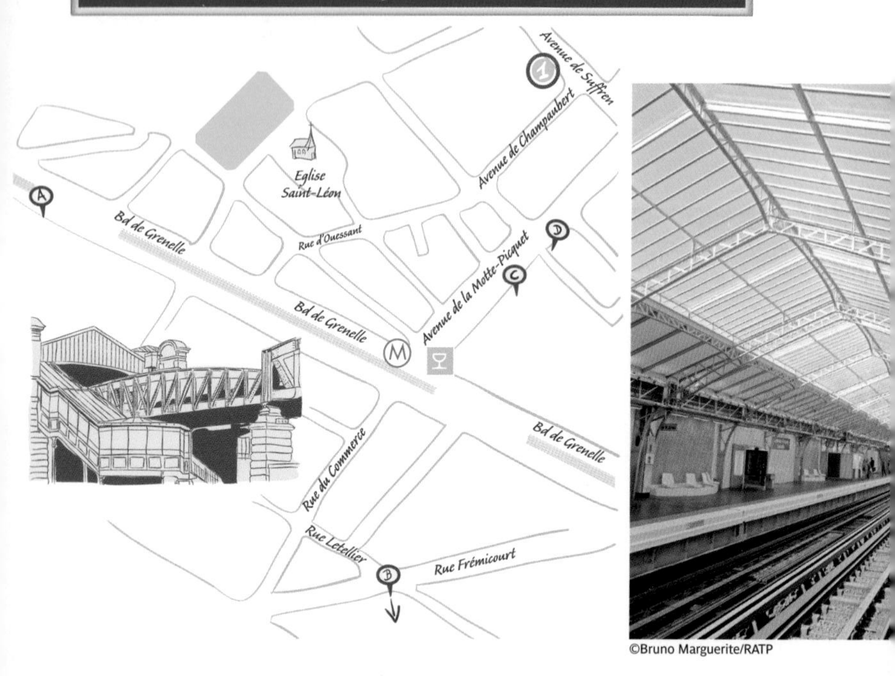

©Bruno Marguerite/RATP

History

La Motte-Picquet station, on the former line 5, opened in 1906. It was named after Admiral Toussaint-Guillaume Picquet de la Motte (1720–1791), and was enlarged in 1913 when the former line 8 was extended to Beaugrenelle station, now renamed Charles Michels. The station was then altered and connected to line 10. However, its real history lies in the connecting corridors decorated with the coats of arms belonging to the Toussaint-Guillaume Picquet de la Motte family. There is also a fresco depicting the Cunette barrier, one of the *Fermiers Généraux* tax gates that surrounded Paris before the Revolution.

SIGHTSEEING

An artistic walk

❶ **Village Suisse:** the 1900 Exposition Universelle (World Fair) was held in the Gros-Caillou district between the Esplanade des Invalides, École Militaire and Champ-de-Mars. Among the international pavilions was a reproduction of a Swiss village that covered a surface area of 21,000 square metres (226,042 square feet), complete with authentic wooden chalets transported all the way to Paris. That has now long gone and Village Suisse has gone up-market and is now a luxury flea market in the heart of Paris. This antiques mall seems a little outdated today but it is still part and parcel of Paris art market, with 150 antique dealers, decorators and art galleries, offering a good choice of furniture and other goodies.

78 avenue de Suffren, 15th.
Tel.: 01-73-79-15-41.
www.villagesuisse.com
Open from Thursday to Monday 10.30am to 7pm.

Address book

The place for a rendezvous

Le Café Pierrot
67 avenue de La Motte-Picquet, 15th.
Tel.: 01-47-34-17-76.
Open daily from 7pm to 2am.

Restaurants

A Au Dernier Métro
A simple and friendly place with an atmosphere straight from rugby-loving southwest of France, so a great place to go when matches are being played—provided you're a fan! You can't go wrong with the *cassoulet*, the duck breast or the duck confit, served with Basque wines. À la carte between €10 and €20.
70 boulevard de Grenelle, 15th.
Tel.: 01-45-75-01-23.
www.audernier metro.com
Open daily noon to 2am.

B El Farès
According to Lebanese sources, this is one of the best Lebanese restaurants in Paris. Don't even try to resist the copious and delicious *mezze* that follow one after the other. Nothing is really out of the ordinary, but a truly delicious *moutabal* (aubergine purée), *hummus* (chick pea purée) and *tabbouleh* (cracked wheat salad). Menus starting from €15.
79 rue Blomet, 15th. Tel.: 01-45-78-10-26.
Open from Monday to Friday noon to 3pm and 7pm to 11.30pm.

C La Gauloise
If you love Parisian *brasseries* you won't be disappointed. Mitterrand used to frequent this one, and it continues to draw business people and politicians alike because of its good food, comfortable décor and welcoming terrace. À la carte from €40.
59 avenue de La Motte-Picquet, 15th.
Tel.: 01-47-34-11-64. Open all week noon to 2.30pm and 7pm to 11pm.

D Le Père Claude
This family restaurant opened in 1988 is another institution, and not just locally but a Parisian one. It attracts the same clients because of its simple but quality traditional food, roasted, grilled or stewed. Menu at €32.
51 avenue de La Motte-Picquet, 15th.
Tel.: 01-45-67-67-46. www.lepereclaude.com
Open daily at lunchtime and in the evenings.

ÉCOLE MILITAIRE

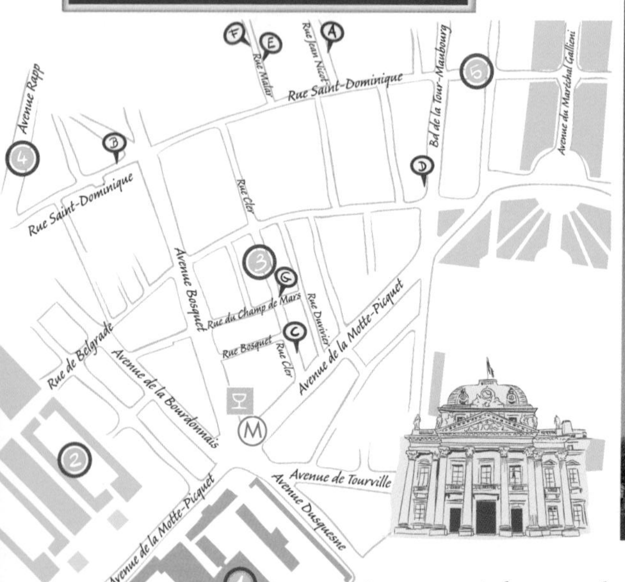

History

École Militaire station was opened in 1913. It is situated between the École Militaire (military academy) and the Champ-de-Mars, but also provides access to the little known neighbourhood of Gros-Caillou, which is a triangular area in the northwest of the 7th arrondissement, between the Eiffel Tower and the Invalides. This area got its name from a boundary stone on the corner of rue Cler and rue Saint-Dominique, which marked the borderline between the Saint-Germain and the Sainte-Geneviève abbeys. Gros-Caillou village grew in the 18th century to become a bustling little working class town with numerous craftsmen as well as *guinguettes* (open air dance halls) and cabarets. It became gentrified over time and acquired its Haussmann elegance in the second half of the 19th century. While there are still many shops on rue Cler and streets surrounding it, this is no longer the case for Avenue Rapp, which has become very sedate.

SIGHTSEEING

Military history

1 **École militaire:** today, École Militaire, as the name suggests, groups together all the military higher education bodies, but the establishment had a tumultuous past. Established by King Louis XV in

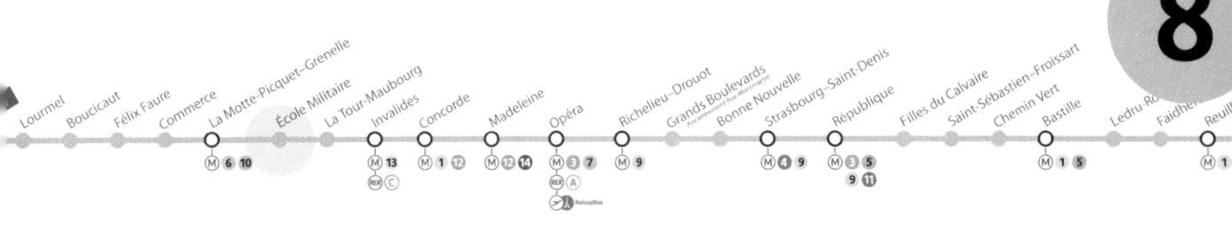

1750, on a suggestion by the financier Joseph Paris Duverney, and with backing from Madame de Pompadour, the king's chief mistress, herself, it was conceived to train officers from modest backgrounds. It opened its doors in 1760 and perhaps the most famous of the many cadets who trained there was young Bonaparte in 1784. Abandoned and pillaged during the French Revolution, the school then became a warehouse, and a barracks for the Imperial Guard. The building was then extended and altered before reverting to its original vocation in 1878, when two military schools were successively established there, the École Supérieure de Guerre, followed by the Centre des Hautes Études Militaires in 1911. You can admire the façade from the Champ-de-Mars, before walking around the building to the magnificent main courtyard on the other side. This is the Cour Morland, now an exercise ground for the cavalry. The inspiration for the École Militaire's architecture came from its prestigious neighbour, the Hôtel des Invalides.

1 place Joffre, 7th.
Tel.: 01-44-42-40-65.
Open from Monday to Friday 7.30am to 7.30pm. Guided tours of the Cour Morland, the library and the chapel by appointment. Admission free.

2 **Champ-de-Mars:** before the École Militaire was built, the Champ-de-Mars was in the countryside among the market gardens that spread across the Grenelle plain. Its fate changed in 1765 when this esplanade became an exercise ground for soldiers and a place for holding military manoeuvres. In the

18th century, nearly 10,000 men trained there every day. During the French Revolution, the Champ-de-Mars was the scene of the Fête de la Fédération festivities organized on 14 July 1790, and was subsequently home to the guillotine. It became a racetrack and then, as the magnificent freestone buildings grew up all around it, a garden. Today it lies at the foot of the Eiffel Tower and is one of the busiest parks in Paris.

An elegant walk

3 **Rue Cler:** this is one of the nicest and liveliest streets in the neighbourhood, mostly because of the food shops that brighten up the pedestrian section. There are a few remarkable Art Nouveau buildings on this street, including one on the corner with rue de Grenelle by the architect Jules Lavirotte, who marked the Gros-Caillou neighbourhood.

4 **Avenue Rapp:** a very beautiful avenue, which also has a few well-known Jules Lavirotte masterpieces. Their ornate 'noodle' style was criticized when the building were first built.

5 **Rue Saint-Dominique:** this is whe Honoré de Balzac located the most beau ful town houses in his *Comédie humai* and not without reason for there are lov examples on both sides of the street. It hard to imagine that this was once a me path, whose name changed over tim Chemin des Treilles (1433), Chemin H bu or Chemin Herbu des Moulins à Ve (1523), Chemin de l'Oseraie (1527), Chem du Port (1530) and Chemin des Vach (1542). In 1631, it finally acquired the nar of rue Saint-Dominique because of t Dominican monastery situated there. T Fontaine de Mars fountain is by the scu tor François-Jean Bralle (1750–1832). walk down this street is a must if you wa to discover the elegant 7th arrondissemen

Address book

The place for a rendezvous

La Terrasse du 7e
2 place de l'École-Militaire, 7th.
Open all week 7am to 2am.
Tel.: 01-45-55-00-02.

Shopping

A Bellota-Bellota
A Spanish wine-cellar-come-delicatessen where you can taste the legendary Bellota-Bellota ham, reputed to be the best in the world. This is a key place for Spanish gastronomy where you will find a good selection of typical produce and dishes.
18 rue Jean-Nicot, 7th.
Tel.: 01-53-59-96-96.
Open Tuesday to Thursday 11am to 10pm and Friday until 11pm; Saturday 10am to 11pm.

Restaurants

B La Fontaine de Mars
This elegant institution offers traditional seasonal cuisine with good wines.
Dish of the day €20.
129 rue Saint-Dominique, 7th.
Tel.: 01-47-05-46-44.
Open daily noon to 3pm and 7pm to 11pm.

C Aux PTT
This good little bistro is known for its oysters to eat there or take away (€9 the dozen to take away).
54 rue Cler, 7th.
Tel.: 01-45-51-94-96.
Open Monday to Thursday 7am to 9pm, Friday and Saturday 9am to 9pm, and Sunday 9am to 2pm for oysters to take away.

D Le Bistrot du 7e
This is where you will find some fine bistro classics, and reasonably priced for this neighbourhood too! Menus €16 and €22.
56 boulevard de La Tour-Maubourg, 7th.
Tel. 01-45-51-93-08.
Open daily noon to 2.30pm and 7.30pm to 11pm Closed for lunch on Saturday and Sunday.

E L'Ami Jean
An establishment that is a veritable institution in the neighbourhood, and has been for decades! The young chef is a lover of the Basque country while the restaurant is very plain and reminiscent of old Paris. Basque specialties are served to large tables full of friends. Approximately €50.
27 rue Malar, 7th.
Tel.: 01-47-05-86-89.
Open from Tuesday to Saturday noon to 2pm and 7pm to 11pm.

F L'Affriolé
A place for excellent and inventive food by chef Thierry Vérola, who changes his repertoire every month but always has a special place for fish. Evening menus €35.
17 rue Malar, 7th.
Tel.: 01-44-18-31-33.
Open daily noon to 2.30pm and 7.30pm to 10.30pm.

Out on the town

G Café du Marché
It's hard to get a table on the terrace when the weather's good. A very pleasant place to have a coffee or a drink after some hard shopping.
38 rue Cler, 7th.
Tel.: 01-47-05-51-27.
Open daily 7am to midnight, and until 4pm on Sunday.

Next station

LA TOUR-MAUBOURG

Le Seven's Coffee
58 rue Saint-Dominique, 7th.

INVALIDES

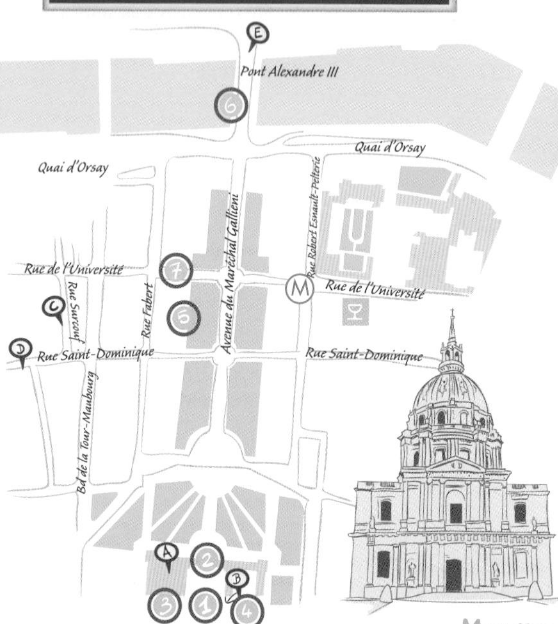

©Gilles Aligon / RATP

History

The Invalides metro station, located on the eponymous esplanade at rue de l'Université level, was named after the Hôtel des Invalides. To the north of the metro entrance lies the Invalides RER line C station (to which there is transit access), and the Air France terminal which runs a bus shuttle service to Orly airport.

SIGHTSEEING

Monuments

1 **Les Invalides:** in 1670, Louis XIV decided to improve the lot of wounded war veterans, many of whom were to be seen wandering around the capital. He decided to establish it on the Plaine de Grenelle and confided the project to the Marquis de Louvois, his Secretary of State for War, who left his mark in the form of a rebus above one of the *œil de bœuf* (round windows, hence 'bull's eye') in the main courtyard. The architect Libéral Bruant was commissioned to design the *hôtel* and the church, while the architect François Mansart designed the dome.
Open daily 10am to 5pm, and 6pm from April to September. Entrance fee.

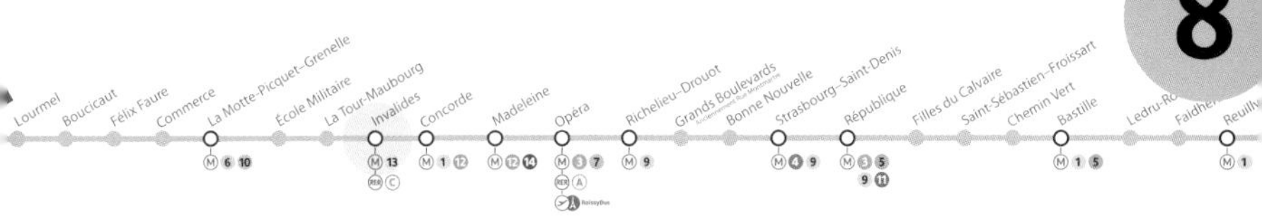

2 **Hôtel des Invalides:** wounded soldiers are still cared for here, free of charge. The establishment used to take in 4,500 patients but only about 100 today. Most of the buildings have been taken over by the military administration and the museums. Guarded by a dozen canons, this is a very imposing building, with a very pure and simple façade with a decorated portal. Simplicity and an almost monastic calm prevail in the main courtyard and the buildings, a tribute to the monasteries that inspired the architecture.

3 **Églises du Dôme and Saint-Louis-des-Invalides:** the two churches were built within the Invalides precinct, the Dôme being for the King, and the smaller Saint-Louis-des-Invalides for the veteran patients of the Hôtel to allow them to hear the same mass as the king but use a separate entrance. The churches are connected by an altar and were separated by a glass window in 1873. When you visit the light-filled Saint-Louis church, where most of the Marshals of France are buried, admire the imposing organ dated 1679, where Berlioz composed his Requiem in 1837. The Dôme church is more richly decorated and the dome itself is impressive, with its two interconnected cupolas. Napoleon's tomb is in the sanctuary.

Place Vauban, 7th Paris.
Tel.: 0810-11-33-99.
www.invalides.org
Open daily 10am to 5pm from October to March, and until 6pm from April to June and in September, or 7pm in July and August. Late night opening Tuesday until 9pm. Entrance fee.

④ **Tomb of Napoleon:** here lie the remains of Napoleon I (Bonaparte), brought back to Paris in 1840 on the orders of King Louis-Philippe who needed to legitimize his power. The work on the crypt was finished in 1861, and the ashes were deposited in a tomb made from red porphyry with a green granite base.
Same opening hours as previous page.

⑤ **Esplanade des Invalides:** this esplanade is a vast lawn bordered on both sides by linden trees, that goes from the Hôtel des Invalides right down to the Seine. It is a popular place on sunny days, when it may turn into something of a sports ground.

⑥ **Pont Alexandre-III:** Nicolas II of Russia, the son of Tsar Alexander III of Russia, laid the first stone of this majestic bridge as a sign of Franco-Russian friendship. It was the first bridge to cross the Seine in a single arch, and was designed for the 1900 Exposition Universelle (World Fair) to connect the Invalides with what would become the Grand Palais and the Petit Palais.

⑦ **Rue de l'Université:** this long street (2.7 kilometres or 1.7 miles), lies just a few meters from the Seine and runs parallel to the river, crossing the entire 7th arrondissement. It was named after the former Paris University, which acquired the land on the banks of the Seine called Pré-aux-clercs in the 12th century. In 1639, the university sold Pré-aux-clercs, and the area then became a new neighbourhood of Paris. The main street became known as rue de l'Université. Today it is a very pleasant street, full of grand and elegant town houses.

Address book

The place for a rendezvous

Café des Ministères

83 rue de l'Université, 7th.
Open from Monday to Friday 7am to 7pm.
Tel.: 01-47-05-43-62.

Culture

A Musée de l'Armée

The military museum opened its doors in 1905, replacing the Musée de l'Artillerie (artillery museum) and the Musée Historique de l'Armée (army history museum). The modern section is devoted to the history of the army from the 17th century to the end of the 20th century. You will also find a section displaying old weapons and armour including weapons used in the two world wars.

129 rue de Grenelle, 7th.
Tel.: 01-44-42-37-72. www.invalides.org
Open daily 10am to 5pm from October to March, and 6pm from April to June and in September, 7pm in July and August. Late night opening Tuesdays until 9pm. Entrance fee.

B Historial Charles-de-Gaulle

A museum opened by the Charles de Gaulle Foundation in 2008 situated in the Invalides. The wealth of documents here retraces de Gaulle's trajectory from his 18 June radio appeal urging the French to resist the Nazis, to his role as liberator or Paris and the head of state. Visitors can delve into the life of the General through photographs, memoirs, and audiovisual recordings.

Access is through the main courtyard, via the Aile d'Orient (west wing).
Tel.: 01-44-42-37-72. www.invalides.org
Open daily 10am to 5pm from October to March, and 6pm from April to June and in September, 7pm in July and August. Late night opening on Tuesdays until 9pm. Entrance fee.

Restaurant

C Le Petit Bordelais

A new little restaurant run by a Chef from Bordeaux. Marvellous tastes with a great regional flavour. Lunch menu €19.

22 rue Surcouf, 7th. Tel.: 01-45-51-46-93.
www.le-petit-bordelais.fr.
Open Tuesday to Saturday 12am to 2.30pm and 7.30pm to 10.30pm.

Out on the town

D O'Briens

This is a real Welsh pub, much appreciated by locals badly in need of a cheerful place for a drink.

77 rue Saint-Dominique, 7th.
Tel.: 01-45-51-75-87. Open daily 5pm to 2am Closes at 3am on Friday and Saturday. Opens around 4pm on Saturdays, depending on sporting events.

E Le Showcase

This nightclub is in a sensational location in a former boathouse under the Alexandre III bridge. It is a vast area, well known for its electronic music and frequented by Paris's young jet set.

Under the Alexandre III bridge,
port des Champs-Élysées, 8th.
Tel.: 01-45-61-25-43. www.showcase.fr
Open every weekend.

Next station

CONCORDE

See line 1, page 22

MADELEINE

History

This station was named after a little 6th century town built on land belonging to the Bishop of Paris that lay to the west of Paris. It acquired the name of La Ville-l'Évêque (bishop town), and in the 13th century its chapel was dedicated to Saint Madeleine, with reference to Mary Madeleine, who wept at Christ's feet when she first met him. This is the origin of the French expression '*pleurer comme une madeleine*' (weeping like a Madeleine). Three metro lines serve the station: line 8, which opened in 1913, line 12, and line 14. Observant passengers will notice the copy of a statue by Brancusi called *The Prayer* (1907), which depicts a kneeling woman with her hands clasped together in prayer. Today the square, Place de la Madeleine, is almost entirely dedicated to sensual gourmet pleasures, dominated by the classic fine food emporia, Hédiard and Fauchon. If you are passing by, stop and visit the public lavatory by the metro station! The entrance is of the right of the church and it has a sublime Art Nouveau mahogany décor with marvellous stained glass windows that were added in 1905.

SIGHTSEEING

rchitecture

Église de la Madeleine: this church is a veritable Greek temple—which is exactly what Napoleon I wanted it to be. In 1764, Constant d'Ivry, the architect, received clear instructions. The edifice was to 'pleasantly' close off rue Royale and face the Bourbon Palace. Then in 1806, the Emperor decided to convert the building into a 'temple to the glory of the French army'. He famously said 'I want a monument such as there are in Athens but none in Paris'. As a result, a forest of Corinthian columns was added around the building, which has neither bell tower or external crucifix. However, it is protected by massive bronze doors depicting the Ten Commandments, and inside, 32 niches harbour the same number of saints. Homage to the church's namesake comes in the form of a marble statue called *The Assumption of Mary Magdalene*, lovingly carved in marble by Charles Marochetti. *4 rue de Surène, 8th.*

2 **Place Vendôme:** the Place Vendôme is a gem, and not only because of the numerous high-end jewellers there, but simply because it is a beautiful square designed by Louis XIV. At a time when streets were dark and narrow, the Sun King wanted a grandiose and magnificent square worthy of him. Jules Hardouin-Mansart was the architect charged with making the monarch's dream a reality. Originally the square had an equestrian statue of the Sun King in the centre, but the revolutionaries destroyed that symbol of royal power in 1792. Napoleon subsequently placed a column there to commemorate the battle of Austerlitz, inspired by the Trajan triumphal column in Rome. Various statues have since adorned the column, depending on the whims of the powers at the time. Today it is a statue of Napoleon I. He gazes out to the horizon draped in a short coat and carrying a sword in his right hand, a globe with a statue of winged victory in his left, and wears an imperial laurel wreath on his head. Opposite stands

the prestigious Ritz Hotel, 'so calm and so splendid' wrote the French poet, Léon-Paul Fargue. The hotel was named after its owner, a Swiss hotelier who also managed the Grand Hôtel in Monte-Carlo. The Ritz was a haven for many famous people including Coco Chanel and Charlie Chaplin. One lively night there, Ernest Hemingway, another regular visitor to the hotel (and especially its bar), allegedly created the first Bloody Mary.

Address book

The place for a rendezvous

🍸 **Le Paris London**
16 place de la Madeleine, 8th.
Open all week 7.30am to 11pm.
Tel.: 01-47-42-33-92.

Shopping

Ⓐ Hédiard
A fine food emporium filled with rare spices, divine chocolate and coffees

with magical names. You'll have a hard time choosing between the old wines, prestige champagnes and rare alcohols. The restaurant with the colonial style décor upstairs, may well tempt you to stop for a bite immediately!
21 place de la Madeleine, 8th.
Tel.: 01-43-12-88-88.
Open from Monday to Saturday 9am to 8.30pm.

Ⓑ Fauchon
Attractively decorated in pink and black, the Fauchon stores are located at numbers 24, 26 and 30 of the square and will delight the palates of any fine gourmet. All the great classics have been revisited here, together with new creations straight from the kitchen, You can buy delicious Danish pastries as well as little *madeleines* (sponge cakes) to take away or eat immediately if you can't wait, as well as selected produce from the world over. Irresistible foie gras, champagne, and *marrons glacés* (candied chestnuts). Menus €27–34.
26 place de la Madeleine, 8th.
Tel.: 01-70-39-38-00.
Open from Monday to Saturday. The fine grocer's, confectioner's and wine cellar from 9am to 8pm (located at no. 30); the bakery 8am to 9pm (8am to 6pm to eat in); the delicatessen and patisserie 8am to 9pm.

Restaurant

Ⓒ Le Foyer de la Madeleine

This place is unimaginable and really off the beaten track. Underneath the église de la Madeleine, volunteers hand out food beneath the vaulted ceiling. The regulars gather in their local canteen, and a priest is on hand if required. Who said that miracles don't exist? Membership required (from €3). Menu €8.

14 rue de Surène, inside the église de la Madeleine (on the Fauchon side, behind the florists), 8th.
Tel.: 01-47-42-39-84.
Open from Monday to Friday 11.45am to 2pm.

Culture

Ⓓ Pierre Cardin's 1900s collection at Maxim's

Fashion designer Pierre Cardin, the co-owner of Maxim's, is mad about Art Nouveau and built up this marvellous collection, which is now on view to the public. You will find a beautifully recreated Belle Époque apartment, complete with sparkling chinaware, Tiffany lamps and Lunéville chandeliers, not to mention paintings by Toulouse-Lautrec, and even a toiletries set belonging to actress Sarah Bernhardt, designed by the famous furniture designer and decorator, Louis Majorelle.

3 rue Royale, 8th.
Tel.: 01-42-65-30-47.
Open Wednesday to Sunday.
Guided tours only (or conference visits) at 2pm, 3.15pm and 4.30pm. Entrance fee.

Next station

OPÉRA

See line 3, page 76

RICHELIEU – DROUOT

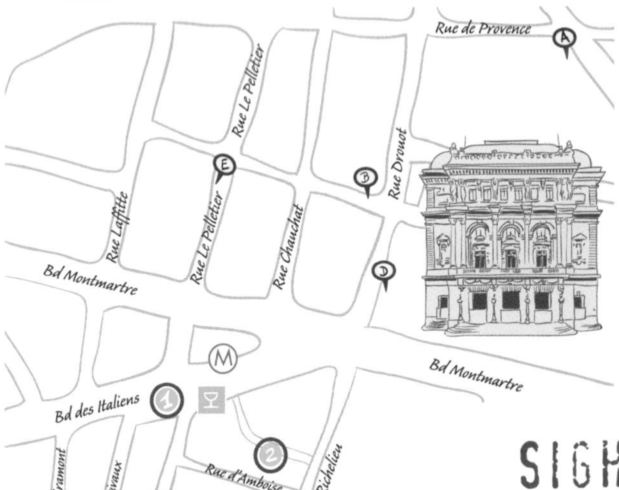

History

Richelieu-Drouot station opened in 1931 on the corner of rue de Richelieu, which was named after Armand Jean du Plessis, Cardinal de Richelieu (1585–1642), and rue Drouot, named after Count Antoine Drouot (1774–1847), the army general who accompanied Napoleon I to the Island of Elba. This metro station has a curious feature in the connection area, namely a large black marble memorial designed by Carlo Sarrabezolles in honour of the Metropolitan Railway (i.e. Paris Metro) employees who died for their country during the First World War.

SIGHTSEEING

A walk in the city

1. **Boulevard des Italiens:** in the 19th century this was the most chic boulevard in Paris, and when you look at some of the opulent facades, you can see why. The current headquarters of BNP Paribas, used to be known as the *'maison dorée'* (golden house) and was the famous Café Hardy (no. 20). Next to it was the no less prestigious Café Riche (no. 16), and the ice-cream parlour Tortoni (no. 22), which stands opposite the Crédit Lyonnais (LCL bank) today (no. 17).

2. **Passage des Princes:** designed in 1860, this is the most recent of the famous Parisian covered arcades. It has not retained a great deal from its magnificence apart from the attractive square floor tiling, its long glass roof, and Art Deco lamp posts. This is a starting point for visiting the neighbourhood art galleries.
5 boulevard des Italiens or 97 rue de Richelieu, 2nd.

Opéra-Comique: along with the Paris Opera House (formerly the Royal Academy of Music), and the Comédie-Française, this is one of the oldest theatrical and musical institutions in France. It was established in 1714, during the reign of Louis XIV, for a new musical genre that was not necessarily funny or comical, but characterised by the fact that it combined song with theatre unlike the opera, which is entirely sung. This genre had a somewhat turbulent albeit prestigious history, and from 1783 opened its seasons in a theatre that acquired the name of a famous librettist, Charles Simon Favart. The Salle Favart, as it became known, burnt down twice and was rebuilt in the same spot. In 1898, the third theatre with that name was built was granted to the Opéra-Comique. A new era began in 2005, when this theatre was listed among France's national theatres. Its history continues and audiences continue to enjoy its very special repertoire.

1 place Boïeldieu, 2nd. Tel.: 0825-01-01-23.
www.opera-comique.com

Address book

The place for a rendezvous

Le Cardinal

1 boulevard des Italiens, 2nd.
Open Monday to Thursday 7am to 2am, Fridays and Saturdays 7am to 5am and Sunday 8am to 2am.
Tel.: 01-42-96-61-20.

Shopping

A À la Mère de Famille

One of the oldest chocolate shops in Paris, situated at thc same address since 1761. In addition to chocolates you will find *Calissons d'Aix*, caramels, marshmallows, nougats and marzipan, all in a lovely 1900 décor. This shop has brought joy to sweet-toothed Parisians for years!

35 rue du Faubourg-Montmartre, 9th.
Tel.: 01-47-70-83-69.

Culture

B Hôtel des Ventes Drouot

The famous auction rooms are a veritable hub for the French and international art market with 21 salesrooms spread over four sites, selling some 600,000 items very year at 2,000 auctions. No. 9 rue Drouot is the oldest and the largest of them. Drouot is rather like a magical and transient museum. Open to everyone, visitors can window shop for the items on auction, consult the catalogues and even get close to the works and place their bids. Auctions are held every day.

9, rue Drouot, 9th.
Tel. : 01-48-00-20-20.
Auctions Monday to Saturday 2pm to 6pm.

Restaurants

C Aux Lyonnais

A typical *bouchon* (Lyon restaurant) in the heart of Paris, established in 1890 and dedicated to that city's renowned cuisine. Lunch menu €28.

32 rue Saint-Marc, 2nd.
Tel.: 01-42-96-65-04.
www.auxlyonnais.com

D J'Go

An ode to the food and wine of southwest France, in a pleasant family atmosphere. Menus €15 and €20.

4 rue Drouot, 9th.
Tel.: 01-40-22-09-09.
www.lejgo.com
Open Monday to Saturday noon to 2.30pm and 7pm to midnight. The bar is open 6pm to 2am.

E Au Petit Riche

Traditional French cuisine, including oysters and seafood. Dishes €18 – 30.

25 rue Le Peletier, 9th.
Tel.: 01-47-70-68-68.
www.restaurant-aupetitriche.com
Open all week noon to 2.30pm and in the evening 7pm to midnight, and 10.30pm on Sunday.

GRANDS BOULEVARDS

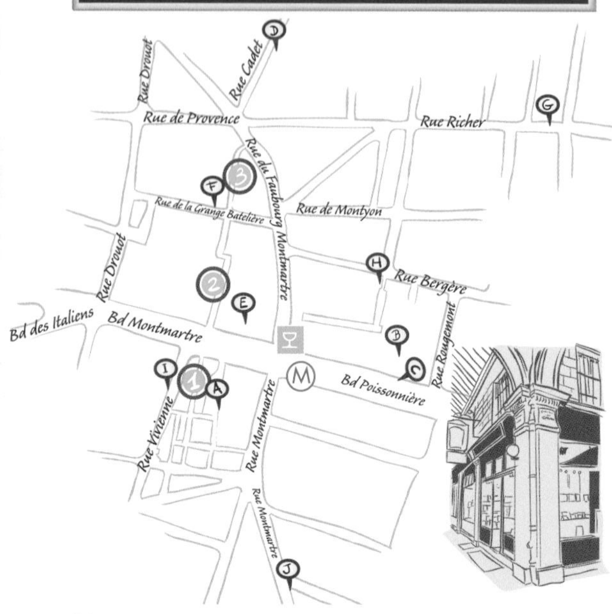

during the reign of Charles V. The 19th century was the apogee of the Grands Boulevards, when they were filled with *brasseries*, cafés and theatres, since this was the when the 'boulevard comedies' reigned supreme. It was extremely chic to be seen strolling along these boulevards in the 1850s but became rather less so in the 1950s, when they attracted a different more 'rank and file' public, which is still the case today.

History

For many years this metro station was called Montmartre and then Rue Montmartre, with reference to the street it served, but in the summer of 1998 it was renamed Grands Boulevards during a general overhaul of the Paris Grands Boulevards. This served to avoid confusion since many tourists thought they were getting off at Butte Montmartre, which is the location of the Sacré Cœur in the 18th arrondissement! This station lies in the heart of the broad avenues known as the Grands Boulevards, that connect Madeleine to Bastille, and located where the former ramparts once stood

SIGHTSEEING

The Parisian arcades

1 **Passage des Panoramas:** the Passage des Panoramas extends between Bourse and Opéra, and is the oldest of the Parisian covered arcades. Open to the public in 1799, the design was inspired by etchings of Oriental bazaars. Its name derives from a popular attraction on nearby Boulevard Montmartre, the projection of *panoramiques* (an early forerunner of the cinema). The arcade rapidly became very popular with worldly Parisians who wanted to see and be seen, while remaining dry, since Paris had neither drains nor pavements at the time. The Théâtre des

Variétés (variety theatre) opened nearby and the arcade got its first gaslights in 1816. Other galleries were connected to it in the 1830s, namely Saint-Marc, Variétés, Bourse, Feydeau and Montmartre.

11 boulevard Montmartre, 9th;
151 rue Montmartre, 2nd;
6–8 rue Saint-Marc, 2nd;
50 rue Vivienne, 9th.
Open daily 6am to midnight.

② **Passage Jouffroy:** this arcade opened in 1847, when it housed a number of prostitutes. Now it has restaurants, the entrance to the Grévin wax museum and a small hotel.

10-12 boulevard Montmartre and 9 rue de la Grange-Batelière, 9th.
Open daily until 9.30pm.

③ **Passage Verdeau:** all kinds of treasures are to be found in this arcade, and it takes time to browse through the shops selling musical instrument, collections of old post cards, posters and newspapers.

You can reach Passage Verdeau at the end of Passage Jouffroy or through no. 4 rue de la Grange-Batelière. Open daily until 9pm (8.30pm at weekends).

Address book

The place for a rendezvous

🍸 **Le Brébant**
32 boulevard Poissonière, 9th.
Open daily 6am to 5.30am. Tel.: 01-47-70-01-02.

Culture

Ⓐ Théâtre des Variétés
This theatre was established in 1807 by a troop of actors obliged to leave the Théâtre Français, and became one of the largest Parisian Boulevard theatres. Offenbach produced his *La Belle Helène* here in 1864.
7 boulevard Montmartre, 2nd.
Tel.: 01-42-33-09-92.
www.theatre-des-varietes.fr

Ⓑ Théâtre des Nouveautés
Just a few steps away from the Théâtre des Variétés is the 'novelty' theatre. It was established here in 1921, although it had moved around over the centuries.
24 boulevard Poissonnière, 9th.
Tel.: 01-47-70-52-76.
www.theatredesnouveautes.fr

Ⓒ Max Linder Panorama
Together with the Rex, the Max Linder is one of the iconic cinemas of the Parisian Grands Boulevards. Originally called Kosmorama, it was taken over in 1914 by the comic actor Max Linder, who renamed it Ciné Max Linder. It changed owners and décor several times before reopening in its present form in 1987, with a wide screen. It has since acquired state-of-the-art technology, and is ideal for seeing films in 3D as well as old movies!
24 boulevard Poissonnière, 9th.
Tel.: 01-48-24-00-47.
http://maxlinder.cine.allocine.fr

Ⓓ Musée de la Franc-Maçonnerie
This freemasonry museum opened in 1889. It was plundered during the German occupation but reopened in 1973, having gradually built up its collection again. In 2003, it acquired 'Musée de France' status from the Ministry of Culture. The museum shows how freemasonry has influenced society, citizenship and life over time, with an important collection of seals, jewels, medals and paintings in addition to manuscripts, patents, engravings, architectural works and photographs.
16 rue Cadet, 9th.
Tel.: 01-45-23-74-09. www.museefm.org
Open Tuesday to Saturday (except holidays) 2pm to 6pm. Entrance fee.

Ⓔ Musée Grévin
This museum opened in the passage Jouffroy in 1882 and displayed realistic wax models of well-known personalities from the outset. It continues to disconcert and attract crowds to this day.
10 boulevard Montmartre, 9th.
Tel.: 01-47-70-85-05. www.grevin.com
Open from Monday to Friday 10am to 6.30pm, and 7pm on Saturdays, Sundays and public holidays. Entrance fee.

Restaurants

Ⓕ I Golosi
Marvellous north Italian food served above an Italian delicatessen. A delight for

everyone, not just connoisseurs. Dishes à la carte €27 – 35.

6 rue de la Grange-Batelière, 9th.
Tel. : 01-48-24-18-63. www.igolosi.com
Open Monday to Friday noon to 3.30pm and 7pm to 11.30, Saturday 11am to 7pm.

G Kiku

A delicious Japanese restaurant, presided over by a chef who is famous for his creative approach. Lunchtime menus at €10.50 and €14.50.

56, rue Richer, 9th.
Tel.: 01-44-83-02-30.
Open from Monday to Friday noon to 2.15pm and 7.30pm to 10.15pm, as well as on Saturday evenings.

Out on the town

H Le Limonaire

An old Parisian bistro (restaurant and bar), which is transformed into something of a subversive cabaret show in the evening when singers and poets take to the stage. Clients pay them what they think they are worth. Cabaret show every Sunday, except for the third Sunday of the month when silent movies are projected.

21 rue Bergère, 9th. Tel.: 01-45-23-33-33.
Open daily except Mondays, show at 10pm on weekdays and 7pm on Sundays.

I Chez Carmen

Ideal for a drink after a show or for insomniacs, since this night bar is filled with clients dancing to lively music until the wee hours.

53 rue Vivienne, 2nd. Tel.: 01-42-36-45-41.
Open Tuesday to Sunday 10.30pm to 9am Saturdays until noon.

J Social Club

An eclectic place that is inquisitive and open to new ideas. Established a year ago, the Social Club hosts a DJ and holds concerts, aftershows, and preview evenings, the aim being to deconstruct styles and categories, and mix different audiences.

142 rue Montmartre, 2nd. Tel. 01-40-28-05-55.

BONNE NOUVELLE

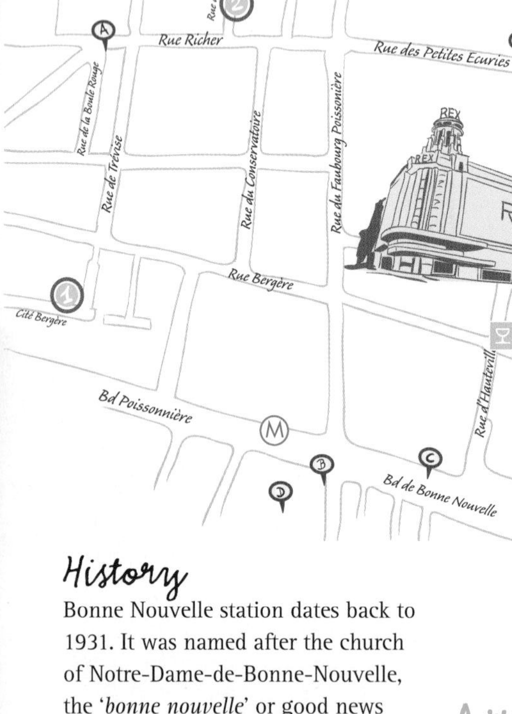

©Bruno Marguerite/RATP

History

Bonne Nouvelle station dates back to 1931. It was named after the church of Notre-Dame-de-Bonne-Nouvelle, the '*bonne nouvelle*' or good news being the Annunciation. The church was built in 1563, but destroyed and rebuilt several times since. During the celebrations of the 100-year anniversary of the Paris Metro, the station was redecorated in a cinema theme. They typography of the station signage on the platforms was designed to resemble the famous Hollywood sign in Los Angeles. The station is located on Boulevard Bonne-Nouvelle, one of the Parisian Grands Boulevards.

SIGHTSEEING

A walk in the city

1. **Cité Bergère:** the attractive facades date back to the Restoration. Today the buildings have nearly all been converted into hotels.
From 6 rue du Faubourg-Montmartre to 23 rue Bergère, 9th.

2. **Cité de Trévise:** a sleepy street with a square in the middle and a lovely fountain. The pretty neo-Renaissance facades are great for lovers of the Romantic Movement.
From 18 rue Richer to 7 rue Bleue, 9th.

Address book

The place for a rendezvous

Le Mistral Café
14 rue d'Hauteville, 10th.
Open from Monday to Saturday 8am to 8pm.
Tel.: 01-48-24-37-50.

Shows

A Folies-Bergère
Behind the Art Deco façade sculpted by Pico in 1929, lies the leading French variety theatre with dancing revues and variety performances ranging from Belle Époque to the Roaring Twenties in style. Today the theatre also puts on musicals, shows and concerts.
32 rue Richer, 9th.
Tel.: 0892-68-16-50.
www.foliesbergere.com

B Grand Rex

Built in 1932 by Jacques Haïk, the owner of the Olympia theatre, this enormous cinema is a duplicate of New York's Radio City Music Hall on a smaller scale. The interior is in the Art Deco style of French Riviera villas, and the cinema has been a success ever since it opened. It is considered one of the most attractive cinemas in Paris. In 1981, the cinema with its Art Deco facade was listed as a protected regional building. The Grand Rex has one of the largest screens in France and remains a real temple to the cinema today.
1 boulevard Poissonnière, 2nd.
Tel.: 0892-68-05-96. www.legrandrex.com

Restaurant

C Le Delaville
Eating in a former brothel built under Napoleon III is an interesting experience, to say the least! All that remains of its history is a lavish marble staircase, a stained glass window, gilded ceiling and yellowing walls. The place is now a trendy bar-cum-restaurant with a large terrace

on the Grands Boulevards.
Le Delaville is especially known for its cheeseburgers.
Dishes €14–22.
34 boulevard Bonne-Nouvelle, 10th.
Tel.: 01-48-24-48-09.
Open all week 8am to 2am and 1am on Sunday.

Out on the town

D Rex Club

A discotheque known for the latest electro rhythms, located inside the Grand Rex complex.
5 boulevard Poissonnière, 2nd.
Tel.: 01-42-36-10-96.
www.rexclub.com
Open Tuesday to Saturday 11.30pm to 7am.

E Le Pompom
It is quite fashionable to queue on the pavement for a beer in this once charming bistro, now ultra-trendy bar. If you prefer not to die of thirst, be sure to get there early!
39 rue des Petites-Écuries, 10th.
Tel.: 01-53-34-60-85.
Open Monday to Saturday 7pm to 2am.

STRASBOURG SAINT-DENIS

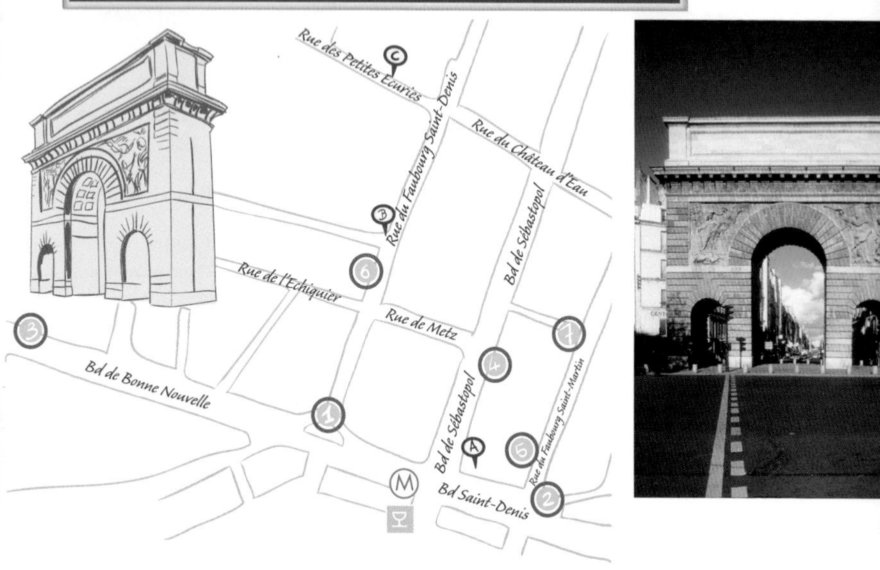

SIGHTSEEING

History

Strasbourg–Saint-Denis is a key station in the Paris Metro system, serving lines 4, 8 and 9. It is also located at a juncture between the 2nd, 3rd and 10th arrondissements. When the station was opened in 1908, it was called Boulevard Saint-Denis, but it was later renamed in reference to the Boulevard de Strasbourg, a vast thoroughfare carved out by Baron Haussmann, and to the rue du Faubourg-Saint-Denis. This station takes you to the most working-class part of the Grands Boulevards, which is still home to numerous theatres.

Monuments

1 **Porte Saint-Denis:** this triumphal arch stands on the corners of rue Saint-Denis, rue du Faubourg-Saint-Denis and the Grands Boulevards. It was commissioned by Louis XIV in 1672, in honour of his victories in the Rhine and Franche-Comté, in the place of a medieval gate in the Charles V era city walls that stood there.

2 **Porte Saint-Martin:** this arch was built two years after its sister arch, the Porte Saint-Denis, on the corners of the rue Saint-Martin, rue du Faubourg-Saint-Martin and the Grands Boulevards (Boulevard Saint-Denis and Boulevard Saint-Martin).

[Th]eatres

[Pa]risian theatre-goers are spoilt for choice in this part of the Grands Boulevards. They include recent places, such as the Comedy Club 3 opened by the French actor Jamel Debbouze, as well as historic or prestigious theatres such as the Théâtre Antoine 4, built in 1881, or the Théâtre de la Renaissance 5, which was sponsored by Alexandre Dumas and Victor Hugo, was rebuilt in 1873, and managed by Sarah Bernhardt.

Comedy Club: 42 boulevard Bonne-Nouvelle, 10th. Tel.: 01-73-54-17-00.
Théâtre Antoine: 14 boulevard de Strasbourg, 10th. Tel.: 01-42-08-77-71.
Théâtre de la Renaissance: 20 boulevard Saint-Martin, 10th. Tel.: 01-42-02-47-35.

[A]n exotic walk

- *Faubourg Saint-Denis:* rue du Faubourg-Saint-Denis is a lively, shop-lined thoroughfare, which runs from the Gare du Nord to the Grands Boulevards. An incredible mix of shops and century-old buildings, it is jostling with Turkish stallholders and narrow covered arcades like the Prado and Industrie. The neighbourhood known as Little India is here, the heart of which is in Passage Brady. Don't miss the Cour des Petites Écuries, a peaceful haven in the lively but noisy atmosphere of this neighbourhood.

- *Faubourg Saint-Martin:* rue du Faubourg-Saint-Martin, which is bordered with clothes wholesaler and African hairdressers, is hardly worth a detour. However, the 10th arrondissement's Town Hall and the Théâtre du Splendid (no. 48) are both attractive. There is one curiosity at no. 39 rue du Château d'Eau, which intersects rue du Faubourg-Saint-Martin by the town hall. This is the smallest house in Paris!

Next station

RÉPUBLIQUE

See line 3, page 86

Address book

The place for a rendezvous

Les Boulevards
112 boulevard de Sébastopol, 3rd.
Open from Monday to Friday 7.30am to 11pm.
Tel.: 01-42-72-20-90.

Culture

A Musée de l'Éventail-Atelier Hoguet
The Hoguet family has been making fans and transmitting their know-how from generation to generation since 1872! This is the last high-end fan maker in France. A little gem for fashion lovers!
2 boulevard de Strasbourg, 10th.
Tel.: 01-42-08-90-20.
Entrance fee.

Out on the town

B Chez Jeannette
An obscure local café with 1970s décor that has become a headquarters for partygoers. If you want to nibble something while you drink you can get good plate of cheese or charcuterie. The beer is cheap, and there's a great atmosphere, especially later in the evening.
47 rue du Faubourg-Saint-Denis, 10th.
Tel.: 01-47-70-30-89.
Open daily 8am to 2am.

C New Morning
A sparse, no-frills place, which is a sort of club-cum-music venue. However, it is a cult jazz club and not only for Parisians.
7 rue des Petites-Écuries, 10th.
Tel.: 01-45-23-51-41.
newmorning.com
Concerts from Monday to Saturday.

FILLES DU CALVAIRE

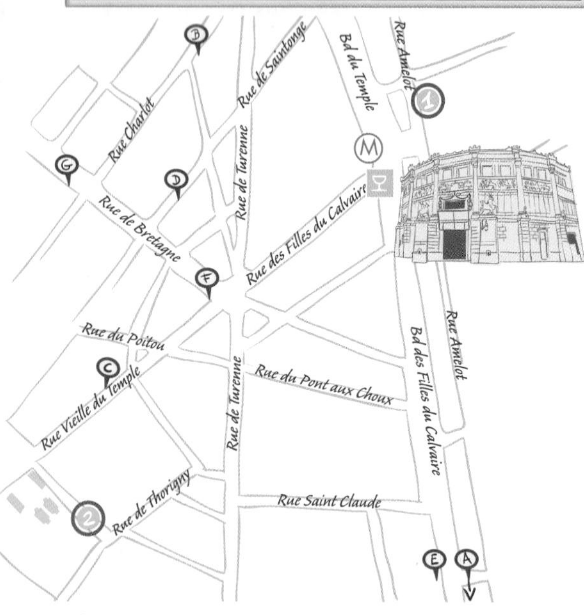

History

The name of this station, which opened in 1931, was a tribute to a congregation of reformed Benedictine nuns, known as the Calvairiennes, or Filles du Calvaire (daughters of Calvary, from the Congregation of Our Lady of Calvary). The order was founded in Poitiers by Antoinette d'Orléans and Father Joseph Le Clerc du Tremblay in 1617 and the convent later moved to the Marais district of Paris. It was closed during the Revolution and being clergy property, was seized and converted to quarters for the cavalry. The station gives onto the rue and the Boulevard des Filles-du-Calvaire, where the convent garden used to be. Today, this part of the upper Marais is a trendy area and its boutiques and restaurants greatly sought after.

SIGHTSEEING

Culture

1. ***Cirque d'Hiver:*** the so-called winter circus was built by Louis Dejean, owner of the Cirque d'Été (summer circus) in 1851 and was first called Cirque Napoléon. It is a legendary place with magnificent interior decoration. It was devoted to the circus from outset, notably with the early flying trapeze artists. In 1934, the four brothers Bouglione took over and their name has been associated with the Cirque d'Hiver ever since. All the circus stars have performed here, including Pauline Borelli, the first female lion tamer, and members of the Fratellini and Zavatta families. It is still highly

successful and the building is occasionally hired out for special events.

110 rue Amelot, 11th.
Tel.: 01-47-00-28-81.
www.cirquedhiver.com

2 **Musée Picasso:** Picasso moved to the Hôtel Salé, a grand town house in the Marais, in 1985. Built in 1659, the first owner of this *hôtel particulier* was Pierre Aubert de Fontenay who grew rich by collecting the *gabelle*, or salt tax, hence the name of the house (salty). The Picasso Museum houses the largest collection of the artists' works in the world, covering all his periods, as well as items from his own collection, which include works by Manet, Cézanne, Renoir, Matisse, le Douanier Rousseau, Derain, Braque, Modigliani, and Miró. At the time of writing the museum was closed for renovation but is due to reopen in spring 2013.

5 rue de Thorigny, 3rd.
Tel.: 01-42-71-25-21.

The place for a rendezvous

Le Barricou
1 boulevard du Temple, 3rd.
Open from Monday to Friday 7am to 8pm, Saturday 8am to 8pm.
Tel.: 01-42-72-20-53. www.lebarricou.fr

Shopping

Ⓐ Merci
A three-storey charity concept store concealed in a marvellous courtyard. Parisians enjoy guilt-free shopping here, since the profits go to charity.
111 boulevard Beaumarchais, 3rd.
Tel.: 01-42-77-00-33.
www.merci-merci.com
Open Monday to Saturday 10am to 7pm.

Ⓑ *Rues des modeuses* (fashionistas' streets)
The upper part of the Marais district is a shoppers' paradise. Fashionable clothing boutiques and trendy accessory stores proliferate along Charlot, Vieille-du-Temple and de Saintonge streets. You may find this to be an expensive walk!

Out on the town

Ⓒ Le Murano
The Murano Hotel is known for having suites with private swimming pools that look over the rooftops of Paris. Visitors can have a drink in the bar or eat in the restaurant. This is hardly typical Paris, but nevertheless a warm and intimate place.
13 boulevard du Temple, 3rd.
Tel.: 01-42-71-20-00.
Open all week 7am to 2am.

Ⓓ Le Progrès
Le Progrès is quite simply an institution on rue de Bretagne, and its terrace area is gradually spreading along the pavement. Typical Parisian waiters and French food, in a very Marais atmosphere.
1 rue de Bretagne, 3rd.
Tel.: 01-42-72-01-44.
Open Monday to Saturday 8am to 2am.

F Grazzie

A relatively new address and it's not easy to get a table. It is well worthwhile though, to enjoy pizzas and cocktails in a magnificent setting.

91 boulevard Beaumarchais, 3rd.
Tel.: 01-42-78-11-96.
Open daily noon to 2.30pm and 7.30pm to 11pm.

Restaurants

E Marché des Enfants-Rouges

This market stands on the place of a 16th century orphanage that took in lost children and dressed them in red, hence the name (red children). Today this charming covered market also offers a broad selection of prepared foods to tempt you on the spot. You can take your pick from a range of world dishes from couscous to sushi and eat right there among the flower and vegetable stalls.

39 rue de Bretagne, 3rd.
Tel.: 01-42-72-28-12.
Open on Tuesdays, Wednesdays and Thursdays 8.30am to 1pm and 4pm to 7.30pm or 8pm on Saturdays. Sundays 8.30am to 2pm.

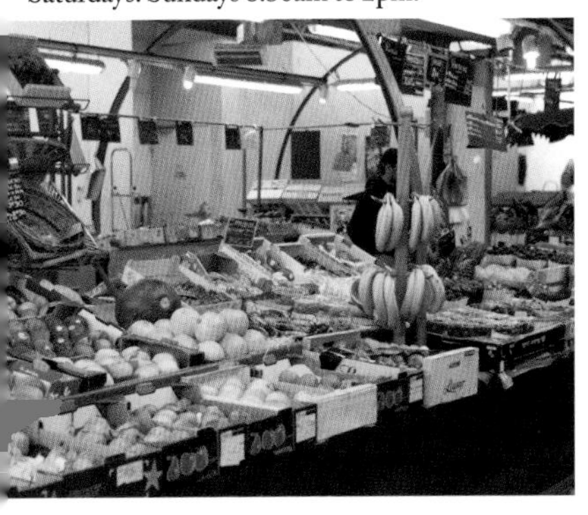

Next station

SAINT-SÉBASTIEN – FROISSART

Bistrot l'Amelot
80 rue Amelot, 11th.

CHEMIN VERT

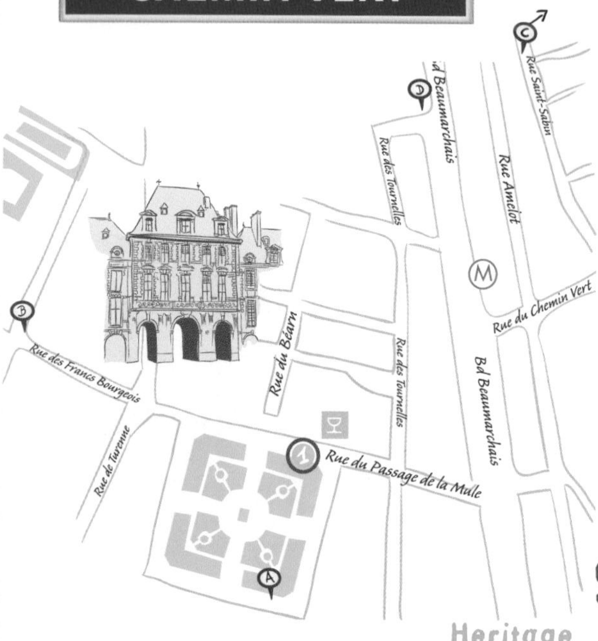

©Denis Sutton / RATP

History

This station has stood here since 1931 and is named after the rue du Chemin Vert (green path) itself named after a path that once wove its way across the market gardens here. The station is on the Boulevard Beaumarchais, which forms a border between the 11th arrondissement and the Marais.

SIGHTSEEIN

Heritage

1 **Place des Vosges:** in the early 17th century Henri IV asked the Duc de Sully to erect a square called Place Royale in place of the former Hôtel des Tournelles. The square was soon surrounded by imposing, identical two-storey buildings with a lovely arcade for shops at street level. The Place Royale was inaugurated by Louis XIII in 1612, and became a favourite walking place for aristocrats. During Paris' tumultuous history it changed its name several times, first during the French Revolution when it was called Place des Fédérés. It acquired its present name of Place des Vosges in 1800, in honour of the Vosges department in eastern France, which was the first to pay its taxes under the French Revolution. Today Parisians en-

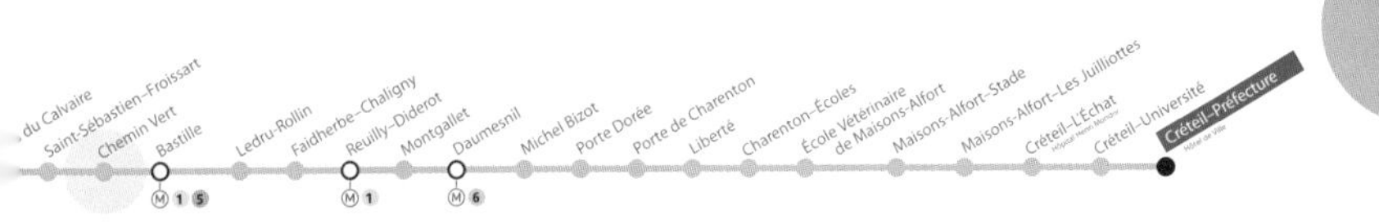

joy strolling there among the art galleries and cafés.

Around Place des Vosges: the streets and alleys in this area at the centre of the Marais rival with each other for charm. The peaceful rue Payenne has lovely façades and the Swedish Cultural Centre is located in a beautiful old town house. The rue des Francs-Bourgeois is prized for its lovely building and numerous boutiques open on Sunday.

Address book

The place for a rendezvous

🍸 **Café Hugo**

22 place des Vosges, 4th.
Open daily 7am to 2am.
Tel.: 01-47-72-64-04.

Ⓐ Maison de Victor Hugo

Victor Hugo lived in a second floor apartment in the Hôtel de Rohan-Guéménée from 1832 to 1848. The Victor Hugo Museum was established in 1902, the 100th anniversary of his birth, at the initiative of his faithful journalist friend, Paul Meurice. Meurice also gave the city of Paris a collection of Hugo's etchings, drawings, books and manuscripts in addition to furniture and other objects belonging to the great poet and writer. He added to these with purchases from many contemporary artists.

6 place des Vosges, 4th.
Tel.: 01-42-72-10-16.
Open Tuesday to Sunday (except on public holidays) 10am to 6pm. Free entrance to the permanent collection.

Ⓑ Musée Carnavalet

Housed in the former Hôtel de Carnavalet as well as the former Hôtel Le Peletier-de-Saint-Fargeau since 1989, the Carnavalet Museum traces the history of Paris from its origins to the present, through an outstanding collection of iconography and decorative arts. Paintings furniture, models and objects transport the visitor in recreations of rooms in Parisian styles from the 17th to the 20th century, including a typical Marais town houses, and Marcel Proust's bedroom.

23 rue de Sévigné, 3rd.
Tel.: 01-44-59-58-58.
Open Tuesday to Sunday 10am to 6pm.
Free entrance to the permanent collection.

Restaurants

Ⓒ Amici Miei

An Italian *trattoria* frequented by film stars amongst others. À la carte dishes €16–35.
44 rue Saint-Sabin, 11th.
Tel.: 01-42-71-82-62.
Open from Tuesday to Saturday noon to 2.30pm and 7.30pm to 11pm.

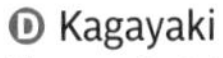

Ⓓ Kagayaki

The perfect *tepanyaki* with excellent, fresh ingredients and flawless Japanese flavours at a reasonable price. À la carte dishes €16–35.
79 boulevard Beaumarchais, 3rd.
Tel.: 01-48-87-61-88.
Open daily noon to 2.30pm and 7pm to 11pm.

Next station

BASTILLE

See line 1 page 40

LEDRU-ROLLIN

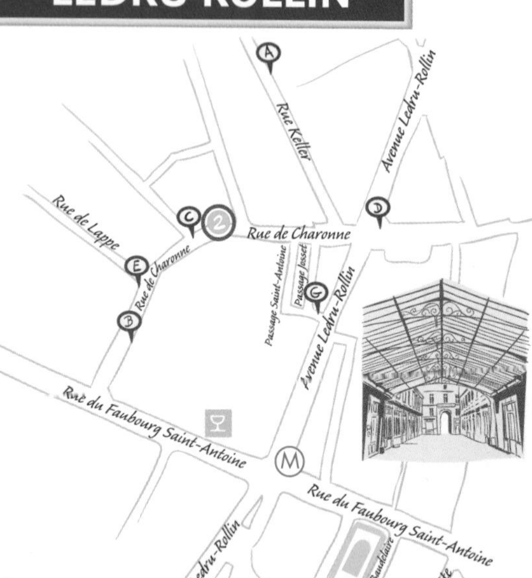

History

The station, which opened in 1931, pays homage to the lawyer Alexandre Auguste Ledru, known as Ledru-Rollin (1807–1874). Ledru-Rollin was a fervent republican and founder of the newspaper *La Réforme*. He promoted universal suffrage in the 1848 legistlative elections and stood against Napoleon Bonaparte in the presidential elections the same year, but was beaten. The station stands at the intersection of the rue du Faubourg Saint-Antoine and Avenue Ledru-Rollin, a trendy Parisian street that combines charming remnants of its working class history with a dynamic population of designers and artists, numerous restaurants, and unlimited night life.

SIGHTSEEING

A walk in the city

1 **Rue du Faubourg-Saint-Antoine:** this is one of the oldest streets in the capital. The Faubourg (or suburb of) Saint-Antoine grew in the Middle Ages around the Saint-Antoine-des-Champs abbey. Because the kings of France protected the abbey, arts and crafts flourished here, notably the cabinetmakers. The abbey was destroyed at the end of the 18th century but the cabinetmaking and carpentry tradition continued in the rue du Faubourg-Saint-Antoine (now fully a part of Paris) and all around it. The rue du Faubourg-Saint-Antoine is a narrow street that starts at the Bastille, and numerous barricades were erected along it in the course of its history. It you stroll along it you will find many interesting

shops and discover the charming courtyards behind the facades, for instance Cour du Bel-Air (at no. 56), Cour des Shadoks (no. 71), and Cour de l'Étoile-d'Or (no. 75).

Rue de Charonne: in the early 17th century this road led to the village of Charonne, which was annexed to Paris in 1860. The street was full of the homes and workshops of the cabinetmakers who specialised in furniture and chairs. After the Opéra Bastille was built in the late 1980s, the neighbourhood changed and now many design studios and photographers have set up in the former workshops. A stroll along the rue de Charonne will reveal numerous gems. At the very beginning of the street (numbers 3 and 5), when coming from rue du Faubourg-Saint-Antoine, there are two courtyards, cour Saint-Joseph and Cour Jacques-Viguès, where the cabinetmakers' workshops were in the 19th and early 20th century. At 51–53, rue de Charonne, you'll see the Hôtel de Mortagne (1661), where the famous inventor and musician Jacques de Vaucanson lived from 1746 to 1782. His inventions were the very first exhibits in the Conservatoire National des Arts et Métiers. Two typical buildings from 17th century Faubourg Saint-Antoine are to be found at numbers 78 and 69. The Palais de la Femme (women's palace) at no. 94 has a marvellous Art Nouveau façade built in 1910. This is a hostel that was acquired by the Salvation Army in 1926 and remains the largest women's hostel in Europe. Give yourself plenty of

time to get lost in the maze of alley that criss-cross the rue de Charonne, such as the Passage Lhomme, Passage Saint-Antoine, Passage Josset, Passage de la Main-d'Or, and the Passage Charles-Dallery. Last, near the Charonne metro station you will see that the crossroads at the intersection of the rue de Charonne and Boulevard Voltaire was named place du 8 Février 1962 by the Mayor of Paris, Bertrand Delanoë, in homage to the demonstration against the war in Algeria held here on that date, that ended with several dead.

Address book

The place for a rendezvous

🍸 Le Petit Café

89 rue du Faubourg-Saint-Antoine, 11th.
Open Monday 1pm to 7.30pm, and Tuesday to Saturday from 10am.
Tel.: 01-43-43-11-63.

Shopping

Ⓐ Rue Keller and Ⓑ rue de Charonne

The capital's most ardent fashionistas roam up and down these streets, because they are lined with boutiques of up-and-coming young designers—as well as many that have already made it.

A few examples

Loulou Addict: many decorative home accessories, as well as toys and ideas for children's rooms.
25 rue Keller, 11th. Tel.: 01-49-29-00-61.
Open Tuesday to Friday 11am to 2pm and 5pm to 7pm, Saturday 11am to 7pm.

Anne Willi: women's and children's fashion.
13 rue Keller, 11th.
Tel.: 01-48-06-74-06. www.annewilli.com.
Open Monday 2pm to 6pm, Tuesday to Saturday 11am to 6pm.

Marci N'oum
1 rue Keller, 11th. www.marcinoum.com

French Trotters
30 rue de Charonne, 11th.
Tel.: 01-47-00-84-35.
Open Monday 2.30pm to 7.30pm, and Tuesday to Saturday 11.30am to 7.30pm.

Sessùn
34 rue de Charonne, 11th.
Tel.: 01-48-06-55-66.
Open Monday to Saturday 11am to 7pm.

Isabelle Marant
16 rue de Charonne, 11th.
Tel.: 01-49-29-71-55.
Open Monday to Saturday 10.30am to 7.30pm.

Culture

Ⓒ Lazy Dog

There's some debate as to whether this is a boutique, a concept store or a bookshop, but it doesn't really matter. You will find graphic arts, fashion, photography, graffiti, contemporary illustrations, music and all kinds of urban trends here. Not to be missed for anyone interested in the arts or simply seeking inspiration.

25 rue de Charonne, 11th.
Tel.: 01-49-29-97-93. www.thelazydog.fr
Open Monday 1pm to 7pm, Tuesday to Thursday 11am to 7pm, Friday and Saturday 11am to 7.30pm.

Restaurants

D Le Bistrot du Peintre

Established in the heart of the historic Bastille district in 1902, the Bistrot du Peintre is a great stopping place for visitors wanting to discover the joys of this Parisian neighbourhood. It typifies all the charm of old Parisian bistros in a terrific Art Nouveau style from the 1900s. It is the oldest bistro in the neighbourhood and has had an eventful past, which has contributed to

its reputation. In front of the bistro you will see the date (1902), as well as the price of a cup of coffee at the time: just 10 centimes!
Dishes €12–17.
116 avenue Ledru-Rollin, 11th.
Tel.: 01-47-00-34-39.
www.bistrotdupeintre.com.
Open all week 7am to 2am, continuous service from noon to midnight.

E Chez Paul

Since the beginning of the last century, artists and the unknown, regulars and others have all flocked to Chez Paul and enjoyed its family atmosphere. The old 1940s telephone cabin bears witness to the pleasant ambiance and good food this agreeable local restaurant has provided since then. Dishes €16–25.
13 rue Charonne, 11th.
Tel.: 01-47-00-34-57. www.chezpaul.com
Open Monday to Friday noon to 3pm and 7pm to 0.30am, Saturday and Sunday noon to 0.30am.

F La Gazzetta

The word 'fusion' acquires real meaning here, thanks to a very creative Swedish chef, the New York atmosphere and a dash of Italy. Highly-prized by the Parisian smart set. Lunch menus €39 and €52 in the evenings.

29 rue de Cotte, 12th.
Tel.: 01-43-47-47-05. www.lagazzetta.fr.
Open Tuesday to Saturday noon to 2.30pm and 8pm to 11pm.

Out on the town

G Le Motel

This bar is the incarnation of all things trendy in the Charonne neighbourhood. A range of musical events, spiced up from time to time with karaoke. Happy hour until 9pm.
8 passage Josset, 11th.
Tel.: 01-58-30-88-52.
Open Tuesday to Sunday 6pm to 2am.

FAIDHERBE – CHALIGNY

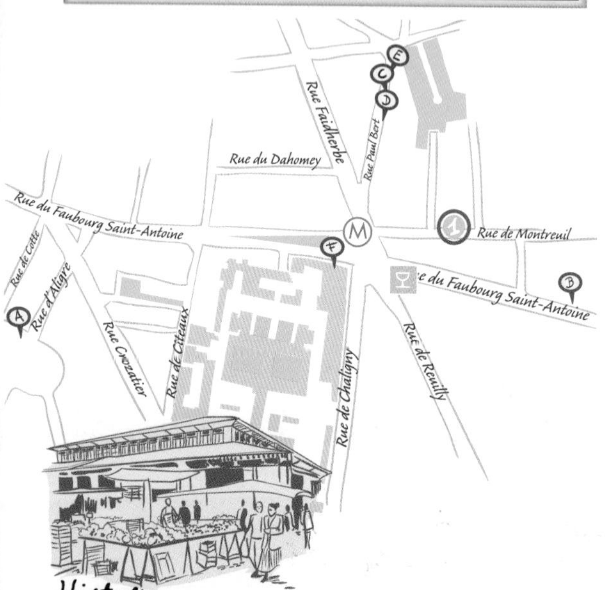

History

This station was opened in 1931 at the intersection of the rue Faidherbe, rue de Reuilly and rue Chaligny. Rue Faidherbe was named after Général Louis Léon César Faidherbe (1818–1889), who was Governor of Senegal from 1854 to 1861 and again from 1863 to 1865. He was then Commander of the Northern Army in 1870–1871, and valiantly resisted the Prussians. Rue Chaligny was named after the Chaligny family of illustrious foundry owners in Lorraine. This is a very endearing neighbourhood, which is still home to numerous cabinetmakers and artisans working in wrought iron. It is also an area with some of the most creative restaurants in Paris.

SIGHTSEEING

Working class history

1 **Around rue de Montreuil:** take the rue de Montreuil as soon as you leave the metro and you will plunge into the history of 19th century urbanisation and the establishment of housing estates and workshops. You will discover the courtyards off the streets, such as Cité de l'Ameublement, Cour de l'Industrie and Cour Saint-Nicolas. Further on you can stroll down rue des Immeubles-Industriels, a phalanstery designed for thousands of workers in 1872, and another former housing estate at 95 rue de Montreuil, relics of the past that confer considerable charm on this neighbourhood.

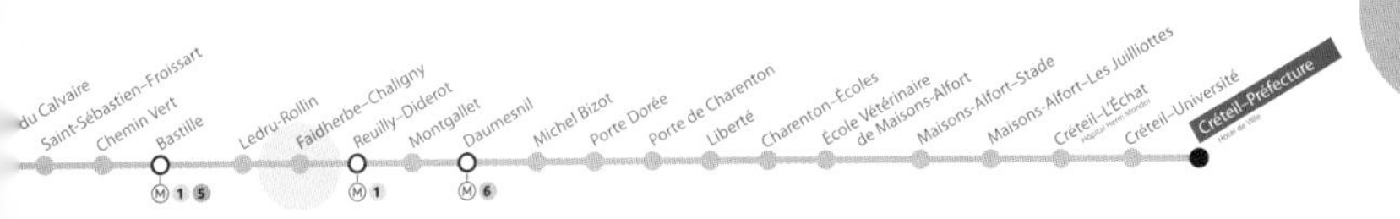

Address book

The place for a rendezvous

Café Pierre
202 rue du Faubourg-Saint-Antoine, 12th.
Tel.: 01-43-73-84-79.

Shopping

Ⓐ Marché d'Aligre
This market really exemplifies neighbourhood community life. Here the locals natter between the flea market stands and the fruit and veg. A truly Parisian experience.
Rue and Place d'Aligre.
Open Tuesday to Sunday 7.30am to 1.30pm.

Restaurants

Ⓑ Chez Ramulaud
The Ramulaud carries the banner of French cuisine on high. You will find a quality, traditional French cuisine here, complete with an *apéritif* at the bar and inventive country cooking. Nothing but the best. Approximately €20–30.
269 rue du Faubourg-Saint-Antoine, 11th.
Tel.: 01-43-72-23-29.
www.chez-ramulaud.fr
Open Monday to Friday noon to 3pm and 8pm to 11pm and Saturday evenings.

Ⓒ Bistrot Paul Bert
An old Parisian bistro that is on its way to becoming an institution. The seasonal menu is mouth-watering, with marvellous meat and produce straight from the market. Approximately €35–45.
18 rue Paul-Bert, 11th.
Tel.: 01-43-72-24-01.
Open Tuesday to Saturday noon to 2pm and 7.30 to 11pm.

Ⓓ Le Chardenoux
Taken over in 2008 by the chef Cyril Lignac, this venerable bistro with its 1900 décor is a gourmet paradise. High quality cuisine in a friendly atmosphere. Lunch menus €25 and €30.
1, rue Jules Vallès, 11th.
Tel.: 01-43-71-49-52.
Open Monday to Sunday noon to 2.30pm (3.30pm on Sunday) and Sunday 7.30pm to 11pm.

Ⓔ L'Écailler du Bistrot
If you love oysters and seafood this is the place to go. Lunch menu at €16.50, €45 in the evenings.
22 rue Paul-Bert, 11th.
Tel.: 01-43-72-76-77.
Open Tuesday to Saturday noon to 2.30pm and 7.30pm to 11pm.

Out on the town

Ⓕ La Liberté
If you fancy starting off the evening with a drink, then head for La Liberté, a 'prehistoric' neighbourhood bar, much loved by the local regulars. A sort of rock'n'roll family place!
196 rue du Faubourg-Saint-Antoine, 12th.
Tel.: 01-43-72-11-18.
Open Monday to Friday 8.30pm to 2am, Saturday and Sunday from 11am.

Next stations

REUILLY-DIDEROT

See line 1, page 43

MONTGALLET

Royal Reuilly Bar
66 rue de Reuilly, 12th.

DAUMESNIL

See line 6, page 165

MICHEL BIZOT

Au Tramway
253 avenue Daumesnil, 12th.

PORTE DORÉE

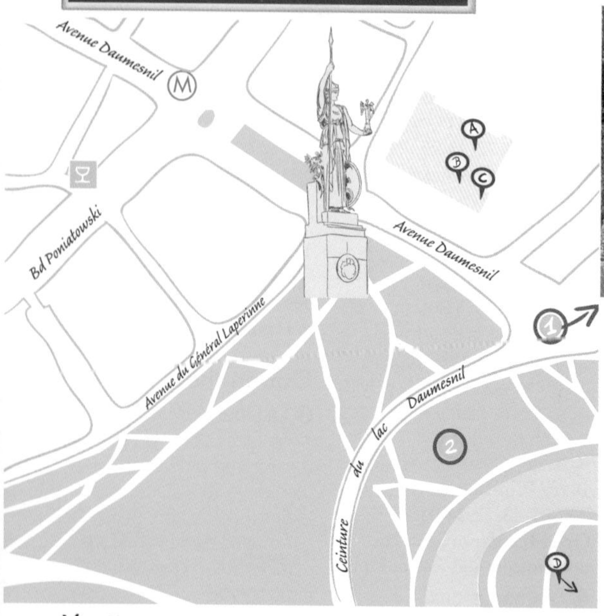

History

Porte Dorée metro station opened in 1931, on the edge of the Bois de Vincennes. Its name may come from a contraction of *'porte de l'orée du bois'* (gate on the edge of the woods), but it may also be from the golden statue of a woman that stands here, bearing a seal from the Rudier foundry.

SIGHTSEEING

Monument

❶ ***Château de Vincennes:*** since it was renovated at the end of the 1980s the Château has gradually regained its noble credentials. Built during the Capetian dynasty it was a royal residence from the 12th to the 17th century, and was then used as a state prison in the 18th century. During the 19th and 20th centuries it was transformed into a military establishment. It was badly damaged during the Second World War, after having been occupied by the Nazis. The donjon tower, which dates back to King Charles V, is not only the tallest in Europe, but also the only medieval donjon still standing.
The main entrance is on avenue de Paris, 94300 Vincennes.
Tel.: 01-48-08-31-20.
www.chateau-vincennes.fr.
Open daily 10am to 6pm from May to August and 1am to 5pm from September to April. Closed on public holidays. Entrance fee.

A walk in the park

❷ ***Bois de Vincennes:*** this wood is really a vast 1,000 hectares (around 2,500 acres) park, filled with oaks and other species, and a place where Parisians come to

study nature. It houses a bird sanctuary in the centre, plated in a stopover point for migrating birds. A large observatory enabled birdwatchers to observe some 180 different species. The Bois de Vincennes also has an arboretum comprising some 2,000 species of trees, and a tropical garden that has recently grown rather neglected. Last but not least, the Parc Floral de Paris has numerous activities for children of all ages and is open all year round.

Address book

The place for a rendezvous

Les Jardins de Reuilly
105 boulevard Poniatowski, 12th.
Open daily 8.30am to midnight.
Tel.: 01-43-43-69-79.

Culture

Ⓐ Palais de la Porte-dorée
Designed for the 1931 Colonial Exhibition, the Palais de la Porte was originally a colonial museum devoted to the history of the conquests and occupied territories. It later became the Museum of the French Overseas Territories until the end of the 1950s. In 1990 it housed artefacts from Africa and the Pacific, until the Quai Branly Museum opened in 2006 and took these over. Today only the Tropical Aquarium and Historic Rooms on the ground floor are still open to the public but the Immigration Museum (Cité Nationale de l'Histoire de l'Immigration) opened here in 2007.
293 avenue Daumesnil, 12th. Tel.: 01-53-59-60. www.aquarium-portedoree.fr. Open Tuesday to Friday 10am to 5.15pm, Saturday and Sunday 10am to 7pm. Entrance fee.

Ⓑ Aquarium Tropical
This tropical aquarium was built in 1931 and is worth the trip if you enjoy looking at rare and amazing fish. The aquarium has a collection of primitive fish, which have looked the same for 300 million years, and there are plenty of thrills to be had in the crocodile pit too!
Inside the Palais de la Porte-Dorée. Open Tuesday to Sunday 10am to 5pm. Entrance fee.

Ⓒ Cité Nationale de l'Histoire de l'Immigration
The various waves of immigration to France are recorded here and tribute is paid to the contribution the immigrants have made to the construction of France over the past two centuries. You will find ever changing exhibitions, artwork, equipment and life histories, as well as a programme of conferences on related issues.
293 avenue Daumesnil, 12th. Tel.: 01-53-59-58-60. www.histoire-immigration.fr Open Tuesday to Friday 10.a.m. to 5.30pm, Saturday and Sunday 10am to 7pm. Entrance fee.

Restaurant

Ⓓ Le Chalet des Îles Daumesnil
Fancy dining on an island? The Île de Reuilly is an island in the heart of the Vincennes woods with a pleasant restaurant surrounded by terraces. A former Swiss chalet, the restaurant was a popular Parisian dance hall at the end of the 19th century. Recently taken over by two talented restaurant owners, it has now been transformed into a contemporary *brasserie*, blending traditional tastes with exotic ones from abroad.
Lac Daumesnil, bois de Vincennes. Tel.: 01-43-07-00-10. www.lechaletdesiles.com.Open daily 9am to midnight.

line 9

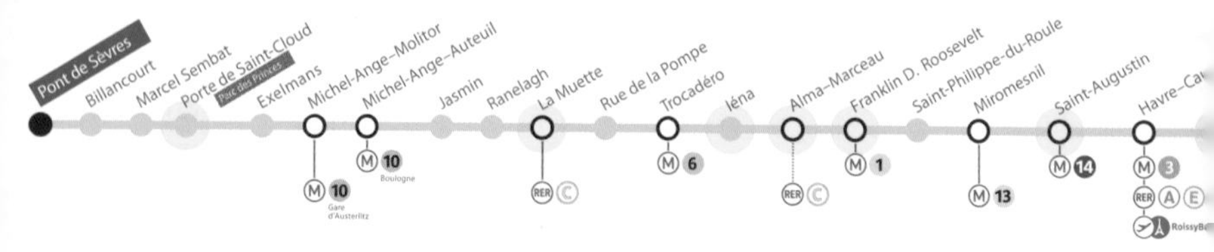

History

This parabola-shaped line covers 19.562 kilometres (12.155 miles) and links the elegant facades of south-west Paris to the working class streets of Montreuil in the east. The first section from Exelmans to Trocadéro was opened between the wars in 1922. The next two sections, from Trocadéro north-east to Chaussée d'Antin and from Exelmans south to Porte de Saint-Cloud, were opened in 1923. This was not an easy line to build since the tunnel under Place de l'Alma was dug 14 metres (15 yards) deep and runs through the water table. Also, the tram companies were pitiless competitors and tried to slow down work on the line. Nevertheless, the extension

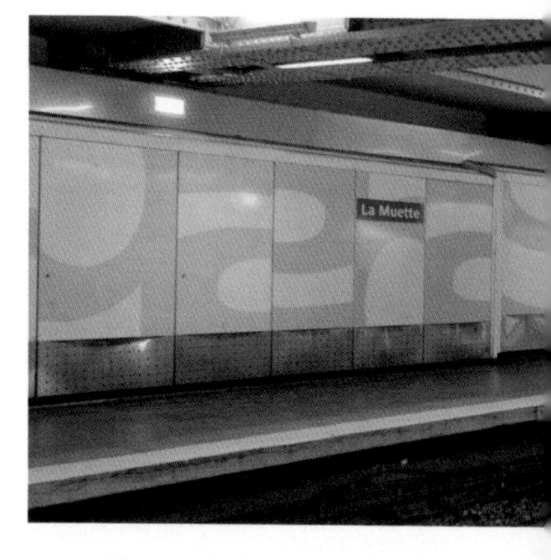

from Chaussée d'Antin east to Richelieu-Drouot was finished in 1928, and by 1933 the line ran to the eastern edge of Paris at Porte de Montreuil. The south-western terminus, Pont de Sèvres, was finished in 1934, while the eastern terminus, Mairie de Montreuil, was opened in 1937.A curious historical snapshot tells us that when British

Pont de Sèvres / Mairie de Montreuil

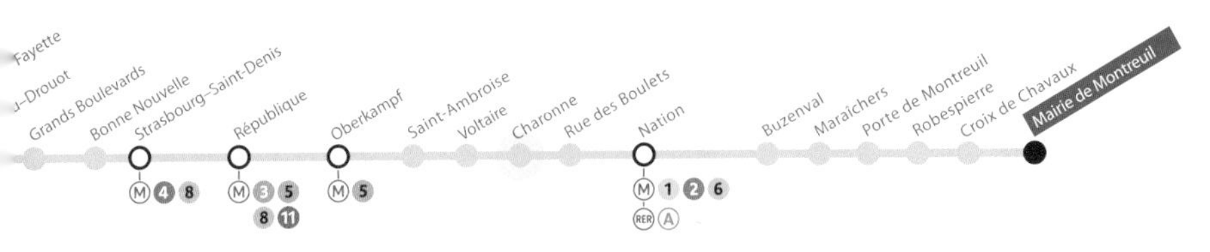

© Guillaume Lacourt / RATP

forces bombarded Renault's factories in Boulogne Billancourt in 1943, although metro stations Pont de Sèvres and Billancourt were seriously damaged, car production at the factories was able to resume just five days later.

PORTE DE SAINT-CLOUD

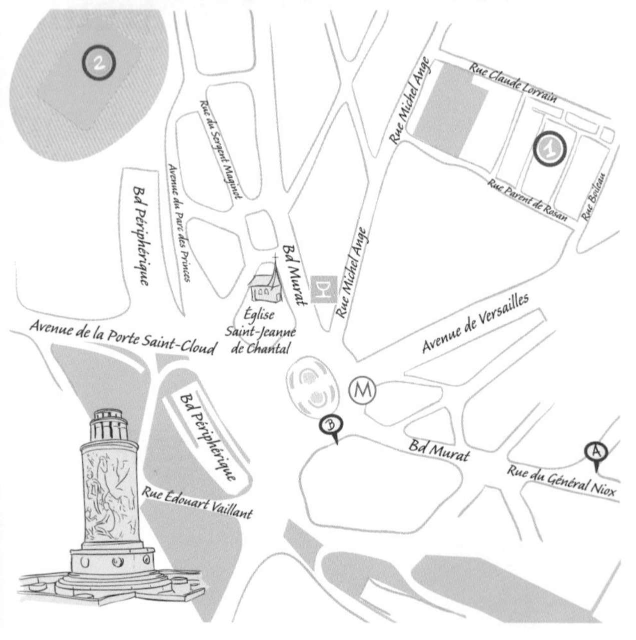

History

This station is situated in Auteuil, one of the 16th arrondissement's classy neighbourhoods. It is unusual in having four platforms, and was the south-western terminus on line 9 from 1923 to 1934. It is normally as quiet as the sleepy neighbourhood it serves, but on nights when there is a football match at nearby Parc des Princes, it is packed. Auteuil itself was an ecclesiastical fiefdom from the 11th century until the French Revolution. It attracted literary personalities who fled the tumult of Paris for the peacefulness of what was then a village known for its vineyards and thermal baths. Molière, Racine and Boileau took the waters here. Chateaubriand, Edmond and Jules de Goncourt and Proust also stayed here. Auteuil became part of Paris in 1860.

SIGHTSEEING

Architecture

1 Les Trois Villas: not the prettiest part of Auteuil, yet it contains a real gem. On tiny cobbled side streets protected from cars, you can find little houses with lovely gardens full of ivy and lilac trees. Look for three villas in particular, Dietz-Monnin, Émile-Meyer and Cheysson, on rue Parent-de-Rosan. At the end of the 19th century workers lived in these houses, which were used as lodgings by the Passy-Auteuil society of working people's housing.
Rue Parent-de-Rosan, 16th.

Parc des Princes: this was a favourite hunting haunt for the king in the 18th century. Then in 1841, Louis-Philippe ordered a wall to be built enclosing a park where the Parisian aristocracy would go, and the Parc des Princes was born. A track was built here in 1897, and in 1903 it was the finishing line for the first Tour de France bycicle race. In 1972 it was replaced by a sports complex designed by contemporary architect Roger Taillibert. The stadium, home to Paris-Saint-Germain football club, can hold nearly 50,000 supporters.

24 rue du Commandant-Guilbaud, 16th.
www.leparcdesprinces.fr

Address Book

The place for a rendezvous

Aux Trois Obus
120 rue Michel-Ange, 16th. Open daily 6am to 10pm.
Tel.: 01-46-51-22-58.

Restaurants

A A&M
A restaurant with cream-coloured, contemporary decor located near the river Seine. The chef, Tsukasa Fukuyama, serves dishes straight out of French gourmet tradition, but adds a touch of Japan. Savour the *hâchis Parmentier de joue de bœuf*, a gourmet version of cottage pie, or pork dishes like *duo de cochon, poitrine rôtie au romarin* and *galette de pied et oreille*. Menus €23–30.
136 boulevard Murat, 16th.
Tel.: 01-45-27-39-60
am-restaurant.com

B Le Cardinal
This family restaurant describes itself as having 'a chic yet cosy contemporary decor playing on natural materials like wood and leather'. Cooking is simple and good, portions generous, and ingredients are chosen carefully, particularly the seafood. Worth a try for its intimate feel. À la carte about €30.
5 place de la Porte-de-Saint-Cloud, 16th.
Tel.: 01-45-27-38-63
lecardinalparis.com

Previous stations

PONT DE SÈVRES
L'Arcouest
100 rue de Sèvres, 92100 Boulogne-Billancourt.

BILLANCOURT
Le B 19
19 avenue du Général-Leclerc, 92100 Boulogne-Billancourt.

MARCEL SEMBAT
Café Édouard
78 avenue Édouard-Vaillant, 92100 Boulogne Billancourt.

Next stations

EXELMANS
Brussel'Café,
71 boulevard Exelmans, 16th.

MICHEL-ANGE – MOLITOR
Café le Jean Bouin
55 rue Molitor, 16th.

MICHEL-ANGE – AUTEUIL
Le Fétiche
53 rue d'Auteuil, 16th.

LA MUETTE

History

There is debate over the true origin of the name 'La Muette', besides its obvious association with the nearby Château de la Muette in the Passy neighbourhood. Some say it derives from *meute*, meaning pack, referring to the hounds used for hunting in the nearby Bois de Boulogne woods. Others suggest it refers to a hunting pavilion near Passy belonging to Charles IX, where *mues*, the antlers deer shed in autumn, were kept. The former château had been a hunting base; princes were raised there and several of the king's mistresses had lived there. It became the property of the state during the French Revolution. The contemporary château was built nearby in 1922 and was the home of Henri de Rothschild. Nowadays it is the headquarters of the Organisation for Economic Cooperation and Development (OECD).

SIGHTSEEING

A walk through history

1 Jardins du Ranelagh: the gardens of Château de la Muette where aviator Jean-François Pilâtre de Rozier took off on 21 November 1783 in the first manned flight in a hot-air balloon, to Butte-aux-Cailles in south-east Paris. Balls were held here during the Second Empire in the rotunda, which was a copy of the rotunda built by an English peer, Lord Ranelagh, in his garden in Chelsea—hence the name of the gardens. They are the only remainder of Château de la Muette's former splendour.
Avenue de Ranelagh, 16th.

Maison de Balzac: Honoré de Balzac lived in this house for seven years under the name De Breugnol to escape from his creditors. He wrote *La Comédie Humaine* while living here. In the house you can see objects that belonged to Balzac, like a coffee pot with his initials and a turquoise-studded cane given to him by Madame Hanska, who would become his wife after they had corresponded for 18 years.

47 rue Raynouard, 16th.
Open Tuesday to Saturday 10am to 6pm.

Address Book

The place for a rendezvous

Tabac de la Muette-Bongrand
6 chaussée de la Muette, 16th.
Open Monday to Saturday 7am to 8.30pm and Sundays 9am to 8pm.
Tel.: 01-46-47-53-39.

Culture

Ⓐ Théâtre du Ranelagh
This 18th-century theatre was originally a concert hall decorated in oak carved in neo-Renaissance style by theatre architect Alban Chambon. On 25 April 1900 the first performance in France of the opera *Das Rheingold* by Richard Wagner was held here, conducted by Camille Chevillard with an orchestra of 24 musicians. In 1931 it became a cinema for independent films, a favourite haunt for celebrities like actor Gerard Philipe or director Marcel Carné. Now the theatre orients its programming around discovering new talent.
5 rue des Vignes 16th.
Tel.: 01-42-88-64-44.
www.theatre-ranelagh.com

Shopping

Ⓑ Galerie Commerciale Passy Plazza
This shopping centre leads off the busy, bustling rue de Passy. There are 26 boutiques to assuage shopaholics' lust. Not far away, those who prefer a bit of history can admire the charming Place de Passy.
53 rue de Passy, 16th.
Tel.: 01-40-50-09-07.
www.passyplaza.com

Previous stations

JASMIN

L'Avenue,
63 avenue Mozart, 16th.

RANELAGH

Café l'Amadeus
54 bis avenue Mozart, 16th.

Next stations

RUE DE LA POMPE

Le Montespan
87 rue de la Pompe, 16th.

TROCADÉRO

See line 6, page 146

IÉNA

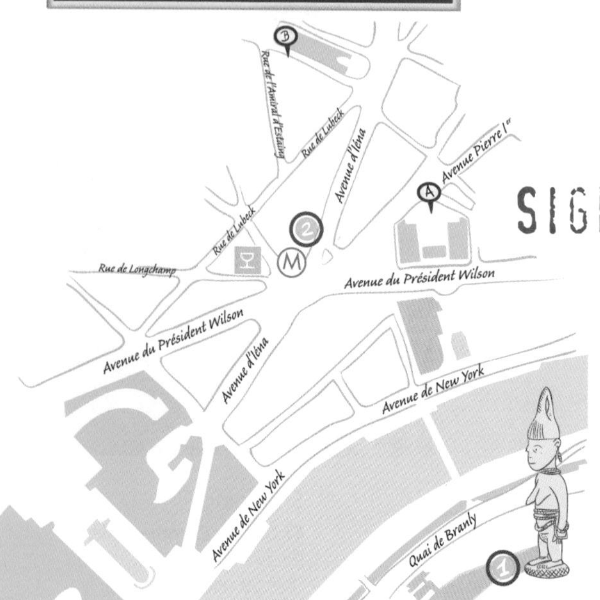

SIGHTSEEING

Culture

1 Musée du Quai Branly: the museum is surrounded by plants, and they also cover its outside walls. Its living walls were designed by botanist Patrick Blanc. This is where you begin your journey from one continent to another in a space conceived by contemporary architect Jean Nouvel. It contains impressive works of tribal art from Africa, Asia, the Americas and Oceania, which create a dialogue and a harmonious whole despite their different styles.

37, quai Branly, 7th.
Tel.: 01-56-61-70-00. www.quaibranly.fr
Entrance fee.

History

This station is named after the German town Jena where a historic battle took place on 14 October 1806. French forces under Napoléon Bonaparte vanquished Prussian armies under the Prince of Hohenlohe-Ingelfingen. The station, opened in 1923, is quite unusual. The railings around its entrance match those of the neighbouring Musée Guimet. The entrance on this side has a Val d'Osne cast iron lamppost, named after the foundry that manufactured them, while the other entrance has an Art Deco Dervaux lamppost, named after architect Adolphe Dervaux.

Musée Guimet: this museum was opened in 1889 during the lifetime of its owner, industrialist and traveller Émile Guimet (1836–1918). He was fascinated by Asian art, and during his travels in the Far East he had put together a collection that allowed him to open his first museum, on religious history, in his home town of Lyon. Gradually other museums entrusted him with artworks from India, Afghanistan, Japan, China and Nepal, among others, to expand his collection.

6 place d'Iéna, 16th.
Tel.: 01-56-52-53-00. www.guimet.fr

Address Book

The place for a rendezvous

P Au Bon Accueil
12 rue de Longchamp, 16th.
Open Monday to Friday 7.30am to 9.30pm, Sundays 9am to 6pm.
Tel.: 01-53-70-92-67.

Luxury

A Palais Galliera – Musée de la Mode
This fashion museum was closed for a while for renovation but has now reopened. Located in the Duchess of Galliera's palace, dating from 1894, it only carries temporary exhibitions because of the difficulty of conserving exhibits. It draws on a stock of 90,000 items, including lace, frills, jewels, canes, hats and umbrellas designed by famous fashion designers and couturiers. A fashion history of the 18th and 19th centuries.
10 avenue Pierre-Ier-de-Serbie, 16th.
Tel.: 01-56-52-86-00.
www.paris.fr

B Galérie-Musée Baccarat
The grand town house that used to belong to arts patron Marie-Laure de Noailles now houses the remarkable collection of crystal glass artworks by Baccarat. It is a surreal, enchanting and poetic place to visit with superb interior architecture designed by Philippe Starck. There is also a shop and a restaurant.
11 place des États-Unis, 16th.
Tel.: 01-40-22-11-00.
Open Mondays and Wednesday to Saturday 10am to 6.30pm.
Entrance fee.

ALMA – MARCEAU

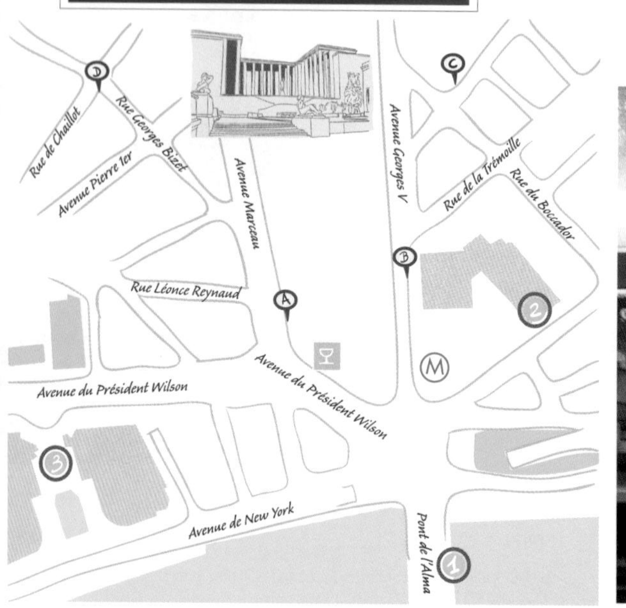

History

This station's name refers to the Pont de l'Alma bridge, Place de l'Alma and Avenue Marceau. The bridge and the square are called after the Battle of Alma, when French and British armies were victorious against the Russians in 1854 during the Crimean War. Avenue Marceau is named after General François Séverin Marceau-Desgravier (1769–1796), a general in the French Revolutionary Wars, who was known for his heroism and honesty. He was originally set to embark on a legal career, but became a solider instead and later put down the rebellion by Vendée royalists in 1793. As for the Battle of Alma, 120 allied regiments had arrived 50 kilometres (31 miles) north of Sebastopol, the British marching on the left, the French in the centre and the Turks on the right. They had to cross the River Alma, which was firmly held by Marshal Menshikov with 37,000 men posted on the hills above the river. The battle began on 20 September in the chill of dawn. Napoléon III commemorated the victory by building the eponymous bridge. As you come out of the metro on Place de l'Alma, you can see the Flame of Liberty, a replica of the flame on the Statue of Liberty, which was a gift from France to the United States. The Flame of Liberty was given to France by the *International Herald Tribune*. The square is also where people come to remember Lady Diana Spencer, Princess of Wales, known affectionately as Lady Di, who died in a car accident in the tunnel under the square in 1997.

SIGHTSEEING

rchitecture

Pont de l'Alma: the bridge was opened by Napoléon III to commemorate his first victory in the Crimean War. It was built by engineer Gariel in 1854 as part of Baron Haussmann's major redesign of Paris. Its three arches have pedestals that used to serve as bases for four giant statues of various types of soldier bearing arms. During the 1970s engineers Lagallisserie, Darcel and Vaudrey were brought in to rebuild it in iron, but without losing its design, and in particular to widen it to accommodate increased river traffic. Three statues were relocated during the renovation. Only the famous Zouave by Georges Diébolt remains. According to legend, André-Louis Gody, a soldier in Napoléon III's army, was chosen by the emperor to be the model for the statue. It wears the distinctive *Zouave* uniform—a fez, a short jacket without buttons, a wide cloth belt, bloomers, leggings and greaves (shin pads). The statue is used as a measure of whether the river Seine is likely to flood. If the river reaches its feet, the Seine is worryingly high. During the famous flood of 1910, people had to swim because the swirling floodwaters came up to their shoulders.

② **Théâtre des Champs-Élysées**

This immaculate theatre was built in 1913 on the prestigious Avenue Mon-

taigne in a district that grew up in a fever of property development. It was to provide a venue for contemporary dance shows and concerts. Sculptor and painter Antoine Bourdelle and painters Maurice Denis, Édouard Vuillard and Ker-Xavier Roussel contributed to its decoration. It has always hosted avant-garde performances and is the Paris venue for the contemporary ballet *Gala des Étoiles*, now in its 14th edition, which mixes classical and contemporary choreography and features star dancers from a variety of different ballet companies.

15 avenue Montaigne, 8th.
Tel.: 01-49-52-50-50.
www.theatrechampselysees.fr

③ **Palais de Tokyo:** this building with imposing white columns was built for the World Fair in 1937 and is dedicated to modern and contemporary art and creation. Its east wing houses the Paris modern art museum, Musée d'Art Moderne de la Ville de Paris. The west wing houses the Palais de Tokyo, and its exhibition space, dedicated to all forms of contemporary art, was opened in 2002. During the Second World War its basement was used to stock goods confiscated from Jews. Nowadays it aims to shake up prejudices and give free reign to ex-

perimentation. Light enters the building from all angles, giving exhibits the best possible showing.

13 avenue du Président-Wilson, 16th.
Tel.: 01-47-23-54-01.
www.palaisdetokyo.com
Open Tuesday to Sunday noon to 9pm. Entrance fee.

Address Book

The place for a rendezvous

La Mascotte
6 avenue du Président-Wilson, 8th.
Open daily 7am to midnight.
Tel.: 01-47-20-83-47.

Out on the town

A Le Baron
There used to be a 'hostess bar' here, but it was closed down in 2002 and Le Baron emerged from its ashes to become one of Paris's hottest discotheques. Entry is highly selective and you need to be on the guest list if possible. Its dim lighting and pearl curtains set the tone for this intimate venue where internationally known artists, singers and actors can be seen. Björk, Sofia Coppola and Quentin Tarantino have been spotted here. A bottle of champagne costs €150.
6 avenue Marceau, 8th.
Tel.: 01-47-20-04-01.

B The Crazy Horse
This venue, founded in 1951 by Alain Bernardin, is the most avant-garde Parisian cabaret and is known for its nude dancing numbers which alternate with cabaret and conjuring shows. The dancers are the only women allowed on stage. Alain Bernardin, who combined his fascination with the female form and the Far West in this venue, gave each of his dancers a stage name, and several became famous in the 1980s. Even nowadays performances here can still create a sensation, like burlesque queen Dita Von Teese's sensual show when she was the first guest star here in 2006.
12avenue George-V, 8th.
Tel.: 01-47-23-32-32.
www.lecrazyhorseparis.com

Restaurants

C La Fermette Marbeuf
It is hard to believe that this sumptuous place, which was classed as a historical monument in 1983, was discovered by chance. It is a jewel of Art Nouveau style with a magnificent, absolutely breathtaking glass roof. The chef, Gilbert Isaac, serves his generous and tasty version of French cuisine using traditional recipes with a twist. This restaurant is just magical with its 19th century ornaments and engraved arches. Menus €23 – 32.
5 rue Marbeuf, 8th.
Tel.: 01.53.23.08.00.
www.fermettemarbeuf.com

D Il Gusto Sardo
This restaurant done up in cream and scarlet is not far from the Galliera Museum. Its chef and cooks are all Italian and from the same Sardinian family. Copious dishes redolent of a sun-kissed, sensual Italy. À la carte dishes about €50.
17 rue Georges-Bizet, 16th.
Tel.: 01-47-20-08-90.
www.restaurant-ilgustosardo.com
Open Monday to Friday 12.15pm to 2.30pm and 7.30pm to 10.30pm, evenings only on Saturdays.

FRANKLIN D. ROOSEVELT

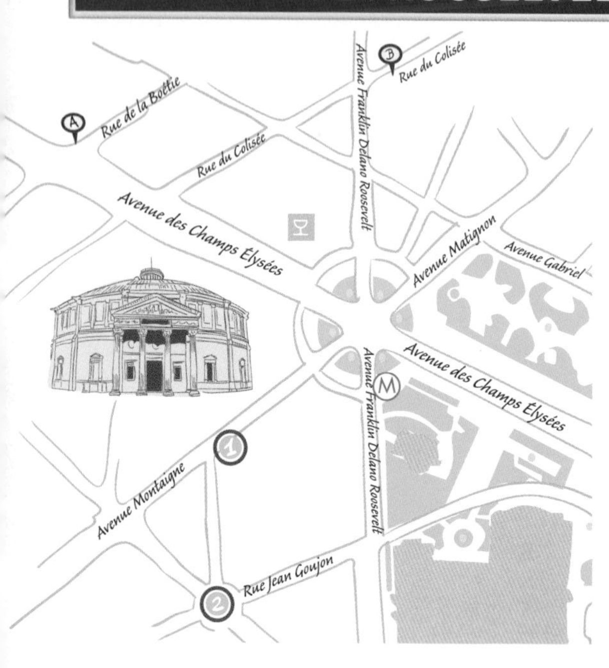

So the station became Franklin D. Roosevelt in 1946. A new technique for joining stained glass called *gemmail* in French and block glass or glass brick in English was used for the station's decoration, but most of that work had disappeared by the 2000s. When the station was opened in 1957, the buffet for guests rolled into the station on two train carriages equipped with tables.

History

Before the Second World War there were two stations here, but line 1 and line 9 were joined here by a corridor in 1942 and a single station was formed called Marbeuf Rond-Point des Champs-Élysées. Its name changed because of post-war politics. The nearby avenue had been called Victor-Emmanuel III, after the king of Italy until 1946. Since Italy had been one of the Axis powers, it was decided to name both the avenue and the station after the President of the United States, the country that had liberated France.

SIGHTSEEING

Architecture

1. **Avenue Montaigne:** this really is a luxury goods paradise with its couturiers and leather goods shops. Pause to admire the Hôtel Plaza Athénée at number 23, opened in 1911 with 45 suites, or the Théâtre des Champs-Élysées with its typical Art Deco style at number 15. The theatre, built before the First World War to liven up the new neighbourhood, is still a temple to music and dance.

2. **François Ier quarter:** this was the first lot to be developed in Paris in 1823. Its promoters, a certain Colonel Brack

and Mr Constantin, called it after the Renaissance monarch because the facade they had had installed on a building at the corner of Cours de la Reine and rue Bayard was said by some to have come from a house the king had built for the Duchess of Étampes. Two splendid grand town houses face each other on Place François Ier: Hôtel de Clermont-Tonnerre and Hôtel de Vilgruy. In the centre is a fountain built in 1864 by architect Jean-Antoine Gabriel-Davioud and sculptor François-Théophile Murguet.

Between avenue Franklin-Roosevelt and avenue George-V, 8th.

Address Book

The place for a rendezvous

Le Madrigal

32 avenue des Champs-Élysées, 8th. Open daily 8am to 2am. Tel.: 01-43-59-90-25.

Shopping

A Le 66

A true fashion paradise where you will find everything, including accessories, books, vintage and designer clothes. All major brands ply their wares in its 1,200 square metres (12,917 square feet), and every month a guest presents a collection of imaginative fashion right under the noses of the Avenue Montaigne couturiers.

66 avenue des Champs-Élysées, 8th.
Tel.: 01-53-53-33-80.

Restaurant

B Le Bœuf sur le Toit

A Parisian cabaret founded in 1921 where Cocteau, Picasso and Poulenc would come. With its Art Deco style and a name that could be taken from a Brazilian song, this restaurant will tempt you with sea-food served à la carte and its piano-bar atmosphere in the evening. Legend has it that the expression *'faire le bœuf'* used by French musicians for a jam session comes from this restaurant. Menus €24–29.90.

34 rue du Colisée, 8th.
Tel.: 01-53-93-65-55.
www.boeufsurletoit.com

Next stations

SAINT-PHILIPE-DU-ROULE

Café l'Arci Boétie

68 rue de la Boétie, 8th.

MIROMESNIL

See line 13, page 344

SAINT-AUGUSTIN

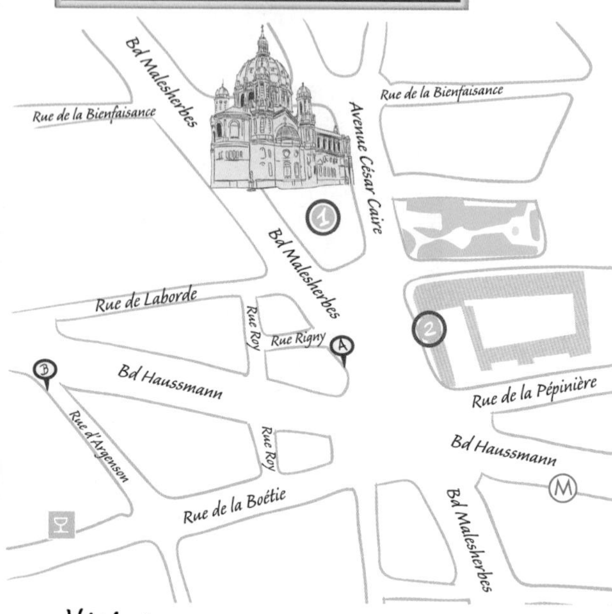

here, and the neighbourhood testifies to the power of finance with its imposing monuments. It was also a very fashionable district for a long time, until the Left Bank became the place of choice for literary circles after the First World War.

History

This station opened in 1923, and since 2004 it is linked by labyrinthine corridors to line 14 at Saint-Lazare. The station is called after the church next to it, Église Saint-Augustin, which itself took the name of one of the earliest major Christian philosophers, Augustine of Hippo (354–430 AD). You may notice that the platform for east-bound trains towards Mairie-de-Montreuil is very wide—it overlays a former garage ramp. The station is in the elegant 8th arrondissement, which was redesigned by Baron Haussmann. Many bank head offices are located

SIGHTSEEING

Architecture

1 **Église Saint-Augustin:** a vast church the size of a cathedral, built in 1861 by architect Victor Baltard in the former Polish quarter, which no longer exists. The church contains all known architectural styles: Roman, Gothic, Renaissance, as well as neo-Byzantine, which together form a neo-Baroque style. It is ethereal, rising to a height of 50 metres (55 yards) thanks to its cast iron structure, which is covered over with stone. *8 avenue César-Caire, 8th.*

Cercle National des Armées: this institution is a grand hotel for officers of the French Army. It was built next to Square Marcel Pagnol during the inter-war period and was inaugurated in 1928 by then President Gaston Doumergue. Four statues surmounting the columns represent a *Turco* (Algerian soldier in the French infantry), a *Poilu* (French infantryman), a *Marin* (marine) and a *Cuirassier* (cavalry soldier) and were the work of Jean-Antoine Injalbert, François-Léon Sicard, Jean Boucher and Paul Landowski respectively. Behind its austere facade is an interior in pure Art Deco style.

8 place Saint-Augustin, 8th.

Address Book

The place for a rendezvous

Café Le Miro

29 rue de la Boétie, 8th.
Open Monday to Saturday 6am to 9pm.
Tel.: 01-42-65-48-16.

Restaurants

A L'Évasion

In this district restaurants are not cheap, but this place is worth checking out. You can rest on its benches and allow yourself to be tempted by the wine of the month or the week, detailed on the slate. To go with the wine, take a culinary tour of France with cooking that uses genuine country ingredients.
À la carte dishes about €45.
7 place Saint-Augustin, 8th.
Tel.: 01-45-22-66-20.
Reservation necessary.

B Pomze

This restaurant has applied the maxim 'an apple a day keeps the doctor away'. Its entire menu is structured around apples (*pommes* in French, hence the name). Upstairs, a former Haussmanian apartment has been converted into intimate dining areas. Photos of orchards on the walls intimate that here, you drink cider. There is a tea house and food store as well.
Main courses from €23.
109 boulevard Haussmann, 8th.
Tel.: 01-42-65-65-83.

Next station

HAVRE – CAUMARTIN

See line 3, page 74

CHAUSSÉES D'ANTIN - LA FAYETTE

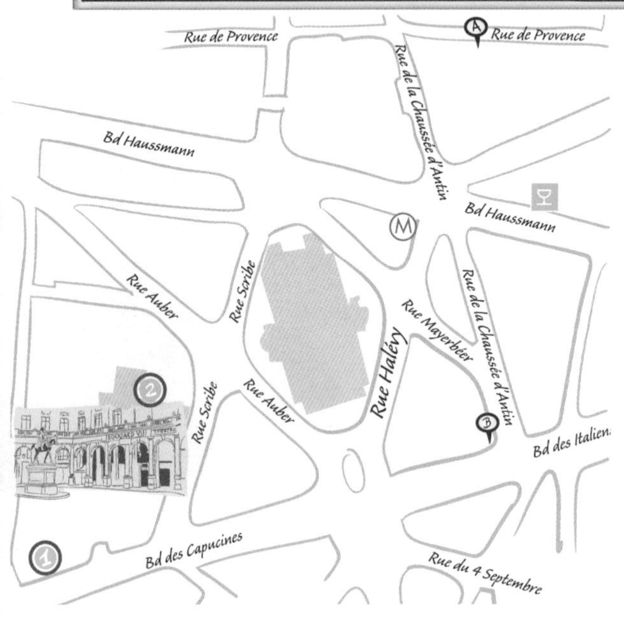

History

This station at the corner of rue de la Chaussée-d'Antin and rue La Fayette dates from 1910. *Chaussée* means causeway, and this road was raised above ground level because of the marshland underneath. It boasts splendid town houses, like the Paris mansion built by the Duke of Antin (1665–1736), son of the Marquis of Montespan, where Louis XV would stay. The road was named after him during his lifetime. In 1977 an excavation at numbers 18 and 22 brought to light 21 heads of the kings of Judah that had been removed from their statues at Notre Dame in 1789 during the Revolution. Rue La Fayette is named after the Marquis of La Fayette (1757–1834), a French aristocrat and general who served under George Washington in the American Revolutionary War and was a major figure in the French Revolution. Contemporary artist Jean-Paul Chambas decorated the station with a vast fresco running along the centre of the platform's roof.

SIGHTSEEING

Entertainment

1 **L'Olympia:** Paris's oldest music hall is a legendary venue. Some of the most outstanding shows have been put on here and many talents revealed. For artists, performing here means they have truly arrived on the scene. The Beatles, the Rolling Stones, Jacques Brel, Edith Piaf and Gilbert Bécaud are among those who have performed in its hallowed hall and occupied its mythical dressing rooms.

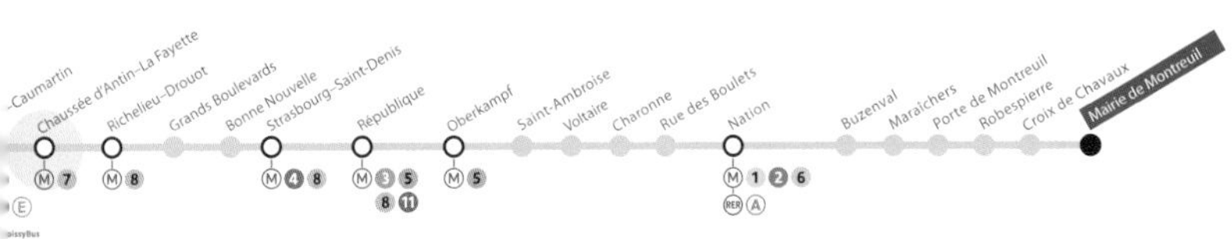

Théâtre Édouard VII: this theatre owes its name to King Edward VII's love of Paris. The British monarch in 1913 asked architect William Sprague to build a theatre in the centre of the square. At first Anglo-American film pioneer Charles Urban operated it as a cinema, but from 1916 a theatre replaced the spools of film. Actors like Sacha Guitry, Sarah Bernhardt, Arletty and Orson Welles performed here.

Address Book

The place for a rendezvous

Le Manoir
34 boulevard Haussmann, 9th.
Open Monday to Friday 7am to 9pm.
Tel.: 01-47-70-90-10.

Restaurants

A Lou Cantou
Copper pans and egg whisks decorate the immaculate walls of this local eating spot. The cooking is simple, warm and welcoming, like family fare. Lou Cantou was first opened by natives of Auvergne in central France in the 1920s. Then it was bought by people from the Alpine province of Savoie, and nowadays the manager is from Sri Lanka. Through all that, its name was carefully preserved. *Cantou* means 'home' in the ancient Occitan language of southern France. Menu €14.
35 cité d'Antin or 63 rue de Provence, 9th.
Tel.: 01-48-74-75-15.

B Le Grand Café des Capucines
This is where night owls come to satisfy their hunger. Situated near the Opéra Garnier, it is an institution in Paris and has lost none of its former splendour. Its totally Art Nouveau décor was conceived by decorator Jacques Garcia, and warm tones of crimson and gold dominate.
4 boulevard des Capucines, 9th.
Tel.: 01-43-12-19-00.
www.legrandcafe.com
Open all day and all night every day.

Next stations

RICHELIEU-DROUOT
See line 8, page 216

GRANDS BOULEVARDS
See line 8, page 218

BONNE NOUVELLE
See line 8, page 222

STRASBOURG – SAINT-DENIS
See line 8, page 224

RÉPUBLIQUE
See line 3, page 86

OBERKAMPF
See line 5, page 134

CHARONNE

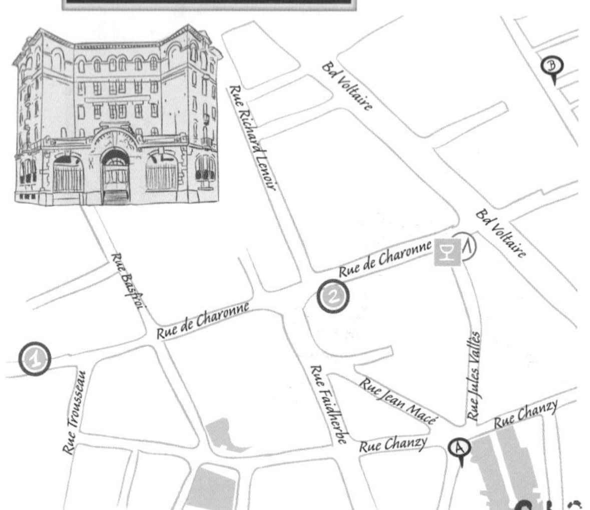

History

This station opened in 1933 and owes its name to the feudal land of the Lord of Charonne, which was sold to the Abbey of Saint-Magloire by King Robert II (972–1031) in 1008. This ancient history has been forgotten, but the station's name is remembered in recent history for the Charonne metro station massacre in 1962. The Communist Party and other left-wing organisations had called a demonstration against the Algerian War and the OAS, the Secret Armed Organisation that continued to resist independence for Algeria. The authorities refused permission for the demonstration, and the then Paris police chief, Maurice Papon, gave the order to break up the demonstration with the agreement of the then president, Charles de Gaulle. Demonstrators sought refuge in the metro station. Eight died on the spot and a ninth died later in hospital.

SIGHTSEEING

Off the beaten track

① ***Hôtel de Mortagne:*** this grand town house surrounded by modern buildings was erected in 1660 by architect Pierre Delisle-Mansart, with a hexagonal rotunda and a facade with mascarons, carvings of faces designed to frighten away evil spirits. In 1746 inventor Jacques Vaucanson came to live here and built most of his machines. It was bought by Louis XVI in 1783

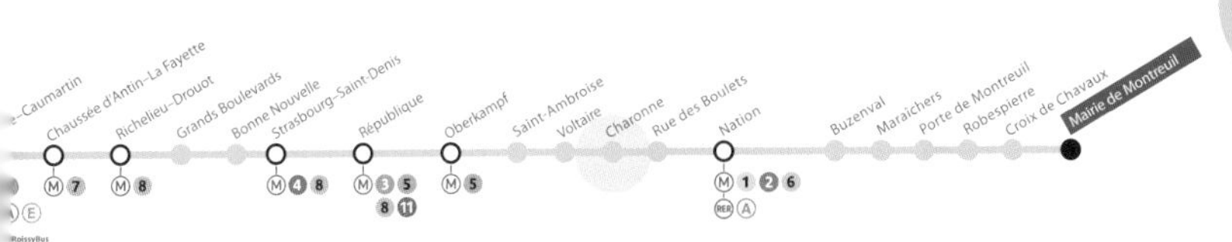

and converted into an industrial museum open to the public, becoming the forerunner of today's Musée des Arts et Métiers (Arts and Crafts Museum), which is now in the 3rd arrondissement.
53 rue de Charonne, 11th.

Palais de la Femme–Fondation de l'Armée du Salut: this Salvation Army foundation opened its doors to single girls and women in 1926. It had been the site of a Dominican convent, Les Filles-de-la-Croix, between 1641 and 1904. Legend has it that Cyrano de Bergerac is buried here. The nuns were expelled in 1792 but returned in 1825. The convent would later be closed and demolished. In 1910 a new building was used as for single men, and it became a war hospital in 1914. Then, from 1919 to 1924, the Pensions Ministry was based here. The Salvation Army launched a massive collection to buy the building, which it managed to do in 1926.
94 rue de Charonne, 11th.

Address Book

The place for a rendezvous

L'Armagnac Café
104 rue de Charonne, 11th.
Open Monday to Friday 7.30am to 2am and from 10am on weekends.
Tel.: 01-43-71-49-43.

Restaurants

A Mélac
This bistro has become a local institution. It has a warm and welcoming atmosphere and tasty cooking with origins in the gastronomic traditions of Averyon, in south-western France. The wine list is amazing and well-documented. You can pick grapes at the local vineyards at Château Charonne in mid-September. Lunch menu about €15.
42 rue Léon Frot, 11th.
Tel.: 01-43-70-59-27.

B Le Fifty-fifty
A trendy, relaxed atmosphere pervades this bistro where you can enjoy good French cooking with exotic influences. There is scampi and scallops done in a wok and *tartare de bœuf* and home-made fries with *fleur de sel* (French sea salt). Choose from the ground floor bistro and a warmer, club-like ambiance in the basement. Main courses about €15.
50 rue Léon-Frot, 11th.
Tel.: 01-77-18-80-24.

vious stations

AINT-AMBROISE

Le Perroquet, 14 rue ie-Méricourt, 11th.

VOLTAIRE

Brasserie Sehrine
132 bld Voltaire, 11th.

Next stations

RUE DES BOULETS

Café Titon
34 rue Titon, 11th.

NATION

See line 1, page 40

line 10

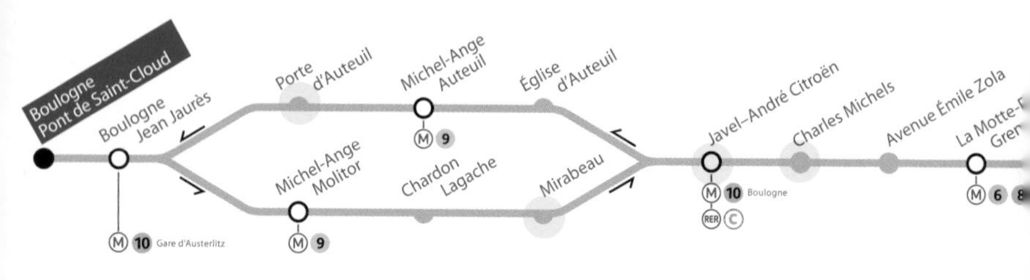

History

Line 10 may be just 11.7 kilometres (7.3 miles) long, but from east to west it serves some of the legendary Left Bank's most prestigious stations. It would take volumes to cover the tumultuous birth of this line. In fact, its route, interwoven with those of lines 7, 8 and 13, has changed enormously over the years. The first section inaugurated in 1923 connected Les Invalides to the Croix Rouge station, closed in 1939. This ghost station took its name from the Croix-Rouge crossroads, named since the 15th century after the red cross worn by Guillaume Briçonnet, Bishop of Meaux. Lively crossroads, it was the scene of executions: in 1721 and 1722, the gallows and the pillory were erected there. This section stretched to Invalides – Mabillon in 1925, then Invalides – Odéon in 1926. In 1930, the line was extended as far as Porte d'Italie, but this route was replaced in 1931 by the Maubert-Mutualité – Jussieu stretch. The Gare d'Austerlitz terminus was inaugurated in 1939 on the eve of the Second World War. That at Boulogne came much later in 1981. The white walls of its tunnels, frequented by dreaming—or dashing—students give it an unequalled luminosity and beauty.

Boulogne – Pont de Saint-Cloud / Gare d'Austerlitz

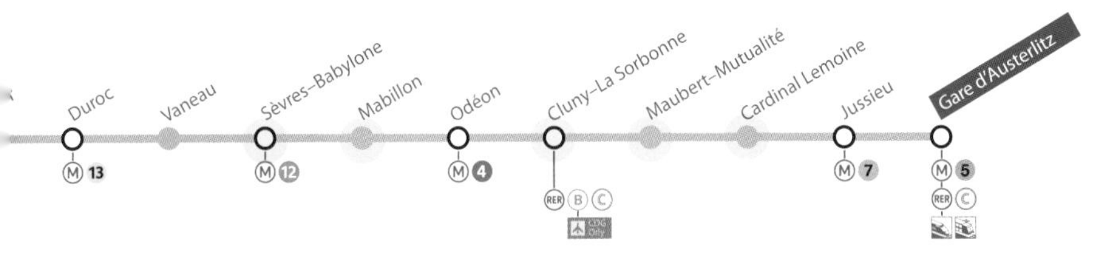

PORTE D'AUTEUIL

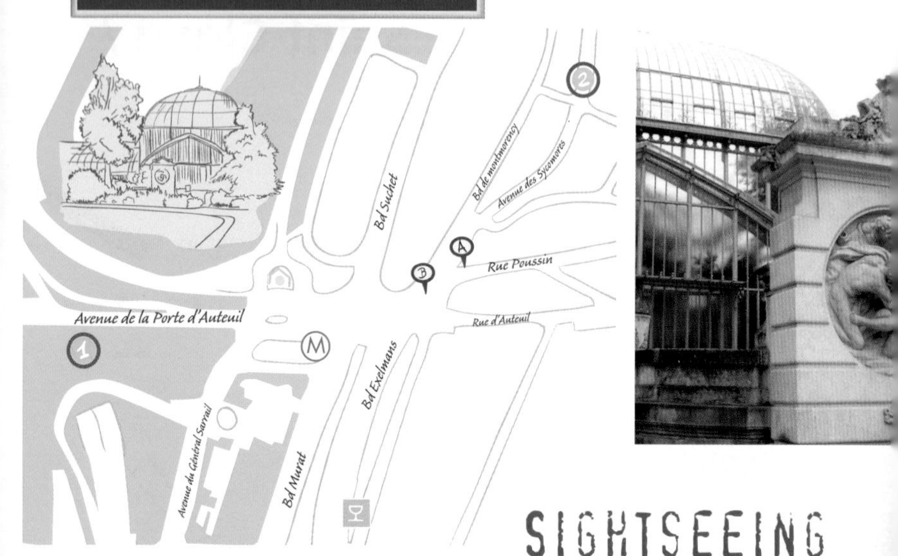

History

Opened in 1913. This station is certainly unusual: its trains run in only one direction, towards Boulogne. It owes its name to the gate to the old village of Auteuil. This entrance made it possible to watch over the traffic on the road to Boulogne. During the Paris Commune of 1871, the Versaillais government troops entered Paris by rue d'Auteuil after taking the gates of Auteuil and Saint-Cloud. The station borders the legendary Auteuil racecourse, the temple of jump racing since 1871. Its star event is the Grand Steeple-Chase de Paris, which takes place each May.

SIGHTSEEING

A walk in the park

1 Jardin and Serres d'Auteuil

Created in 1898 by the architect Jean-Camille Formigé, the Jardin d'Auteuil is situated on the very site of Louis XV's old nurseries. Today, it serves as the nursery for the whole Paris municipality. Its flowers, orchids and azaleas among others, adorn the interiors of all the arrondissement town halls. Within its walls, one also finds a botanical garden where plant lovers can discover numerous species and plant collections. Like a small cathedral, the 99 metre (325 feet) long grand hothouse dating from the late 19th century is crowned by a 16-metre (52 feet) dome. It forms the backdrop for a palm grove and luxuriant tropical flora.

3 avenue de la Porte-d'Auteuil
or 1 avenue Gordon-Bennett, 16th.

Boulogne – Pont de Saint-Cloud · Boulogne Jean Jaurès · Porte d'Auteuil · Michel-Ange Auteuil · Église d'Auteuil · Michel-Ange Molitor · Chardon Lagache · Mirabeau · Javel-André Citroën · Charles Michels · Avenue Émile Zola · La Motte-Picquet Grenelle · Ségur · Duroc · Vaneau · Sèvres-

Secret Paris

Villa Montmorency: this tiny private hamlet, which shelters 80 houses, is extremely guarded and regulated. Without a doubt, you have arrived in a ghetto of the elite, inhabited by business magnates and showbiz stars. Grand residences colonised by wisteria, town houses in stone... this is one of the most secret and charming places in Paris, plunged in torpor, yet only seconds from the Bois de Boulogne.
12 rue Poussin, 16th.

Address book

The place for a rendezvous

Le Congrès d'Auteuil
144 boulevard Exelmans, 16th.
Open daily 8am to 1am.
Tel.: 01-46-51-15-75.

Restaurants

A Le Beaujolais d'Auteuil
This bistro, near the Auteuil racecourse, has been rejuvenated by the arrival of chef Nicolas Duquenoy, formerly at the Relais Louis XIII and La Ferrandaise. Simmered dishes revisit the classics with a zing. While waiting for your horse to come home, peacefully savour a foie gras consommé or a *blanquette* of veal. Menu €32.
99 boulevard de Montmorency, 16th. Tel.: 01-47-43-03-56. Open daily 11.30am to 2.30pm, 7.30pm to 10pm.

B Tsé
An elegant, cossetted restaurant mixing four different atmospheres. You come here for the stylish decor as well as the fusion menu, which gives an Asian touch to even the most traditional French dishes. Around €40 à la carte.
78 rue d'Auteuil, 16th. Tel.: 01-40-71-11-90. Open daily noon to 3 pm, 7pm to 11 pm, Friday and Saturday until 11.30pm.

Previous stations

BOULOGNE – PONT DE SAINT-CLOUD

Le Gaulois, 35 rue de Bellevue, 92100 Boulogne-Billancourt.

BOULOGNE JEAN-JAURÈS

Le Bougainvillier, 73 route de la Reine, 92100 Boulogne-Billancourt.

MIRABEAU

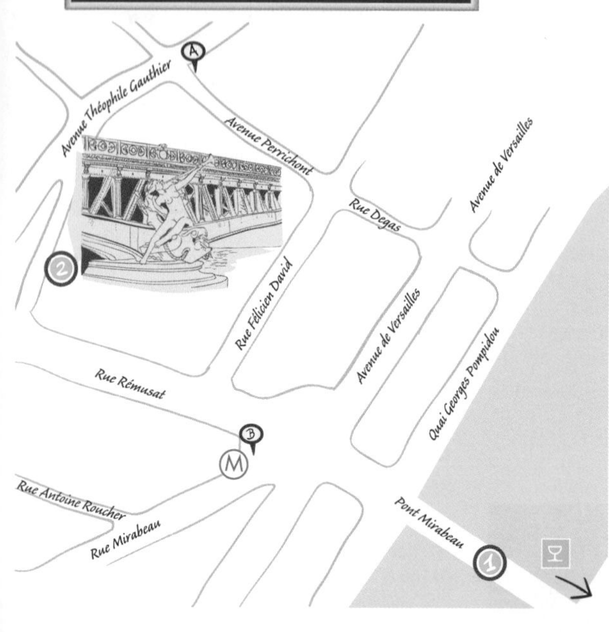

© Denis Sutton / RATP

History

The builders of this one-way station created in 1913 took care to ensure that it was sufficiently deep to pass right by the foundations of the Église d'Auteuil. It is dedicated to Mirabeau. This writer and politician—of a 'grandiose and astonishing ugliness', according to Victor Hugo—first became known as a revolutionary. During the Royal Session of 23 June 1789, he made a declaration to the Marquis de Dreux-Brézé, who had come bearing orders to dissolve the Assembly: 'Go and tell those who sent you that we are here at the will of the People and we will leave only by the force of bayonets!' After his death, the discovery of a hidden cabinet in the Tuileries palace revealed his double game: he was in reality... one of Louis XVI's most loyal supporters!

SIGHTSEEING

A walk through history

1 **Pont Mirabeau:** 'Under the Pont Mirabeau flows the Seine', wrote Apollinaire. Immortalised thanks to this poem, taken from the collection of poems *Alcools* (1913), this metal bridge with an aerial appeal was built between 1895 and 1897 at the instigation of President Sadi Carnot, assassinated in1894. The cutwaters are adorned by four allegorical statues by Jean-Antoine Injalbert, representing the city of Paris and the spirits of Commerce, Navigation and Abundance.

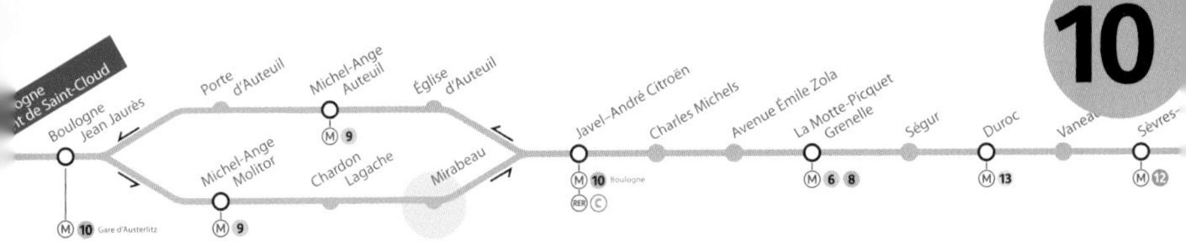

Russian Catholic Church of the Holy Trinity: escaping the 1917 revolution, Russian Catholics found refuge in Paris. Not having a place of worship, the community gathered in an apartment in the 16th arrondissement. To resolve the problem, in the 1930s a vicar-general of Paris bought the studio of painter François Gérard and transformed it into a chapel. In 1960, the studio was demolished and a new chapel was constructed in the basement. Around 1980 a fixed iconostasis was installed, the work of the Jesuit Egon Sendler.

39 rue François Gérard, 16th.

Address book

The place for a rendezvous

Le Muguet
7 rond-point du pont Mirabeau, 16th.
Open daily 8am to 8pm.
Tel: 01-45-78-12-22.

Restaurants

Ⓐ Le Bistrot 31
Enter into the shadowy interior of the B31 and sample its Franco-Italian inspired cuisine. Your tastebuds will tingle for *al dente* pasta with truffles or foie gras, or San Daniele ham accompanied by rocket. Whether in the dining room, at the bar, a high table or on the terrace, the experience is unforgettable. Lunch menu €16.50.
31 avenue Théophile-Gautier, 16th.
Tel: 01-42-24-52-31.
www.bistro31.com

Ⓑ La Terrasse Mirabeau
This cream and red restaurant will seduce you with its mix: traditional yet tinged with modernity, the cuisine here is both playful and refined. Feast on a fried fillet of Breton shad, nettle cream soup or Spanish Bellota black pork belly. The pretty terrace allows you to profit as soon as the sun comes out. Lunch and dinner menu €45.
5 place de Barcelone, 16th.
Tel.: 01-42-24-41-51.
www.terrasse-mirabeau.com
Open Monday to Friday noon to 2.30pm, 7.30pm to 10.30pm.

Previous stations

MICHEL-ANGE MOLITOR

See line 9, page 245

CHARDON LAGACHE

Le Tunnel
48 boulevard Exelmans, 16th.

JAVEL–ANDRÉ CITROËN

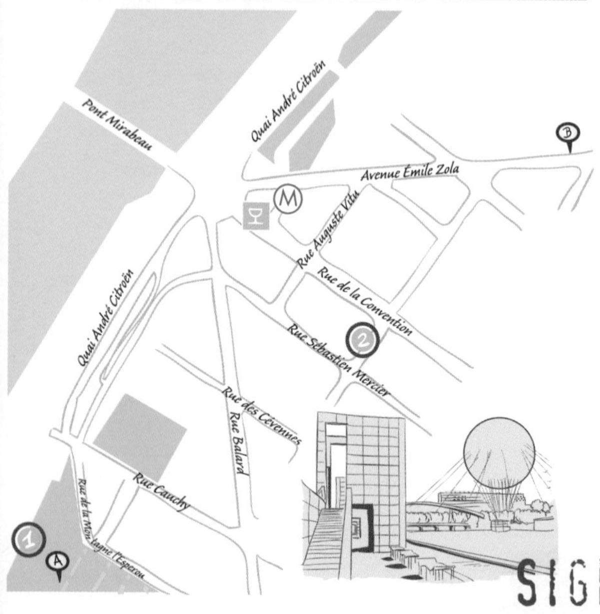

History

'Miracle without a name at Javel station', as Charles Trenet used to sing. Opened in 1913, it pays tribute to the celebrated factory and to the hamlet of Javel, a little fishing port where pleasure boats used to gather as early as the 15th century. In 1777, a manufacture of chemical products opened: *eau de Javel* or bleach was born. Much later, during the First World War, André Citroën, then a lieutenant, set up a missile factory on Quai de Javel. 13,000 workers produced 23 million munitions during four years of conflict. Once peace was signed, the factory converted into an automobile manufacture. Despite the success of the Traction Avant and the DS, Citroën's passion for gambling and the colossal debts of the company had the better of the factory. It closed in 1970, giving birth to a vast urban renewal project whose results we can now admire.

SIGHTSEEING

A walk in the park

1 **Parc André-Citroën:** order and disorder is how this 14-hectare (35-acre) garden all in glass, concrete and metal could be defined. It was created as the result of an international competition won by a team of French architects and landscape designers. Delighted promenaders will discover its thematic gardens, nestled on the site of the old Citroën factory: the mineral White Garden, the shady Black Garden, the Garden of Metamorphoses, the wild and disordered Garden in Movement and six gardens in series with six little glasshouses. Two gigantic glasshouses frame a peristyle of 120 jets of water. Sloping gently down to the Seine, the central space is a huge rectangle of lawn, inviting relaxation. Canals,

waterfalls and jets of water make water an architect in its own right in this modern creation.

Quai André-Citröen, 15th.

Architecture

Église Saint-Christophe de Javel

Inaugurated in 1933, this church designed by Charles-Henri Besnard is constructed in reinforced concrete. The mural painted by Henri-Marcel Magne portrays Saint Christopher surrounded by travellers begging for his protection. On the vault, train, cruise liner, hot air balloon, plane and car surround the patron saint of travellers, doubtless a reference to the nearby Citroën factory.

4 rue Saint-Christophe, 15th.

Leisure

A Air de Paris Balloon

Take off on board the biggest hot-air balloon in the world! From 150 metres (164 yards) high, you have an unbeatable view over the capital. The balloon, which can carry up to 30 passengers for ten minutes, informs Parisians on air quality: it is lit up according to the level of pollution.

Parc André-Citroën, 15th.
Tel.: 01-44-26-20-00

www.ballondeparis.com
Open daily 9am until 40 minutes before the park closes, depending on weather conditions.
Entrance fee.

Restaurant

B La Mousson

Over lunch or dinner, take a trip into the heart of ancient Cambodia. At the meeting point between Indian and Chinese cuisine, discover a sweet and sour cuisine in the image of the 'middle way' advocated by Buddha! A journey to the heart of Khmer colours and flavours. Around €25 à la carte.

45avenue Émile-Zola, 15th.
Tel.: 01-45-79-98-52.
Open daily noon to 3pm, 7pm to 11pm.

Address book

The place for a rendezvous

Le Régalia : 1 rue de la Convention, 15th. Open Monday to Friday 6.30am to 1.30am, Saturday from 8am, Sunday 9am to 9pm. Tel: 01-45-77-97-00.

Previous stations

MICHEL-ANGE AUTEUIL

See line 9, page 245

ÉGLISE D' AUTEUIL

Café le Ribera

60 rue Jean-de-la-Fontaine, 16th.

CHARLES MICHELS

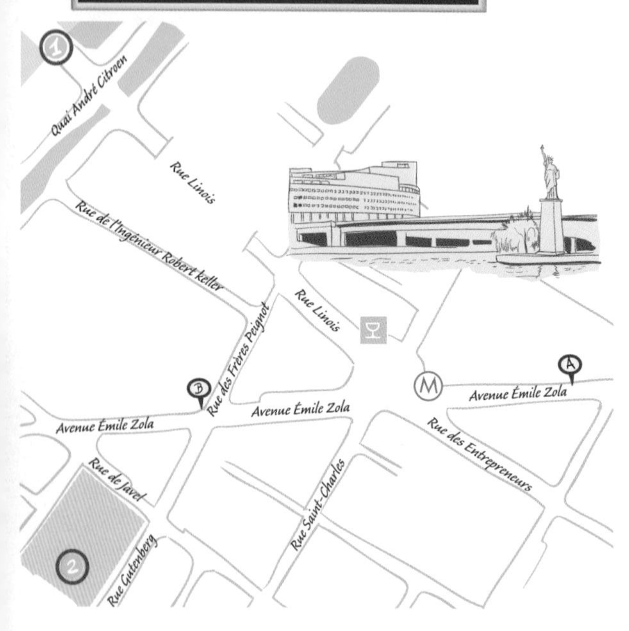

History

The station wasn't always called this. Opened in 1913, it was originally called Beaugrenelle, after the brilliant advertising gimmick–beautiful Grenelle–thought up by property developers during the urbanisation of the Grenelle district. It was on 14 July 1945, France's national holiday, that it lost its original name to pay homage to Charles Michels, the Communist deputy of the 15th arrondissement executed by the Nazis in 1941. This young man with an athletic build and wavy blond hair remains in the collective memory as one of the heroes of the Résistance, one of 26 hostages shot at Châteaubriant, along with Guy Môquet, in retaliation for the successful attack against the Feldkommandant of Nantes, Karl Hotz.

SIGHTSEEING

Monuments

1 **Pont de Grenelle:** an earlier wooden bridge having collapsed, the decision was taken in 1884 to reconstruct it in cast iron. Two engineers, Vaudrey and Passon, constructed a metal bridge that was itself replaced in 1968. You are not imagining it: at the tip of the Allée des Cygnes, the Statue of Liberty, a small version of Bartholdi's sculpture, stands facing the river. Offered to the City of Paris by the American community in 1885, it was installed in 1898 for the 1900 World Fair. Restored in 1990, it has a majestic bronze-coloured patina.

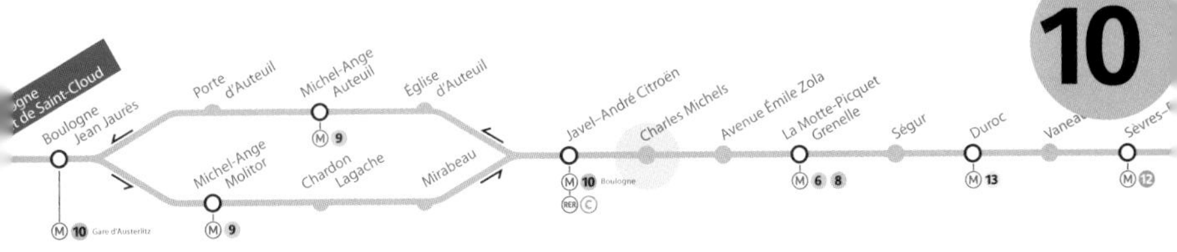

Ministère des Affaires Etrangères, former Imprimerie Nationale: this huge red brick building, bathed with large windows was the home of the state printworks since 1921. It is the fruit of an eventful history: as early as 1538, François Ier created the 'Royal Printers for the Grec' (the name of a new typeface), replaced in 1640 by the Royal Printworks of Cardinal Richelieu. A last remnant of Paris's industrial heritage, the building was sold in 2003, then reacquired by the state in 2007 to house the Ministry of Foreign Affairs.

27 rue de la Convention, 15th.

Address book

The place for a rendezvous

Le Lutétia
49 rue Linois,15th.
Open daily 6am to 1am.
Tel.: 01-45-77-65-65.

Restaurants

Ⓐ L'Épopée
Quintessentially Parisian, this elegant restaurant knows how to delight you with its authentic cuisine. On the blackboard menu, the chef's Burgundy and Lyonnais references are evident: beef fillet with *grenaille* potatoes, langoustine ravioli with satay await you. Menu €35.
89 avenue Émile-Zola, 15th.
Tel.: 01-45-77-71-37.
Open daily noon to 2pm, 7.30pm to 10pm, closed Sunday lunch.

Ⓑ Sawadee
Nothing is left to chance at this temple of Thai cuisine, from the striking blood-red decor to the exotic dishes marrying coconut milk and basil. In short, it's tasteful and tasty. Menus €21 – 33.
53 avenue Émile-Zola, 15th.
Tel.: 01-45-77-68-90.
Open Monday to Saturday noon to 2pm, 7.30 to 10pm.

Next stations

AVENUE ÉMILE ZOLA
Le Cosmos, 10 rue Henri-Duchêne, 15th.

LA MOTTE-PICQUET – GRENELLE
See line 8, page 202

SÉGUR
Le Ségur, 156 avenue de Suffren, 15th.

DUROC
Le François Coppée
1 boulevard du Montparnasse, 6th.

VANEAU
Le Deauville
87 rue de Sèvres, 6th.

SÈVRES – BABYLONE

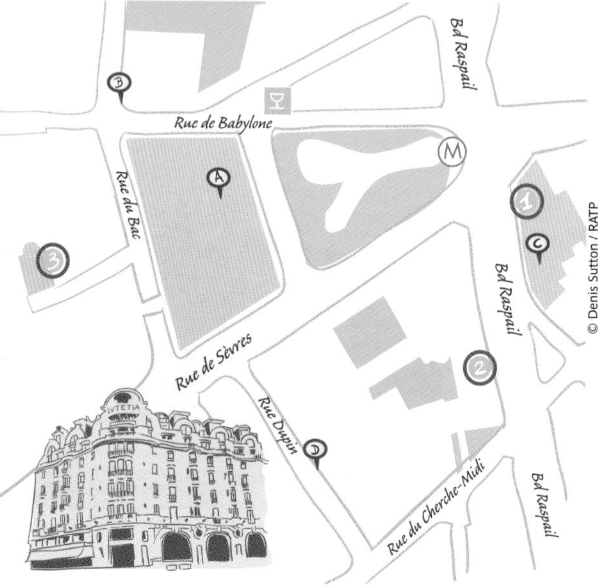

© Denis Sutton / RATP

History

Created in 1910, the station bears the double name of the rue de Sèvres, an ancient track that led in the 18th century from Paris to Sèvres, and the rue de Babylone, a lane that disappears into the Grenelle district. Since 1673, it owed its name to the Bishop of Babylone, Bernard de Sainte-Thérèse. The history of this station is that of a fusion that was not without scars. Originally, the line 10 station, run by the Compagnie du Métro Parisien (CMP), should have been called Babylone, and the line 12 station, owned by the Nord-Sud company, should have been called Sèvres. The city forced the two companies to make a joint station. The companies gave in in bad grace, and the station's walls bear the traces of this battle: on line 10 the platform indicates 'Sèvres-Babylone' but 'Babylone' is more visible. On line 12, 'Sèvres' is spread out bigger. A few steps from the station, Le Bon Marché department store rises proudly against the Parisian sky. Its metal-framed structure and its large glazed roof lights are the work of an inspired Gustave Eiffel. Facing it, the immaculate Hôtel Lutetia rivalises it in grandeur. There's no mistake: you have indeed arrived at Sèvres-Babylone station.

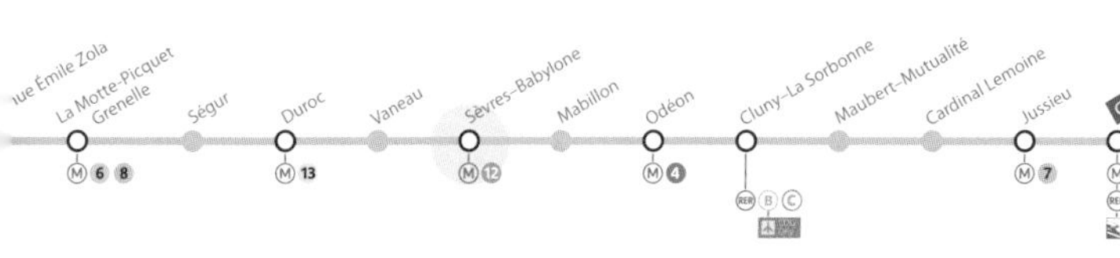

SIGHTSEEING

rchitecture

Hôtel Lutetia: how beautiful is this hotel put up in 1910! We owe it to Madame Boucicaut, owner of Le Bon Marché, 'so that its important clients from the provinces were lodged in a nearby establishment corresponding to their lifestyle when they came to do their shopping in Paris.' It was conceived by the architects Boileau and Tauzin, and some of the sculptures on its facade are by Paul Belmondo, father of the film star. Between the wars, the Lutetia was the hub for all the great intellectuals and artists: Picasso, Matisse, Gide, Beckett, Saint-Exupéry, Malraux… Albert Cohen wrote *Belle du Seigneur* there. Josephine Baker's children ran in its corridors. General de Gaulle himself spent his wedding night there. When the German army entered Paris on 14 June 1940, it immediately requisitioned the hotel to install its information and intelligence services. The owner then walled up the cellar to hide the best wines stored there. At the Liberation, to restore an image tarnished by the enemy occu-

pation, the Lutetia took in the deportees returning from the concentration camps. A plaque at the entrance recalls this difficult period in history. The hotel has a permanent display of sculptures by Hiquily, Arman, César and Chemiakin, as well as paintings by Bisch. In 1985, it was decorated by the fashion designer Sonia Rykiel.
45 boulevard Raspail, 6th.

2 **Fondation de la Maison des Sciences de l'Homme:** this modern building houses a foundation devoted to the human and social sciences. The concrete and glass construction one can admire today is the work of the architects Beauclair, Capelle, Depondt, Lods and Malizard. It was built on the site of the Cherche-Midi prison, the old military prison of Paris, demolished in 1961. Dreyfus was locked up there. Resistants, among them the famous Estienne d'Orves, were incarcerated there under the Occupation.
54 boulevard Raspail, 6th.

Monument

3 **Chapelle de la Médaille Miraculeuse:** on 19 July 1830, Catherine Labouré, a young novice at the convent of the Filles-de-la-Charité, was woken in the middle of the night by a small child who told her: 'Go to the chapel, the Holy Virgin is waiting for you.' Still half-asleep, Catherine got up and followed the child. The Holy Virgin was there, glowing with light. 'Have a medal-

lion made. The people who wear it will receive Holy blessings.' Hearing these phrases, Catherine felt Heaven descend on Earth: she gave the world this miraculous medallion that is now worn by millions of Catholics.
140 rue du Bac, 7th.

Address book

The place for a rendezvous

Le Babylone

12 rue de Babylone, 7th.
Open Monday to Saturday 7.30am to 9pm.
Tel.: 01-45-48-56-12.

Shopping

A Le Bon Marché

'A cathedral of commerce for a race of clients,' is how Émile Zola presented it in his novel *Au bonheur des dames*. In 1838 the birth of the Bon Marché saw the first French department store, still the only one on the Left Bank. The concept of the shop invented by Aristide and Marguerite Boucicaut was totally innovative at the time: to sell within a single space a large variety of merchandise, theatrically displayed and at fixed prices. The modern spaces of this prestigious shop have a refined decoration, including an escalator signed by Andrée Putman, assuring its unequalled reputation: L'Entre-Temps, the Théâtre de la Beauté, l'Appartement de Mode, Balthazar, la Grande Épicerie de Paris. Today prestigious luxury brands compete to be displayed here.

24 rue de Sèvres, 7th.
Tel.: 01-44-39-80-00.
Open Monday to Saturday 10am to 8pm, Thursday and Friday until 9pm.

B Conran Shop

Housed in Bon Marché's former warehouse designed by Gustave Eiffel, the Conran Shop overflows with surprises assembled over its 1,700 square metres (18,300 square feet) of display space. Scandinavian furniture, lights by young designers and accessories of all sorts make it a reference for anyone interested in design and decoration.

117 rue du Bac, 7th.
Tel.: 01-42-84-10-01.
www.conranshop.fr
Open Monday to Friday 10am to 7pm, Saturday until 7.30pm.

Out on the town

C Bar du Lutetia

This legendary bar was immortalised by Eddy Mitchell in a song paying tribute to Serge Gainsbourg. Writers and artists cross its threshold to savour the particular taste of these privileged moments. Its flamboyant carmine red and gold colour scheme give a refined touch to the decor. In the evening it is animated by a few notes on the piano.

45 boulevard Raspail, 6th.
Tel.: 01-49-54-46-46.
Open daily 10am to 1am.

Restaurant

D L'Épi Dupin

François Pasteau, a follow of Joël Robuchon, astonishes with his creativity, that leads him to endlessly change his menu. He will propose you a meal worthy of a star chef for a price defying all competition, amid the exposed stone and beams of his pretty restaurant. Parisians in the know flock here, so be prepared to be patient to discover the cuisine of this little genius at the stove. Menu €33. Reservation essential for the first dinner sitting.

11 rue Dupin, 6th.
Tel.: 01-42-22-64-56.
www.epidupin.com
Open Monday dinner and Tuesday to Friday noon to 3pm, 7pm to 11pm.

MABILLON

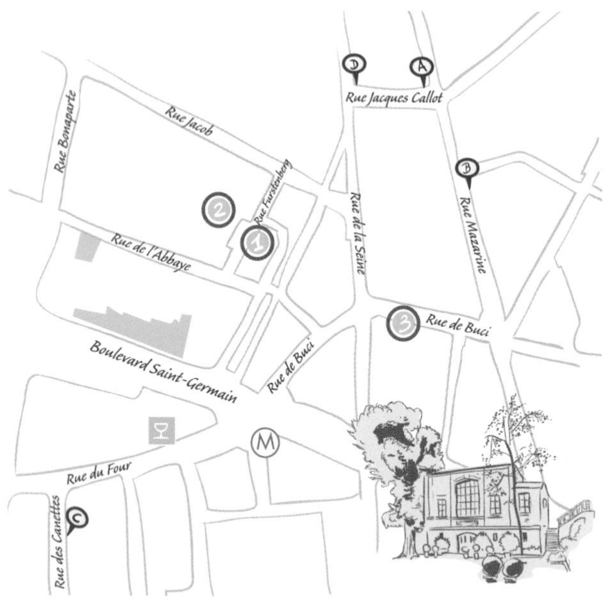

History

Inaugurated in 1925, this station gets its name from rue Mabillon, named after the Benedictine monk Jean Mabillon (1632–1707). Writer and intellectual, monk of the Benedictine reformed congregation of Saint-Maur, he became treasurer of the Abbaye de Saint-Denis in 1653, but some of his peers already recognised his great ability. In 1664, he was sent to Saint-Germain-des-Prés to join a learned circle around the abbey librairian, Jean-Luc d'Achery. His first mission was to patiently assemble documents in view to publishing the acts of the order of Saint Benoît. He devoted such an effort to this huge task that he was considered the author of the work. In 1681, in the treatise *De re diplomatica*, he wrote an answer to Daniel van Papenbroeck, a Dutch Jesuit, who had questioned the authenticity of some of the charters of the Abbaye de Saint-Denis, and won the intellectual battle. However, this soon made him some enemies and saw him in dispute with the Abbot of La Trappe on the role that study and manual labour should play in monastic life. In 1701, he was made a member of the Académie Royale des Inscriptions et Médailles by the king. He died in 1707 in Saint-Germain-des-Prés.

SIGHTSEEING

romantic promenade

Place de Fürstenberg: this incredibly charming square owes its name to Cardinal Guillaume Egon de Fürstenberg, Abbot of Saint-Germain-des-Prés in 1689. At the end of the 17th century it formed the forecourt of the abbey palace, visible at the end of the street. The ground floor of the buildings on the square used to be mews destined for dusty carriages and tired horses. The stage coach staff were lodged on the floor above. Between the wars, the religious art workshops of Desvallières et Denis used the premises 'to train artists and craftsmen in the practice of Christian art' and to 'supply churches, especially churches damaged by the war, with religious works that are both aesthetic, traditional and modern.' Four paulownia trees majestically frame a lamppost with five globe lamps, which glows like a lighthouse on this unbelievably romantic square.

2 **Musée Delacroix:** from 28 December 1857 until his dying breath on 13 August 1863, Delacroix lived on the square at no. 6, on the site of the former abbey dependences built by Cardinal Fürstenberg in the 17th century. The painter had moved to this peaceful place, bathed in light, to be nearer to the church of Saint-Sulpice, where he had undertaken the decoration of the Saint-Anges chapel. The most disturbing painting on show is surely *Mary Magdalene in the Desert,* much loved by Baudelaire. Portraits, palettes and brushes that belonged to Delacroix will move those who adore this major Romantic artist.

6 rue Fürstenberg, 6th.
Tel.: 01-40-20-51-77.
Open Wednesday to Monday 9.30am to 5pm. Entrance fee.

③ **Marché Buci:** on leaving the museum wander down picturesque rues Cardinale and Bourbon-le-Château to reach the animated rue de Buci. Stalls of flowers, shellfish, delicatessens and patisseries give this very Parisian street a provincial air. After a deserved pause on a shady café terrace, you'll be ready to wander through the nearby streets. Thus, on rue Mazarine, no. 27 conceals an interesting alleyway. Two steps away, part of Philippe Auguste's city wall hides... in a car park! On rue de Seine, numerous *hôtels particuliers* (town houses) conceal pretty paved courtyards. They carry such an aura of mystery that it's impossible not to dream for a moment of the life you would lead if you resided in these places.

Address book

The place for a rendezvous

Le Pré Saint-Germain
4 rue du Four, 6th.
Open daily 7am to 5am.
Tel.: 01-40-46-93-22.

Culture

Ⓐ Galerie Pièce unique
Founded in 1988, the gallery exhibits just one 'unique piece': a work created especially for the space by a contemporary artist in the unique *pièce*—or room—on the ground floor

of the gallery. Separated from the street by an immense window, it invites passers-by to contemplate it. Even nightbirds can profit from this ephemeral show: the work remains illuminated until 2am. In February 2000, Pièce Unique opened a second space at 26 rue Mazarine, which presents the work of artists represented by the gallery.

4 rue Jacques-Callot, 6th.
Tel.: 01-43-26-54-58.
Open Tuesday to Saturday 11am to 1pm, 2.30pm to 7pm.

Restaurant

Ⓑ L'Alcazar

This restaurant conceived by Terence

Conran is an ode to New York lofts with its immense atrium inundated by light, its open kitchen, waxed zinc bar and suspended mezzanine. On Monday, opera arias reunite music lovers and gourmets in a Fellini-esque atmosphere, while upstairs, from Wednesday to Saturday, the gilded youth of Saint-Germain sips cocktails to the sound of fashionable DJs. Evening menu €40.

62 rue Mazarine, 6th.
Tel.: 01-53-10-19-99.
www.alcazar.fr
Open daily noon to 3pm, 7pm to midnight.

Out on the town

Ⓒ Chez Georges

Georges is no more but the soul of this bistro, with its

pretty vaulted cellar, lives on. On the walls, portraits of singers from another era are pinned around the old wooden bar. It dates from 1928 and would surely have many a tale to tell of the nightbirds who have propped it up glass in hand. When it gets too crowded, follow the throng outside for a breath of fresh air in front of the carmine facade.

11 rue des Canettes, 6th.
Tel.: 01-43-26-79-15.
Open Tuesday to Saturday 2pm to 2am.

Ⓓ La Palette

The art café, sitting on the terrace art students flirt gently in the sun. Beside them, artists and gallerists come to breathe in the atmosphere and contemplate the street action. Don't judge by the few modern impulses, a nonchalent glance at the ceiling and you will be reassured to see that this café dates from the very start of the 20th century. In the middle of this cheerful crowd, you can nibble delicious open sandwiches, accompanied by a glass of burgundy.

43 rue de Seine, 6th.
Tel.: 01-43-26-68-15.
Open daily 8am to 2am, Sunday from 10am.

Next station

ODÉON

See line 4, page 106

CLUNY - LA SORBONNE

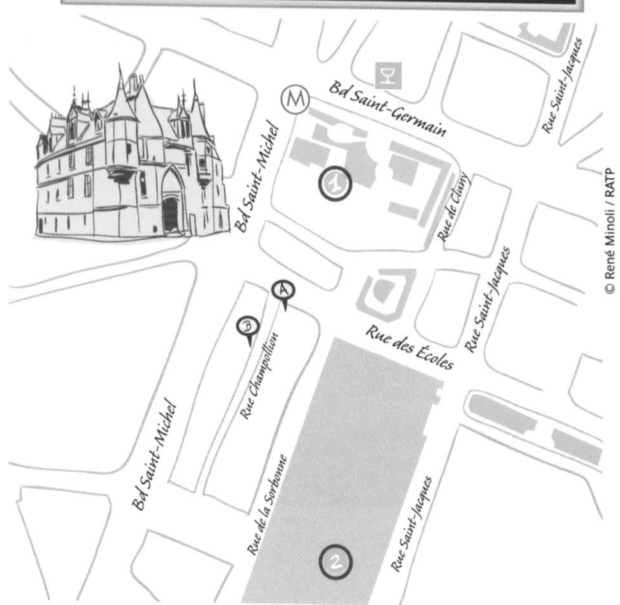

© René Minoli / RATP

History

Admired today by all its users, this station had a strange destiny. Opened in 1930, it was then closed for almost half a century. During a period of austerity, it was considered superfluous. The ghost station only came back to life in 1988 to provide an interchange with lines B and C of the RER, via station Saint-Michel-Notre-Dame.
It is named after the France's most prestigious university and the abbots of Cluny. Waiting in its chrysalis during its forced hibernation, the station was clothed in its best finery, its ceiling was decorated for the reopening with glazed enamel mosaics by Jean Bazaine. Colourful, timeless, pared back could be the adjectives to describe his work. Embued with spirituality mixed with poetry, the mosaic frieze reproduces the signatures of illustrious Latin Quarter personnalities from Rabelais to Robespierre, Molière to Richelieu, poets, writers, philosophers, artists, men (and one token) woman of science, king and French statesmen. These representations of a tiny bit of their personality–their signature–brings back with emotion their gestures, whether hesitant or confident, on the illuminated vault.

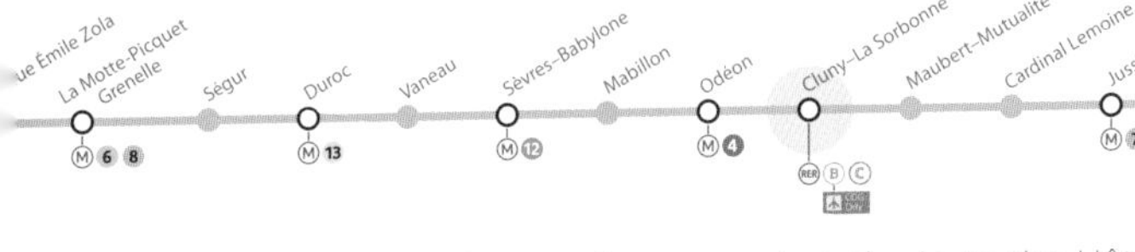

SIGHTSEEING

onuments

Thermes and Hôtel de Cluny: the Musée National du Moyen-Âge is sheltered within, on one hand, the Roman bathing complex and, on the other, the town house of the abbots of Cluny. The architect Alexandre-Albert Lenoir was given the task of restoring the two buildings in 1844. Along with the amphitheatre on rue Monge, the baths are one of the last remnants of 2nd and 3rd century Lutetia. As to the Hôtel de Cluny, it is the finest example of medieval civil architecture in Paris, together with the Hôtel de Sens. The baths follow the model of the large public bathing establishments of the Roman Empire: a warm room (*caldarium*) used for massages and hot steam baths, a tepid room (*tepidarium*) containing the individual bathtubs and a cold room (*frigidarium*), the best-preserved part with its three cradle vaults. Historians attribute its foundation to the Paris waterman's corporation, which held the water monopoly. The water was brought here by the Arcueil aqueduct. The system was

already equipped with sewers and underground corridors. During the Hun and Norman invasions, the baths served as a refuge for the terrified population. Built between 1485 and 1498, the Hôtel de Cluny was originally the property of Pierre de Chaslus, Abbot of Cluny-en-Bourgogne. It served as a guest house for the Cluniac abbots when visiting Paris. Reconstructed by Jacques d'Ambroise, it took on the Flamboyant Gothic style. Its exterior wall is prettily crenelated and its important doorway is decorated by an arch with angels and demons. The interior is full of treasures, such as the abbots' splendid little chapel and the Lady and the Unicorn tapestry cycle woven in Flanders in the 15th century.

6 place Paul-Painlevé, 5th.
Tel.: 01-53-73-78-16 or 01-53-73-78-00. Open Wednesday to Monday 9.15am to 5.45pm. Entrance fee.

② **The Sorbonne:** a huge liner dedicated to knowledge, the Sorbonne has crossed the sea of ages and bears the indelible marks of the three historic epochs that have shaped it: medieval, royal and republican. It was founded in 1257 by Robert de Sorbon and Saint Louis to welcome almost 10,000 deprived theology students. Cardinal Richelieu, Dean of Sorbon's college, had it rebuilt in 1625. Closed during the Revolution, it was reopened by Napoleon in 1806. Under the impetus of the Third Republic, Nénot gave it its current appearence in 1885. Only the chapel designed by Lemercier, built in 1635, remains from earlier epochs. Inside is Richelieu's majestic tomb sculpted by Girardon, which was saved from revolutionary destruction. Seat of uprising in May 1968, the Sorbonne has occasionally been the stage of violent student revolt.

1 rue Victor-Cousin, 5th (not open to the public).

Address book

The place for a rendezvous

Le Stop Cluny
94 boulevard Saint-Germain, 5th.
Open Monday to Saturday 7am to midnight, Sunday from 9am.
Tel.: 01-46-33-30-74.

Culture

A Le Champo

The soul of Jacques Tati and his curls of pipe smoke linger over your head in this cinema. On its 50th anniversary, the cinema paid homage to the film director in rebaptising itself 'Le Champo Espace Jacques-Tati'. Black and white stills from his films decorate the hall, while a rare poster of *Jour de Fête* is displayed not far from an illuminated silhouette of the director straight out of *Les Vacances de Monsieur Hulot*. This cinema certainly has a soul. An arts cinema that is proud of its programme, it is a meeting place for film buffs come to see the most imaginative films since 1938. Each of the cinemas has an original touch that makes it unique: the projection in cinema no. 1 is made with the help of a periscope, the ceiling of no. 2 glitters with 3,000 stars. Le Champo is renowned for its retrospectives: Woody Allen remained on the programme for two years, David Lynch one year. All the films of Louis Jouvet, Sacha Guitry, Cary Grant, Louis Malle, Marcel Carné and, of course, Jacques Tati have been devotedly screened here. It is the waking dream of every film lover, you can even spend the night here to watch three films, with breakfast included. What are you waiting for?
51 rue des Écoles, 5th.
Tel.: 01.43.54.51.60.
www.lechampo.com
Open daily.

Restaurant

B Le Reflet

On the walls, like rare, precious specimens, are black and white photos of actors and scenes taken during film shoots, illuminated by genuine cinema spotlights. Tucked just opposite the Reflet Médicis cinema, this restaurant is itself an ode to cinema. David Bowie, the Beatles and the Doors provide musical accompaniment to this cavern furnished with a sofa that has seen better days. The atmosphere is welcoming and regulars crowd along the bar. The food is simple but tasty, such as *croque provençal* on toasted rye bread garnished with melted goat's cheese, a delicious baking hot crumble with caramelised apples flavoured with cinnamon. You are at last ready to go to Le Champo, which is waiting nearby. Dish of the day €11.
6 rue Champollion, 5th.
Tel.: 01-43-29-97-27.
Open Monday to Saturday 11am to 2am.

MAUBERT – MUTUALITÉ

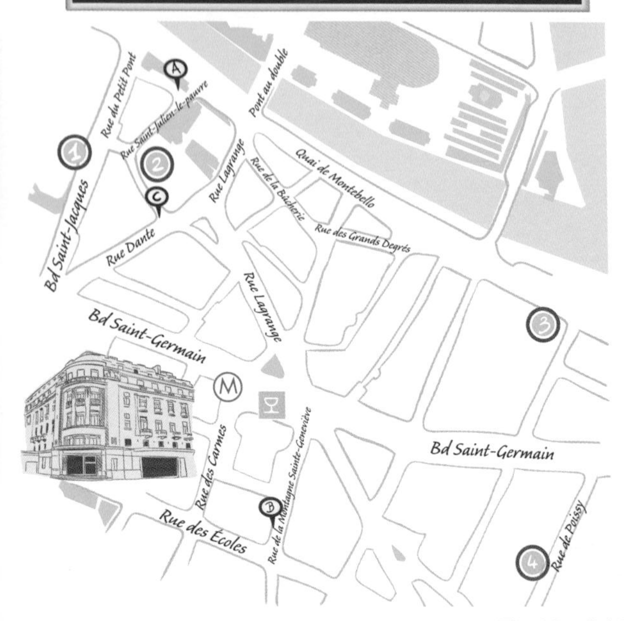

History

The station's name evokes Place Maubert and the nearby Maison de la Mutualité. This charming square dates from the early 13th century. Its name is said to come either from a deformation of the name Aubert, Abbot of Sainte-Geneviève, who established butchers' stalls on this site in the 12th century, or from that of Maître Albert, Dominican monk, philosopher and theologian, best known as the teacher of Thomas Aquinas. On 12 May 1588 during the eighth War of Religion, the first barricade of the Catholic League, which supported the tumultous Duc de Guise, was set up on the square on the Journée des Barricades (named in reference to the barrels amassed to build them). The population's animosity towards King Henri III, suspected of wanting to designate Henri de Navarre (future Henri IV) as his successor, was at its height.

The Marché Maubert, founded in 1547, is one of the oldest markets in Paris. The square was used for outdoor lectures in theology and philosophy to interested or anxious spectators. The Art Deco Maison de la Mutualité was inaugurated as a theatre in 1931 by the politician Paul Doumer. Headquarters of the Fédération Mutualiste de Paris (FMP), it is used for animated congresses and political meetings and has become a rallying place for left-wing militants. Majestic concerts have been held here. Great singer Léo Ferré often performed here out of loyalty to the Anarchist Federation, which he supported passionately.

SIGHTSEEING

spiritual walk

Église Saint-Séverin: the choir of Saint-Séverin is protected by the splendid forest of columns of the double deambulatory in Flamboyant Gothic style, illuminated by modern stained glass by Jean Bazaine. In its centre is an admirable twisted column, from which flow the 14 ribs of the infinitely graceful vault of the apse. Its belfry preciously hides the oldest bell in Paris, dating from 1412.

5 rue Saint-Séverin, 5th.

2 Église Saint-Julien-le-Pauvre

Standing opposite Square Viviani, where the oldest tree in Paris, a robinier planted in 1602 flaunts its age with pride, the church impresses by the solidity of its buttresses, characteristic of 12th-century architecture. Built on the site of a Merovingian burial ground, this little chapel at the junction of two Roman roads was given as a ruin by king Henri I to the chapter house of Notre-Dame in 1045.

Cistercian monks from the Abbaye de Longpont (Aisne) patiently rebuilt it in 1165. The university and its rectors held a court here until it was sacked in 1524 because of a contested election. Partially demolished in the 17th century, a salt store during the Revolution, it was finally given to the Greek Melkite Catholic church in 1889. On its south columns, don't be afraid, four harpies are watching you.
79 rue Galande, 5th.

Culture

③ **Musée de l'Assistance Publique**
Founded in 1934 and housed in the 17th century Hôtel de Miramion, this astonishing little museum retraces the history of hospitals from the Middle Ages to the early 20th century, against the background of the separation between Church and State,

from a reserve of 10,000 objects and paintings. The hotel is named after its original owner, Madame de Miramion, founder of a lay community dedicated to teaching poor children and caring for the sick. At the time the *miramiones* made remedies here from medicinal plants that you can see in wandering around the garden.
47 quai de la Tournelle, 5th.
Tel.: 01-40-27-50-05.
Open Tuesday to Thursday and the first Sunday of the month 10am to 6pm.
Entrance fee.

④ **Collège des Bernardins:** founded by the Cistercians in the 13th century, this medieval college educated monks from all over Europe. The architects Wilmotte and Baptiste have recently given it a new life as a place of dialogue between the church and society, much desired by Cardinal Lustiger. Lectures, exhibitions and concerts intermingle to animate this cultural centre resolutely focused on sharing and exchange.
20 rue de Poissy, 5th.
Tel.: 01-53-10-74-44.
www.collegedesbernardins.fr

Address book

The place for a rendezvous

Le Village Ronsard
47 boulevard Saint-Germain, 5th.
Open daily 6am to midnight.
Tel.: 01-43-25-07-95.

Culture

A Shakespeare & Co

Be warned: this bookshop is a trap! It's impossible not to stay here for hours looking and leafing through each tome lovingly displayed by the great-granddaughter of the poet Walt Whitman. This English-language bookshop will bowl you over you with its range of new and second-hand books and its setting brimming with charm.
37 rue de la Bûcherie, 5th.
Tel.: 01-43-25-40-93.
shakespeareandcompany.com
Open Monday to Friday 10am to 11pm, Saturday and Sunday from 11am.

Out of the ordinary

B La Lucha libre
This explosive place is a true curiosity. One has to admit there are few restaurants in Paris where you can dress up as a Mexican wrestler and put on a sumo costume to take part in a combat in a real boxing ring. Fans, take note. La Lucha Libre is a small Mexican cantina where you can sip a cocktail upstairs before sending your friends into the ropes. It organises professional wrestling fights on the first and third Friday of the month. You can also dance here on Fridays and leave proudly with a semi-pro wrestler's mask.
10 rue de la Montagne-Sainte-Geneviève, 5th.
Tel.: 01-43-29-59-86.

C The Rocky Horror Picture Show
A cult film in a cinema that is equally so, Studio Galande. Released in 1975, this musical film directed by Jim Sharman is a direct adaptation of Richard O'Brien's crazy London stage musical. At the time, critics accused it of all the evils: poor parody of science-fiction and B movies, holes in the plot, a cartoon mood and over-sexed atmosphere. Yet, despite being a flop on its release, many years later *The Rocky Horror Picture Show* has attained the status of cult film. More than 35 years after it was first screened, it is still on the programme of several cinemas around the world, among them the Studio Galande. The entertainment is not just on the screen, it is also in the room: up on the stage, over-excited actors perform at the same time as the film is projected and make spectators participate...
Be prepared, don't come smartly dressed: the screening has its risks and dangers.
42 rue Galande, 5th.
Tel.: 01-43-26-94-08.

CARDINAL LEMOINE

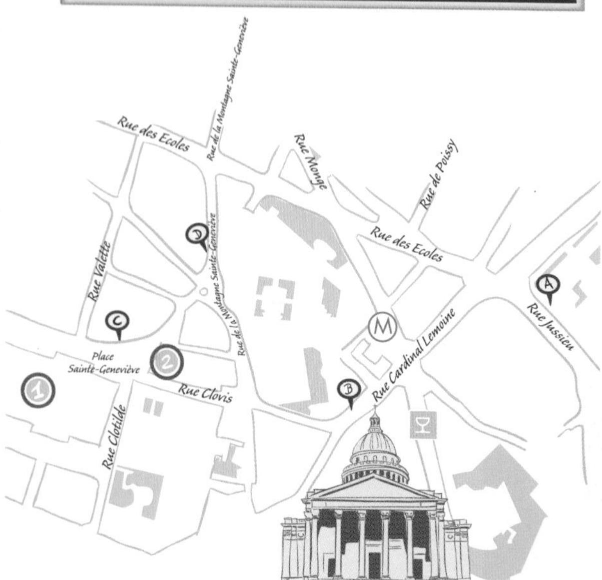

History

This station inaugurated in 1931 pays tribute to Cardinal Jean Lemoine (1250–1313). First as Dean of Bayeux cathedral, then as Bishop of Arras, he led a double career as Papal Legate between France and Rome. Thus he was emissary of the pope to try and appease the quarrel with the Capetian king Philippe le Bel (Philip the Fair) and put an end to the conflict between France and England. Nicknamed 'the Marble King' by his enemies, Philippe le Bel provoked numerous scandals during his reign. The king not wishing to cede again, the pope ordered the cardinal to issue an interdict against the kingdom and obliged Nicolas de Fréauville, the king's confessor, to come and explain in Rome. The legate succeeded in delaying the interdict, which the pope transformed into an excommunication against the king. Warned in advance, the French king had Lemoine placed under surveillance. The cardinal succeeded in leaving Paris during the night and speedily returned to Rome. Jean Lemoine is also remembered as the founder of a chapel nicknamed the 'Altar of the Lazy', in the nave of Notre-Dame Cathedral. Through a contract made in Rome, he next purchased the Maison du Chardonnet, rue Saint-Victor, and its adjoining land, from the monks of the Couvent des Grands Augustins. There he founded a college and offered 100 scholarships to worthy students. The prestigious college disappeared only with the Revolution. Called the Maison du Cardinal, it was renamed the Collège du Cardinal-Lemoine after his death. Rue du Cardinal Lemoine, which remembers it, leads to the place de la Contrescarpe. You are at the heart of the student quarter: schools, institutes and universities rub shoulders to breathe life into this effervescent place of knowledge.

SIGHTSEEING

'great men' walk

Panthéon: the Panthéon originally owed its existence to the desire of Louis XV, who on his deathbed in 1744 had vowed to build an immense church to replace the Abbaye de Sainte-Geneviève, which was in ruins, if God granted him a cure. Over the course of the ups and downs of history, this church was first dedicated to Saint Geneviève, then transformed into a republican temple before rediscovering its vocation as a place of worship under Louis-Philippe. The remains of Mirabeau, Voltaire, Rousseau and Marat were the first to be brought here. Renamed the Panthéon in 1830, the building recovered its role as a secular and patriotic lay temple, of which the golden letters on the pediment sculpted by David d'Angers affirm the unchangeable motto: 'To the great men recognised by the homeland'. A rebel base during the Commune in 1871, during which Jean-Baptiste Millière was coldly shot on the steps by government troops, the edifice was definitively transformed into

a republican monument in 1885, at the moment of the grandiose funeral of Victor Hugo. Soufflot's project, in 1764, originally sought, in his own words, to: 'reunite the lightness of Gothic architecture with the magnificance of Greek architecture.' The architect was heavily inspired by the Pantheon in Rome, in the conception of the 32 columns and the triangular pediment to make it a place inundated by light and carried by grace.

Place du Panthéon, 5th.

Tel.: 01-44-32-18-00. http://pantheon.monuments-nationaux.fr.
Open daily 10am to 6.30pm April to September, 10am to 6pm October to March. Entrance fee.

2 Église Saint-Étienne-du-Mont

Begun under François Ier (Francis I), the construction of the church was completed only during the reign of Louis XIII, which explains the charm of its unbalanced style. It majestically allies Flamboyant Gothic, with its pointed arches and ogival vaulting, with Renaissance style. Inside, it contains the only rood screen in Paris, elegantly adorned by two spiral staircases in sculpted stone dating from the beginning of the 17th century. Since 1803, the church has housed the shrine of Saint Geneviève, who has given her name to the 'mountain'. The legendary heroine remained in Paris during the barbarian invasions of the 5th century and was buried there in around 502. In

Address book

The place for a rendezvous

Les Petits Écoliers
32 rue Monge, 5th.
Open Monday to Friday 7am to 6pm.
Tel.: 01-43-26-90-32.

Culture

A Collection des Minéraux de Pierre et Marie Curie
The geology collection presents over 2,000 examples from around the world, chosen carefully among the most extraordinary and unusual minerals in earth sciences or for their industrial and artistic applications. The presentation in 24 panoramic showcases is directly inspired by the Museum of Crown Jewels in Iran. Unique in France, this sparkling collection is one of the most remarkable in the world. You reach its new location by entering the university campus, descending to level -2, by stairs or lift, on your right immediately on entering the parvis.
4 place Jussieu, 5th.
Tel.: 01-44-27-52-88.
Open Wednesday to Monday 1pm to 6pm. Entrance fee.

B Collège de France
In 1530, at the initiative of the great humanist scholar Guillaume Budé, François Ier decided to create a royal college where the subjects scorned by the very religious University of Paris would be taught, although it only moved to its current location during the reign of Henri IV. First named the Collège des Lecteurs Royaux, then Collège Royal de France, it took its current name during the Revolution. Neither university nor *grande école*, the Collège de France remains an unusual institution: it doesn't award any degrees and is open to all. It does not only recruit academics. Paul Valéry taught there. The courses by Henri Bergson were sought after, and Lévi-Strauss, Duby and Foucault built up its current reputation.

508, an abbey was built on the site where the Panthéon stands today. The church of Saint-Étienne-du-Mont contained the saint's remains, before receiving those of King Clovis. Pascal and Racine were buried in this timeless place, whose pediment, sculpted by Bay, represents the Resurrection. The church stands on the rather solemn, barren square today laid out around the Panthéon. On either side of the church are the Lycée Henri-IV and the neoclassical Bibliothèque Sainte-Geneviève. Built by Labrouste in 1844, on the site of the Collège de Montaigu, known for its iron discipline, this metal-framed library shelters three million volumes, including the precious tomes from the Abbaye Sainte-Geneviève.
Place Sainte-Geneviève, 5th.

11 place Marcelin-Berthelot, 5th.
Tel.: 01-44-27-12-11.
www.college-de-france.fr
All the courses are accessible without enrolment.

Out on the town

Ⓒ The Bombardier

This wood-panelled English pub overlooks the superb Church of Saint-Étienne-du-Mont, on the spot where Woody Allen shot a scene of *Midnight in Paris*. Inside, the atmosphere is convivial, laidback and cheerful. Come here to taste the Bombardier beer, the house brew, evidently.
2 place du Panthéon, 5th.
Tel.: 01-43-54-79-22.
Open daily noon to 2am, food served noon to 2pm.

Ⓓ Le Violon Dingue

A young, studenty crowd gathers in this appealing little bar, with its handful of wooden tables. On the ground floor, the mood is like a pub, mixing nonchalence and energy. A large array of beers and whiskies and huge list of cocktails are proposed by considerate barmen. The attractive vaulted stone cellar hosts dancers into the early hours.
46 rue de la Montagne-Sainte-Geneviève, 5th.
Tel.: 01-43-25-79-93.
Open Tuesday to Sunday 8pm to 4am.

Next stations

JUSSIEU

See line 7, page 180

GARE D'AUSTERLITZ

See line 5, page 136

line 11

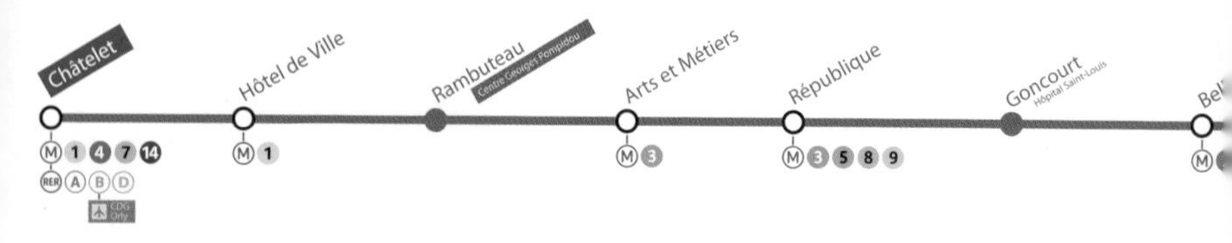

History

Entirely underground, the line 11 is decidedly odd. At just 6,286 metres (6,874 yards) long, it is the shortest line in Paris. Moreover—and unusual enough to be noteworthy—none of the line's stations have changed name since it opened in 1935. The line then served stations from Châtelet to the Porte des Lilas. Only in 1937 could hurried voyagers take the metro as far at the Mairie des Lilas. Decided in 1922 by the Paris City Council, this line was intended to serve the working-class districts of northeast Paris and replace the funicular tramway of Belleville that had closed in 1924. The work was far from simple because of the unstable nature of the ground and the depth of some of the stations, such as Télégraphe, which is buried over 20 metres (66 feet) deep in the guts of Paris. From May 1944 to 1945, the line was requisitioned by the Wehrmacht. In the 1950s and 60s, an experimental line saw the day, at the initiative of the RATP. A showcase of modernity, in 1956 line 11 was the first metro in the world to be equipped with rolling stock running on tyres. Today, its extension further east is under discussion. Work should begin in 2013 to open in 2019. Patience!

Châtelet / Mairie des Lilas

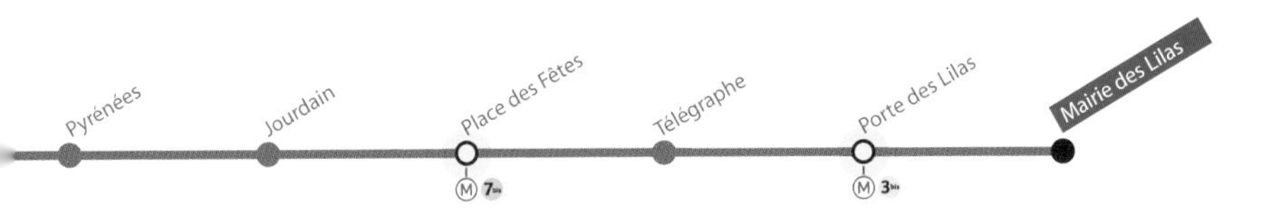

PLACE DES FÊTES

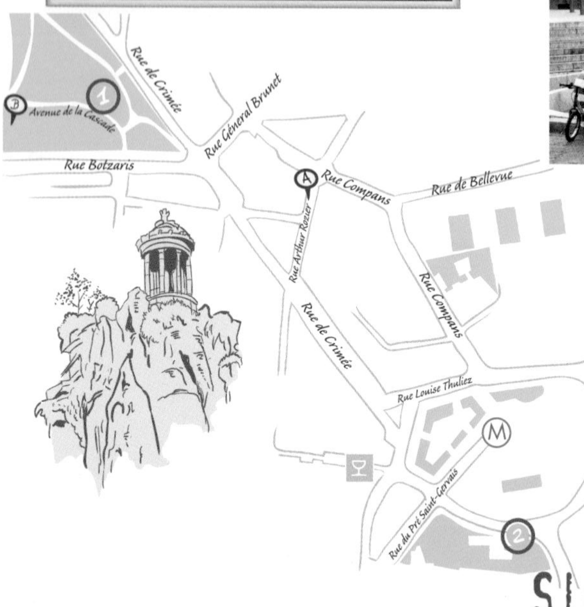

History

Opened in 1911, the name of this station recalls the old *fêtes* (parties) organised by the village of Belleville in front of the church that used to stand on the square. This agora saw the light of day in 1836. It changed its character in the 1970s, when the construction of vast tower blocks disfigured the square forever. Even though it was renovated in the mid 1990s by architect Bernard Huet, the place des Fêtes has lost its joyful and festive atmosphere of old. Since 1987, it has contained a fountain-labyrinth in the (concreted) centre, by Hungarian-born French sculptor Marta Pan, who was a friend of Brancusi and Le Corbusier. In it water ripples over the ground in the corridors of a maze, while a translucent obelisk lights up the night.

SIGHTSEEING

A walk in the park

1 Parc des Buttes-Chaumont

Inaugurated in 1867, this terribly Haussmannian park created by Napoleon III is perched on ancient gypsum quarries. Reputed for its quality, some of its production was exported to the United

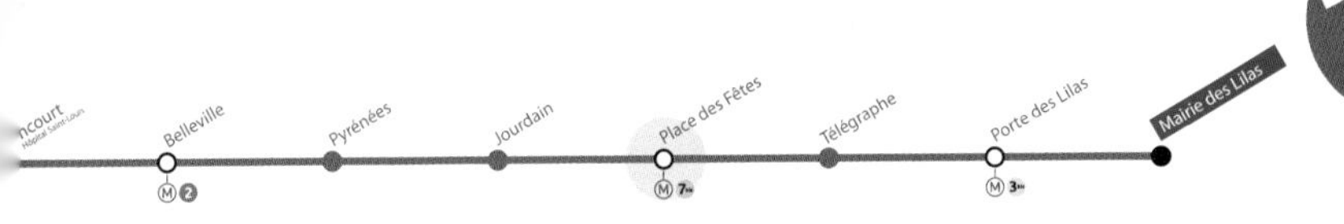

States, giving this area the name 'Quartier des Amériques'. The park's creator, the engineer Jean-Charles Alphand, modelled the landscape with blasts of dynamite to create a mountainous relief around a lake, which is overhung by a mountain all in rock and concrete, pierced by a cave, above which rises a temple. One reaches the latter by two bridges, one in brick, the other a suspension bridge.
1 rue Botzaris, 19th.

Regard de la Lanterne: at the corner of rues Compans and Augustin-Thierry, a regard dating from 1583. It is a relic of the system of underground aqueducts built in the 12th century, which used to bring water from Belleville to the abbeys of Paris. It formed the head of the Belleville aqueduct. Nearby, stroll along rue de Mouzaïa to discover its little streets of houses invaded by lilacs, wisteria and roses. You will succumb to the unbelievable charm of these little garden cities framing cobbled streets so typical of the workers' districts of the 1840s.

Address book

The place for a rendezvous

Le Bistrot du Marché
17 rue des Fêtes, 19th. Open daily 5.30am to 9pm, Saturday until 7pm. Tel.: 01-40-18-35-09

Restaurants

A L'Heure Bleue
A little hidden, this welcoming restaurant with a jazzy ambience knows how to charm. As well as some vegetarian specialities, you could equally be tempted by an entrecôte steak sprinkled with Guérande sea salt, washed down with wines from small producers. The desserts are astonishing. Just the thing for building up strength before climbing to the summit of the Buttes-Chaumont. Around €25 à la carte.
57 rue Arthur-Rozier, 19th. Tel.: 01-42-39-18-07. www.heure-bleue.fr Open Monday to Saturday noon to 2.15pm, 7.30 to 10.15pm.

B Rosa Bonheur
Passionate about freedom and nature, Rosa Bonheur was one of the most famous animal painters of the second half of the 19th century. Packed in fine weather, this animated *guinguette* dance hall is the place of choice for young Parisians, who hurry here for an evening drink, to dance and find... happiness. Snacks €5 to €8.
2 allée de la Cascade, 19th. Tel.: 01-42-00-00-45. www.rosabonheur.fr Open Wednesday to Sunday noon to midnight.

Previous stations

CHÂTELET
See line 1, page 32

RAMBUTEAU
La Station Rambuteau, 20 rue Beaubourg, 4th.

RÉPUBLIQUE
See line 3, page 86

HÔTEL DE VILLE
See line 1, page 34

ARTS ET MÉTIERS
See line 3, page 84

GONCOURT
Le Voyageur
138 avenue Parmentier, 11th.

BELLEVILLE
See line 2, page 62

JOURDAIN
La Gitane
3 rue Lassus, 19th.

PORTE DES LILAS

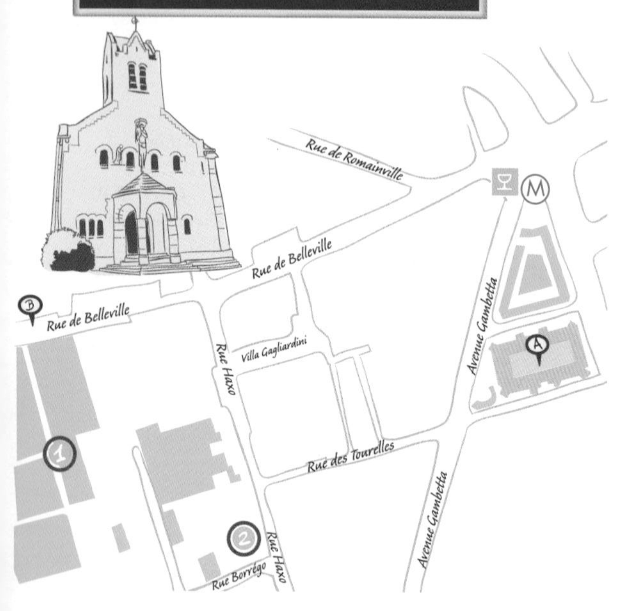

History

'Je suis le poinçonneur des Lilas, le gars qu'on croise et qu'on ne regarde pas' ('I am the ticket collector at the Lilas, the chap who one passes and doesn't look at'), sang Gainsbourg. What no-one remembers is that through his lyrics the cabbage-head man evokes a bit of the station's history. At the time, hurried passengers could travel without changing from the Porte des Lilas to Levallois-Perret. Moreover, this history is complicated, because of junctions, disjunctions and, even, a ghost station. A stop called Porte des Lilas-Cinéma, hidden not far from here, is used as a film set. The metro scenes in *Amélie* and the pop video for Jean-Jacques Goldman's song *Elle a fait un bébé toute seule* were shot in its tunnels.

© Denis Sutton / RATP

SIGHTSEEING

Off the beaten track

1 **Cimetière de Belleville:** from this site dominating the whole of Paris, Claude Chappe, who sought a high point, tried out his optic telegraph between 1790 and 1798. But his invention was vandalised by the revolutionaries, convinced that he was communicating with the royal family imprisoned in the Temple. Today the trees

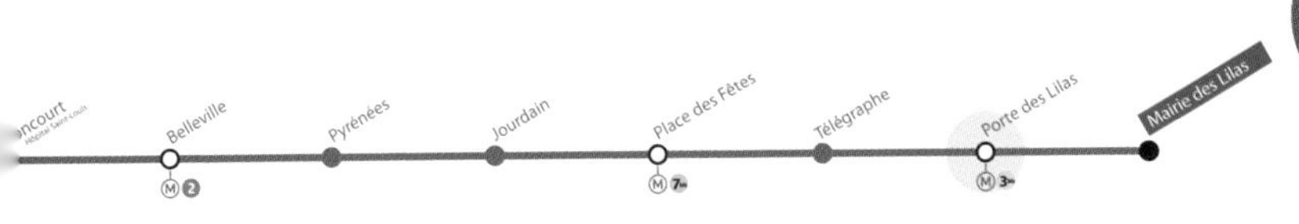

in the cemetery are the only traces of the Parc de Saint-Fargeau that occupied the site at the time. It was unfortunately broken up at the Revolution, like its château. The Belleville reservoir abuts the cemetery at the very place where the main building of the Le Peletiers, the estate's last owners, once stood. In its calm alleyways, you will perhaps meets the ghost of Léon Gaumont. This Bellevillois, a great man of cinema, rests here in peace.

40 rue du Télégraphe, 20th.

2 Église Notre-Dame-des-Otages

Stage of one of the bloodiest events of the Commune on 26 May 1871, the remains of a wall, visible from rue du Borrégo, indicates the execution site of the 52 hostages, both National Guard and clergy, held by the Fédérés or Communards. The district has changed over the years and the chapel constructed on the site has since been replaced by a Jesuit church inaugurated in 1938.

81 rue Haxo, 20th.

Address book

The place for a rendezvous

Au Métro des Lilas
261 avenue Gambetta, 20th.
Open Monday to Friday 5.30am to 11.30pm, Saturday and Sunday from 7am.
Tel.: 01-43-64-57-10.

Leisure

A Piscine Georges-Vallerey
Also known as the 'Piscine des Tourelles', this swimming pool is the temple of watersports in Paris. Constructed for the 1924 Olympic games, it notably witnessed the 400-metres freestyle record by Johnny Weissmuller, future Hollywood Tarzan. The French swimming championships and the Meeting International de la Ville de Paris are held here each year.
148 avenue Gambetta, 20th.
Tel.: 01-40-31-15-20.
www.paris.fr

Restaurant

B Le Bollywood Palace
Go through the door and plunge straight into the heart of Indian delicacies. Starters marinated in spices and yoghurt, saffron rice and tandoori specialities cooked in a wood fire in a traditional terracotta oven leave no doubt as to where you are. Express lunch menu €6.50.

275 rue de Belleville, 19th.
Tel.: 01-42-38-99-30.
www.bollywood-palace.com

Previous station
TÉLÉGRAPHE
Le Mistra
253 rue Belleville, 19th.

Next station
MAIRIE DES LILAS
Les Lilas
80 rue de Paris, 93260 Les Lilas.

line 12

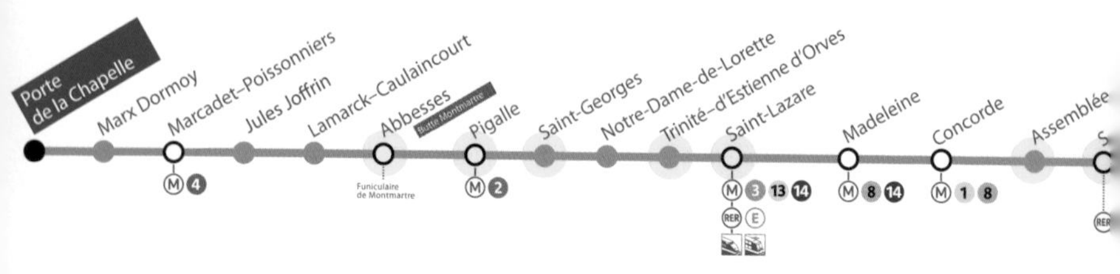

History

This line traces a tortuous path through Paris over 13.8 kilometres (8.6 miles) from the north to the southwest. The engineer behind the plan, Jean-Baptiste Berlier (1841 – 1911) wanted to excavate the line deep underground and line it with metal tubes, like the London Underground. This innovative method drew praise because it meant the line could be built in the straightest possible line. So the section from Porte de Versailles to Notre Dame de Lorette was opened in 1910 with much pomp and circumstance. The press marvelled at the smooth ride, the turquoise colour of the carriages and the brightly lit stations.
The section was extended first to Pigalle in 1911 and to Jules Joffrin in 1912. This extension was particularly difficult, as the tunnel had to be blasted through the hill at Montmartre, which is made of gypsum. While this was being done, workers were surprised to discover several quarries that were not on the plans, and the route of the line had to be changed to bypass them. At Abbesses, which is 36 metres (39 yards) underground, and Lamarck-Caulaincourt, which is 25 metres (27 yards) underground, arches were built to support the stations' roofs and withstand the enormous weight of the gypsum. The terminus at Porte de la Chapelle station was finally opened four years later, and at Mairie d'Issy in 1934.

Porte de la Chapelle / Mairie d'Issy

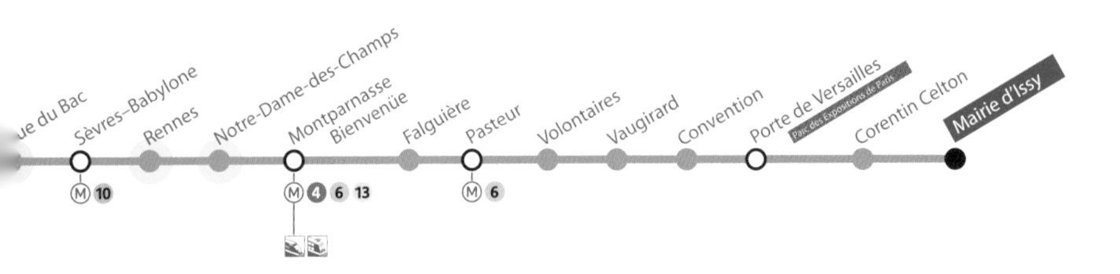

ABBESSES

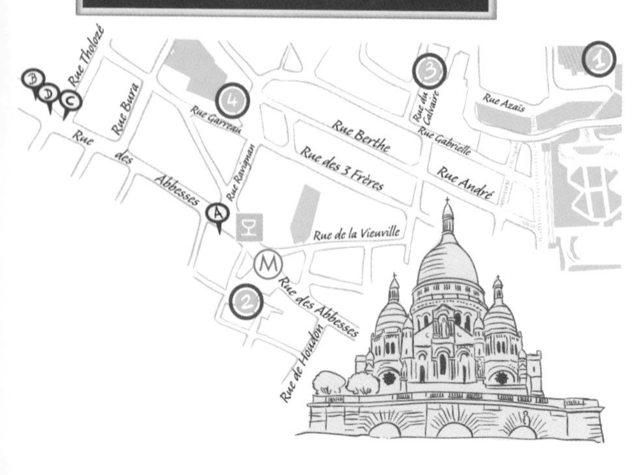

History

This station is just like its neighbourhood–unusual. It was opened on 31 October 1912 and is the deepest in Paris. Its platforms are 36 metres (39 yards) below the metro entrance. If you are fit enough, you can use the spiral staircase to reach them. It was renovated in 2007 with photographs by Jacques Habbas running the full height of the stairwell. That would give you a foretaste of the multitude of steps that make Montmartre's charm. At the bottom of the hill the metro entrance, an Art Nouveau Guimard edicule, is equally spectacular. Its majestic canopy in wrought iron and glass makes it a work of art. It was classified as a historical monument in 1978. The only other stations which still have these distinctive Art Nouveau entrances are Porte Dauphine and Châtelet, at Place Opportune. The edicule here was originally located at Hôtel de Ville station, and was relocated to Abbesses in 1974. You can admire it from the shade of the plane trees in Place des Abbesses, which is the heart of this attractive neighbourhood. The station takes its name from the Benedictine Abbey of the Dames of Montmartre, which was founded in 1133 on the summit of the hill by King Louis VI (1081–1137) and his wife, Adelaide of Savoie, and was for centuries a place of pilgrimage. It is thought there were 45 abbesses there before the abbey was destroyed during the Revolution. The only monument that remains from this history is the Saint-Pierre church.

SIGHTSEEING

Monuments

1 ***Basilique du Sacré-Coeur:*** there is a breathtaking view across Paris from the Basilica of the Sacred Heart, which is right on top of the hill. Its white facade and Roman-Byzantine domes have come to symbolise Montmartre, but it was far from easy to build—work began in 1877 and was finished nearly 40 years later. There were numerous technical difficulties, as the builders had to redesign its foundations because of all the quarries that run through the hill. And it was also built against a backdrop of political tension in the wake of the Paris Commune. As a church, it was supposed to atone for the sins of France and implore the mercy of the Sacred Heart of Jesus. On a more secular level, it was identified with Republican opposition and the Radical Party founded by Georges Clemenceau. It was designed by architect Paul Abadie and is 94 metres (103 yards) high. A crypt covers the entire surface under its flagstones. There is one of the largest mosaics in the world in the chancel's vast dome, representing Christ glorified by the Church and France. Sacré-Cœur also has an imposing hexagonal bell known as 'La Savoyarde'. You can climb the 237 stairs up to the dome's gallery for an incomparable view of the chancel itself and of Paris.
35 rue du Chevalier-de-la-Barre, 18th.

② **Église Saint-Jean-de-Montmartre:** standing on Place des Abbesses, the church is known by locals as Notre-Dame-des-Briques, or Our Lady of the Bricks. It was built by Anatole de Baudot between 1894 and 1904 and was the first church to be made of reinforced concrete. This earned it much criticism from opponents of its Art Nouveau style.

18 rue des Abbesses, 18th.

A walk through (art) history

③ **Place du Tertre:** this square caters not so much for Parisians but rather for tourists and artists of variable talent. You can see some beautiful 18th century mansions here. In the early years of the 20th century, Picasso and Utrillo, the Impressionist painter who was born in Montmartre, would walk here undisturbed. Take a stroll through the adjacent cobbled streets all the way down to the Place des Abbesses to savour the peacefulness of Montmartre, which still retains its village spirit despite being in the heart of Paris.

④ **Bateau-Lavoir:** this building was the cradle of the artistic revolution proclaimed by the founders of Fauvism, Cubism and other types of Futurism. Among famous artists who stayed here were Picasso, Braque, Modigliani and Gauguin, testifying to the artistic effervescence this iconic building nurtured within its walls.

13 place Émile-Goudeau, 18th.

Address Book

The place for a rendezvous

Le Saint-Jean
23 rue des Abbesses, 18th.
Open daily 7am to 2am.
Tel.: 01-46-06-13-78.

Culture

Ⓐ Théâtre des Abbesses
Located at the bottom of the hill in Montmartre, this theatre was established in 1996 as an offshoot of Théâtre de la Ville at Châtelet. Several contemporary artists contributed to the project, including Daniel Buren, Loïc Le Groumellec, Jean-Charles Blais, Robert Barry and Patrick Corillon.
31 rue des Abbesses, 18th. Tel.: 01-42-74-22-77. Ticket office open Tuesday to Saturday 11am to 8pm, closes 7pm on days with no performance.

Ⓑ Galerie W
Founded in 1998 by art dealer Eric Landau, the gallery has grown over the years to become an essential address for creativity and contemporary art. A special exhibition is scheduled each month, and there are also temporary exhibitions. The gallery also features permanent exhibitions for 20 artists, including CharlÉlie, Jean-Marc Dallanegra, Troy Henriksen, Denis Robert and Miss Tic.
44 rue Lepic, 18th. Tel.: 01-42-54-80-24. www.galeriew.com Open daily 10am to 7pm.

Restaurants

Ⓒ Un Zèbre à Montmartre
This cosy restaurant with a bright red street front is right in the heart of Montmartre at the corner of rue des Abbesses. Regulars come here and tourists drop in to sit at its terrace. You will be served specialties from Lyon made in-house, such as tender chuck steak. There are also gourmet salads, beef *tartare* and tuna steak to choose from at a restaurant that aims to brighten up your lunches and dinners. Lunch menu €14.
38 rue Lepic, 18th. Tel.: 01-42-23-97-80. Open Monday to Saturday 9am to 2am, Sunday from 10am.

Ⓓ Pomponnette
Not far from Le Zèbre you will find this restaurant with a history going back a full century. It was founded by Arthur Delcroix and named after a village in Seine-et-Marne. It has become legendary for being the place where poster artist Francisque Poulbot and other local artists launched 'the Republic of Montmartre', a cultural and charitable foundation, in 1921. You can enjoy festive and tasty French cooking here. The walls are full of oil painting and drawings. The founder's descendants believe in keeping it in the family and still run the restaurant. Menu € 34.
42, rue Lepic, 18th. Tel.: 01-46-06-08-36. www.pomponnette montmartre.com Open Monday evenings 7pm to midnight, Tuesday to Saturday noon to 3pm and 7pm to midnight.

Previous stations

PORTE DE LA CHAPELLE

Bar Restaurant de la Gare
82 rue de la Chapelle, 18th.

MARX DORMOY

Café de la Poste
1 rue Ordener, 18th.

MARCADET - POISSONNIERS

See line 4, page 95

JULES JOFFRIN

Saint-Isaure
4 rue Saint-Isaure, 8th.

LAMARCK - CAULAINCOURT

Le Refuge
72 rue Lamarck, 8th.

PIGALLE

History

This station opened in 1902 and is named after Jean-Baptiste Pigalle, who lived locally and was Madame de Pompadour's favourite sculptor. At the end of the 19th century the square and surrounding streets were full of artists who revolutionised their art. One of the neighbourhood's literary cafés, La Nouvelle Athènes, counted Toulouse Lautrec and Emile Zola among its customers. It is true to say that Pigalle has always fed the popular imagination. The musician Georges Ulmer immortalised it in these lines:
'A little fountain, a metro station, bistros with imagination, Pigalle ...'
The district is synonymous with Parisian nightlife and has a *risqué* reputation, but it is changing. Until recently it was essentially an area with sex shops and erotic cabaret shows, but gradually trendy discothèques are moving in, which draw young people like a magnet.

SIGHTSEEING

Off the beaten track

1 **Cité du Midi:** Pigalle may be better known for its night life than its monuments, but it nevertheless contains some

surprises. This is one. It is an astonishing concealed enclave on Boulevard de Clichy which offers a haven of peace despite being only a short distance from the bustle of Pigalle's sex shops. Plants have won the day over urbanism in this cobbled cul-de-sac with a provincial charm. At number 12, the former Pigalle bath house with its blue tiles is the last reminder of a time when homes hardly ever had running water.

48 boulevard de Clichy, 18th.

2 **Avenue Frochot:** like Cité du Midi, Avenue Frochot is a quiet haven behind a massive iron gate. You can just make out pretty houses with trees in this oasis of greenery in the heart of Paris's red light district. Gypsy guitarist Django Reinhardt lived here. Toulouse-Lautrec painted here. Both Renoir and his son took walks here. Perhaps the spirits of these immense artists still pervade this mysterious place. In any case, legend has it that one of the houses is haunted.

Avenue de Frochot, 9th.

Address Book

The place for a rendezvous

Les Omnibus
13 place Pigalle, 9th.
Open daily 8.45am to 2am.
Tel.: 01-42-26-82-04.

Out on the town

A Le Bus Palladium
From the 1960s to the present day, everyone who marked the history of rock'n roll has performed here, from Johnny Hallyday to Mick Jagger. Le Bus has recently been done up and is always full. Night owls can have dinner and dance the night away.
6 rue Fontaine, 9th.
Tel.: 01-45-26-80-35.
www.lebuspalladium.com
Tuesday: live acoustic music and DJ; Friday and Saturday: concerts from 10pm to 12:30am; nightclub from 12.30am to 6am.

B La Fourmi
Not far from the famous La Cigale (the grasshopper) is another famous concert hall named after an insect. *Fourmi* means ant, and the names evoke the fable *The Ant and the Grasshopper* by Jean de la Fontaine. This unusual bar has a very heterogeneous clientele. You need sharp elbows to get to the zinc bar, and you eat without ceremony. With its bistro chairs and huge chandelier, the furniture looks as if it comes from a second-hand shop.

74 rue des Martyrs, 18th.
Tel.: 01-42-64-70-35.
Open Monday to Friday 8.30am to 2.30am, Saturdays 8.30am to 4am and Sundays 10am to 4.30am.

SAINT-GEORGES

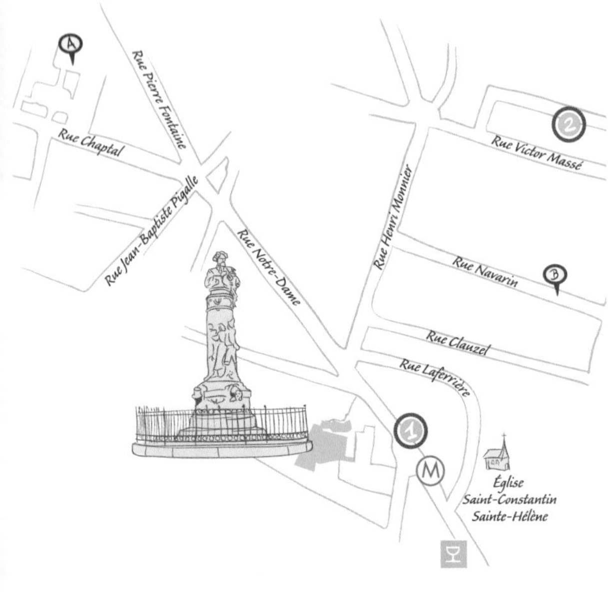

History

This station opened in 1911 and was named after Saint George, who symbolises the ideal of chivalry. It was renovated in the early 2000s using a style named after the Nord-Sud company that operated three Paris metro lines until 1931. Purists may say it does not truly follow that style's rules, as the saint's name is neither in ceramic, nor is it brown to denote that it is not possible to change lines at the station, as would normally be the case. Nevertheless, the station still has its charm. Note the curved access staircase. Another unusual feature is its underground ticket office at platform level. You will see daylight and trains going by.

SIGHTSEEING

A walk in the city

1 **Place Saint-Georges:** in the centre of this small square is a neoclassical fountain where tired horses were allowed to drink in olden times. Nowadays a lovely bust of caricaturist Paul Gavarni is mounted there. On the pedestal is a relief showing a scene from the Carnival of Paris. This area was called La Nouvelle Athènes (New Athens) because of its profusion of Doric columns and other arcades. It was a favourite spot for the Romantics. George Sand and Frederic Chopin would rub shoulders with Georges Bizet in Square d'Orléans. At number 27 stands Hôtel Thiers, where Adolphe Thiers, who was prime minister under Louis Philippe,

was arrested during Napoleon III's coup d'état in 1851. Truffaut filmed *The Last Metro* in the nearby theatre at the top of rue Saint-Georges.

2 **Cité Malesherbes:** a gate protects this enclosed street that acts as a dividing line between the New Athens and Montmartre crowds, near Avenue Frochot (see Pigalle, page 305). It has beautiful balconies enclosed in glass. Ludovic Lepic, one of the founding artists of the Impressionist movement, lived at number 5.

Address Book

The place for a rendezvous

Le Bergerac
13 rue Notre-Dame-de-Lorette, 9th.
Open daily 8am to midnight.
Tel.: 01-45-26-66-77.

Culture

A Musée de la Vie Romantique
This Italian-inspired house is more than a museum, it takes you into the very essence of Romanticism. You can see mementos of George Sand and paintings by Ary Scheffer. You will succumb to the infectious charm of this place where writer Alphonse Lamartine and artist Eugène Delacroix would come. The host would receive them in his verdant courtyard with its border of beautiful roses.
16 rue Chaptal, 9th.
Tel.: 01-55-31-95-67.
Open Tuesday to Sunday 10am to 6pm.
Admission free for permanent collections.

Restaurant

B Hôtel Amour
You can lunch in the sun in the courtyard of this hotel which is just a stone's throw from Place Saint-Georges, or dine here far from the bustle of Paris in a restaurant full of antique furniture. The menu is very basic, serving up bistro-style food. The main attractions are to sip coffee in the retro décor or to laze on the lovely terrace.
About €30.
8 rue Navarin, 9th.
Tel.: 01-48-78-31-80.
www.hotelamourparis.fr
Open daily from 8am for breakfast, restaurant open noon to 12.30am.

Next station

NOTRE-DAME-DE-LORETTE

La Rimaudière, 2 rue Martyrs, 9th.

TRINITÉ – D'ESTIENNE D'ORVES

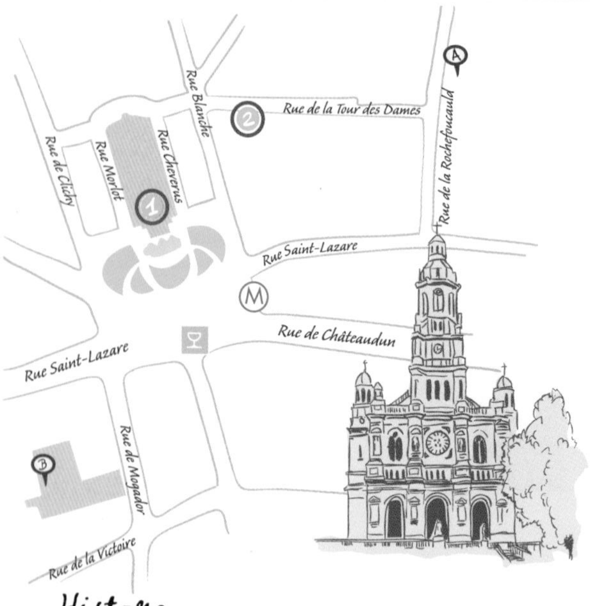

© Gilles Aligon / RATP

History

This station dates from 1910 and is named after both the neighbouring Trinity Church and Count Honoré d'Estienne d'Orves, a naval officer who joined General de Gaulle during the war. The square in front of the church is also named after him. He was a hero of the Resistance and established the first radio link between occupied France and London, but he was betrayed and transferred to Berlin. The German court was so impressed by his great dignity and unwavering courage that it requested a reprieve from Hitler. He was nevertheless executed by firing squad on Mount Valerian on August 29 1941, to serve as an example, after the first attack against the occupying forces that succeeded in inflicting casualties which had been organised by Pierre Georges, also known as Colonel Fabien.

SIGHTSEEING

Architecture

1 **Église de la Trinité:** this church with its remarkable bell tower was designed to be seen from the Opéra Garnier. In 1861 Baron Haussmann commissioned the church from architect Théodore Ballu. Its facade is inspired by the Italian Renaissance, featuring bold pediments, protruding pilasters and immaculate statues. You can see a magnificent painting of the Holy Trinity and the angels by Félix-Joseph Barrias above the chancel. There is also a play on the

number three, in tune with its name. There are three fountains and a triple basin over which there are three statues that depict the three theological virtues: Faith, Hope and Charity.

Place d'Estienne d'Orves, 9th.

2 ***Rue de la Tour des Dames:*** this street in the heart of New Athens, the intellectual hub of the early 19th century, clearly owes its name to its mills, which were owned by the abbesses of Montmartre. Famous people who lived in the neo-classical mansions here include actress Mademoiselle Mars, who acted in the first romantic dramas, at number 1. Mademoiselle Duchesnois, a friend of Victor Hugo and tragedian with François-Joseph Talma's company, lived at number 3. Talma himself lived at number 9.

Address Book

The place for a rendezvous

Café du Mogador
57 rue Chaussée-d'Antin, 9th.
Tel.: 01-48-74-85-19.
Open Monday to Friday 7am to 2am and Sundays 8am to 1am.

Culture

A Musée Gustave-Moreau
This museum was set up by Gustave Moreau, a figure in the Symbolist movement, during his lifetime. His paintings, inspired by mythology, are exhibited in the mansion where he lived. There are nearly 850 paintings and cartoons, 350 watercolours, over 13,000 drawings and sketches and 15 wax sculptures. He taught Matisse and strongly influenced André Breton, who was deeply affected by his visit to the museum.
14 rue de La Rochefoucauld, 9th.
Tel.: 01-48-74-38-50.
www.musee moreau.fr
Open Wednesday to Monday 10am to 12.45pm and 2pm to 5.15pm, and 10am to 5.15pm Friday to Sunday.
Admission fee.

B Theatre Mogador
This temple to the musical was the brainchild of a British financier, Sir Alfred Butt, who had it built in 1913 with a London Music Hall as its model. At first it was called the Palace Théâtre, but later took the name Mogador, which used to be the name of the town of Essaouira in Morocco. It was inaugurated in April 1919 by Franklin Delano Roosevelt, who would go on to become president of the United States.
25 rue de Mogador, 9th.
Tel.: 0-820-88-87-86 or 01-53-32-32-32.
www.mogador.net

SAINT-LAZARE

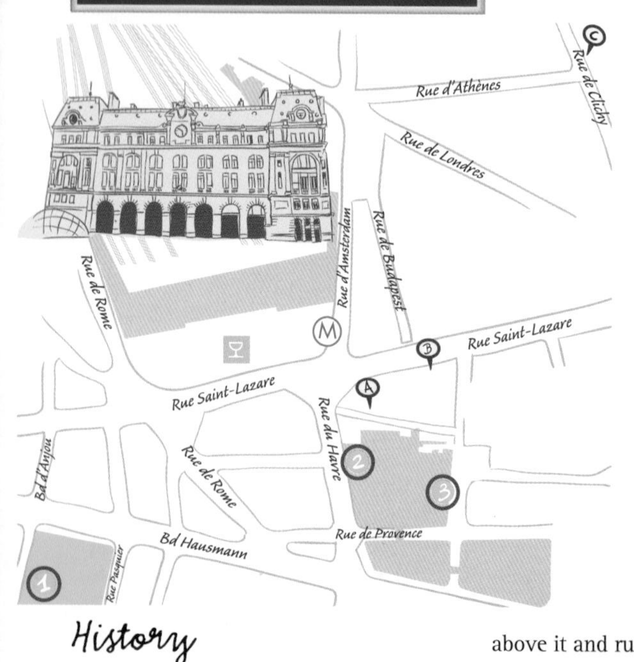

History

This station opened in 1904, and new lines have constantly been added to its repertoire, which makes it one of the busiest stations in Paris. At the front of the station, the metro entrance on Cour de Rome is a modern glass *édicule* (kiosk) by contemporary architect Jean-Marie Charpentier. He based his design for this half-moon-shaped glasshouse on the old Art Nouveau *édicules* in glass and metal. However, it stands on the ground rather than being supported by railings. Modern artist Arman contributed two works that stand in Cour du Havre and Cour de Rome. One is called *L'Heure pour Tous (The Time for All)* and consists of a pile of clocks, while the other, called *Consigne à Vue (Left Luggage on View)*, is a stack of suitcases. The station takes its name from the railway terminus above it and rue Saint-Lazare. In 1837, during the reign of Louis Philippe, a railway line was built from Paris to Saint-Germain to the west. At the time a temporary station was built in wood and called L'Embarcadère de l'Ouest, on Place de l'Europe, close to today's station. Nowadays no less than 450,000 passengers taking 1,600 trains every day transit through its corridors, making it one of Europe's busiest stations. The old concourse, dating from 1854, would remain the centre of the station. With its magnificent glass roof and metal frame, it is classed as a historic building. Monet painted it in 1877, when he lived in the neighbourhood.

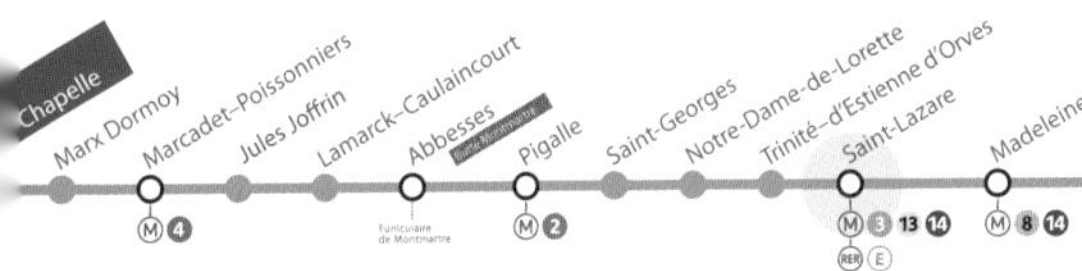

SIGHTSEEING

Monuments

1 **Chapelle Expiatoire:** the chapel was built in 1861 at the place where Louis XVI and Marie Antoinette were buried before their remains were transferred to the Basilica of Saint Denis in 1815. Louis XVIII decided to build this memorial chapel at his own expense. However, the word *expiatoire* (atonement) was never used officially. The king commissioned the chapel from architect Pierre François Léonard Fontaine, who gave it a Greco-Roman style. The altar in the crypt is said to mark the precise place where Louis XVI was originally buried. The building contains two white marble sculptures: one of Louis XVI with an angel pointing to the sky, by François-Joseph Bosio; and the other of Marie Antoinette supported by Religion, by Jean-Pierre Cortot. Chateaubriand said the chapel was 'perhaps the most remarkable monument of Paris'.

29 rue Pasquier, 8th.

❷ Lycée Condorcet: this school, a former Capuchin convent, was founded in 1803 and had some exceptional students and teachers. Its name was changed for political reasons, from Bonaparte, to Bourbon, to Fontanes, and finally to Condorcet. It is the work of architect Alexandre Théodore Brogniart, who also designed the church of Saint-Louis d'Antin. The facade is in neoclassical style and it has a cloister with Doric columns. For much of the 19th century the school had a relatively flexible curriculum, and progressive-minded bourgeois families liked to send their children there. It is among the few private schools in Paris that never took in boarders. Pupils who could not stay at their parents' homes would stay with the district's *maîtres de pension*, people with official recognition to put up schoolchildren. Alexandre Dumas and Marcel Proust were pupils. Classes to prepare pupils for high school were given by famous teachers, including Alain Desjardins, Jean Jaurès, Stéphane Mallarmé, Jean-Luc Merleau-Ponty, Marcel Pagnol, François Poulenc and Jean-Paul Sartre.

8 rue du Havre, 9th.

❸ Église Saint-Louis d'Antin: in 1782 Louis XVI asked the Capuchins to take over a convent which Brogniart had built on rue de la Chaussée d'Antin. After the Revolution, the Chapel of Saint-Louis d'Antin was given back to the Church in 1795 and designated as a parish in 1802. Its walls feature paintings from the second half of the 19th century. The organ, by Auguste Cavaillé-Coll, can be heard from time to time here.

63 rue Caumartin, 9th.

Address Book

The place for a rendezvous

Brasserie Mollard
115 rue Saint-Lazare, 8th.
Open daily noon to 12.30am.
Tel.: 01-43-87-50-22.

Shopping

Ⓐ Centre Commercial du Passage du Havre
This busy shopping centre just around the corner from Paris's two main department stores is on two levels and has many store franchises. It also has a huge glass roof.
10 rue Saint-Lazare, 9th.
www.passageduhavre.com
Open Monday to Saturday 10am to 8pm.

Culture

Ⓑ Les Cinq Caumartin
This cinema with character in the heart of the Saint-Lazare district has survived for over 80 years – it has existed since

1939. The top film at the time was *The Baker's Wife* by Marcel Pagnol. Decorated in red and white and kitted out with small tables and chairs, the cinema also has a counter full of all types of sweets. One of its theatres shows films that are no longer showing in other cinemas. Its quality programming and atmosphere make you want to venture in and treat yourself to an ice-cream.

101 rue Saint-Lazare, 9th.
Tel.: 0892-68-81-07.
www.cinqcaumartin.com
Open daily.

Ⓒ Casino de Paris

In 1730 the Duke of Richelieu commissioned a building for his own personal entertainment called La Folie Richelieu, which then became a theatre open to the public until 1811. It was replaced by Le Tivoli, a vast amusement park run by Claude Ruggieri, a fireworks expert. Then the Church of the Trinity was built on its site, but in 1861 Baron Haussmann had it dismantled and rebuilt nearby as part of his grand plan for Paris. A huge hall with a skating rink was built in the newly vacant space, and in 1880, the Palace Théâtre was built on part of the ice rink. Spectators could watch the attractions on a large podium from the theatre's Belle Époque décor. The Casino de Paris finally became a music hall during the First World War. In 1930 its director hired African-American singer Josephine Baker and put her on stage with a leopard named Chiquita, creating a sensation at the Colonial Exhibition of 1931. She sang what became her signature song, *J'ai deux amours* ('I have two loves'). Shows resumed here after the Second World War, and in 1959 actress Line Renaud launched her show, 'Pleasures of Paris', with over a hundred people on stage and dazzling costumes and scenery. It enjoyed huge success and played for four years.

16 rue de Clichy, 9th.
Tel.: 08-926-98-926
casinodeparis.fr. Open Monday to Saturday 11am to 6pm and one hour before the show.

Next stations

MADELEINE

See line 8, page 212

CONCORDE

See line 1, page 22

ASSEMBLÉE NATIONALE

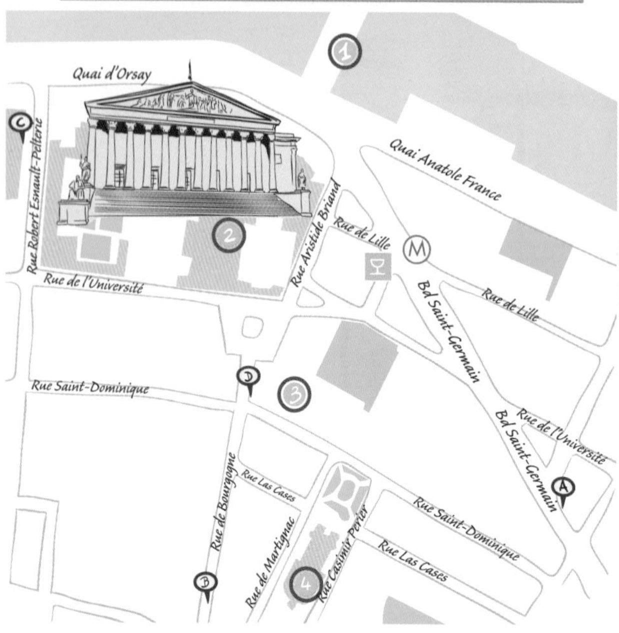

History

This station is situated under the legendary Boulevard Saint-Germain and was opened in 1910. However, it has not always had the same name. Until 1969 it was called Chambre des Députés, although this name for the lower house of Parliament was brought in under the Third Republic and had not been in use since 1946. In 1990 the station was given a new look by modern artist Jean-Charles Blais who is renowned worldwide for his paintings on recycled materials and work with ripped posters. He produced a vast frieze of posters printed with colourful geometric patterns. In 2008, to celebrate 50 years of the Fifth Republic, a new frieze was presented to the public. It takes the form of a symbolic dialogue, from one platform to another, between the executive arm of government and the legislature. Even though embassies and ministries have taken over the area and official cars have replaced the carriages of olden times, some say that the local inhabitants are the descendants of the great families who came to settle here centuries ago. This illustrates how Paris has been fashioned by historical upheavals—a neighbourhood with aristocratic antecedents becomes home to one of the most important Republican institutions.

SIGHTSEEING

Monuments

1. **Pont de la Concorde:** the bridge connects Quai des Tuileries and Quai d'Orsay. Its arches were built with stones from the Bastille prison. Architect Jean-Rodolphe Perronet, founder of the prestigious École des Ponts et Chaussées (School of Civil Engineering), completed it in 1791. The bridge's width was subsequently doubled between 1930 and 1932. It is a place where you can fall in love with Paris, as it offers one of the most enchanting views of the Seine.

2. **Palais Bourbon:** the Garde Républicaine stands guard at the entrance to the seat of the National Assembly, the lower house of Parliament, in the Palais Bourbon. Its construction was completed in 1726 by architect Pierre Lassurance, and in 1806 architect Bernard Poyet added the Corinthian columns we see today. The facade replicates the Église de la Madeleine, and faces it across the river, giving the impression that the two monuments are on the same axis. Inside the Palais Bourbon there is a hive of activity day and night, according to the calendar of Parliamentary sessions.
126 rue de l'Université and 33 quai d'Orsay, 7th.

③ ***Hôtel de Brienne:*** this mansion is decorated with angels. It was built in the 18th century and is now the Ministry of Defence. It is named after Compte de Brienne, a military officer and Secretary of State for War who was guillotined in 1794. It is fair to say that the building has kept its association with war. It was sold to the mother of another fearsome warrior, Napoleon Bonaparte. Then it was bought by the state in 1817 and became the official residence of the Minister of War. It was from here that Georges Clemenceau meticulously organised a victory from 1917. General de Gaulle had his headquarters here twice in difficult times, first as Secretary of State for War in June 1940, then as head of the provisional government from 1944 to 1946.

14 rue Saint-Dominique, 7th.

④ ***Basilique Sainte-Clotilde:*** its spires have risen to the sky since 1856. Its neo-Gothic style was inspired by architect François Gaud, who came from Cologne in Germany. He drew his inspiration from the cathedral in the city of his childhood. Théodore Ballu completed the facade and erected the two spires. It was consecrated in 1857 and became a basilica by edict of Pope Leo XIII for the 19th centenary of the baptism of Clovis (466–511), King of the Franks, to honour his wife Clotilde. Composer César Franck, a major figure in French music, was appointed organist at the basilica and played the famous Cavaillé-Coll organ here.

23bis rue Las Cases, 7th.

Address Book

The place for a rendezvous

Le Concorde

239 boulevard Saint-Germain, 7th.
Tel.: 01-45-51-43-71.
Open Monday to Friday 7am to 9pm and Saturdays 8am to 7pm.

Shopping

Ⓐ Galerie Taporo

Strolling along Boulevard Saint-Germain, passers-by will be intrigued by the plethora of designer boutiques. The most unlikely

creations are given free rein here. Their windows are like miniature museums or temples to modernism. And one of the most unusual is Galerie Taporo, where everything for sale is made of concrete. It is polished, waxed or coloured as minimalist furniture or art objects.
260 boulevard Saint-Germain, 7th.
Tel.: 01-53-59-94-89.
Open Tuesday to Friday 11am to 1pm and 2.30pm to 7pm, and 11am to 7pm on Saturdays.

Out on the town

Ⓑ Club des Poètes

Founded in 1961 by poet Jean-Pierre Rosnay 'to make poetry contagious and inevitable' because, he said, it 'de-pollutes mental space and is the counterweight and antidote to a life that tends to make us robots.' This place is unusual and captivating. Poets, actors and singers recite poems ranging from the *Song of Songs* to Baudelaire. Drinks €7.50, dinner €20.
30 rue de Bourgogne, 7th.
Tel.: 01-47-05-06-03.
www.poesie.net
Open Tuesday, Friday and Saturday night.
Dinner 8pm, poetry reading 10.15pm.

Restaurants

Ⓒ Chez Françoise

This restaurant was set up by Air France in 1949 to cater for the first ever air travellers, and is now the restaurant of choice for members of the French Parliament. They go for its refined, traditional cuisine and the discreet charm of a restaurant hidden right inside the Air France terminal. Musical evenings with jazz are held on Saturday nights. In summer you may prefer its sunny terrace to the refined décor of its restaurant. Menus €26 to 54.50. .
Aérogare des Invalides, 7th.
Tel.: 01-47-05-49-03. Open daily noon to 3.30pm and 7pm to 11.30pm.

Ⓓ Tante Marguerite

This elegant, refined restaurant near the Assemblée Nationale was acquired in 1999 by the famous chef Bernard Loiseau, who died in 2003. It serves Burgundy cuisine

like roast saddle of lamb and Charolais rib eye steak washed down with local wines. The owner may no longer be with us, but the food perpetuates his spirit, talent and creativity. Dinner menu €49.
5 rue de Bourgogne, 7th.
Tel.:01-45-51-79-42.
Open Monday to Friday noon to 2.30pm and 7pm to 10.30pm.

SOLFÉRINO

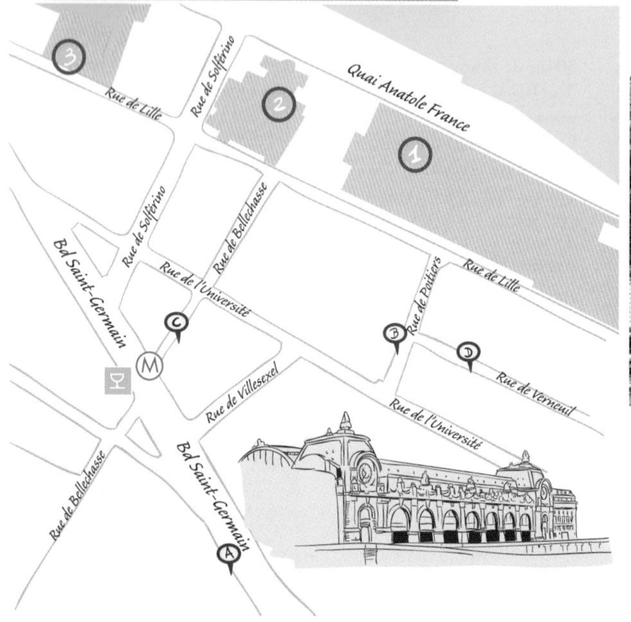

History

This station, which dates from 1910, celebrates the French-Italian victory against the Austrian empire at Solférino in Lombardy. On June 24 1859, the first shots rang out soon after 3am. Under a blazing sun 300,000 men braved the extreme heat and went into battle, falling, rising to fight again or dying. During the afternoon the Austrians successively abandoned their positions. When night fell, the ground was strewn with nearly 40,000 corpses. French troops under Napoleon III, allied with the Sardinian army, defeated the Austrian Emperor Franz Joseph. This particularly bloody battle would change the life of Swiss businessman Henry Dunant forever. He witnessed the atrocities and alerted public opinion by describing the savagery of the fighting in a book entitled *A Memory of Solférino*, published in 1862. Henry Dunant is considered as one of the founders of the Red Cross. The first Geneva Convention in 1864 adopted many of his proposals. He was awarded the Nobel Peace Prize in 1901 and died in 1910.

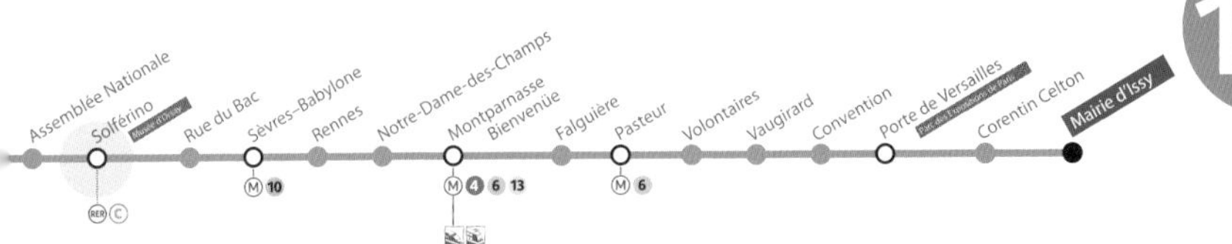

SIGHTSEEING

Culture

1 ***Musée d'Orsay:*** this former railway station was destroyed by the Paris Commune in 1871. It was earmarked for demolition in the 1970s, but media coverage aroused popular support, in the same way as Les Halles (see page 98) in central Paris was saved. Fortunately, its carved cast iron beams and exquisite glass roof were preserved. The museum is structured around its nave and central aisle, off which there are ochre-coloured hallways and terraces. Natural light penetrates everywhere, allowing the artworks to be appreciated. The exhibits include paintings, sculptures, architecture, photographs, decorative arts and graphics, reflecting the cultural expansion during the second half of the 19th century and early 20th century. It is an enchanting place where academic art and modern pioneers can be found in the various halls, to the delight of art lovers.

62 rue de Lille, 7th.
Tel.: 01-40-49-48-14.
www.musee-orsay.fr
Open Tuesday to Sunday 9.30am to 6pm, Thursdays until 9.45pm.
Admission fee.

② Palais de la Légion d'Honneur

This building is also called Hôtel de Salm and was built by architect Pierre Rousseau in 1782. It was burned down during the Paris Commune and rebuilt according to plans by architect Anastasius Mortier. Thomas Jefferson was one of its most fervent admirers and painter Jean-Charles Landon wrote a eulogy of the view from its salon overlooking the River Seine between the Tuileries gardens and Place de la Concorde. Nowadays, its green dome and Doric colonnade leading to a frontispiece of Corinthian columns provide the headquarters of the National Order of the Legion of Honour. Its

museum contains some of Napoleon's personal belongings. He founded the Legion of Honour in 1802 to recognise talent and courage in the service of the nation.

2 rue de la Légion d'Honneur, 7th.
Tel.: 01-40-62-84-25.
www.musee-legiondhonneur.fr
Open Wednesday to Sunday from 1pm to 6pm. Admission free.

③ Hôtel de Beauharnais:

in 1713 architect Germain Boffrand laid the foundation stone for the magnificent Hôtel de Beauharnais and the adjacent Hôtel de Seignelay. The story of this mansion with a garden overlooking the river bank owes much to the imperial period. It was owned by Eugène, son of Joséphine de Beauharnais, Napoleon Bonaparte's wife. She wanted her son to have a dwelling worthy of his rank, and carefully oversaw its interior decoration, in the elegant style of the Consulate and early Empire. References to Napoleon, who was then Consul for life, abound in this unique place. The building's architecture is enriched by an Egyptian-style portal overlooking the courtyard, designed by architect Jean-Augustin Renard and considered to be a rare reminder of Napoleon's Egyptian campaign. Prince Eugène sold the mansion to the Prussian delegation in 1817. Nowadays it houses the German Embassy in Paris.

78 rue de Lille, 7th.

Address Book

The place for a rendezvous

🍸 The Mucha Café
227 boulevard Saint-Germain, 7th.
Open daily 7am to midnight, closes Sundays at 9pm.
Tel.: 01-45-51-06-30.

Restaurants

Ⓐ La Maison de l'Amérique Latine

The House of Latin America occupies the Hôtel de Varengeville and Hôtel d'Amelot de Gournay, and has a French-style garden. After a visit to its temporary exhibitions you can enjoy French cuisine on the shady terrace or taste Latin American specialties with delicious cocktails at the bar. Lunch menu €37.
217, boulevard Saint-Germain, 7th.
Tel.: 01-49-54-75-10.
Open Monday to Friday noon to 2.30pm and 7.30pm to 9.30pm.

Ⓑ La Maison des Polytechniciens Restaurant Le Poulpry
This discreet restaurant located in the Maison des Polytechniciens, an 18th century town house, is open to all. Top political figures and captains of industry discuss in its elegant Second Empire décor. Chef Pascal Chanteloup serves a noble version of traditional cooking: *saisie de foie gras* with caramelised balsamic vinegar on a bed of lentils; *mousse* of langoustine in a chicken *consommé*; roast rack of lamb and pasta shells with *morille* mushrooms and crumbled *souris d'agneau*; which will delight even the most discerning palates.
À la carte €38–50.

12 rue de Poitiers, 7th.
Tel.: 01-49-54-74-54.
Open Monday to Friday noon to 2.30pm and 7.30pm to 9.30pm.

Ⓒ Le 20 de Bellechasse
Everyone is won over by the charm of this Art Deco bistro. You can enjoy roasted goat cheese with aubergine and marinated peppers or lentil salad with bacon pieces while sitting comfortably on its bright red moleskin benches.
À la carte €25–45.
20 rue de Bellechasse, 7th.
Tel.: 01-47-05-11-11.
Open Monday noon to 2:30pm and 7.30pm to 10pm, Tuesday to Friday noon to 11pm and Saturdays noon to 2.30pm.

Ⓓ Tan Dinh
This small restaurant with its décor of speckled mirrors is one of the best Vietnamese restaurants in Paris. Located on the same street as French singer-songwriter Serge Gainsbourg's house, the Vifian brothers bring Vietnamese cuisine to life here before your eyes with exotic flavours and exquisite wines. Their wine cellar is well supplied with Pomerol and Château Petrus wines and is without doubt one of the best in Paris. À la carte €50–75.
60 rue de Verneuil, 7th.
Tel.: 01-45-44-04-84.
Open Monday to Saturday noon to 2pm and 7.30pm to 11pm.

RUE DU BAC

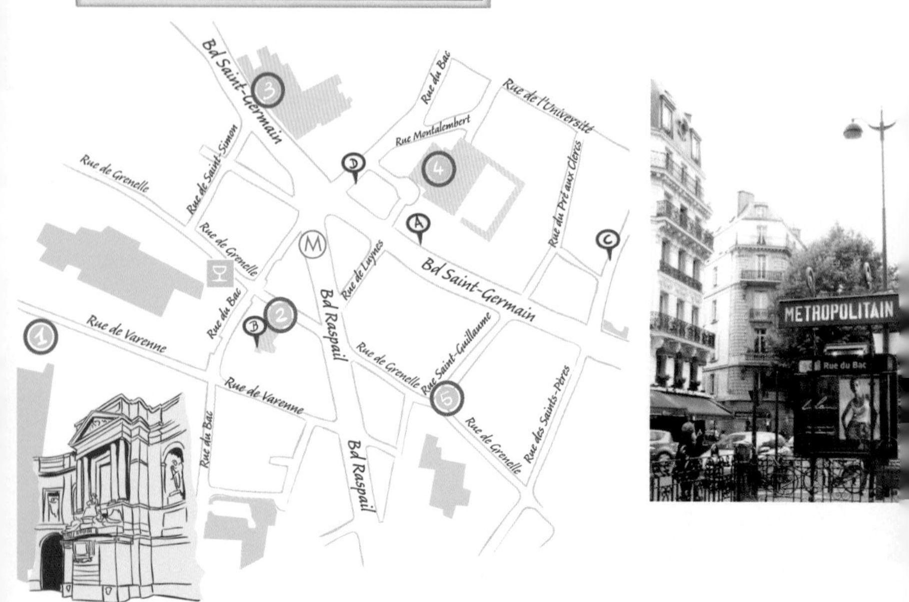

History

This station opened in 1910 and was renovated in 'Motte' style in 1984. This style uses white décor and bevelled tiles and was used in hundreds of stations. Colour is used in strip lighting and on seats. The station is named after a path that used to wind down to the Seine. At the end was a *bac*, a type of large flat-bottomed boat. The *bac* was installed in1550 on the present-day Quai Voltaire for transporting heavy stones from the Vaugirard quarries to the Right Bank for use in building the Tuileries Palace. Novelist Antoine Blondin (1922–1991), who was known for his heavy drinking and who lived in the area, wrote about this street in his 1970 novel *Monsieur Jadis ou l'École du Soir*: 'The taxi stopped at the corner of rue du Bac, where at this hour, under its sleepy facades, there is an ebb and flow of adventurous stirrings by its population of tax inspectors, honorary cobblers and poets. While he was counting his change, his attention was drawn to the lit rectangle of the Bar-Bac, the last obstacle between him and his orderly life.' With the novelist's death, some of the street's bohemian feel also disappeared. The bookshops and other bars he loved have now gone and been replaced by modern merchants with

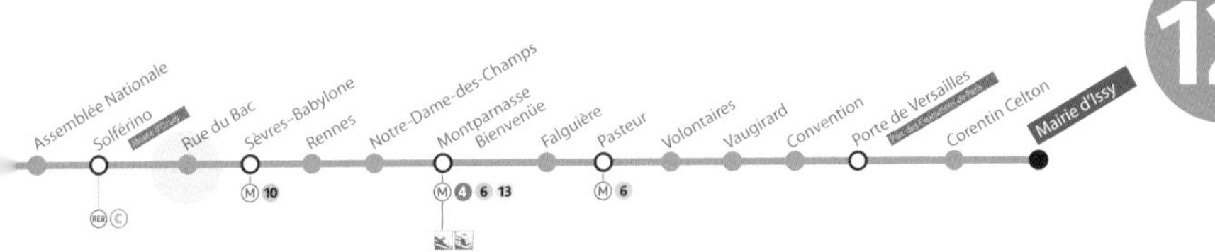

their interior decoration stores. Strolling along the pavement here you can get a feel for the past life of this district which used to be populated by night owls who defied the darkness without restraint, and whose entire world was to be found in this strip of tarmac and a plethora of *bars-tabacs*.

SIGHTSEEING

Architecture

1 ***Hôtel Matignon:*** this is the official residence of the Prime Minister of France and is not far from the other ministries. Begun in 1722, it was the work of architects Jean Courtonne and Jean Mazin. It is a typical 18th century building which for a time belonged to diplomat Charles-Maurice de Talleyrand-Périgord. Talleyrand, a former Bishop of Autun, organised lavish receptions here. It is in the shape of a half moon, which allowed carriages to manoeuvre more easily. Its gardens stretch over three hectares (7 acres) and were designed by Achille Duchêne in 1902.

57 rue de Varenne, 7th.

2 ***Fontaine des Quatre-Saisons***

This semi-circular fountain is an inventive work by sculptor Edmé Bouchardon, who adapted it to a narrow space. It was originally intended to supply water to the neighbourhood and also pays homage to King Louis XV. The scale of the fountain in such a narrow street drew strong criticism, including from Voltaire, who derided the gigantism, excess and pretension of the project in a letter to the Comte de Caylus in 1739.

57–59 rue de Grenelle, 7th.

3 Hôtel de Roquelaure: this mansion is now headquarters to the Ministry for Ecology, Sustainable Development, Transport and Housing. Building work began in 1722 under Pierre Lassurance (1675 – 1724), and was completed in 1724 by Jean-Baptiste Leroux. Despite its austere facade with its *mascarons* (carved faces supposed to frighten off evil spirits), its 18th century interior is breathtaking. The Rococo-style salon is particularly splendid.
246 boulevard Saint-Germain, 7th.

4 Église Saint-Thomas d'Aquin
The church was built on the site of a Dominican chapel. Work began in 1682 under architect Pierre Bullet, but construc-

tion was not finally completed until 1769, when the facade, designed by Brother Claude, a monk at the Dominican monastery, was finished. The church was given a parish in 1791 and placed under the patronage of Saint Thomas Aquinas—it had originally been consecrated as Église Saint-Dominique. In 1723, the dome of its Saint-Louis chapel was embellished by a painting of the Transfiguration by Rococo artist François Lemoyne, who committed suicide after his wife died, an event which brought the fashion for large allegorical ceilings to an end.
Place Saint-Thomas-d'Aquin,
corner of rue du Bac and boulevard Saint-Germain, 7th.

5 Maison de Verre: the House of Glass can only be visited by appointment. However, you can see its superb iron and glass facade from the street. It was custom-built on three floors by architect Pierre Chareau from 1928 and 1931 for Dr Jean Dalsace, who wanted a house that was open to light. The steel beams are painted black and are used as decorative elements.
31 rue Saint-Guillaume, 7th.
Tel.: 01-45-44-91-21.
Tours Thursday afternoons on written request by e-mail to mdv31@orange.fr

Address Book

The place for a rendezvous

Le Florès

80 rue de Grenelle, 7th.
Open Monday to Friday 6am to 11pm and weekends from 7.30am.
Tel.: 01-45-48-96-96.

Culture

Ⓐ Musée des Lettres et des Manuscrits

The Museum of Letters and Manuscripts is housed in a building dating from 1608. Its exhibits are rare and valuable, touching and intimate, beautiful and haunting. Nearly 250 original documents are exposed to public view, including a love letter from Napoleon to Joséphine, a rare Mozart score, a song by Serge Gainsbourg and Louis XVI's declaration to the French people before his flight to Varenne. The authors of these missives live on in the ink they put to paper. You will also see a '*boule de Moulins*', a zinc container used to send mail down the Seine from the central post office in Moulins to Paris when it was under siege by the Prussian army in 1870. No more letters could reach the capital. The zinc tubes could contain nearly 700 letters, and they had ballasts that kept them afloat—usually. When they got to Paris they were taken to their destination in large nets. The last one was discovered in 1980. There are said to be about 20 of these *boules* at the bottom of the Seine.

222 boulevard Saint-Germain, 7th.
Tel.: 01-42-22-48-48.
www.museedeslettres.fr
Open Tuesday to Sunday 10am to 6pm , Thursdays to 9.30pm.
Guided tour Sundays 3pm.
Admission fee.

Ⓑ Musée Maillol

This museum was created by Dina Vierny, model and companion to sculptor Aristide Maillol (1861 – 1944). It features Maillol's sensuous paintings and sculptures as well as works by other great 20th century painters like Gauguin, Bonnard, Redon, Kandinsky or Poliakoff. It is a small museum but has very good temporary exhibitions. Enjoy...

61 rue de Grenelle, 7th.
Tel.: 01-42-22-59-58.
www.museemaillol.com
Open daily 10.30am to 7pm and on Fridays until 9.30pm.
Admission fee.

Shopping

Ⓒ Maison de chocolats Debauve et Gallais

Sulpice Debauve, King Louis XVI's pharmacist, opened this lovely chocolate shop in 1800 with his nephew, Antoine Gallais. Its reputation earned it the status of official supplier to Louis XVIII, then to Charles X and Louis Philippe. The shop has a majestic facade designed by First Empire architects Charles Percier and Pierre Fontaine. Its delicious chocolate will melt in your mouth.

30 rue des Saints-Pères, 7th.
Tel.: 01-45-48-54-67.
Open Monday to Saturday 9am to 7pm.

Ⓓ Deyrolle

This store opened in 1931 and is a reminder of how wildly popular natural curiosities were in the 18th century. Nowadays the shop sports stunning collections of insects and shells as stuffed lions, giraffes, zebras and bears

46 rue du Bac, 7th.
Tel.: 01-42-22-30-07.
www.deyrolle.com
Open Tuesday to Saturday 10am to 7pm and Mondays 10am to 1pm and 2pm to 7pm.

Next station

SÈVRES-BABYLONE

See line 10, page 272

RENNES

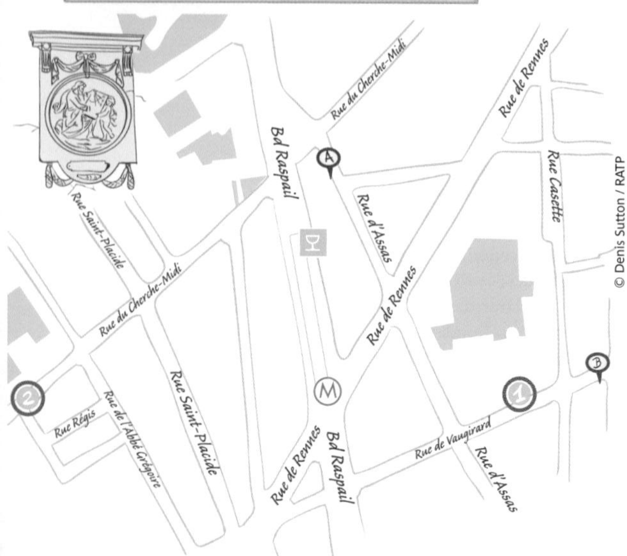

© Denis Sutton / RATP

History

The thing you find most of in this area is shops. The station was previously one of the Paris metro's 'ghost stations', but now serves the busy shopping street after which it is named. It was closed in 1939 as part of a government plan to save money, and remained closed after the Second World War because it was not considered profitable enough. But local residents mobilised, it was finally reopened in 1968. However, it had reduced opening hours until 2004–it used to close at 8pm and on Sundays and public holidays. Rue de Rennes itself was built during the Second Empire. It used to lead directly to the Montparnasse rail terminal, where trains leave for Rennes, a prominent city in Brittany.

SIGHTSEEING

A walk through history

1 **Chapelle Saint-Joseph-des Carmes:** despite its peaceful atmosphere today, this chapel has witnessed

some bloody events since it was built in 1620. During the French Revolution the neighbouring Carmelite monastery became a prison, and many inmates were victims of the massacres of September 1792. Altogether, 116 priests were killed. Nowadays the chapel is part of the Catholic Institute.

70 rue de Vaugirard, 6th.

Rue du Cherche-Midi: it is said that the road's name derives from a sundial in the street. It was formerly a Roman road called Chasse-Midi and was renamed Chemin de Vaugirard in 1388. Walking this street takes you into the history of the iconic figures who have lived here. Number 40 was the home of Comte de Rochambeau, who was sent to aid George Washington by Louis XVI and led the French troops who won the Battle of Yorktown in the American Revolutionary War. Dominique-Joseph Garat, who succeeded Georges Danton as Justice Minister in 1792, lived at number 44, a pleasant 18th century mansion. Garat is known for having proclaimed Louis XVI's death sentence. Laura and Paul Lafargue, Karl Marx's daughter and son-in-law, lived at number 47. Paul Lafargue wrote the provocative book *The Right to be Lazy*. They committed suicide together in 1911 to avoid the trials and tribulations of aging. The Hôtel du Petit-Montmorency at numbers 85 and 87 was built in 1743. It was home and studio for 19th-century painter Ernest Hébert and became a museum for his works in 1933.

Address Book

The place for a rendezvous

Le Tourne Bouchon
71 boulevard Raspail, 6th.
Open Tuesday, Friday and Sunday 6am to 8pm, from 7.30am on Mondays, Wednesdays and Thursdays.
Tel.: 01-45-44-15-50.

Restaurants

Ⓐ Hélène Darroze
This restaurant is certainly expensive, but then the chef is Michelin-starred. La Salle à Manger, the gourmet restaurant on the first floor, is cosy yet elegant. There is a more informal tapas bar called Le Salon on the ground floor. In Le Boudoir you can sample the specialties of the house in a smaller, more intimate setting. Discovery menus €85–105.
4 rue d'Assas, 6th.
Tel.: 01-42-22-00-11.
www.helenedarroze.com
Open Tuesday to Saturday 12.30pm to 2.30pm and 7.30pm to 10.30pm.

Ⓑ La Maison du Jardin
Just by the beautiful Luxembourg Gardens, this restaurant serves inventive and refined dishes like *pastilla* of duck *parmentier*, roasted rockfish with artichokes, or a *waterzoï* (Flemish stew) made with free-range chicken and flavoured with Thai lemon grass.
A menu to please lovers of French or exotic cuisine.
À la carte €22–35.
27 rue de Vaugirard, 6th.
Tel.: 08-99-78-83-36.
Open Monday to Saturday noon to 10pm.

NOTRE-DAME-DES-CHAMPS

© Bruno Marguerite / RATP

History

Like most of the stops on line 12, this station was opened in 1910. It is decorated with coloured tiles which were manufactured by a dynasty of French industrial ceramics makers, the Boulengers, from the mid-19th century at their pottery at Choisy-le-Roi near Paris. The station is named after the church nearby on Boulevard Montparnasse. It is the underground gateway to a terrestrial Garden of Eden–the Luxembourg Gardens, which have been shaped by the history of kings and battles. People who come here often refer to the gardens affectionately as 'Luco'. They will tell you that it has a prestigious feel to it, but they are nevertheless very fond of the place, almost as if it were their own garden. When it is covered in freshly fallen snow its silent, frozen beauty is breathtaking. In summer you will be transported by the nonchalant atmosphere that reigns there which is occasionally interrupted by a burst of impetuosity. Going to the Luxembourg Gardens is like a tryst. There is joy mixed with anticipation and, once through the majestic gates, the feeling that time stretches into infinity.

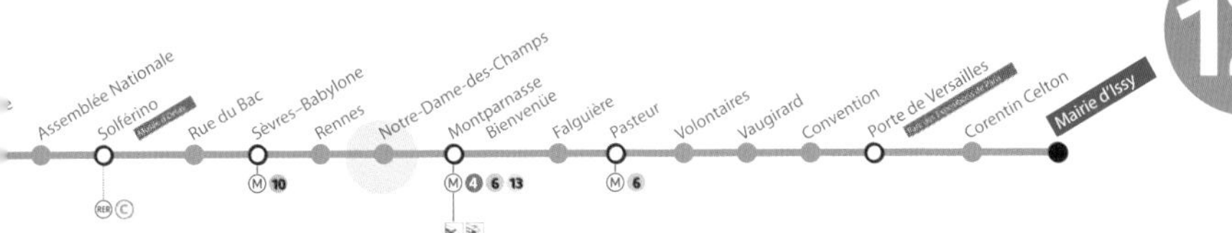

SIGHTSEEING

walk in the park

Jardin du Luxembourg: it would take pages to fully describe these wonderful gardens. They were created in 1617 by garden designer Boyceau de la Barauderie for Maria de Medici, Henry IV's widow, who was homesick for her native Florence. He designed it around a majestic central *parterre* flowerbed which was surrounded by pleasant alleys. The Queen was still unhappy, however, because the perspective of her beautiful garden was broken by the wall of a Carthusian monastery to the south. But the monks refused to allow her to extend the gardens onto their land. Even Cardinal Richelieu himself was unable to oust the monks from their monastery. So for a long time the gardens were extended laterally before they could expand on a north-south axis. In 1635 André Le Notre, Louis XIV's gardener, added more sumptuous *parterres*. Then

the Revolution put an end to the Carthusian monks' resistance and the gardens expanded in the late 18th century. All that remains of the monastery nowadays are the beehives, the rose garden and the orchard. Under the First Empire, architect Jean-François-Thérèse Chalgrin extended the central perspective and created an English garden. But Baron Haussmann's redesign of Paris amputated the gardens' former glory in favour of urban development. Writers and artists have found inspiration under its chestnut trees—like painter Jean-Antoine Watteau (1684–1721), and philosophers Jean-Jacques Rousseau and Denis Diderot. Romantics like François-René Chateaubriand, Frederic Chopin and George Sand came here too. German poet Reiner Maria Rilke wrote a few verses about its merry-go-round. The Medici Fountain inspired Joseph Kessel's book of the same name. Amedeo Modigliani admired the sculptures of the queens of France. The Sénat, the upper house of Parliament, is located in the gardens.

Place Edmond-Rostand,
rue de Vaugirard and rue Guynemer, 6th.

2 Palais du Luxembourg, le Sénat

In 1612, after the death of her husband, King Henry IV, Maria de Medici remained at the Louvre Palace, but she was not happy there. She commissioned architect Salomon de Brosse to design a palace that would remind her of her youth in Florence. The building has suffered several abrupt changes. It has been a royal palace, a prison, and, since 1792, a National Palace belonging to the state. The Revolution robbed it of its magnificent works of art, as it was ransacked during the Revolutionary period and turned into a prison. Revolutionaries Georges Danton, Philippe Fabre d'Eglantine and Jacques-Louis David were imprisoned here, and their families were the only visitors in the gardens at that time. Later, the Directory, one of the governing bodies after the Revolution, would use it as its headquarters. In 1814 Alphonse de Gisors created the vast semicircular parliamentary chamber. Each chair is made individually and has slightly different proportions. The unruly mix of décor here contrasts with the orderliness of lawmaking.

Address Book

The place for a rendezvous

Le Funzy Café
3 rue Bréa, 6th.
Open Monday to Saturday 7am to 10pm.
Tel.: 01-40-51-80-90.

Culture

A Musée Zadkine
Follow the narrow path through a lush little garden where ivy lines the walls to find a splendid statue of Orpheus. It shows you the way to this charming museum. Sculptor Ossip Zadkine was born in 1890 in Vitebsk, then part of Russia. He left behind the rigour of the Russian winter for the cosmopolitan atmosphere of Montparnasse from 1910.

His bronze sculptures are exhibited in the beautiful little white house where he created them. His wife, painter Valentine Prax, was the driving force behind turning the house into a museum. In 1981 she donated his artworks for the museum dedicated to her husband's work. She bequeathed everything to the French state when she died in 1991.
110 bis, rue d'Assas, 6th.
Tel.: 01-55-42-77-20.
Open Tuesday to Sunday 10am to 6pm.
Admission fee.

Ⓑ Théâtre des Marionnettes

Children have enjoyed the puppet show here since 1933 when French puppet character *Guignol* took up residence in the Luxembourg Gardens. They love the show. This small theatre founded by Robert Desarthe is located inside the Gardens and has lost none of its verve. His son, Francis Claude Desarthe, took over and works on creating new shows to please his young audience.
Jardin du Luxembourg, 6th.
Tel.: 01-43-26-46-47.
40-minute performances Wednesdays, Saturdays and Sundays, public holidays and during school holidays.

Ⓒ Le Lucernaire

This is a theatre, an independent cinema, a photo gallery, a bookstore and a restaurant. The programming is generally thought to be quite innovative, a major attraction for this lively venue. Lunch menus from €8.50.
53 rue Notre-Dame-des-Champs, 6th.
Tel.: 01 45-44-57-34 for theatre reservations and 01-45-48-91-10 for the restaurant.
Open Monday to Saturday noon to 3pm and 6pm to 11pm (10pm on Mondays), and Sundays noon to 10pm.

Restaurant

Ⓓ Le Timbre

This restaurant is no bigger than the postage stamp of its name, and the cooking is decidedly French even though the chef is English. You can see into the kitchen and watch him working. Elegant dining and impeccable service for lunch or dinner. Saturday night menu €30.
3 rue Sainte-Beuve, 6th.
Tel.: 01-45-49-10-40.
www.restaurantletimbre.com
Open Tuesday to Saturday noon to 2pm and 7.30pm to 10.30pm.

Next stations

MONTPARNASSE-BIENVENÜE

See line 4, page 114

FALGUIÈRE

L'Ancienne Commune, 131 rue de Vaugirard, 15th.

PASTEUR

See line 6, page 157

VOLONTAIRES

Café les Volontaires
227 rue de Vaugirard, 15th.

VAUGIRARD

Le Vaugirard
18 place Adolphe Chérioux, 15th.

CONVENTION

Café du Rond-Point Vaugirard, 198 rue de la Convention, 15th.

PORTE DE VERSAILLES

Café Dupont
386 rue de Vaugirard, 15th.

CORENTIN CELTON

Café Français,
2 place Paul-Vaillant-Couturier, 92130 Issy-les-Moulineaux.

MAIRIE D'ISSY

Brasserie du Parc
28 rue André-Chénier, 92130 Issy-les-Moulineaux.

line 13

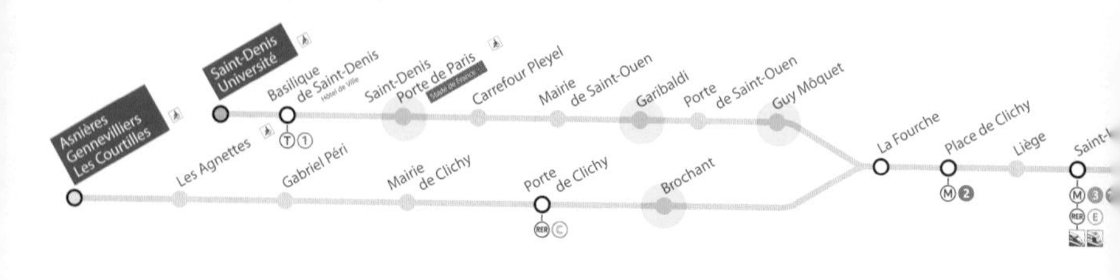

History

Line 13 was created from the merger of the old line B from the Nord-Sud (north-south) network and former line 14 run by the original operating company CMP, forerunner of the RATP. The line crosses Paris and connects the suburban municipalities of Saint-Denis, Asnières, Clichy and Gennevilliers in the north, with Châtillon and Montrouge in the south. It is 22.5 kilometres long (13.98 miles) and the longest line in the Paris Metro network. In 2009, it carried 610,050 passengers per day and it is practically saturated now because of the dense population areas it crosses with its two northern branches, the considerable extension into the suburbs, and the economic growth of the sectors it crosses.

Asnières – Gennevilliers Saint-Denis Université / Châtillon – Montrouge

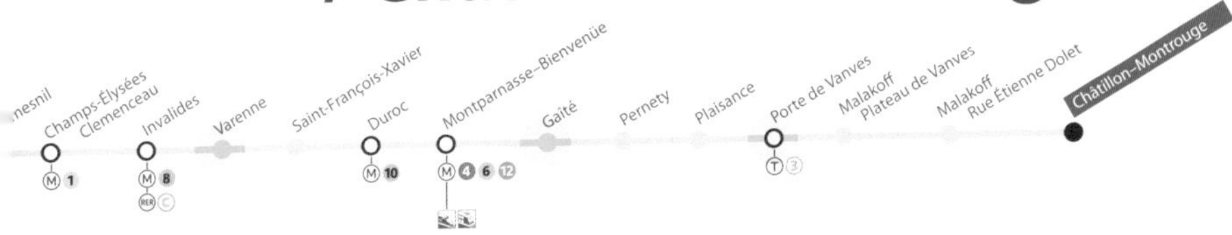

SAINT-DENIS – PORTE DE PARIS

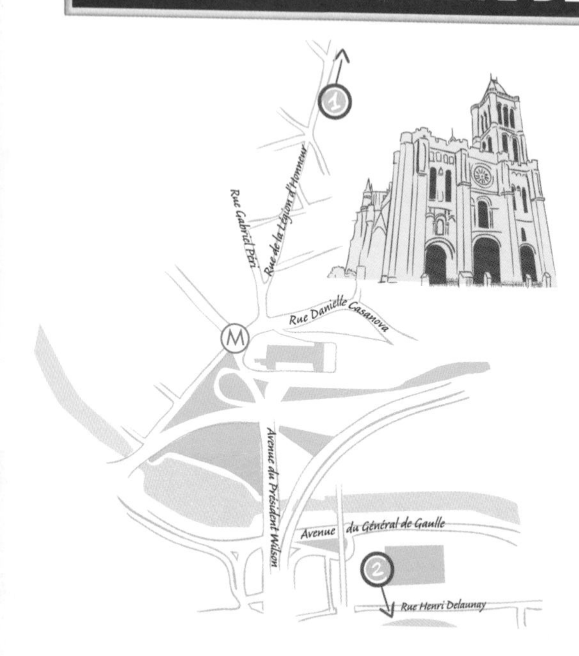

Basilique de Saint-Denis station is in the Saint-Denis town centre in the Seine-Saint-Denis sub-prefecture and connects it to Paris. Its interior design is a tribute to its proximity to the Saint Denis basilica and the town's historic past.

History

At the northern end of line 13, three stations serve the suburban commune of Saint-Denis: Saint-Denis–Porte de Paris and Basilique de Saint-Denis, which opened in 1976 when line 13 merged with the former line 14, and Saint-Denis Université, which opened in 1998. Saint-Denis–Porte de Paris station serves the north of the Plaine Saint-Denis area as well as the south part of Saint-Denis city centre. It was renovated when the Stade de France sports stadium was opened in order to handle the large passenger flows.

SIGHTSEEING

Monuments

1. **Basilique Saint-Denis:** the basilica is not just a royal burial place but a masterpiece of gothic art. The original church was built in the 5th century over the tomb of Saint Denis. An abbey later grew up around this sanctuary, and was richly equipped by the Merovingian dynasty, including King Dagobert who was buried here in 693, and later by the Carolingians. Thanks to Abbot Suger, it became the official burial place for the kings of France in 1122. Over the centuries it lost its lofty status and Louis XIV placed it in the care of the Bishop of Paris.

The church was badly damaged during the Revolution but Louis XVIII reverted it to its former status as a royal necropolis by transferring the remains of Louis XVI and Marie-Antoinette there. Napoleon I began the renovation work, which was continued by Viollet-le-Duc under Napoleon III. Both the Saint-Denis basilica and its garden are classified historical monuments.

1 place de la Légion-d'Honneur, 93200 Saint-Denis.
Tel.: 01-48-09-83-54. Open from April to September 10am to 6pm, Saturday and Sunday noon to 6.15pm; from October to March 10am to 5.15pm, Saturday and Sunday noon to 5.15pm. Entrance fee.

2 **Stade de France:** this is the largest French stadium with a capacity of up to 81,000 spectators for football or rugby matches. It was designed by four architects, Michel Macary, Aymeric Zublena, Michel Regembal and Claude Constantini, and was inaugurated on 28 January 1998 by the then President Jacques Chirac, on the occasion of a France-Spain football match. Although it was built for the World Cup, which France hosted in 1998, it was also designed to cater to other events, both sporting (such as athletics and car racing) and cultural. Some famous French singers, such as Johnny Hallyday have held concerts in the stadium, which has also been the setting for spectacular operatic productions, including *Aïda*. Stade de France is the only stadium in the world to have hosted both a World Cup football final and a World Cup rugby final!

Rue Francis-de-Pressensé, 93210 Saint-Denis.
Tel.: 0892-70-09-00.
www.stadefrance.com
Entrance fee.

Next stations

CARREFOUR PLEYEL

Les Bons Vivants, 5 boulevard d'Ornano, 93200 Saint-Denis.

MAIRIE DE SAINT-OUEN

Auberge de la Poste, 8 avenue Gabriel-Péri, 93400 Saint-Ouen.

GARIBALDI

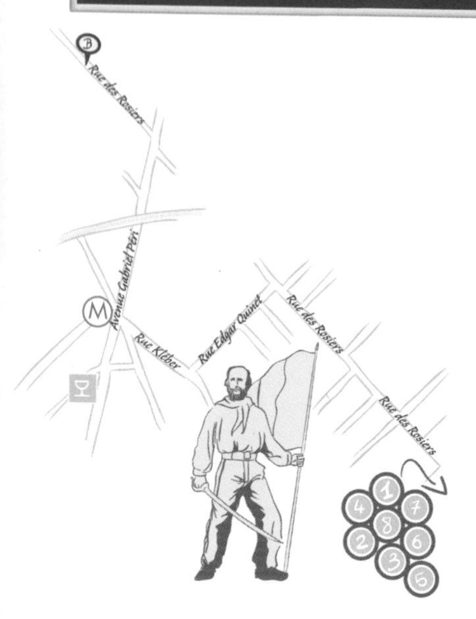

History

Garibaldi station is in the commune of Saint-Ouen, at the gates of Paris. Opened in 1952, it was named after Giuseppe Garibaldi (1807–1882) who helped to unify Italy. Garibaldi was a fervent Republican and wanted Rome to be the country's capital. He defeated Austria in1859, the Kingdom of Naples in 1860 and the papacy in 1867. Garibaldi station is one way of getting to the Saint-Ouen flea market, among the biggest in the world. Every weekend, some 150,000 visitors flock here, Parisians and tourists alike, to stroll around the 2,500 stands and 16 markets. Check out a map before

plunging into this very different aspect of Paris. Start off with rue des Rosiers, which will take you to most of the markets.

SIGHTSEEING

Flea markets

1. **Marché Vernaison:** the Paris Saint-Ouen flea market started here. This is the oldest market, and while it is a little less lively today, it still has that garage-sale atmosphere and interesting prices. A sort of junk paradise.
99 rue des Rosiers or
136 avenue Michelet.

2. **Marché Antica:** this is a miniature market with barely a dozen stands selling a fine selection of antiques, including tap-

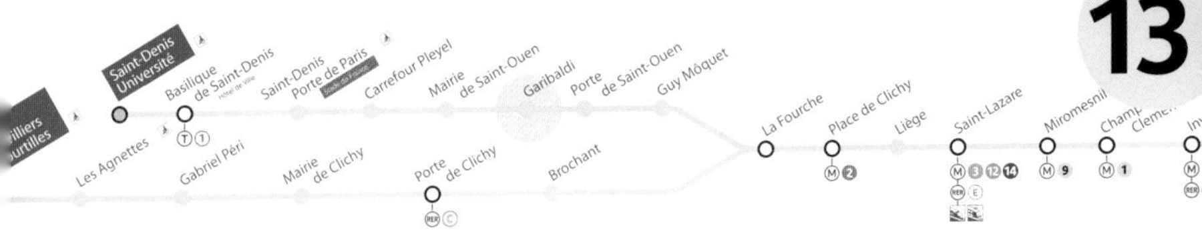

estries, artefacts, Art Deco and Napoleon III era objects in a rather plush part of the market.

Marché Antica is next to Marché Vernaison.

3 **Marché Malassis:** one of the most recent markets here, which has more of a 'gallery' feel about it, with antique dealers-cum-decorators, numerous themed boutiques and shops specialising in 20th century objects.

142 rue des Rosiers.

4 **Marché Dauphine:** the imposing architecture was inspired by the prestigious Baltard Pavilion (all that remains of the Halles). The 6,000 square meter market (64,583 square feet) is full of quality antiques from the 18th and 19th centuries, as well as prints and etchings.

132 – 140 rue des Rosiers.

5 **Marché Biron:** this market is a must for the high-end international clientele, which heads straight for the luxurious central alley, and the second rather more cosy and friendly one.

85 rue des Rosiers or 118 avenue Michelet.

6 **Marché Serpette:** this market with its covered alleyways is the smartest — and also the most expensive. The place for furniture, Art Nouveau objects and silverware.

110 rue des Rosiers.

7 **Marché Paul Bert:** this open-air market is more for modern trends and where you might just make a find at any moment…

96 rue des Rosiers or 18 rue Paul-Bert.

8 **Marché des Rosiers:** this market is home to a dozen specialists in late 19th century and early 20th century Art Deco lighting, glassware and bronzes.

3 rue Paul-Bert.

Address book

The place for a rendezvous

Le Louis XV
94 avenue Gabriel-Péri, 93400 Saint-Ouen.
Tel.: 01-40-10-81-55.

Culture

A Festival de Jazz Musette
Every June, this accordion jazz festival shakes up the flea market with its Manouche music. Musicians wander up and down the alleyways playing among the visitors and going from bar to bar. Occasionally well-known French musicians such as Thomas Dutronc also join in. Don't miss this festival!
www.festivaldespuces.com

Restaurant

B La Puce
A favourite stop for hungry shoppers, this bistro provides good and original food. Try out the *croque-monsieur,* usually a toasted ham and cheese sandwich, but here made with foie gras! Lunch menu on weekdays at €16, à la carte €40.
17, rue Ernest-Renan, 93400 Saint-Ouen.
Tel. : 01-40-12-63-75.

Next station

PORTE DE SAINT-OUEN

L'Imprévu, 115 boulevard Ney, 18th.

GUY MÔQUET

History

When the station opened in 1911 it was called Marcadet, and a year later it changed its name to Marcadet-Balagny. After the war, on 27 January 1946, it was renamed again in honour of a young militant French Communist who was shot by the Nazis at the age of 17. A contemporary fresco on the platforms depicts the young hero. Guy Môquet station is on Avenue de Saint-Ouen at a junction between the lower part of Montmartre and the neighbourhood known as Épinettes.

SIGHTSEEING

A walk in the city

❶ **Village des Épinettes:** the small neighbourhood of Épinettes is a real working class village, and has long been an integral part of Batignolles. It is located in the triangle marked off by Avenue de Clichy and Avenue de Saint-Ouen, and is gradually acquiring quite a *'bobo'* reputation. The name 'Épinettes' apparently came from the word *épine* or thorn, from the brambles that once covered the land, or alternatively from a white variety of *pinot blanc* grape known as *épinette blanche*, which was grown in the area. You can stroll among the quiet streets here, or the busier rue de la Jonquière, and then rest in the charming Square des Épinettes.

Access by rue Félix-Pécaut to the north or rue Maria-Deraismes to the east, Collette from the south and rue Jean-Leclaire to the west.

Cité des Fleurs: a private street full of flowers and lined with middle-class houses in a variety of styles. Cité des Fleurs is something of a village within a village. Built in 1847, it has kept a serenity and charm that is quite unique in Paris. In 1943 the French film star, Catherine Deneuve was born in one of the two clinics in Cité des Fleurs, as was her sister Françoise Dorléac a year earlier.

You can reach it via the Avenue de Clichy at Brochant station level or from rue de la Jonquière.

Cimetière des Batignolles: the Batignolles cemetery opened in 1833, and is one of the four largest cemeteries in Paris, as big as the Montmartre cemetery. Among its 900-odd trees lie the cemetery's 'residents', which include André Breton, Paul Verlaine, Blaise Cendrars and Ray Ventura.

8 rue Saint-Just, 17th.

Address book

The place for a rendezvous

Le Christophe Colomb
265 rue Marcadet, 18th. Open Monday to Saturday 7am to 10pm. Tel.: 01-44-85-74-55.

Shopping

A Marché de l'avenue de Saint-Ouen
Every day, at about Guy Môquet station level, the Avenue de Saint-Ouen is transformed into an open-air food and flower market.

Restaurants

B Irène et Bernard
This restaurant may be one of the signs of the *'bobo'* invasion of a working class neighbourhood. A pretty bistro with a pleasant terrace and a good menu. Approximately €15–20.
58 rue Gauthey, 17th. Tel.: 01-42-29-56-16. Open all week 8am to 1am, and from 9am on Sunday. Lunch served noon to 3.30pm, dinner 8pm to 10pm..

C Le Refuge des Moines
Traditional French dishes matched by a superb selection of excellent wines, with well-known names as well as more accessible ones. About €25–30.
85 rue des Moines, 17th. Tel.: 01-42-28-92-52. www. baravin lerefugedes moines.com Open Monday to Friday noon to 2.30pm and 7.30pm to 10.40pm, and Saturday evening.

D Au Père Pouchet
A real neighbourhood institution! A good and straightforward restaurant with simple food that can make you forget you are in Paris. About €30.
55 rue Navier, 17th. Tel.: 01-42-63-16-73. Open Monday to Friday 9am to 1am, and from 10am Saturday. Lunch served noon to 2.30pm, dinner 7.30pm to 10pm.

BROCHANT

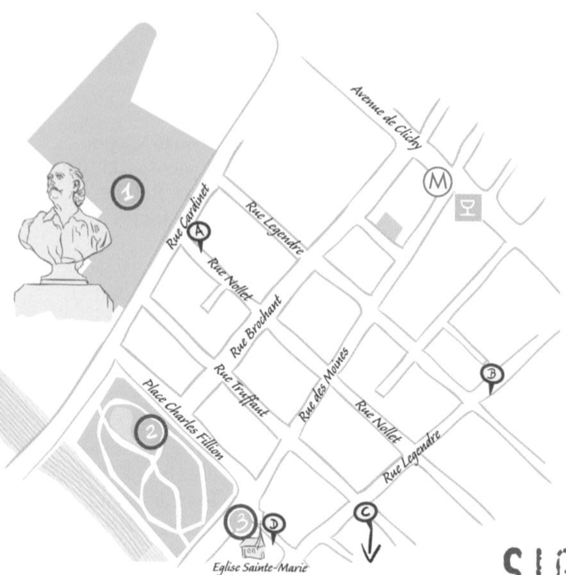

History

This station opened in 1912 and took its name from the mineralogist André Brochant de Villiers (1772–1840), who was a director of the Manufacture de Saint-Gobain (a historic glass and mirror company) and member of the French Academy of Sciences. The station stands on Avenue de Clichy, and serves both Batignolles and Épinettes.

SIGHTSEEING

A walk in the park

❶ **Parc Clichy-Batignolles Martin-Luther-King:** a number of parks have sprung up in Paris since the 1970s, to improve Parisians' quality of life. Some are little more than small gardens but there have also been several large parks, such as the Georges-Brassens Park, the Jardin des Halles, Belleville Park, the themed André-Citroën Park, the Jardin Atlantique and Bercy Park. This one is a vast 100,000 square metre park (24.7 acres) created a few years ago over what used to be the Batignolles freight station. It has three themes: the seasons, sport and water. This is a great place for children, athletes and all nature-loving city-dwellers. In 2008, when the first phase of work on the park was completed, it was named after

Martin-Luther-King to mark the 40th anniversary of his assassination.
Rue Cardinet, 17th.

Square des Batignolles: Batignolles Square, which is more of a park, is just a few feet from Brochant station. This elegant and bucolic garden was created under Baron Haussmann, who followed Napoleon III's wishes to plant several English-style gardens in Paris during the Second Empire. The hilly park comprises a grotto, a river, a cascade, a miniature lake, and some fairly exotic vegetation. Lovers of *pétanque* meet in the area of the park devoted to that game, bordering on rue Cardinet.
Place Charles-Fillon, 17th.

walk in the city

Village des Batignolles: on leaving the park you will see the Batignolles church, which stands over a tiny village square surrounded by small restaurants. After visiting the church you can wander around the small Batignolles streets dotted around busy high streets such as rue des Moines, rue des Batignolles and rue des Dames, that take you to Place de Clichy.

Address book

The place for a rendezvous

Café Le Soleil
134 avenue de Clichy, 17th.
Open daily 7am to 2pm.
Tel.: 01-58-59-27-93.

Restaurants

A Vatel Institute
The Vatel Institute is a hotel school and its restaurant is where future chefs are trained. That means that you can get good food here at a very reasonable price! Lunch and evening menus from €33.
122 rue Nollet, 17th.
Tel.: 01-42-26-26-60.

B Les Puces des Batignolles
An up-and-coming neighbourhood restaurant that has opened an annexe just steps away from this one. The chef's specialty is the smoked beef *en cocotte*! About €35.
110 rue Legendre, 17th.
Tel.: 01-42-26-62-26.

C Le Club des 5
This very popular local restaurant is a real trip down memory lane thanks to its vintage deco and amusing dishes. Dish of the day €10.50 on weekdays, à la carte €25–35.
57, rue des Batignolles, 17th.
Tel.: 01-53-04-94-73.
www.leclubdes5.fr

D L'Endroit
An excellent place for a bite or just a drink. À la carte €33.
67 place du Docteur-Félix-Lobligeois, 17th.
Tel.: 01-42-29-50-00.

Next stations

LA FOURCHE

La Fourche Royale
66 avenue de Clichy, 17th.

LIÈGE

Le Royal Europe, 47 rue d'Amsterdam, 8th.

PLACE DE CLICHY

See line 2, page 56

SAINT-LAZARE

See line 12, page 310

MIROMESNIL

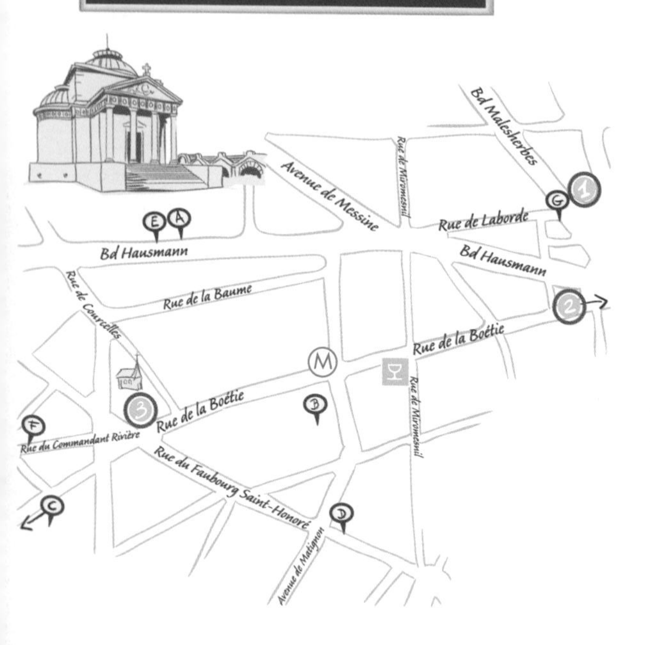

History

Miromesnil station in the heart of the 8th arrondissement, opened to serve line 9 in 1923. In 1973, it also started serving line 13. The station was named after a magistrate, Armand Thomas Hue de Miromesnil (1723–1796), who was also the minister of justice from 1774 to 1787. He abolished the *question préparatoire*, which entailed torturing the accused. This station was the first on line 13 to be equipped with glass platform safety doors. The station serves an area with austere buildings, full of offices and flanked by the large Haussmann era boulevards, but that nevertheless hides a few hidden treasures.

SIGHTSEEING

Monuments

1 *Église Saint-Augustin*

During the Second French Empire, Baron Haussmann criss-crossed Paris with large straight avenues. Their crossroads required imposing edifices to be built on them and one of these was Saint-Augustin church at the crossroads of Boulevard Haussmann and Boulevard Malesherbes, in the neighbourhood known as Petite-Pologne (little Poland). The church was built by Victor Baltard (who also built Les Halles, the famous central market in Paris, now gone) between1860 and 1871. Its special feature is that it has a stone-covered metal framework, which made it possible to erect the massive 50-metre (164-feet) dome. The church's eclectic style has adopted elements from Roman, Gothic, Renaissance and neo-Byzantine art.

8 avenue César-Caire, 8th. Tel.: 01-45-22-01-35.

② **Chapelle Expiatoire and Square Louis-XVI:** the chapel was built in Louis-XVI Square between 1815 and 1826 and according to the writer and politician Chateaubriand, was 'perhaps the most remarkable monument in Paris'. Louis XVIII decided to have it built at his own expense, and asked the architect Pierre-François-Léonard Fontaine to do so, to commemorate Louis XVI and Marie-Antoinette, who had been buried here before being transferred to the Saint-Denis Basilica. The altar and the crypt mark the exact spot where Louis XVI was buried. Some 3,000 victims of the French Revolution were also buried there, including well-known names such as Charlotte Corday, Madame du Barry, and Danton.

29 rue Pasquier, 8th.
Tel.: 01-44-32-18-00. .
Open Thursday to Saturday 1pm to 5pm. Entrance fee.

③ **Église Saint-Philippe-du-Roule**
This church was built between 1774 and 1784, and is one of the most remarkable churches to be built in the tradition of an early Christian basilica, which launched the fashion for neo-Romantic churches. In addition to its basilican layout, note the four-column portico and the 1855 painting by Théodore Chassériau, Descente de Croix (descent from the cross).

154 rue du Faubourg-Saint-Honoré 8th.

Address book

The place for a rendezvous

Café Le Miro
29 rue de la Boétie, 8th.
Open Monday to Saturday 6am to 9pm.
Tel.: 01-42-65-48-16.

Culture

Ⓐ Musée Jacquemart-André
This former grand town house on Boulevard Haussmann is a museum devoted to the art collection of two 19th century art lovers, Edouard André and Nellie Jacquemart. This delightful little museum is much loved by Parisians, and well worth a visit. It houses some treasures of Italian Renaissance painting

(including Botticelli's *Virgin and Child*), works by French 18th century artists such as Chardin, Boucher, and Fragonard, as well as works by Northern School artists such as Rembrandt and Van Dyck. Apart from the rich collection itself, the visit is a marvellous opportunity to discover a grand 19th century home with state apartments, private apartments and a winter garden.

158 boulevard Haussmann, 8th.
Tel.: 01-45-62-11-59.
Open Monday to Sunday 10am to 6pm. Entrance fee.

B Salle Gaveau

An prestigious concert call built in 1908, Salle Gaveau is still a Mecca for classical music in Paris, particularly for piano concerts and chamber music. The beautiful building was closed for renovation work in the 1990s and has now recovered all of its past glory, having reopened in 2001.

45 rue La Boétie, 8th.
Tel.: 01-49-53-05-07.
www.sallegaveau.com

Out on the town

C Charlie Birdy

Charlie was the name of Winston Churchill's parrot. The may give you some idea of the atmosphere in this comfortable and friendly lounge bar, designed as something of a journey from New York to colonial India, and devoted to live music and good cocktails. The house speciality is the Long Island!

124 rue La Boétie, 8th.
Tel.: 01-42-25-18-06.
www.charliebirdy.com
Open daily 10am to 5 am.

D Le Bristol

You must have at least one elegant stopover in this neighbourhood, so how about a cup of tea or a drink at the bar of the Bristol? The bar is gorgeous, the service impeccable, and the clientele both smart and cosmopolitan. It is hard not to remember the famous people who one frequented Le Bristol, including Ava Gardner, Marilyn Monroe, Grace Kelly, and Charlie Chaplin.

112 rue du Faubourg Saint-Honoré, 8th.
Tel.: 01-53-43-43-00.
Open daily 7am to 11pm, noon to 2.30pm and 7pm to 10.30pm.

E Café Jacquemart-André

If you fancy a snack or a brunch in one of the prettiest tearoom in Paris, go to the former dining room of the Jacquemart-André Museum (see above). The interior furnishings include beautiful 18th century tapestries, a magnificent fresco by Tiepolo, and carved and gilded Louis XV tables serving as sideboards. You'll find delicate cakes and pastries from Stohrer and Michel Fenet's 'À La Petite Marquise', two of the very best Parisian patisseries.

158 boulevard Haussmann, 8th.
Tel.: 01-45-62-11-59.
Open all week 11.45am to 5.30pm, Saturday brunch 11am to 3pm.

Restaurants

F Misia

This restaurant is the solution to a tricky problem in this neighbourhood: how to eat well *and* cheaply! Thanks to its set meals, Misia is just the ticket for a perfect and delicious lunch. Lunch menus €18–34, evenings €26–34.

5–7 rue du Commandant-Rivière, 8th.
Tel.: 01-42-56-38-74. Open Monday to Thursday noon to 2.40pm and 7.15pm to 10.30pm, Friday to 11pm.

G L'Évasion

A chic bistro with an elegant clientele, and regional French cooking. The wine list in impressive and includes some organic wines. Evening menu on weekdays €35, à la carte €65.

7 place Saint-Augustin, 8th.
Tel.: 01-45-22-66-20. Open Monday to Friday noon to 2.30pm and 7.30pm to 10.30pm.

Next station

CHAMPS-ÉLYSÉES CLEMENCEAU

See line 1, page 20

INVALIDES

See line 8, page 208

VARENNE

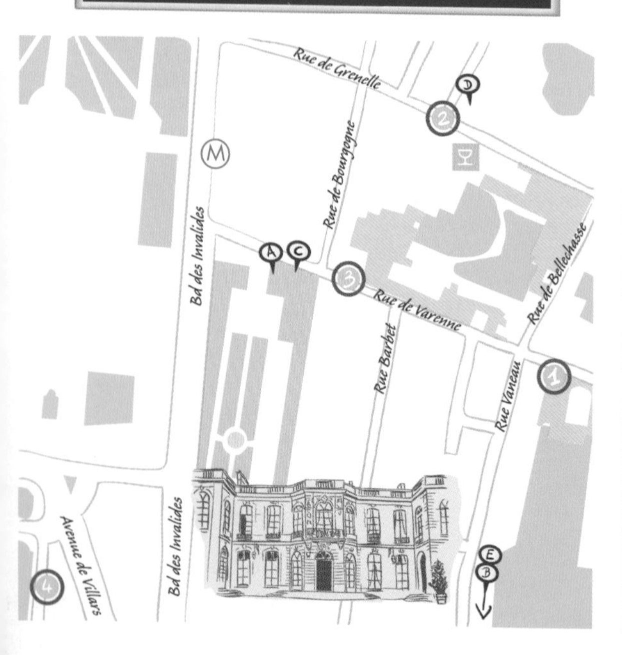

History

The station was opened in 1923 to serve line 10. In 1937 it was connected to line 14 and in 1976 to line 13. The station has strip lighting, seating and tiling, in typical Andreu-Motte style (after the names of the two architects). Being close to the Rodin Museum, it also has copies of Rodin's famous statues, *The Thinker* and *Monument to Balzac* on the platforms. The only exit has a Val-d'Osne lamp post-cum-metro sign in front of it. The station is named after rue de Varenne, which it serves, an important location in French government. The name originally came from a locality called Varenne (or Garenne), which belonged to the Saint-Germain-des-Prés abbey and not, as one might have thought, the place where King Louis XVI was arrested when he fled the Revolution. During the Second World War the station was closed because the government was in Vichy and there was no reason to stop at the grand government houses here. The station only reopened on 24 December 1962.

SIGHTSEEING

Monument

1 **Hôtel de Matignon:** one of the most beautiful of the town houses here has been the French president's residence since 1937. It is easy to recognise by the half-moon gate and the ornate façade, in contrast with the more sober neighbouring town houses. It was built in 1720 by the architect Jean Courtonne, and was successively the home of the Comte de Matignon, and the Princes of Monaco. It then belonged to Talleyrand and Napoleon I. The French government acquired it many years later, in 1922. Once a year on the *Journée du Patrimoine* (heritage day) it is possible to visit the Hôtel de Matignon and discover the lavish interior as well as the gardens, which extend as far as rue de Babylone.

57 rue de Varenne, 7th.
Tel.: 01-42-75-80-00.

A walk in the city

2 **Rue de Grenelle:** this street winds its way around Invalides, and is framed by tall government buildings, the best known of which is the Éducation Nationale (state education) building at

the corner of rue de Bellechasse, at no. 110. If you fancy a quiet walk forget this busy and traffic-filled thoroughfare even though you do get glimpses of the detailed facades of some town houses. If you do venture down it, note Hôtel du Châtelet at no. 127, the little Hôtel de Villars at no. 118, which is where Delacroix's workshop was, and the larger Hôtel de Villars, now the 7th arrondissement Town Hall. Lastly there is the Hôtel d'Avaray (no. 85) and Hôtel d'Estrées, which houses the Russian Embassy.

3 *Rue de Varenne:* you will find a different, quieter atmosphere in the pretty rue de Varenne, which was once a woodland many years ago. Allow yourself to linger in front of the grand homes and town houses all along the street, especially Hôtel de Boisgelin (at no. 47) and Hôtel Gallifet (no. 50), which is now the Italian Embassy.

4 *Avenue de Breteuil:* take Avenue de Breteuil from Place Vauban, in front of the Hôtel des Invalides. This long Haussmann era street is named after a former minister called François Victor Le Tonnelier de Breteuil. It is an agreeable avenue bordered with linden trees on either side of a long lawn, and one of the smartest avenues in Paris. Many of the capital's richest inhabitants live here.

Address book

The place for a rendezvous

Le Telex
124 rue de Grenelle, 7th.
Open Monday to Saturday 7am to 8pm.
Tel.: 01-47-05-53-67.

Culture

A Musée Rodin
Located in the former Hôtel Biron, the museum was set up in the early 20th century and is entirely devoted to the artists work as

well as his own collections. Hôtel Biron was built in 1730 and originally stood in the middle of a splendid park. Many people owned this mansion over the years, until Rodin, Jean Cocteau, Henri Matisse and other artists set up their workshops there. When the government decided to buy the building, Rodin suggested giving all his collection to the State on condition that a museum be devoted to his work after his death. That project was completed in 1919, two years after the artist's death. This is a peaceful and enchanting place to visit and see Rodin's monumental and timeless statues, including *The Man with the Broken Nose*, *The Thinker*, *The Kiss*, and *The Gates of Hell*. You will also find works by Van Gogh, Monet and Renoir in the rooms, and one room is entirely devoted to Camille Claudel, who played an important part in Rodin's life. Last but not least, don't forget to stroll around the beautiful gardens.

79 rue de Varenne, 7th.
Tel.: 01-44-18-61-10.
www.musee-rodin.fr

Ⓑ Cinéma La Pagode

This is certainly the most unusual cinema in the whole of Paris. It is an independent art house cinema well known for its Japanese style interior and its garden. It had romantic origins but without the happy end, because it was built in 1896 by François-Émile Morin, one of the three directors of the famous department store, Le Bon Marché, as a present for his wife. Unfortunately, she left him for his associate almost as soon after it was completed. La Pagode was a place for parties and receptions until it closed in 1927. It was opened to the public again in 1931, and became an avant-garde art house cinema. Jean Cocteau screened the premiere of his *Orpheus* here in 1959. During the 1960s all the French New Wave directors screened their films here, including François Truffaut, Éric Rohmer and Jacques Rozier.

57 rue de Babylone, 7th.
Tel.: 01-45-55-48-48.

Restaurants

Ⓒ The Rodin Museum café

If you want an outstanding place for breakfast or a bucolic setting for a drink or dinner, this is the place to go.
À la carte €12.
79 rue de Varenne, 7th.
Tel.: 01-44-18-61-10.

Ⓓ Le Basilic

Vegetarians stay away! Hidden in a quiet tree-filled square in the centre of the government ministry district, this is one of the most famous *rôtisseries* in Paris, known especially for its roast lamb. Not to be missed on any account, if you're a meat eater!
À la carte €30–40.
2 rue Casimir-Perier, 7th.
Tel.: 01-44-18-94-64. www.restaurant-le-basilic.fr

Ⓔ Au Pied de Fouet

A little bistro set in a former post office that serves traditional food to a clientele of regulars, with good, fresh produce at decent prices.
À la carte €11–20.
45 rue de Babylone, 7th.
Tel.: 01-47-05-12-27.

Next stations

SAINT-FRANCOIS XAVIER

Le Paris-Dusquene
41 avenue Dusquene, 7th.

DUROC

See line 10, page 271

MONTPARNASSE-BIENVENÜE

See line 4, page 114

GAÎTÉ

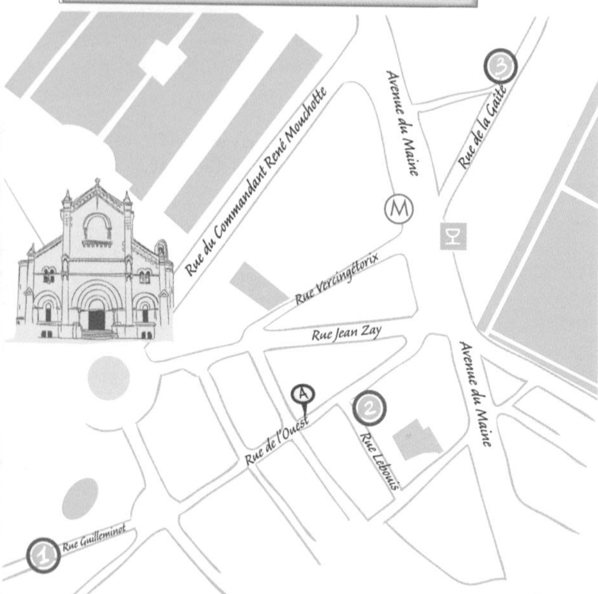

History

When it opened in 1937, this station on the Avenue du Maine served line 14 but was also connected to line 13 in 1976. It was named after rue de la Gaîté, once a mere path that gradually grew into a lively thoroughfare in the Montparnasse neighbourhood, filled with dance halls, restaurants and theatres.

SIGHTSEEING

Monument

1 **Église Notre-Dame du Travail**
Built between 1899 and 1901 by the architect Jules Astruc, Notre-Dame-du-Travail church (meaning Our Lady of Labour) was set up to cater to the working class population in the neighbourhood.
36 rue Guilleminot, 14th.
Tel.: 01-44-10-72-92.

Culture

2 **Fondation Henri Cartier-Bresson:** this is a Mecca for photography in the French capital. The foundation was established in 2003 under the aegis of Henri Cartier-Bresson, Martine

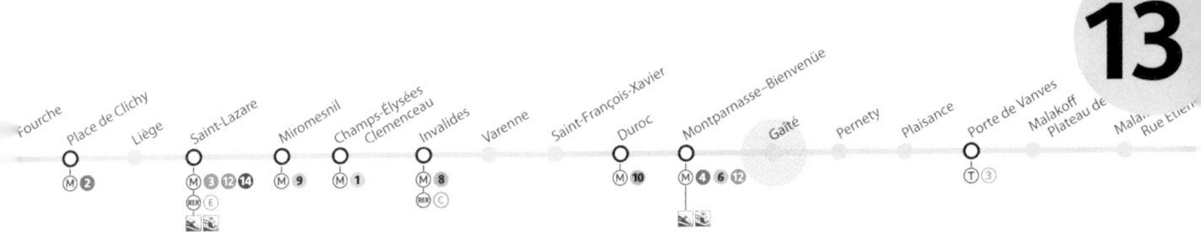

Address book

The place for a rendezvous

L'Indianna Club
77 avenue du Maine, 14th.
Open Sunday to Thursday 9am to 2pm, and to 4am on Friday and Saturday.
Tel.: 01-43-22-50-46.

A Marché biologique
This is one of the three organic food markets in Paris, the other two being Raspail and Batignolles.
Place Constantin-Brancusi, 15th.

Franck and their daughter Mélanie. It is housed in a former artist's workshop in Montparnasse, built by Molinié in 1912 and then renovated by Ceria & Coupel. You will find all the works by this famous photographer, who died in 2004. Thanks to his talent and his eye, Cartier-Bresson succeeded in capturing all the great events of the past century since the 1930s. He believed that photography was 'putting one's eye and one's heart in the same sight line. It's a way of life.' Three times a year, the two exhibition areas alternate between exhibitions of Henri Cartier-Bresson's works and those by other photographers.

2 impasse Lebouis, 14th.
Tel.: 01-56-80-27-00. www. henricartierbresson.org.
Open Tuesday to Friday 1pm to 6.30pm, Saturday 11am to 6.45pm. Late night on Wednesday to 8.30pm. Entrance fee.

A walk in the city

3 **Rue de la Gaîté:** the atmosphere here is very different from that in the nearby Tour Montparnasse (the only skyscraper in central Paris). Rue de la Gaîté still retains is centuries-old ambiance, when this little street was still outside Paris proper and full of theatres, brothels, restaurants and dance halls. It wakes up gradually in the evenings. Stroll along it and admire the facades of the old theatres or go to a show. Théâtre Bobino was a music hall built in 1867, which closed in 1980 and was recently renovated. Some famous French singers have performed here, including Fernandel, Barbara, Léo Ferré, and Georges Brassens. The charming Théâtre du Montparnasse (at no. 31) is famous for having staged Jean Anouilh's plays, and you can also admire the Comédie Italienne (no. 17) and Théâtre de la Gaîté Montparnasse (no. 26).

Next stations

PERNÉTY

Café Losserand
77 rue Raymond-Losserand, 14th.

PLAISANCE

Le Bouquet
94 rue Raymond-Losserand, 14th.

PORTE DE VANVES

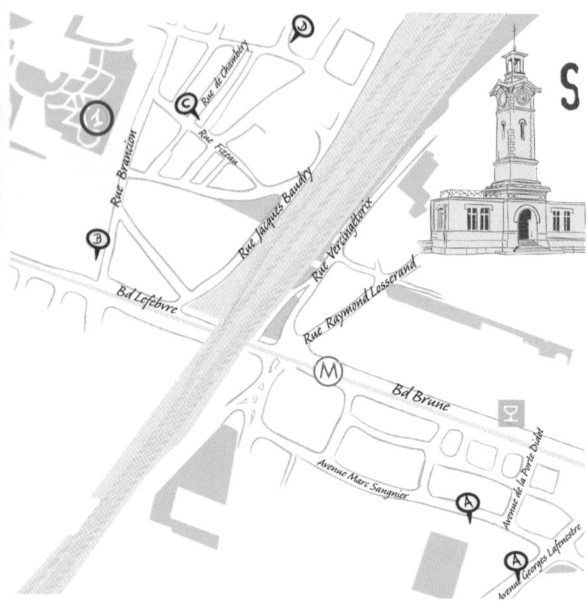

SIGHTSEEING

A walk in the park

1 Parc Georges-Brassens: this park stands on what used to be the small town of Vaugirard, which was attached to Paris in 1860. Vineyards once grew here and later market gardens before slaughterhouses for horses were built between 1894 and 1974. When these were demolished in 1985 the vast area of 8.7 hectares (21.5 acres), became a park and was named after the singer and songwriter Georges Brassens, who lived nearby for many years, first at no. 9 impasse Florimont (14th arrondissement), and later at 42 rue Santos-Dumont (15th arrondissement). Many architectural features of the old slaughterhouses were integrated into the park landscape, with which also has a tree-covered hill with belvedere on top, in addition to play areas for children, a rock climbing area and a bandstand. Nature lovers will enjoy the rose garden, the little vineyard, and the scented garden containing 80 different fragrant species. The park also has its own beehives and once a year a honey festival is held here, usually in the first or second weekend of October, to sell the park's honey harvest.

Rue des Morillons, 15th.

History

Porte de Vanves station opened on 21 January 1937. For nearly 40 years this was the terminal for line 14, which served the Left Bank from Invalides. The line was then extended to Châtillon-Montrouge in 1976 and became part of line 13, after which Porte de Vanves served line 13. The rows of shell seats on the platforms were designed by Motte and outside no. 1 exit you will see an original Dervaux lamp post-cum-Metro sign.

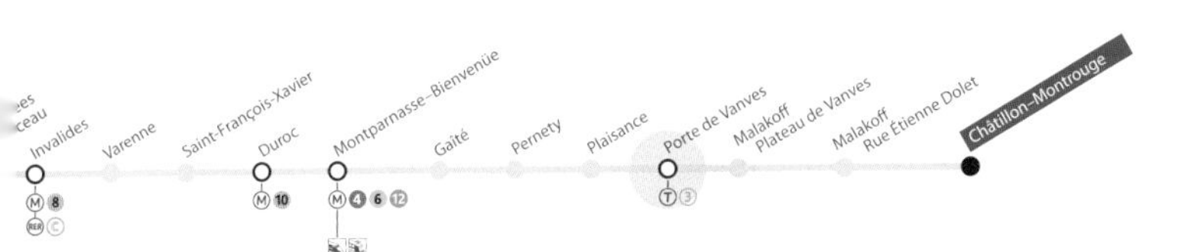

Address book

The place for a rendezvous

Le Paris Sud

57 boulevard Brune, 14th. Open daily 7am to midnight. Tel.: 01-74-30-13-41.

Shopping

Ⓐ Puces de la Porte de Vanves

The Porte de Vanves flea market is the only worthwhile one if you are looking to unearth treasure in a pleasant backdrop. Open every Saturday and Sunday all year round, come rain or shine, some 380 stalls set

up on Marc-Sangnier and Georges-Lafenestre avenues, with their weekly finds and curiosities. You will see 18th and 19th century furniture and objects, as well as Art Deco, oddments from the 1950s and 1970s, old clothing and textiles, jewellery, books and old papers.

Avenue Marc-Sangnier, 15th. Open Saturday and Sunday 7am to 1pm.

Ⓑ Marché du Livre Ancien et d'Occasion

This antique and second-hand book market has been held every weekend since it first opened in 1987. Some 60 book sellers set up in the former covered market in Georges-Brassens Park.

104 rue Brancion, 15th. Open Saturday and Sunday 9am to 6pm.

Restaurants

Ⓒ Diet Éthique

Allow yourself to be tempted by Francine's healthy and inventive cooking, with ultra-

fresh ingredients, deliciously prepared with no fat. À la carte at lunchtime €17, evenings €21.

27 rue de Chambéry, 15th. Tel. : 01-48-28-65-50. www.dietethique.com

Ⓓ Le Grand Pan

When you enter the restaurant, you are greeted with a quotation by Georges Brassens which roughly translates as 'When the great god Pan reigned, god protected drunkards'. An excellent neighbourhood restaurant providing Basque cuisine and cheerful service. Menus €15–30.

20 rue Rosenwald, 15th. Tel.: 01-42-50-02-50.

Next stations

MALAKOFF – PLATEAU DE VANVES

Café Brasserie de l'Hôtel de Ville
2 place du 11-Novembre, 92240 Malakoff.

MALAKOFF RUE ÉTIENNE DOLET

Au Métro, 70 rue Paul-Vaillant Couturier, 92240 Malakoff.

CHÂTILLON – MONTROUGE

Le Sologniot
226 avenue Marx-Dormoy, 92120 Montrouge.

line 14

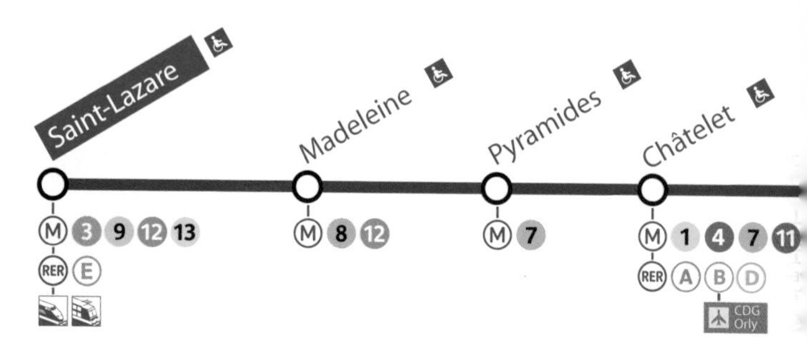

History

Line 14 is Paris's newest metro line, opened in October 1998. It succeeds an earlier line 14 that used to link Invalides to Porte de Vanves and which disappeared in 1976 when it merged with line 13. The current line 14 follows a completely different route to the old one. It crosses Paris diagonally from Saint-Lazare to Olympiades. It was the first automatic line in the capital. Within the framework of the Grand Paris project, the line may be extended northwards between Mairie de Saint-Ouen and Saint-Denis Pleyel, and then between Olympiades and Orly to the south. The architecture of the line 14 stations privileges light and transparency, in a resolutely contemporary spirit, playing on large volumes, modern materials and abundant light.

Saint-Lazare / Olympiades

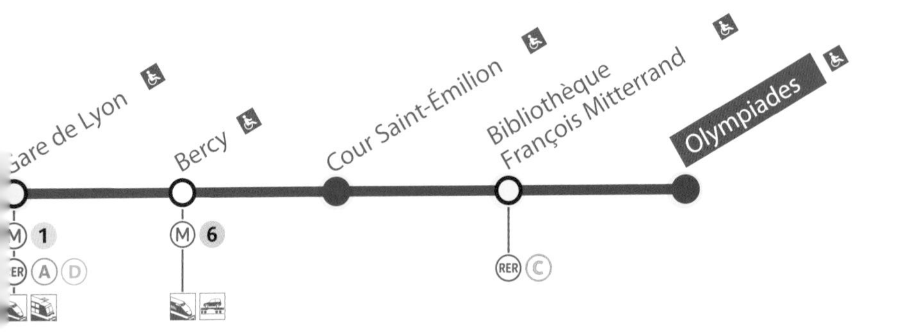

GARE DE LYON

History

Gare de Lyon is one of the oldest stations on the Paris Metro network, opened with the first metro line on 19 July 1900. It is still proof of the technical prowess used to tunnel underneath Paris. It was the first station to be constructed by the cut and cover method, following the route of the streets above. Almost a century later on 15 October 1998, it was joined to line 14. The line 14 station has a decor sheltering a dozen varieties of plants and rocks, renewed over time. It also has cultural spaces, with showcases presenting temporary exhibitions of young artists.

SIGHTSEEING

Monuments

1 **Gare de Lyon:** Paris's third train station by its traffic, with some 83 million voyagers a year, serves a large corner of southeastern France, as well as international destinations in Switzerland and Italy. Originally just a simple wooden platform when it was built in 1849, the station was reconstructed for the World Fair of 1900, adorned with the 64 me-

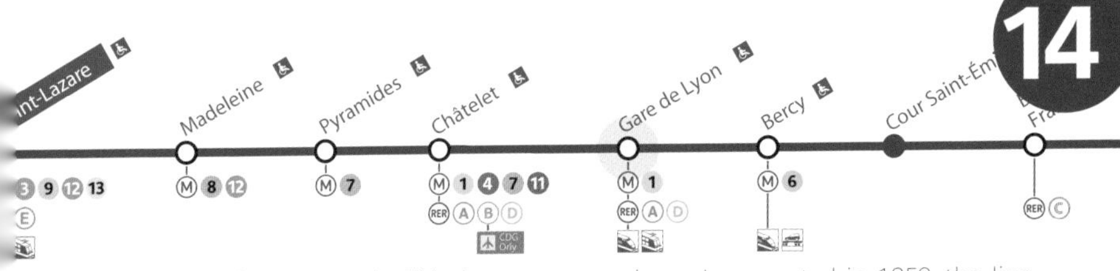

tre-high (210 feet) Tour de l'Horloge clocktower, with its clock faces on each side. The station was later rehabilitated to meets the needs of the developing metro and the RER. It is a listed historic monument and the interior has some southern touches: scattered palm trees as well as a large fresco representing the towns served.

Place Louis-Armand, 12th.

2 **Viaduc des Arts:** in 1853, a concession was awarded to the private Paris-Strasbourg rail company to open a line between the Bastille and Vincennes, along the route of the current avenue Daumesnil. The Viaduc de la Bastille

was born. Inaugurated in 1859, the line was abandoned roughly a century later, after the creation of RER line A, which uses its old route outside Paris. In 1990, the City of Paris decided to rehabilitate the viaduct, which had been abandoned for several decades, restoring its pink brick and stone arches to transform them into a new Parisian conservatory for craftsmanship. Above, the railway has been replaced by a planted promenade, part of the green corridor connecting Place de la Bastille to the Bois de Vincennes. The renovation was completed in 1994 and the Viaduc des Arts has become a showcase of French craftsmanship, welcoming more than 50 workshops. Parisians have quickly adopted the abandoned railway as a favourite place for a weekend stroll.

Avenue Daumesnil, 12th.

A nature walk

3 **Promenade Plantée:** this 4.5 kilometre (2.8 miles) long green path crosses the length of the 12th arrondissement as far as the *Périphérique* on the trace of an old railway, which went out of service in 1969. The terminus was at the Bastille, where the opera house now stands, and trains went as far as Saint-Maur, to what is now the RER A station. The green corridor starts just behind Opéra Bastille, at the level of the Viaduc des Arts. From the square, take rue de Lyon as far as Avenue Dausmesnil, then climb the steps up to the suspended gardens. The promenade stretches along the avenue, in a string of flowerbeds and little pools as far as the

Jardins de Reuilly, which it spans with a wooden footbridge. Once past the lawn, it runs into allée Vivaldi, the commercial section of the promenade. Then it continues eastwards along tunnels and cuttings via the Square Charles-Péguy and finishes by joining Porte Dorée and the Bois de Vincennes. During your walk, pause for a while in the Jardin de la Gare de Reuilly and in the square Hector-Malot.

4 **Jardins de Reuilly:** created in the 1990s by architect Pierre Colboc and landscape designers Paysage, this small lush park replaced a former goods station, roughly on the site of the Château de Reuilly, built by the Merovingian kings in the early Middle Ages. Bordered on one side by the glass facade of the Piscine Reuilly swimming pool, the park has an agreeable lawn, an imaginative children's playground, a water garden and a series of small gardens planted with ferns, bamboo, heather or roses.

Rue Albinoni and avenue Dausmesnil, 12th.

Open daily, times vary from winter 8am to 5.45pm to summer 8am to 9.30pm; Saturday and Sunday from 9am.

Address book

The place for a rendezvous

Brasserie La Tour
193 rue de Bercy, 12th. Open Monday to Friday 6am to 8.30pm.
Tel.: 01-43-45-86-37

Craftsmen and women

A Crafts Workshops of the Viaduc des Arts
Adjoining the Faubourg Saint-Antoine, a district historically devoted

to crafts and furniture making, the Viaduc des Arts today houses under its arches some 50 craftsmen and craftswomen exercising different skills. Each workshop nestles inside an arch, visible from the street to passers-by fascinated by the savoir-faire on show and conscious of the tradition and artistic heritage displayed before their eyes.

Ⓑ Ateliers Le Tallec

Founded in 1928, this is one of the last French workshops for hand-decorated porcelain. Here artisans decorate Limoges porcelain, which is entirely hand painted following the tradition of its founder Camille Le Tallec.

93–95 avenue Daumesnil, 12th.
Tel.: 01-43-40-61-55.
www.atelierdetallec.com
Open Monday to Friday 9.30am to 6pm and by appointment on Saturday.

Ⓒ Atelier du Cuivre et de l'Argent

Return to a lifestyle of old and forgotten refinement in this workshop where French silverwares and old-fashioned objects from another era are made, such as the moustache spoon and the valve spoon.

113 avenue Daumesnil, 12th.
Tel.: 01-43-40-20-20.
www.atelier-culinaire.fr
Open Monday to Saturday 10am to 7pm.

Restaurants

Ⓓ Le Train Bleu

This is not simply an institution and breathtaking place, but it is also one of Paris's top *brasseries*. Situated facing the platforms in the middle of Gare de Lyon, it owes its glory to its construction for the World Fair of 1900. The restaurant was originally called the Buffet de la Gare de Lyon. It was renamed Train Bleu in 1963, after the mythic 'Paris – Ventimiglia' line, and subsequently listed as a historic monument in 1972 by André Malraux. The dining room is simply magnificent, decorated on the walls and ceilings with 41 paintings worthy of a museum, representing the landscapes of the destinations served by trains from this station. Prestigious guests have included Coco Chanel, Brigitte Bardot, Jean Cocteau, Salvador Dalí and Jean Gabin. The excellent French cuisine doesn't disappoint either. Menus from €55.

Place Louis-Armand, 12th, 1st floor of Gare de Lyon, facing the platforms.
Tel.: 01-43-43-09-06.
Open daily 11.30am to 3pm, 7pm to 10pm.

Ⓔ Goûter l'Instant

For a simple meal, take a seat around this large communal table with its whiff of Belgium. Open sandwiches, tarts, soups and salads, accompanied by imported beer, are served in a relaxed atmosphere. Around €15 – 20.

24 rue Taine, 12th.
Tel.: 01-43-47-33-01.
Open Monday to Saturday noon to 3pm, in the evening by reservation for a group of at least 10 people, Sunday brunch 10.30am to 6pm.

Previous stations

SAINT-LAZARE
See line 8, page 31

PYRAMIDES
See line 7, page 18

MADELEINE
See line 8, page 212

CHÂTELET
See line 1, page 32

Next station

BERCY
See line 6, page 162

COUR SAINT-ÉMILION

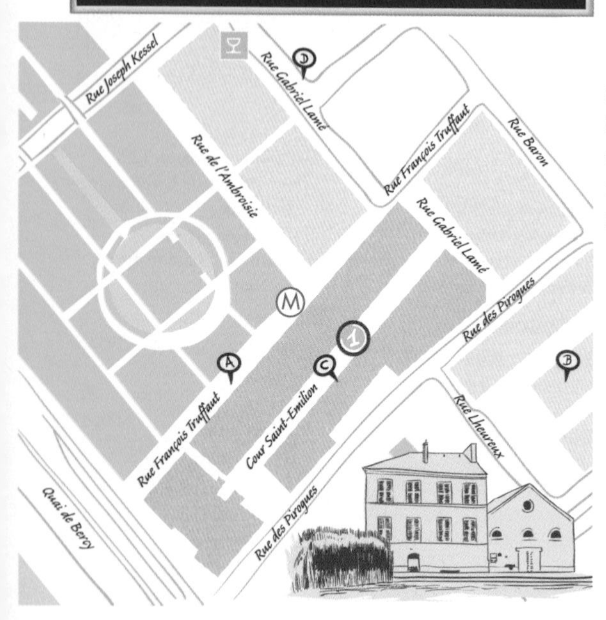

moderation' to meet the Loi Évin, concerning alcohol advertisements. It was therefore decided to name it Cour Saint-Émilion.

History

This station opened on 15 October 1998. It is situated within part of the old Bercy goods station, which used to receive trains bringing wines from the South of France. The huge, cathedral-like space is decorated with light, noble materials, laid out with vast spaces and fluid circulation, and it is endowed with a mezzanine giving access to the platforms. It was initially going to be called Pommard Saint-Émilion in tribute to the nearby rue Pommard and Cour Saint-Émilion, which would have obliged the RATP to add the health warning 'Alcohol abuse is harmful for health, to be consumed with

SIGHTSEEING

A walk in the city

1 **Cour Saint-Émilion:** situated south of the Parc de Bercy, its origins go back to the warehouses and wine cellars of Bercy and it is named after Saint-Émilion wines. The listed buildings held an important place in the wine trade in the 19th and early 20th centuries. In the middle of the street, one can still see the rails that were used to transport the wine. The wine warehouses that border it have been restored and now contain shops and restaurants. Cour Saint-Émilion has become a fashionable pedestrianised alley that makes a pleasant stroll.

Address book

The place for a rendezvous

L'Edeilweiss de Bercy
2 rue de Dijon, 12th.
Open daily 6am to midnight.
Tel.: 01-40-02-09-28.

Shopping

Ⓐ Bercy Village
Bercy Village is the name given to the cluster of 30 or so shops and restaurants installed in the heart of the district. There is also a multiplex cinema, the UGC Ciné Cité Bercy.
28 rue François-Truffaut, 12th.
Tel.: 01-40-02-90-80.
www.bercyvillage.com
Open daily 11am to 9pm.

Culture

Ⓑ Musée des Arts Forains
This museum is unique in Paris, both for its extraordinary collection of objects, hunted out with passion over the past 35 years by its founder, Jean-Paul Favand, and its unique atmosphere. A living museum, it recreates the atmosphere of 19th-century fairgrounds, with its wooden merry-go-round horses, old-fashioned sweets and thrills of yesteryear. Lose yourself like a child in this museum, which has lost its sense of direction, where restored antique fairground attractions mingle with thousands of rare curios from the theatre, music hall and fun fairs. It is one of the biggest collections of fairground art in the world. Now private, the museum is open for groups of 15, so if you are in a smaller group, enroll on its website.
53 avenue des Terroirs-de-France, 12th.
Guided visits for groups Monday to Friday by reservation on 01-43-40-16-15, it is possible to join an exisiting group.
www.arts-forains.com
Entrance fee.

Restaurants

Ⓒ Chai 33
This restaurant installed in the wine warehouses at the heart of the Cour Saint-Émilion is naturally devoted to wine. A huge contemporary *brasserie*, with two pleasant terraces, Chai 33 proposes attractive fusion cuisine with Asian accents. The oenological touch is the 'wine key' placed on the table, which opens the door to the wine cellar where everyone is invited to go down to choose their bottle from more than 300 references. Around €25.
33 cour Saint-Émilion, 12th.
Tel.: 01-53-44-01-01.
www.chai33.com
Open daily 8.30am to 2am.

Ⓓ L'Auberge Aveyronnaise
In the Terroirs-de-France district, this is the place to sample *aligot* (mashed potato with melted Tomme cheese) and southwestern specialities. Situated in a calm street, this inn lives up to its name, proposing a friendly welcome and tasty food. Dinner menus €35–30.
40 rue Gabriel-Lamé, 12th.
Tel.: 01-43-40-12-24.
Open daily noon to 2.30pm, 7pm to 11pm.

BIBLIOTHÈQUE FRANÇOIS MITTERRAND

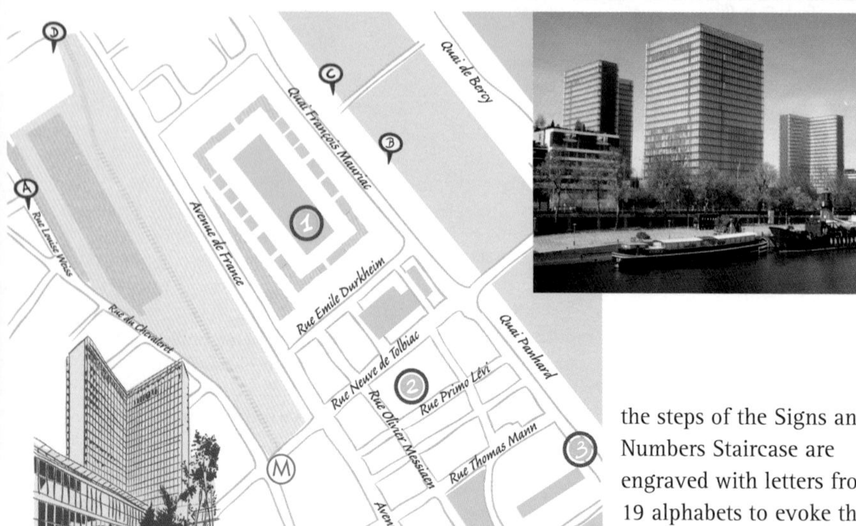

History

Bibliothèque François Mitterrand station was inaugurated on 15 October 1998 as the terminus of line 14, before its extension to Olympiades in 2007. Designed by architect Antoine Grumbach, it contains a 'shower of quotations' plucked from worldwide literature by the writer Jean-Christophe Bailly. Placed on the walls and the ground, they are reproduced on bronze discs, 12 centimetres (5 inches) in diameter. On the glass partitions, they appear transparently in circles of the same size. The station was conceived like an amphitheatre suitable for cultural dialogue. In the metro-RER interchange, the steps of the Signs and Numbers Staircase are engraved with letters from 19 alphabets to evoke the diversity of the language and forms used by humanity. The exceptional volume of this hall was made possible because the station was constructed rather than excavated.

SIGHTSEEING

Architecture

1 Bibliothèque François-Mitterrand

Since the 16th century, the National Library of France has had the weighty task of preserving all that is published in France. This temple of heritage located on rue de Richelieu threatened to overflow with knowledge in the 1980s, so François Mitterrand, then President of the Republic, decided to build a new edifice, which would be the jewel in the new Paris-Rive Gauche district. The project of architect Dominique Perrault won the competition, with its concept of four towers conceived as four open books facing each other. To ensure maximum protection for the works within, the glass towers are equipped with wooden shutters. In the middle of the towers hides a garden that is inaccessible to the public. The 13 million books, 350,000 sets of newspapers, two million musical scores, etc. are stored in cases located in the plinth and in the towers. A sophisticated system allows them to be delivered rapidly on request. The public library is situated on the upper garden level, and the research library reserved for academics is on the lower garden level. The site also puts on exhibitions in its galleries.

11 quai François-Mauriac, 13th.
Tel.: 01-53-79-53-79.
www.bnf.fr
Open Tuesday to Saturday 10am to 7pm, Sunday 1pm to 7pm.
Entrance fee.

2 Les Frigos: after the First World War, in the 1920s, a huge refrigerated railway warehouse was constructed on what was then called Quai de la Gare. With the closure of Paris's wholesale market at Les Halles and the opening of Rungis, they were gradually abandoned to become an industrial wasteland in the 1970s. It was then that artists and craftsmen in need of studios squatted the disaffected building, attracted by the quality of its volumes and by its good thermal and sound insulation. After a long battle, the inhabitants succeeded in saving the building from demolition and in regularising their situation by occupation contracts and by paying rents. This impressive place, which cannot fail to make an impression, ideally situated in the heart of the Paris-Rive Gauche district, between the Bibliothèque Nationale de France and Denis-Diderot University, has become a major place of artistic creation and production.

19 rue des Frigos, 13th.
http://les-frigos.com

3 Grands Moulins de Paris
From its construction by architect Georges Wybo during the First World War to its closure in 1996, this former industrial flour mill transformed millions of tonnes of wheat into flour. It closed down when its activities were transferred to Gennevilliers and Verneuil-l'Étang. While the adjoining buildings were destroyed, the main building with its quadrangle plan in neoclassical style and the largest storeroom were preserved and rehabilitated by architect Rudy Ricciotti between 2004 and 2006. The converted Grands Moulins now house the university Paris VII-Denis Diderot.

73 quai Panhard-et-Levassor, 13th.
Tel.: 01-57-27-57-27.

Address book

The place for a rendezvous

Le Charber Café
75 rue du Chevaleret, 13th.
Open Monday to Friday 6.30am to 9pm.

Culture

A Air de Paris
Last survivor of the bunch of art galleries that colonised a row of modern shops beneath an annex of the Ministry of Finance at the end of the 1990s, Air de Paris gets its name from Marcel Duchamp's famous glass phial

of Parisian air. Something of the same spirit is evident in the mainly conceptual artists exhibited here. You will find French and international names there, including Sarah Morris, Liam Gillick, Carsten Höller and Philippe Parreno and the collective Claire Fontaine (itself named after a popular French brand of stationery), who work in all media—installation, video, photography, wall painting—often with an experimental edge. An adjoining, self-contained window space, dubbed Random Gallery, is used for one-off, site-specific installations.

32 rue Louise-Weiss, 13th. Tel.: 01-44-23-02-77. www.airdeparis.com, open Tuesday to Saturday 11am to 7pm.

Leisure

Ⓑ Piscine Joséphine-Baker

A swimming pool floating on a river is hardly usual. Its forerunner the Piscine de Deligny had finished by sinking, but this one has proved its worth and, after a few incidents, opened definitively in 2008 to the satisfaction of east Parisian swimmers. Conceived by architect Robert de Busni, it consists of a glass and steel structure supported on 20 metal floats. In summer, the roof comes off the two pools: a 25-metre pool and a paddling pool reserved for children. One can also profit from the sun on its two huge sunbathing decks. For the more courageous, there is also a gym, with view of the river. At the end of a fitness class, one has access to the saunas, Turkish bath and jacuzzi..

8 quai François-Mauriac, 13th. Tel.: 01-56-61-96-50. Open daily, times on the website www.paris.fr

Restaurant

Ⓒ Le Batofar

The now mythic lighthouse ship concert venue, whose programme is as sharp as it is electronic, has gained a much talked-about restaurant. Regional produce, traditional dishes, spit-roast meat and good little wines are all served until 5am. One can also breakfast and brunch here. Around €15–25.

11 quai François-Mauriac, 13th. Tel.: 01-53-60-17-30. www.batofar.org. Open Tuesday to Saturday noon to 2.30pm, 7.30pm to 11.30pm.

Sortir

Ⓓ Djoon

A soulful club? In any case a restaurant, lounge bar and club, whose two spaces designed like a New York loft, host some of the greatest French and international DJs, such as Derrick May, Little Louie Vega and Lil Louis.

22 boulevard Vincent-Auriol, 13th. Tel.: 01-45-70-83-49. www.djoon.com Open Friday and Saturday midnight to 5am, Sunday 6pm to 2am. Entrance fee.

OLYMPIADES

East Asian origin—some 35,000 people from ten or so different nationalities. Try to visit on Sunday, when the district is particularly animated.

History

Olympiades station, opened in 2007, marks the terminus of line 14. It was named in reference to the ensemble of buildings towering over it. Its architecture remains faithful to the spirit of the line: with light-coloured concrete vaults, wooden ceilings, larger than average platforms and high ceilings. Its individual touch appears in the orange lighting of the wall at the end of the platform towards Bibliothèque. Olympiades station is at the heart of a densely populated districted that is poorly served by the metro. Here one finds notably the Parisian Chinatown, where one in two inhabitants is of South-

SIGHTSEEING

An Asian walk

1 **Chinatown:** a visit to the Parisian Chinatown is hardly bucolic but it is worthwhile for a momentary trip to Asia. Lose yourself in the triangle situated between Avenue de Choisy, Avenue d'Ivry and Boulevard Masséna. Pause for a moment on the esplanade of the Olympiades Very lively during Chinese New Year it is not very welcoming the rest of the time Flanked by towerblocks each named after a city that has organised the Olympic games, the esplanade nonetheless offers numerous boutiques and restaurants One can easily imagine oneself somewhere in an Asian megalopolis.

Between avenue de Choisy, avenue d'Ivry and boulevard Masséna, 13th.

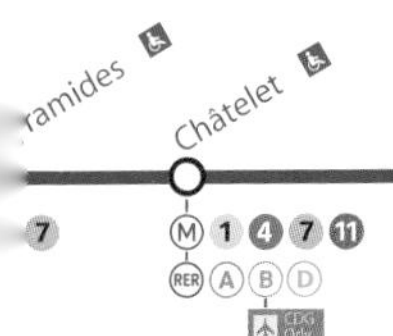

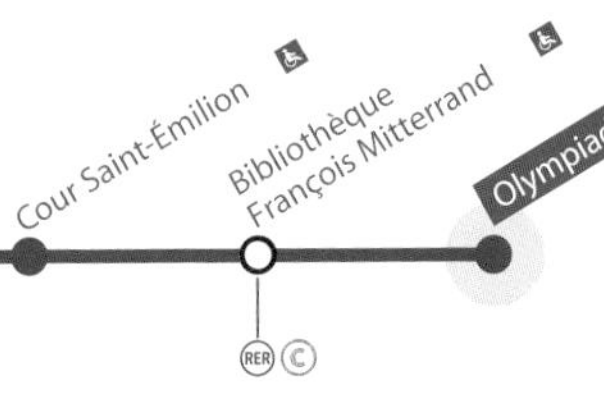

Olympiades

14

Address book

The place for a rendezvous

Brasserie La Roseraie

47 rue de Tolbiac, 13th.
Open Monday to Friday 6am to 10pm, Saturday and Sunday 8am to 8pm.
Tel.: 01-45-83-23-23.

Buddhist temples

A Temple de l'Arfoi

At the foot of the Helsinki Tower, in the pagoda of the Association for French Residents of Indochinese Origins, the faithful gather here not just to pray, but also for conversation, to drink tea and make offerings.

37 rue du Disque (entrancy by 70 avenue d'Ivry), 13th.
Tel.: 01-45-86-80-99.
Open daily 9am to 6pm.

B Temple des Teochew

This is the temple of Chinatown's ethnic majority. The same ancestral rituals and unique atmosphere. An exotic trip is guaranteed.

Behind the Anvers Tower, esplanade des Olympiades, 13th.
Tel.: 01-45-82-06-01.
Open daily 9am to 5pm.

Shopping

C Tang Frères

An institution throughout Paris. If you have not yet been initiated, then learn that this is the Asian supermarket par excellence where one can find everything one wants. It is also the largest Asian supply hub in Europe. That takes place underground in warehouses worthy of Rungis, which see tons of rice, fruit, vegetables and dried shrimps pass through here in transit towards the whole of Europe. A genuine experience.

48 avenue d'Ivry, 13th.
Tel.: 01-45-70-80-00.
Open Monday to Friday 10am to 8pm, Saturday 10am to 9pm.

D Galerie Marchande d'Oslo

This Asian supermarket is located on the esplanade des Olympiades.

22, rue du Disque, 13th.

Restaurants

E Lao Lane Xhang 2 and Lao Douang Chan

Two exquisite little Laotian restaurants.

Lao Lane Xhang 2.
Around €20–25.
102 avenue d'Ivry, 13th.
Tel.: 01-58-89-00-00.
Open Thursday to Tuesday noon to 3pm, 7pm to 11pm.

Lao Douang Chan.
Around €11.
161 avenue de Choisy, 13th.
Tel.: 01-44-24-80-80.
Open Thursday to Tuesday noon to 3pm, 7pm to 10.30pm.

F Chinatown Olympiades

The Mecca of Chinese restaurants on two storeys with karoake and a dance floor. Menus from €11.

44 avenue d'Ivry, 13th.
Tel.: 01-45-84-72-21.
Open daily noon to 3pm, 7pm to 2am.

THE TYPES OF TICKETS AVAILABLE FOR VISITING PARIS BY METRO

You will find some practical information below. To find out more, check out the RATP's website: www.ratp.fr

Ticket t+ for occasional travel

Unit price: €1.70

Pack of 10 tickets (full price): €12.70

Pack of 10 tickets (reduced price): €6.35

Where to buy them:

- At the ticket offices and automatic vending machines in the metro stations, bus stations, train stations and RER stations (single ticket or packs of 10).
- from RATP-approved retailers (in packs of 10).
- In the buffet cars of certain TGV trains (single ticket or packs of 10).

'Paris Visite' is an unlimited travel pass for 1, 2, 3 or 5 consecutive days for zones 1 – 3 or 1 – 5.

The day begins at 5.30 am and end at 5.30 am the following morning.

'Paris Visite' pass for adults

	1 day/€	2 days/€	3 days/€	5 days/€
zones 1-3	9.75	15.85	21.60	31.15
zones 1-5	20.50	31.15	43.65	53.40

'Paris Visite' pass for children aged 4-12

	1 day/€	2 days/€	3 days/€	5 days/€
zones 1-3	4.85	7.90	10.80	15.55
zones 1-5	10.25	15.55	21.80	26.70

Where to buy them:

- At the ticket offices and automatic vending machines in the metro stations, bus stations, train stations and RER stations (single ticket or packs of 10).

The 'Navigo' pass is for regular and frequent travellers residing or working in the Île-de-France area.

The 'Navigo Découverte' pass is for all visitors and costs €5.

Both passes provide unlimited travel in the zones selected at the time of purchase for a period of one week or a month.
One week in zones 1-2: €19.15
One month in zones 1-2: €62.90

The annual 'Navigo' pass is for regular and frequent travellers residing or working in the Île-de-France area for a full year.
Zones 1-2: €649.50 (+€7.60 application fee)
You can buy them on line on the RATP website at www.ratp.fr or in a RATP sales office.

The 'imagine 'R' pass provides unlimited travel for school children, secondary school pupils and students under the age of 26 for a full year.
Zones 1-2: €306.50 (€8.00 application fee included)
Available from RATP points of sale.

The 'Améthyste' pass (free) and the 'Emeraude' pass are for seniors and disabled people. They are income dependent and the price depends on the departmental council in the applicant's place of residence.

How to apply: the free 'Améthyste' pass is provided by the social services in the department or arrondissement of the applicant's place of residence.
Applications for the 'Emeraude' pass are made to the Centre d'Action Social (social services centre) in the arrondissement of the applicant's place of residence.

All rates are indicative and may be revised annually by STIF.
Prices quoted here are valid at 1 January 2012.

Contents

Line 11 292

Line 12 298

Line 13 334

Line 14 356

A to Z of the metro stations

Index of monuments and key places listed in the guidebook

Palais Bourbon	Line 12	Assemblée Nationale	315
Palais Brongniart	Line 3	Bourse	79
Palais de Chaillot	Lines **6**, 9	Trocadéro	147
Palais de Justice	Line 4	Cité	103
Palais de l'Élysée	Lines **1**, 13	Champs-Élysées - Clémenceau	20
Palais de la Découverte	Lines **1**, 13	Champs-Élysées - Clémenceau	21
Palais de la Femme	Line 9	Charonne	261
Palais de Tokyo	Line 9	Alma-Marceau	252
Palais du Luxembourg (Sénat)	Line 12	Notre-Dame des Champs	330
Palais Galliera - Musée de la Mode	Line 9	Iéna	249
Palais Omnisport de Bercy	Lines **6**, 14	Bercy	163
Panthéon	Line 10	Cardinal Lemoine	289
Parc André-Citroën	Line 8	Balard	198
Parc André-Citroën	Line 10	Javel-André Citroën	268
Parc de Bercy	Lines **6**, 14	Bercy	163
Parc de la Villette	Line 5	Porte de Pantin	124
Parc des Buttes-Chaumont	Lines 7bis, **11**	Place des Fêtes	294
Parc des Princes	Line 9	Porte de Saint-Cloud	245
Parc Georges Brassens	Line 13	Porte de Vanves	354
Parc Monceau	Line 2	Courcelles	54
Petit Palais	Lines **1**, 13	Champs-Élysées - Clémenceau	21
Pierre Hermé	Line 4	Saint-Sulpice	113
Place Dauphine	Line 7	Pont-Neuf	174
Place des Vosges	Line 1	Saint-Paul	37
Place des Vosges	Line 8	Chemin Vert	230
Place du Tertre	Line 12	Abbesses	302
Place Vendôme	Lines **8**, 12, 14	Madeleine	213
Pont Alexandre III	Lines **8**, 13	Invalides	210
Pont de Bir-Hakeim	Line 6	Bir Hakeim	155
Pont de Grenelle	Line 10	Charles-Michels	270
Pont de l'Alma	Line 9	Alma-Marceau	251
Pont de la Concorde	Line 12	Assemblée Nationale	315
Pont des Arts	Line 4	Saint-Germain-des-Prés	111
Pont Mirabeau	Line 10	Mirabeau	266
Printemps	Lines **3**, 9	Havre-Caumartin	75
Sainte-Chapelle	Line 4	Cité	102
Shakespeare & Co	Line 4	Cité	103
Shakespeare & Co	Line 10	Maubert-Mutualité	287
Sorbonne	Line 10	Cluny-La Sorbonne	282
Square des Batignolles	Line 13	Brochant	343
Square du Vert-Galant	Line 7	Pont-Neuf	174
Stade de France	Line 13	Saint-Denis - Porte de Paris	337
Synagogue de la rue Vauquelin	Line 7	Censier-Daubenton	190
Théâtre des Abbesses	Line 12	Abbesses	303
Théâtre des Champs-Élysées	Line 9	Alma-Marceau	252
Théâtre des Variétés	Line 8	Grands Boulevards	220
Théâtre du Palais-Royal	Lines **7**, 14	Pyramides	170
Théâtre du Ranelagh	Line 9	La Muette	247
Théâtre du Vieux Colombier	Line 4	Saint-Sulpice	113
Théâtre Edouard VII	Lines 7, **9**	Chaussée d'Antin- La Fayette	259
Théâtre Mogador	Line 12	Trinité-d'Estienne d'Orves	309
Théâtre National de Chaillot	Lines **6**, 9	Trocadéro	149
Thermes and Hôtel de Cluny	Line 10	Cluny-La Sorbonne	281
Tour de Jean-sans-Peur	Line 4	Etienne Marcel	96
Tour Eiffel	Line 6	Bir Hakeim	154
Tour Montparnasse	Lines **4**, 6, 12, 13	Montparnasse-Bienvenüe	115
Tour Saint-Jacques	Line **1**, 4, 7, 11, 14	Châtelet	33
Village Suisse	Lines 6, **8**, 10	La Motte-Picquet Grenelle	202

Do help us update this guidebook by sharing your own finds in Paris. Feel free to send us your good ideas and be sure to include names and addresses. Our authors will be delighted to check them out and include them in the next edition of the guidebook.

You can write to us at: guidedeparisenmetro@editionsduchene.fr
Thank you for your help.

You can find us at www.guidedeparisenmetro.fr

This guidebook was produced from an original idea by Fabienne Kriegel, Managing Director of Éditions du Chêne.

www.editionsduchene.fr

Project editor: Volcy Loustau
Graphic design: Gaëlle Junius
Production: Nicole Thiérot-Pichon
Writers: Anne-Claire Ruel, Aurélie Clair, Catherine Taret
Local Paris maps: Ulric Maes
Photographers: Gilles Targat and Anne-Claire Ruel
Proofreading/corrections: Carine Merlin, Myriam Blanc and Marion Baugier

Coordination for the English edition: Olivia Roussel
Page layout: ELSE
English translation: Natasha Edwards, Krystyna Horko and Sue Landau

Printed in Italy
Copyright registration: March 2012
978-2-81230-552-8
34/8444/1